WORKS BY STANLEY BARON

Fiction

END OF THE LINE

ALL MY ENEMIES

FACTS OF LOVE

MATTERS OF CONCERN

THE KINDNESS OF STRANGERS

General

PEOPLE AND AMERICANS

BREWED IN AMERICA

Brewed in America

Brewed

IN AMERICA

A History of
Beer and Ale in the United States

BY Stanley Baron

LITTLE, BROWN AND COMPANY · BOSTON · TORONTO

Published simultaneously in Canada
by Little, Brown & Company (Canada) Limited

PRINTED IN THE UNITED STATES OF AMERICA

Acknowledgments

I would like to express my gratitude for help received from the following institutions:

Adriance Memorial Library, Poughkeepsie
American Philosophical Society Library, Philadelphia
Arizona State Department of Library and Archives, Phoenix
Baker Library, Harvard Graduate School of Business Administration
Bancroft Library, University of California, Berkeley
California Historical Society, San Francisco
Carnegie Library, Pittsburgh
Chicago Historical Society
Cincinnati *Enquirer* Library
Cleveland Public Library
College of William and Mary Library, Williamsburg, Virginia
Colonial Williamsburg Research Library
Dallas Public Library
Darlington Memorial Library, University of Pittsburgh
Denver Public Library
Detroit Public Library
East Hampton Free Library, East Hampton, New York
Free Library of Philadelphia
Henry E. Huntington Library, San Marino, California
Historical and Philosophical Society of Ohio, University of Cincinnati
Historical Society of Pennsylvania, Philadelphia
Historical Society of Western Pennsylvania, Pittsburgh
Historical Society of York County, York, Pennsylvania
Howard-Tilton Memorial Library, Tulane University of Louisiana
John Carter Brown Library, Brown University

Library of Congress
Library of the United States Brewers Association, New York
Maryland Historical Society, Baltimore
Massachusetts Historical Society, Boston
Milwaukee County Historical Society
Milwaukee Public Library
Minnesota Historical Society, St. Paul
Missouri Historical Society, St. Louis
New England Historical Genealogical Society (Directory Library), Boston
New Orleans Public Library
Newport Historical Society
New-York Historical Society
New York Public Library
Ohio Historical Society, Columbus
Oregon Historical Society, Portland
Rhode-Island Historical Society, Providence
Seattle Public Library
State Historical Society of Colorado, Denver
State Historical Society of Wisconsin, Madison
State House (Archives), Providence
Thomas Jefferson Memorial Foundation, Charlottesville, Virginia
University of Illinois Library, Urbana
Virginia Historical Society, Richmond
Western Reserve Historical Society, Cleveland
Widener Library, Harvard University

My thanks are also due to the managements of the various breweries I have visited all over the country, for valuable time I used up, for answers to my questions and for facilitation in gathering materials for this book.

For advice, criticism and support I am particularly indebted to Mrs. Dorothea D. Reeves, Miss Mary C. Dunnigan, Dr. Thomas P. Govan and Mr. Berton Roueché.

S. B.

Introduction

BEER HAS ALWAYS been part of man's diet. Every society studied by archaeologists and historians yields evidence of a traditional beverage which may be called beer. At certain periods of history, it has been regarded primarily as a food product, nourishing, stimulating and wholesome; at others, it has been used as a medicine or a tonic. Since the word "beer" itself embraces such a wide variety of beverages, it is certain that the beer drunk five thousand or more years ago barely resembled the beers of today. It may be granted, however, that common to both of them are the process of fermentation and the use of some sort of grain (usually barley) as basic ingredient.

Most people are apt to think of hops as the characteristic element in the recipe for beer, but in fact hops are mostly a flavoring device, much like vanilla in baking, and have appeared relatively recently in the history of brewing. This is only one of many misconceptions about beer and brewing. It is the object of this book to correct some of these prevalent mistakes and to clarify for the general reader not only what brewing is in the United States today, but what it has been in the past and what it has meant.

Contrary to the popular notion, beer did not appear suddenly in this country around 1850 when German-born brewers began to introduce a specific type well known in their homeland, *lager*. There was a brewing tradition in America which had begun some two hundred years before. This earlier, English style of brewing had become established during the Colonial period and was carried on with fair success after the Revolution. The conduct of this trade and the men who were engaged in it form an integral part of early American history. Indeed, brewing was one of the earliest native industries.

But there is no contesting the fact that the homesick German brewers and their *lager bier*, once established, to all intents and purposes took over the American brewing industry and have ever since been dominant. Only the ale we drink today, and — in special localities — the stout and porter, can in any way be identified with the English brewing tradition that preceded the German. Those drinks, so dear to our eighteenth-century forebears, were lustier, more alcoholic, darker and flatter than the ruling beverage of today. George Washington, who was a great fancier of porter, would probably have found twentieth-century beer an insipid concoction; but on the other hand, the beer-drinker of today would frown on the original porter as distastefully muddy and bittersweet.

The modern lager, with its emphasis on lightness, dryness and sparkle, is an American adaptation of the original German brew and may be considered, in both its character and its method of production, as an indigenous creation. The lager first produced here was more like what is brewed in Germany today: slightly sweeter, slightly heavier and with a stronger flavoring of hops than our current American brands. One brand even advertises nowadays that it provides only "the kiss of the hops" — evidently this subtlety of flavor suits the contemporary American taste. American beers have generally been more highly carbonated than others: that, too, has been a native development, evolving out of the lager as it was first introduced here. Clarity has also become a prime feature of American beers. The traditional British brews, such as the "mild" and "bitter" widely drunk in Great Britain today (and completely nonexistent in the United States), are comparatively translucent and leave a harmless sediment at the bottom of the glass.

But these conditions, no matter how firmly rooted they seem to be at any given time, are subject to fluctuations, and there is no telling what sort of beer will be most popular in 1975. Though imported lagers constitute only a tiny fraction of the American market, even that small popularity may indicate that a taste for more of the hop-flavor is reawakening. The rise in sales of ale (though ale and lager are made currently by methods that are similar in many respects) may prove a significant factor. It has taken a hundred years to arrive at the beer most popular today, and it may take just as long to develop any noticeable difference. This is an industry which has never been given to tampering with its product and changes dictated by consumer preference have been cautious and slow.

Beer was once a universal beverage prepared by every pioneer housewife in the kitchen. It has grown since those days into one of the leading industries in the country, even surviving a long attempt to extinguish it. An examination of its roots, growth and foliation may give some indication of what lies in store for it.

Contents

List of Illustrations

List of Illustrations

Part One

ONE

The Universal Beverage

TO SPEAK of the origins of brewing in America is to speak of the origins of the nation itself. Beer, in one form or another, arrived on these shores with the first of the colonists; at least there was always beer on the ships that brought those courageous, ambitious, or simply adventurous people here. And those who remained in the promised (but untamed) land and were deprived, because of lack of brewing equipment and suitable ingredients, of their daily beer were quick to complain. When the ship which had brought the first contingent of permanent settlers to Virginia in 1607 started back for England, "there remained neither taverne, beer house, nor place of reliefe," according to Thomas Studly, one of their number. "Had we beene as free from all sinnes as gluttony, and drunkennesse, we might have been canonized for Saints." Their president, however, not burdened by so much virtue, kept for his private use such decent provisions as were available and offered the others only a mess of boiled grains: "our drinke was water." [1]

Reluctantly and with ill grace, these settlers drank water while they survived by the skin of their teeth. Because of hard winters, shortage of supplies, and Indian enmity, they nearly faded away like the "Lost Colony" of Roanoke Island, which had preceded them by some twenty years. After the so-called "Starving Time" of 1609-1610, the seventy survivors were ready to call it quits and return to England. They did, in fact, go as far as setting sail, but they were met at the mouth of the James River by Lord Delaware, their governor-in-chief, just arriving from England with abundant supplies and a new company of settlers.

Almost by chance, as it were, the colony was reprieved and the basis of an enduring settlement in America was assured.

The records of the London Company show that the question of beer supplies for the Virginia colonists was prominently considered. Those original settlers of June 1607 were reinforced, though inadequately, in the winter of the same year by "the First Supply," which arrived from England in charge of Captain Christopher Newport. Beer was among its provisions.[2] A large quantity, however, was more or less confiscated by the sailors for their own use and thus never reached the thirsty settlers.

As a general rule, if the Virginia settlers were not properly supplied by those in charge at the home base, it was because Virginia was not consistently in a top-priority position from the London Company's point of view. The sugar-rich islands of the Caribbean promised (and produced) quicker dividends.

Captain John Smith (hero of the Virginia settlement as a result of a combination of fact, fiction and fancy) complained that, because of false reports in England about the prosperity of the precarious Virginia beachhead, many men were brought over "without victuals," and that these men stole the tools so sorely needed by the colony, in order to use them for trade with the Indians or as exchange with the sailors for "Butter, Cheese, Beefe, Porke, Aquavitae, Beere, Bisket, Oatmeal, and Oyle."[3]

The London Company, however, was not always unmindful of the needs of the Virginia colony, and sought to establish some sort of brewing enterprise there. Their aim apparently was only to supply the settlers' requirement; they had other, harebrained schemes for making money out of the colony — the manufacture of glass, wine, potash, and the raising of silkworms.

The Governor and Council of Virginia advertised in 1609 for two brewers to be sent to the colony.[4] But the situation was still fairly desperate in 1613, according to a letter of appraisal written by a Spaniard to his government:

> There are about three hundred men there more or less; and the majority sick and badly treated, because they have nothing but bread of maize, with fish; nor do they drink anything but water — all of which

is contrary to the nature of the English — on which account they all wish to return and would have done so if they had been at liberty.[5]

In 1621 there appeared in a list of certain Walloons and Frenchmen who were prepared to emigrate to Virginia the names of Jacques de Lecheilles and Pierre Quesnée, both called brewer and "marrying man." Though the records indicate that no objection was raised to the query of the Virginia Company about the usefulness of these prospective immigrants, no notice of their arrival has yet been discovered.[6]

The minimum ingredients for manufacturing beer were considered to be available in the new country. The very first reference to barley in America was probably that of Thomas Hariot, writing in the 1580s of the Roanoke episode: "For barlie, oates and peaze, we haue seene proof of, not beeing purposely sowen but fallen casually."[7] In 1605 Captain George Weymouth claimed to have grown barley in the northern part of Virginia:

> We digged a Garden the 22. of May, where among our garden-seeds we sowed Pease and Barley, which in 16. dayes grew up 8. ynches, although this was but the crust of the ground, and much inferiour to the mould we after found in the mayne.[8]

With barley and water available, there was no reason why beer should not be produced in the new colony. Transporting the beer from England was difficult; it took up valuable space in the cramped ships, and besides there was no certainty that it would arrive in drinkable form. Letters addressed to England show a constant disgruntled preoccupation with the condition of imported beer. The Governor and Council of Virginia wrote to the Earl of Southampton on 3 April 1623, "Beg that strict orders be given that the provisions for the ship will be well conditioned for it is certain that Dupper's beer hath been the death of a great number of passengers."[9]

"Dupper" doubtless refers to the brothers James and Jeffrey Duppa, both of them brewers, whose names appear in the Second Charter of the Virginia Company dated 23 May 1609.[10] Perhaps they were among the Company of Brewers who bought shares in the Virginia Company when it was incorporated. The Duppas either were very poor brewers or they were dumping spoiled supplies on the faraway settlers: obviously they did not give satisfaction. George Sandys wrote from Newport News on 8 April 1623 to John Ferrar, a member of His Majesty's Council for the Virginia Company, that "it would well please the Country to hear he [Ferrar] had taken revenge of Dupper for his Stinking beer, which . . . hath been the death of 200." [11]

The Governor and Council had to insist once more on 30 January 1624:

> Again put the Company in mind how the ships are pestered, victualled with musty bread & stinking beer, heretofore so earnestly complained of, in great part the cause of that mortality which is imputed alone to the Country.

The letter also advised that new emigrants should carry with them "malt, cider, butter, cheese, &c., & not make too sudden a change in their diet." [12]

The availability of beer was considered to be essential to the maintenance of good health. The governor, Sir Francis Wyatt, wrote to England sometime between 1623 and 1624 that there had been great sickness in the colony because of "want of beere, poultry, mutton, &c."

> To plant a Colony by water drinkers was an inexcusable errour in those, who layd the first foundacion, and have made it a recieved custome, which until it be laide downe againe, there is small hope of health.[13]

It must be remembered that, in the seventeenth century, beer was the universal beverage of Englishmen and those who lived on the Continent. The water was, generally speaking, not to be trusted; by tradition it was considered unwholesome — and with good reason, of course, since contamination of common water supplies was hardly surprising in an age when hygiene was not understood.[14]

In 1619, when the Pilgrims in Holland were mulling over the possibility of emigrating to America, one of the first doubts raised was that "The change of air, diet and drinking of water would infect their bodies with sore sicknesses and grievous diseases." [15] When matters were finally arranged between the Pilgrims and the London Partners, who put up the money for the enterprise in hopes of eventual profits, one of the conditions was that all the colonists would "have their meat, drink, apparel, and all provisions out of the common stock of the said colony." [16] The problem of beverages, in other words, was as important as that of food and clothing.

Preparations for the outfitting and transportation of the Pilgrim group were difficult and long-winded. Robert Cushman, among those sent from Leyden to England to make provisions for the voyage, wrote to John Carver, one of the prime organizers, on 10 June 1620, that he was running over the budget. "We shall come short at least £300 or £400. I would have had something shortened at first of beer and other provisions." [17]

It was just as well, though, that the beer supply carried on the *Mayflower* was not reduced because, as it was, the amount proved insufficient. The fact appears to be well established that the leaders of the Pilgrim party, when they left Plymouth in England, were not headed for Cape Cod or the Massachusetts coast, but presumably for the "Hudson's River." As a result of somewhat uncertain navigation, as well as the vagaries of the winds, landfall was made at an area recognized by the mariners as Cape Cod. An attempt to sail southward was frustrated by the appearance of "dangerous shoals and roaring breakers"; the vessel turned back toward the Cape.[18] The Pilgrims had to give up their idea of settling farther to the south. The ship's master and the mariners were eager to be rid of their strange load of passengers and return to their home port in England. What was more, "we could not now take time for further search or consideration, our victuals being much spent, especially our Beere." [19]

The final decision to settle in Plymouth was reached then, in some desperation, and the passengers "were hasted ashore and made to drink water that the seamen might have the more beer." [20] Fortunately, the Pilgrims found that the water was both fresh and pure in that area: the first they drank, because of their great thirst, was "as pleasant to them as wine or beer had been in foretimes." [21] Unlike the settlers in Virginia, the Pilgrims did not complain of being sickened by having to drink water. In 1624, while answering an objection from England that the water in New England was not wholesome, Bradford wrote:

If they mean, not so wholesome as the good beer and wine in London
. . . we will not dispute with them; but else for water it is as good as
any in the world . . . and it is wholesome enough for us that can be
content therewith.[22]

Another writer in 1634 remarked that those who drank New England
water were as "healthful, fresh and lusty as they that drink beer." [23] The
Pilgrims were willing to put up with drinking water, as they put up with
many other hardships, but they would have preferred beer, and indeed
had beer as soon as it was possible.

The seamen on the *Mayflower* may seem to have been selfish in practically forcing the emigrants ashore in order to retain sufficient beer for
the homeward journey. Bradford certainly felt little affection for them
and tells one incident in particular to illustrate their insensitive behavior during the nearly four months they remained at anchor (15
December 1620 to early April 1621). The Pilgrims ashore in Plymouth
were suffering an epidemic of scurvy and other maladies. One of those
who were sick (Bradford himself),

> desiring but a small can* of beer, it was answered that if he were their
> own father he should have none. The disease began to fall amongst
> them [the crew] also, so as almost half of their company died before
> they went away, and many of their officers and lustiest men. . . At
> which the Master was something strucken and sent to the sick ashore
> and told the Governor he should send for beer for them that had need
> of it, though he drunk water homeward bound.[24]

The crew, as it happened, depended on beer as a preventive of
scurvy, a vitamin-deficiency disease especially prevalent on ships, where
fresh vegetables were not available. It was certainly known in the seventeenth century that the "Iuyce of Lemons well put up, is good either to
prevent or cure the Scurvy." [25] But citrus fruits were not to be had in
great supply, and besides they were perishable. Until the eighteenth
century sailors (mistakenly, no doubt) depended on their beer ration,
and later on their tot of rum.

In any case, when the *Mayflower* turned back toward England, its
former passengers were left beerless. They had acquired, however, an additional and much-needed member for their band: John Alden, the

---

* Seventeenth-century term for drinking receptacle.

cooper, who had ostensibly been hired only to look after the hogsheads*
of beer during the westbound voyage, decided to stay in the new
world.[26] Surviving this new colony's "Starving Time" (1620-1621) along
with some fifty others, out of the nearly one hundred settlers who had
landed in Plymouth, Alden became, mainly for romantic reasons, one of
its best-known citizens.

By 1629, when the Massachusetts Bay Company was formed in England to finance the establishment of a third settlement on the American coast, the hardships and mistakes of both the Virginia and Plymouth colonists were well known. Every attempt was therefore made to
avoid some of those pitfalls. John Winthrop, leader of the Puritans
who emigrated to Massachusetts Bay, was a rich and intelligent man,
who had achieved notability in the practice of law. Among various
other writings, he drafted a bill for the House of Commons, "For Preventing Drunkenness," in which he maintained that the potency of
beer and ale should be controlled — "to that proportion of strength, as
may be wholesome for our bodye, and not influencing to drunkenness,"
specifically 2½ bushels of malt to one hogshead of beer or ale.[27]

In 1628, an advance group of settlers, under the leadership of John
Endicott, was dispatched to the coast of Massachusetts, somewhat north
of Plymouth; and two years later, the large emigration took place. Its
size alone (nearly a thousand people) and its superior outfitting made
it a decidedly more viable operation than either the Virginia or Plymouth settlements had been, and yet it too barely survived the first winter
— a particularly brutal one.

Winthrop himself sailed on the ship *Arbella*, which had among its
provisions "42 Tonnes of Beere [about 10,000 gallons] " and "4 Pompes
per water and beere." [28] There were obviously other liquid refreshments
on board, for Winthrop records the case of "A maid servant," who, because she was "stomach sick,"

> drank so much strong water, that she was senseless, and had near
> killed herself. We observed it a common fault in our young people,
> that they gave themselves to drink hot waters very immoderately.[29]

* A large barrel or cask; in seventeenth-century England, equal to 48 ale gallons or
54 beer gallons.

His disapproval of "strong water" and obvious approval of beer is typical of his period, particularly among the Puritans, to whom the notion of temperance was fitting and appealing. Moreover, beer was considered to be a means of maintaining good health on an ocean crossing. Richard Mather, the Puritan minister, made a point of this when he took the voyage in 1635:

> And a speciall means of ye healthfulnesse of ye passengers by ye blessing of God wee all conceyved to bee much walking in ye open ayre, and ye comfortable variety of our food; . . . we had no want of good and wholesome beere and bread.[30]

William Wood, writing at about the same time, recommended "sixeshilling Beere" among ship's provisions, and also advised prospective settlers in New England to carry malt with them.[31]

Upon his arrival in Massachusetts Bay, Winthrop was greeted on board by William Peirce and John Endicott, who had, as it were, laid the groundwork for him. He returned with them to the shore, where "they supped with a good venison pasty and good beer." [32] He does not tell us, however, what we would like to know: whether the beer had been brewed in America or brought over from England in one of the ships.

If this particular beer was not brewed in America (and most likely it was not), brewing certainly began shortly afterward in Winthrop's colony. In 1633, Emmanuel Dowling wrote from England to his nephew, John Winthrop, Jr., about

> a furnace for brewinge or boylinge salt or sope etc. since the shippinge hereof I haue caused another to be made wh Sir [Richard] Saltonstall hath bought on me, for the price I paid the worke-man, but he should not have had the same, had he not promised to send it to the plantation wh accordingly he hath done.[33]

All through 1633, there are references in the Winthrop letters to the shipping of malt from England. Barley had not yet been successfully grown in sufficient quantity for any extensive malting to be possible in America, though Winthrop, Sr., does remark, as of 1632: "This week they had in barley and oats, at Sagus"; [34] and the records of Charlestown around 1640 give "maulsters lane" as an address.[35]

As early as 1634, only four years after Winthrop's arrival, steps were being taken by the Governor and Company of the Massachusetts Bay Colony to regulate the local "ordinaries" (taverns or inns). On 3 September, for instance, "It is ordered, that no person that keeps an ordinarie shall take above 6d. a meal of a person, and not above 1d. for an ale quart* of beer." [36]

By an order of 4 March 1635, no person was allowed to keep a "common victualing howse, without license from the Court," [37] and as a result of widespread drunkenness, a General Court held at Newtown on 20 November 1637 laid down a number of stringent rules for inn- and tavern-keepers. They were to sell or have in their houses only wine, spirits or beer that could be sold by law for no more than 1d. a quart; they were not to brew their own beer but to buy from a "common [commercial] brewer." What was more, the "common brewer" had to be licensed by the General Court or the Court of Assistants, and the prices he could demand were also specified. At this particular court, Captain Robert Sedgwick, who had "before this time set up a brew house at his great charge, & very commodious for this part of the countrey," was named as licensed common brewer.[38]

Sedgwick, who certainly must rank as one of the earliest American commercial brewers,† owned property in Charlestown (now a part of Greater Boston), and it was there that this brewhouse was located.[39] What its size was, what equipment it contained: these facts were not recorded. Sedgwick's operation was undoubtedly modest. All that was needed was several vats — or even barrels would do: one for the mashing, one for cooling, another perhaps for fermenting. (In home brewing, even a single vat would have been enough.) Sedgwick was interested in a good many other things than his brewing, for he was an active soldier as well as merchant. He helped in the organization of the Massachusetts Military Company, and was three times its captain. In his commercial career, he was successful enough to endow Harvard College

---

* In early English liquid measures, the ale quart contained more than the beer quart. An ale hogshead contained 192 quarts, a beer hogshead 216. See note on page 9.

† There appear to have been two other brewers in this family: Stephen Sedgwick, probably Robert's uncle, and a brother, John Sedgwicke, of St. Saviour's, Southwark, England (Pope, p. 406).

in 1647 with what the records call merely a "shop." He particularly distinguished himself in military service under Cromwell, with the ultimate rank of major-general, and died in Jamaica in 1656.[40]

Nearly a year after those 1637 laws were enunciated, a law was passed permitting innkeepers to brew "the beer which they sell in their houses, or to agree with the brewer as they can." And this liberalizing trend continued in a law passed on 22 May 1639, repealing all former orders about "restraint of beer." [41]

It may be that Sedgwick was unable to supply all the beer that was called for. As noted before, the Puritan leaders were generally consistent in favoring the use of beer, as a wholesome and nourishing beverage, over spirits or brandy, which they considered too quickly intoxicating and therefore conducive of immodest behavior. By restricting the manufacture of beer, however, and placing it exclusively in the hands of Captain Sedgwick, they probably brought about a shortage which, in turn, led to an increase in the use of spirits — the very opposite of their intention. Consequently, they had to reverse themselves in 1639, and make it legal for more people to brew commercial beer.

At this same period, during the 1630s, similar regulatory laws were being enacted in both the Plymouth and Virginia colonies. The latter was, by then, of course, no longer weak and ailing, but firmly established, blossoming, and finding its way into an agricultural prosperity based on tobacco. Back in England, John Smith wrote a general history of Virginia in 1629, in which he stated that the colony had two brewhouses:

> For drink, some malt the Indian corne, others barley, of which they make good Ale, both strong and small, and such plentie thereof, few of the upper Planters drinke any water; but the better sort are well furnished with Sacke, Aquavitae, and good English Beere.[42]

Smith was doubtless trying to paint a glowing picture of the colony, in order to attract more settlers to it. In the same way, a frequently quoted pamphlet published in London in 1649 made Virginia out to have every possible blessing:

10. That they have plenty of barley, make excellent malt.
11. That they have six publick brew-houses, and most brew their own beer, strong and good.
12. That their hops are fair and large, thrive well. . . .

38. That they have health very well, and fewer die in a year there, according to the proportion, than in any place of England; since that men are provided with all necessaries, have plenty of victual, bread, and good beer, and housing, all which the Englishman loves full dearly.[43]

This anonymous report reads suspiciously like tourist-agency propaganda; and yet, added to the statement of Smith twenty years earlier, it must be partially accepted as indicating that there certainly were brewing activities in Virginia prior to 1650, and that Virginians were drinking beer brewed either in their homes or by licensed brewers as well as that which was imported from the home country.

✎§ *TWO* ৡ◈

The Art and Mystery of Brewing

W HAT WAS this beer that our seventeenth-century forebears found so necessary to their well-being? How was it made? And how did it differ from or resemble twentieth-century beer?

First, a basic definition: beer (used as a generic term meaning malt liquor) is the product of fermentation of an infusion or a decoction* of cereal malt. Ingredients and taste vary widely, but any beverage that may be correctly called "beer" must go through the following stages: the original cereal must first be dampened to induce germination, then heated and dried to cut off germination, thereby producing *malt*; the malt must be ground and infused or decocted with water, a process called "mashing"; the resulting "wort," after straining and cooling, must then have yeast introduced into it to cause fermentation. It is in this last stage, through the yeast's feeding on the sugar content of the malt, that alcohol and carbonic-acid gas (carbon dioxide) are formed.

While it is true that beer is made up of these ingredients, they do not simply add up to "beer": the end product is something less tangible — something greater than its ingredients. It is useful to think of brewing as a form of cooking — which, indeed, it is. The word "brew" is a distant etymological relation of words like "broth" and "boil."

A great variety of cereals have been used during the five thousand years since malt liquors were first made. But barley, as early as in the pe-

---

* In a decoction, the solid substance is introduced into water and then they are boiled up together; in an infusion, the substance is immersed in hot boiled water and steeped, like tea.

riod of ancient Egypt, was preferred above all others, because of the superior beverage it produced.

In England, the art of brewing goes back at least as far as the third century,[1] and the beverage which remained popular through the Middle Ages and on into modern times was "ale." But the word "ale" specifically meant, until the seventeenth century, the traditional English malt beverage which contained no hops, and was differentiated from "beer," a hopped malt beverage which had been introduced into England by Dutch brewers in the fifteenth century.

The original English ale has been described as sweetish — stronger and more perishable than hopped beer. According to an article on this subject in a recent special edition of *The Times*, ale "had about three times the potency of the 'single' or cheapest beer of the Elizabethans and nearly twice that of their 'double' beer." [2] A useful interaction took place between ale and beer, as understood at that time. Beer, the "artful beverage," as it was called, taught ale how to keep, and from ale it learned how to be stronger.[3]

"Beer is a stranger, a Dutch upstart, come," begins an early seventeenth-century ballad,

> Whose credit with us sometimes is small;
> But in records of the Empire of Rome,
> The old Catholic drink is a pot of good ale.[4]

The drinking of wine was generally taken, in the seventeenth and eighteenth centuries, to be a prerogative of the privileged classes. On the other hand, beer and ale were not specifically the province of the poor; even royalty was known to indulge a taste for beer. The contrast between country and city tastes, however, seems to be the only real distinction that existed between ale and beer during the sevententh century, for both at this time were hopped. Not until the introduction of *porter* in the 1720s was a real semantic distinction possible again, but even in modern times there is a justifiable confusion over the difference between the two terms. When Thomas Hariot, in the sixteenth century, wrote of the feasibility of making ale from corn,* he added, "So likewise by the help of hops thereof may bee made as good Beere,"

* See page 17.

going along with the prevailing notion of a somewhat earlier age that ale was not hopped.[5]

The author of a brewing manual published in England in 1692 speaks interchangeably of "beer" and "ale," [6] and similar treatises published even in the early part of the nineteenth century distinguish between ale and beer only in terms of the color of malt used,* the ratio of hops to malt, and the temperature and timing of the mashing. A typical unembellished statement of this kind is that beer "is distinguished from ale by having a greater quantity of hops, whence it is more bitter, and will keep longer." [7] (In modern times, beer and ale have come to be differentiated mainly by the type of yeast used in their brewing.)

It was a common practice until well into the nineteenth century to refer to "strong beer," "table beer," "ship's beer" and "small beer." These were distinctions of strength, depending on the amount of time the malt was allowed to boil or steep in hot water, and also on the alcoholic content. "Small beer" was the weakest and was meant to be drunk immediately after being brewed. The strongest beers, in both taste and alcoholic content, were those which kept best: gentlemen in those days, after all, kept barrels of beer in their cellars along with wine.

The beer or ale brought over from England by the colonists was doubtless a hopped beverage made of barley malt, brewed to extra strength in order to survive the buffeting of an ocean voyage. The beer first made in America, however, may well have been unhopped; though hops were native to America and found growing wild, they were not available to the early settlers in any quantity and even imported supplies were far from adequate.

But the settlers brought with them an English tradition of using substitute ingredients whenever necessary. Wheat or oats would certainly do if barley was lacking. But they also experimented with persimmons, pumpkins and the Jerusalem artichoke.[8]

> The fruit, seeds and all, was crushed, mixed with wheat bran, then baked in cakes. As occasion arose, the cakes were soaked in water and the beer brewed.[9]

* Depending on the temperature at which malt is dried, it will come out darker or lighter. The darkest malts are used in brewing stout and porter; lighter malts and mixtures of dark and light malts go into the brewing of brown ale, amber ale, pale ale, dark and light beers, etc.

A kind of imitation beer could also be made of molasses, but it was the native Indian corn, or maize, that the colonists were most anxious to use as a basis for brewing. Thomas Hariot gave the earliest report of beer produced from maize: "Wee made of the same in the countrey some mault, whereof was brued as good ale as was to be desired." [10] Later, a writer of 1620 remarked optimistically that the Virginia settlers had found a way to make a beverage from maize, which he himself preferred to English beer.[11] The problem of malting maize also engaged the attention of John Winthrop, Jr., son of the original governor of Massachusetts, and himself governor of Connecticut. In 1662, after being admitted to membership in the Royal Society in London, the leading scientific institution of his day, he presented a paper on that very subject: making malt of maize.*

Though maize was easy to grow in the new country, where it had been discovered, and proved to be extraordinarily useful, it did not become popular as a basis of beer manufacture, for the records show that malt was constantly imported from England, and at the same time increasing amounts of barley for malting were being grown in the colonies.

When hops were not readily available (as was probably the case until about 1640, although four hundredweight of them are supposed to have been shipped over to Massachusetts in 1629),[12] sassafras, spruce, or a variety of herbs could be used to replace them. Spruce beer, which had a certain vogue even into the late eighteenth century, was supposed to be especially efficacious against scurvy.

The most characteristic aspect of brewing in the seventeenth century, however, was its chanciness. Brewers understood very little about the technology of their trade, and the chemistry involved was a total blank to them. Even measuring devices, such as the thermometer, the hydrometer (to measure strength) and the attemperator (for control of the temperature of brews in process), did not come into practical use until the second half of the eighteenth century.[13] Everything about their brewing was inaccurate and capricious; they could not explain why one brew came out well and the next poorly. The properties and control of yeast remained unexplored until the researches of Pasteur and Han-

* See Appendix One.

sen in the 1870s. No wonder we find references to "the art and *mystery* of brewing."

The wonder, indeed, is how they were able, with a completely empirical approach, to produce a palatable brew as regularly as they did. Their success is probably best seen in terms of a baker or cook who, by practice and instinct, can usually make a decent loaf of bread or an admirable stew — though carelessness may occasionally lead to an out-and-out failure.

Brewing in New Netherland

A T THE TIME when America began to be seriously colonized, the Dutch, on a world-wide scale, were the most powerful mercantile competitors of the English. It was no surprise, then, that the Dutch should have been seeking to establish a colony on the American mainland at about the same time as the English. One year after the Pilgrims had made their precarious crossing of the Atlantic, a West India Company was formed in Holland. Speculators, investors, merchants joined together for the main purpose of exploiting the fur resources of the upper Hudson River and the Mohawk Valley areas, where intrepid Dutch traders had been operating independently for nearly ten years. The first permanent settlement was made, under the auspices of the West India Company, in 1623; two small colonies were established that year at Fort Orange (which subsequently became part of Albany) and Fort Nassau (the site of Camden, New Jersey) on the Delaware River. It was probably not until 1626 that Peter Minuit made his canny purchase of Manhattan Island and began the settlement of New Amsterdam.

The tenuous colony did not develop rapidly; in 1629 there were only 350 people there. About three years later, however, the West India Company saw fit to build a brewery not far from the fort, on a street which became known afterward as "Brouwers [Brewers'] Straet." [1] The Dutch were, if anything, even more partial to beer than the English. The company brewery continued in operation, supplying the settlement's needs, until 1651, when Peter Stuyvesant, needing as many taxes as he could procure, saw the wisdom of letting some private brewer (of which there were a good number) take over the company's business.

The Dutch had found, as early as 1626, that the ingredients for brewing could be grown in the new world.[2] One of the contemporary chroniclers wrote that the Dutch in New Amsterdam could "brew as good beer here as in our Fatherland, for good hops grow in the woods."[3] Indeed, in their New Amsterdam farming, the Dutch concentrated on "rye, barley, wheat, oats and hops, which could be distilled into hard liquor or brewed into strong beer."[4]

One of the means by which the West India Company sought to attract more emigrants to New Netherland was the "patroon" system. Large tracts of land were granted under advantageous charters to individuals who were willing to settle, at their own expense, a colony of fifty adults. The most notable of these "patroons" was Kiliaen van Rensselaer, an Amsterdam jeweler and director of the company, who acquired extremely valuable and spacious land near Fort Orange up the Hudson. Shortly after he obtained his grant, Rensselaer (who never came to America but managed his property efficiently from afar) wrote that "as soon as there is a supply of grain on hand, I intend to erect a brewery to provide all New Netherland with beer, for which purpose there is already a brew kettle there."[5] That brew kettle caused Rensselaer to write at least one more letter about its disposal; chances are good that it finally came to rest in the brewery that was built, possibly before 1637, on the patroon's land. This enterprise, which was supervised at first by Rutger Hendricksen van Soest (a 1630 arrival in New Netherland), was supposed to have the exclusive account of all retail dealers in the Manor of Rensselaerwyck. Private brewing for home consumption was allowed, but unlicensed brewing for retail sale was not. There is record of one particular offender, Cornelis Segersz, who was accused in 1646 of presuming "to meddle with what is not his business — with beer brewing — directly contrary to the grant and authorization given to the brewery of this colony." He was warned either to stop at once or to pay a fine.[6] On the other hand, an independent brewer was authorized around the same time — probably on payment of license fees. His name was Evert Pels van Steltyn; he arrived from the Netherlands on the ship *Houttuyn* about 1637 and providently brought along with him on the ship some two or three hundred bushels of malt.[7]

Similarly, the patroon's carpenter, Jean Labadie, obtained permission on 15 June 1647 to build a house at Fort Orange for use as a brewery "without injury to the Interests of the Company, promising that he shall pay annually for this favor six merchantable Beavers to the company," and also to continue his carpentering.[8]

The patroon's brewery was rented in 1649 by Goosen Gerrittsen van Schaick and Rutger Jacobsen van Schoenderwoerdt, progenitor of the distinguished New York brewing family called Rutgers. The rent of the brewery came to 450 guilders paid yearly; in addition, one guilder was collected for every tun of beer brewed.[9]

The fact that the patroon owned an official brewery did not interfere with the fact that his son, Jeremias, when he came over to be director of the colony in 1658, set about remodeling for himself a dwelling which had a brewhouse attached to it. Jeremias married, in 1662, the daughter of Oloff Stevensen van Cortlandt, New Amsterdam brewer. They lived in his newly rebuilt house until 1666, when an accumulation of ice on the river caused flooding and ruin to the house and "the barn and the brewery, the new as well as the old." Two years later he was building again, but this time on high land north of Albany; by June 1668 he had already erected his brewery, though the new house itself was not ready until a year later.[10]

Another of the patroons, David Pieterssen de Vries, had a less extensive property than Rensselaer's, situated on land near Tappan and called Vriesendael. He also had a farm on Staten Island, which suffered a fierce Indian attack in February 1643. Livestock, crops and barns were destroyed, but an intervention at the last minute by an Indian who owed de Vries a favor saved the main house and the brewery.

The company manufactured beer in New Amsterdam, the patroons manufactured beer, tavern-keepers manufactured beer, and many of the colonists were busy making beer in their own houses. When other things went short, there always seemed to be a sufficiency of inexpensive beer, and even enough to sell or barter to Virginia during the 1640s.[11] To make doubly sure, beer was even imported from the Netherlands.

By 1638, when Willem Kieft replaced the hopeless Wouter van Twil-ler as governor, it was estimated that one-fourth of the city consisted of houses in which tobacco and beer could be bought — seventeen licensed taverns and about seven more where beer and spirits were sold illegally.[12]

New Amsterdam was the first cosmopolitan city on the American mainland; small in area, but teeming with life and resembling Amster-dam itself in its rows of narrow brick buildings with their crow-stepped gables. Dutch and foreign ships found it convenient to anchor there; in the streets a babel of languages could be heard: Flemish, French, Eng-lish. The director boasted to a visiting Jesuit missionary in 1646 that there were "men of eighteen different languages" in the bustling town.[13] One of the public places in which these people met was the White Horse Tavern, run by a Frenchman, Philip Gérard, and his wife, Marie Pollet. The tavern (not far from what later became known as the Battery) is described as consisting of one room, measuring eighteen by twenty-five feet, with a single door and window.

> It was always crowded with drinkers during the legal drinking hours, which were from early morning until ten in the evening, and did a brisk business after hours as well as during church service on Sunday, when drinking was also banned.[14]

The favorite tavern of Long Island farmers, who came into the settle-ment to sell their vegetables, was owned by Sergeant Daniel Litschoe on the East River shore, quite near to the White Horse Tavern. Another well-known tavern-keeper of Dutch Manhattan was Martin Kregier, who was captain of the burgher guard as well, and evidently a most energetic citizen.

The company also invaded the tavern business in 1642, when Director Kieft ordered a handsome little stone inn to be erected. It was called the "Stadt Herberg" (City Tavern), and its purpose was apparently to relieve Kieft from having to entertain the many passing traders and visitors to New Amsterdam in his personal quarters at the fort. Traffic between New England and Virginia was increasing and New Amsterdam was a suitable stop en route. The tavern provided shelter and sustenance to a multitude of visitors until 1653, when it became the "Stadt Huys" (City Hall), meeting place of the newly established city magistracy.[15]

The director had to spend a good deal of his time issuing regulations for taverns (legal hours of business, prohibition of sales to Indians, keeping of the Sabbath, licenses, etc.) — in fact, so much time that the only conclusion to be drawn is that the Dutch settlers were an unruly crowd who rarely bothered to observe the law in spite of severe penalties.

As for those who brewed privately, the records are full of references to property sales "including brewhouse."* Except for the immediate family needs, however, and perhaps in times of short supplies, the home-brewer could probably do better by patronizing one of the commercial breweries that were established in the '40s and '50s. There were at least ten of these, a generous number in view of the population (1600 in New Amsterdam when the British took over the colony in 1664); and it is a point of interest that so many of those Dutch brewers became men of wealth and authority, with names that are famous in New York history.

Oloff Stevensen van Cortlandt, who arrived at New Amsterdam in 1637 as an employee of the West India Company, took up the brewing business in 1648. He had obtained a lot for a house and garden in 1645; here (on Marketfield Street) he eventually built a brewery which was called "extensive." [16] Van Cortlandt participated in municipal politics and was appointed, in 1650, president of a citizens' group called "Nine Men," who sought to extend the right of self-government in opposition to the iron rule of Director Peter Stuyvesant.

Jacob Wolfertsen van Couwenhoven, an immigrant from Amersfoort in the Netherlands, obtained land for a house and brewery on 12 December 1645.[17] The fact that there was a good well on this property no doubt contributed to his brewing plans. After several false starts, he managed to get the brewery built about ten years later; but he launched his business with a load of debts and was never able to recover. By 1656, a fellow-brewer and friend, Isaac de Foreest, applied to the city council for permission to draw up a contract with van Couwenhoven for all the strong beer the latter could brew in a year,

* Hendrick Jansen, tailor, for example, sold his house and barn in 1641, but reserved for himself his brewhouse and two brew kettles. In an inventory of the property of the widow of Jonas Bronck, dated May 1643, "agricultural and brewing implements" are included. A house and brewery, belonging originally to Reyndert Jansen Hoorn and bought in 1661 by a Frenchman, François de Bruyn, was reported up for sale by the City Marshal in 1663. (Stokes, vol. 4, pp. 94, 224; Wilson, *Memorial History*, vol. 1, p. 225.)

so that such a well-situated brewery as that [of van Couwenhoven] may not be abandoned, but to the contrary may become the means to maintain decently that man with his family, while otherwise his ruin might be unavoidable.[18]

Van Couwenhoven appears to have been one of those improvident businessmen who are doomed, through bad organization and financial incompetence, to eventual failure.

Van Couwenhoven had a more successful younger brother, Peter, who set up a brewing establishment of his own in New Amsterdam. For six years he served as Schepen (magistrate) of the city, and distinguished himself in the fight against the Indians in the area of Esopus, up the Hudson. In later years, as a result of his disfavor with the English, Peter van Couwenhoven left New York to settle in New Jersey. His New York brewery was sold in 1670 to Isaac van Vleck, who seems to have made a success of the business and — like so many of his co-brewers — served in the municipal government in 1684 and 1686.[19]

Jacob Kip, son of one of the earliest Dutch settlers, had a position at first with the city magistrates. After taking up the trade of brewing in 1658, he eventually became one of New York's foremost merchants. His marriage to the widow of Guleyn Verplanck was fortunate in adding a considerable amount of property to his interests.[20] The area in New York City called Kip's Bay is named for this family.

The Bayard brothers — Nicholas, Balthazar and Peter — doubtless profited from the fact that they were nephews of Director Stuyvesant. Arriving shortly after Stuyvesant made his first appearance in New Amsterdam (1647), they all engaged in brewing and became prominent citizens of the colony. Balthazar married a daughter of Govert Loockermans, a wealthy merchant whose brewhouse appears in the record of a legal suit in which he was involved.[21] Balthazar eventually became owner of extensive city properties, and in 1691 was listed as alderman.

Nicholas, outside of his prominence as a brewer, became an important factor in political events after the changeover from Dutch to English control. He was a conspicuous opponent of Jacob Leisler, the curious German who took the management of New York into his own hands and held out against the English from 1689 to 1691. Nicholas Bayard was one of the loyalist leaders, and during that period was often in jail and on the verge of execution.

William Beekman, both of whose names have remained in constant use as a means of geographical identification, came to New Amsterdam in 1647, at the time of Stuyvesant's appointment, and served in a variety of administrative positions for the company and later for the city. At one period, he was in charge of the settlements on the Delaware River. He is stated to have been in the brewing business as early as 1658,[22] and according to the old city records, in 1670 (after the Dutch administration), he bought a farm situated outside the city wall, and made use of the brewhouse which had been erected and operated there by the former owner, Thomas Hall, an Englishman.[23] In 1674, Beekman's fellow-citizens appointed him burgomaster.

A business establishment mentioned in 1660 was the Red Lion Brewery, owned by Isaac de Foreest (the friend and would-be supporter of Jacob van Couwenhoven), Joannes Verveelen (owner of a tavern) and Johannes de la Montagne.[24] It is likely that this was at first the property of de Foreest alone, and that he took in Verveelen as his partner in 1660. Doubtless the first example of a brewery in America that operated under a company name, so to speak, it eventually was turned over entirely to Verveelen and his brother, Daniel. In 1663, the latter took it on alone. The building was demolished in July 1675.[25] De Foreest, a man of great enterprise, seems to have owned at least one other brewery — on Stone Street (the former "Brouwers Straet") — which was bought in 1693 by Harman Rutgers.

Sometime in the 1650s, a commercial brewery was erected by Jan Damen, at the foot of a hill pasture called the Claaver Weytie, where there was a good water supply. The brewery was operated by Damen's stepson, Jan Vinje, who is supposed to have been the first male born of European parents in New Netherland.[26] Upon Damen's death, it was sold for 1375 guilders, but several years later it passed back into Vinje's hands. The brewery is described as occupying "a rear position in the spacious enclosure which was about eighty feet front by one hundred and sixty in depth." The street it stood on later became known as Pearl Street.[27]

The beer produced by the Dutch at these various breweries received numerous compliments over the years. The patroon David de Vries wrote that New Amsterdam beer challenged that made in the Netherlands.[28] Nicasius de Sille, councillor for the West India Company and eventually sheriff of New Amsterdam, wrote back to The Hague shortly after his arrival in America: "This country suits me exceedingly well. I shall not try to leave it as long as I live. . . . Beer is brewed here as good as in Holland, of barley and wheat. . . ." And a few months later, in the same vein, "This country is good and healthy. . . . They brew good beer here, but the wine still comes from the fatherland." [29]

Because the beer was so pleasing and so plentiful, and because the Dutch and their visitors drank so much of it, it was inevitable that the colonial administration would seek to obtain revenue from it. The first step in this direction was during a period of war with the Indians. Kieft and the Council ordered an excise tax* on liquors and beaver skins, to provide money for the payment of troops and the prosecution of war. As far as the brewers and tavern-keepers went, two guilders were to be paid for each half-barrel of beer tapped — one half payable by the brewer, and one half by the tapster.[30] The receiver of the excise must have been in a desperately unhappy position, for everything written about this tax points to the fact that brewer and tapster alike were extraordinarily delinquent in the payment of it. On the formal level, through their appointed citizen-representatives, they protested that the director had no right of taxation. Only the company at The Hague could levy taxes.

On 28 October 1644, Kieft issued even more rigorous instructions; the brewers were to make an exact return of the quantity they might brew, and to pay a tax of three guilders on every barrel.[31] The brewers refused to pay this tax, and the matter was officially brought into court. Since the court consisted only of Kieft and the Council, who were appointed by him and completely dependent, the brewers were readily found guilty, their beer being confiscated and handed over to the soldiers.

This excise on beer and spirits kept relations between the director and

---

* A tax on the consumption, sale or manufacture of products within the country. The first English excise tax, copied from one existing in the Netherlands, was established on 28 March 1643 and included ale and beer. The term was used "from the excision of a part of the article taxed." (Stephen Dowell, A History of Taxation and Taxes in England, vol. 2, p. 9.)

citizens in a state of incessant friction. When there was a real crisis, the brewers and tavern-keepers would contribute what they considered appropriate to their own defense, but as soon as the crisis was over, they would again refuse to pay. The burghers found this tax so irksome that the "Nine Men" drew up a long list of grievances against the colonial administration, which they called a *Remonstrance*. They sent three of their most distinguished and responsible citizens — including Jacob van Couwenhoven, the brewer — to deliver the *Remonstrance* to the directors of the West India Company and to try some personal persuasion as well.

The crucial struggle, however, occurred later between Peter Stuyvesant and the citizens. While the company in The Hague vacillated, war with the English was threatening in the colony. Stuyvesant, hard-pressed for funds, had imposed additional excise taxes, above and beyond those of his predecessor. In losing the struggle, as he did in 1653, Stuyvesant unwittingly paved the way for self-government. The citizens had demanded that the liquor excise, which had been going into the treasury of the company, should instead belong to the city. Stuyvesant was forced by the circumstances of the moment to capitulate, and the foundation of authoritarianism was shaken. The first application for a municipal form of government which had been made in 1649 included among the signatures of the "Nine Men" four brewers: Jacob van Couwenhoven, Michiel Jansen, Thomas Hall and Hendrick Hendricksen Kip.[32] It took four years for them to achieve this objective, for Stuyvesant was a formidable, ruthless opponent and the struggle a hard one.

The Dutch, as mentioned above, depended not just on their Amsterdam breweries, but set up brewing establishments in every one of their holdings. In the settlement of Beverwyck, which developed later into Albany, a brewery was started, probably before 1650, by Captain Volkest Janse Douw, from Frederickstadt, who collaborated in this enterprise with Jan Thomase Witbeck.[33] Their brewery, which extended to the river, was sold in 1675 to Harman Rutgers, only son of that Rutger Jacobsen van Schoenderwoerdt* who had rented the patroon's brewery. Harman Rutgers sold his Beverwyck brewery two months after buying it,

* See page 21.

but maintained one that he had inherited from his father. Harman continued here with apparent success (one of his clients being the Dutch Church, to which he supplied beer for funerals) until 1693, when the repeated incursions of hostile Indians made it advisable for him to take his family away from Albany to New York.[34] There he acquired a brewery belonging to Isaac de Foreest,* and brought up his two sons, Anthony and Harman II, in the brewing tradition. They each had breweries of their own, and eventually, *their* sons in turn came into the business. In the sense that four consecutive generations remained in the brewing business, the Rutgerses may be spoken of as the first of the "brewing families" in America.

The Hudson River settlement of Esopus (in the Kingston neighborhood) apparently produced a memorable brew which came to be called " 'Sopus ale." † The water of the river that far up has been credited by tradition with making a particularly delicate product.[35] The earliest reference to a brewer in Esopus appears in a 1663 "Journal of the Second Esopus War," kept by Captain Martin Kregier, the New Amsterdam tavern-keeper; the man is simply called "Jacob, the Brewer." [36] And Esopus was the scene of open dissatisfaction in 1666, after the Dutch capitulation, when the English commander arrested the village brewer — possibly the same Jacob mentioned by Kregier. The villagers were so outraged by this provocative act that they "gathered in fierce excitement; one of them was killed by a soldier, and Nicolls [the English commander] was only able to suppress the rising by severe measures." [37] The stolid Dutch could always be aroused when a question of their drinking supplies was involved.

As for the settlements on the Delaware, they had not amounted to much. There was some trifling competition from the Swedes, who, with the help, incidentally, of Peter Minuit, established a small colony, called Fort Christina, at a location which later became Wilmington. Colonization was not seriously undertaken by the Swedes until about 1642, when a governor, Johan Printz, was sent out with a small group of colonists. These people, few as they were, remained tenaciously, although they

---

* See page 25.
† The tradition apparently carried on into the nineteenth century. An official study of manufactures published in 1833 refers to a brewery then in Esopus, capable of brewing four to five thousand barrels of ale during the season.

can hardly be said to have flourished. Printz was replaced in 1654 by Johan Rising, but growing tensions between New Sweden and New Netherland in America culminated the following year in a series of mutual attacks, ending with a foreseeable Dutch victory and consequent annexation by Stuyvesant of the Swedish settlements, which became known then as New Amstel.

The second vice-governor of that colony, Jacob Alrichs, complained in a report written upon his arrival in 1657 that "there is neither baker nor brewer here," and that the colonists were using "Manhattan beer." [38] This need not necessarily mean that the Swedes had not engaged in brewing before the Dutch victory — in fact, there is some evidence that they had. David de Vries, for example, reports that he sailed up the Delaware River in 1643, and that at Fort Christian, "Captain Prins [the governor] had a silver mug brought, with which he treated the skipper with hop beer." [39]

Among the supplies carried by the 1642 immigrants, in two ships, is listed "malt for their brewing." [40] In his 1644 report to the Noble West India Company in Sweden, Printz commented that "everything is fearfully dear here. One barrel of malt, Swedish measure, is worth seven, yes even eight, rix-dollars,* a pound of hops, half a rix-dollar." [41]

In 1650, he wrote that the colonists were sowing rye and barley.[42] His successor, Johan Rising, offered a business suggestion in his first report in 1654: "With brewery and distillery and alehouses and well-fitted inns there would be a good profit for the company to be made." Rising decidedly had beer on the mind: in his 1655 report he requested a variety of workmen from Sweden, including "hop-garden masters,"[43] and he is often quoted as having specified, in writing back to Sweden for a wife, that she must number among her domestic accomplishments the ability to make malt and brew ale.[44]

The Dutch Vice-Governor Alrichs, who continued to agitate for a brewing operation in New Amstel, must have been satisfied in his wish to some extent, for in 1661 the name of Adam Dortmans, brewer, appears among the colony's bills payable.[45] And two years later, ever on the search for ways of making some income for his employers, Alrichs sug-

---

* Scandinavian silver coin, no longer used.

gested that since the English in Maryland did not brew strong beer (presumably for lack of materials), perhaps the New Amstel colony would do well to sell barley and buckwheat to the Maryland settlers.[46] No doubt Alrichs would have continued to propose new means of bringing prosperity to New Amstel, but in 1664, the settlement fell, like the rest of the Dutch colony in America, under English control, and many changes naturally took place. This transfer of ownership simply reflected the outcome of the power struggle which had been going on between those two imposing rivals all over the world. But in the case of the American possessions in particular, the Dutch appear to have hastened their disinheritance by mismanaging their affairs badly; in dealing with the Indians they were remarkably maladroit; and the English, with the help of political-economic conditions at home, were able to plant many more dedicated and durable emigrants in the new territories than the Dutch ever could.

FOUR

Seventeenth-Century Brewing

B Y THE SECOND half of the seventeenth century, the colonies which then existed on the eastern Atlantic coast of America were individually well rooted, and by 1675 England had established firm control of them all. Yet there were too many squabbles going on at home, too many back-and-forth transfers of authority, too many administrative changes and confusions — not to speak of constant military excursions against the Indians as well as the prodding French — for the colonists to feel sufficiently secure to risk a significant expansion of their mercantile activities. Indeed, the colonies continued to represent a financial loss to their London backers. Land was still the greatest source of prosperity, because of the tobacco and grain that could be raised in exportable quantities. In the New England colonies, shipping, shipbuilding, fishing and the manufacture of rum were on the way toward laying down an important basis of wealth. Various of the original schemes for quick fortunes had wisely been tossed on the discard pile. On the other hand, there were strong hopes for the successful manufacture of iron, tar, resin and potash.

As for the infant brewing industry, it was barely out of the crib in the second half of the century, although popular drinking habits (except for the gradual introduction of rum) changed little.* In the main, beer was produced in the home for daily table use. The most prosperous or pretentious households tended to use beer imported from London, either directly or through provisioners. Such commercial breweries as were

* See page 12.

actually operating in America fulfilled a demand, not of any great proportions, somewhere between those two extremes.

In Virginia the records show only one licensed brewer in this period.* The Assembly on 25 November 1652

> ordered that Mr. George Fletcher shall have to himself, his heires, ex'rs. and adm'rs. liberty to distill and brew in wooden vessels which none have experience in but himself for fourteen years.[1]

The general situation at that time was described by a Virginia historian in the following terms:

> In some places, beer was, about the middle of the century, the most popular of all the liquors drunk in the Colony, the greater proportion of it being brewed at this time in the houses of the planters.[2]

A contemporary pamphleteer, however, took the planters' wives to task in 1656 for being "negligent or idle; for it is not for want of Corn to make Malt with (for the Country affords enough) but because they are sloathfull and carelesse." [3]

As more and more land was devoted to the fantastically profitable tobacco, barley became a scarce crop in Virginia, and malt for brewing was imported increasingly from England. In a letter dated 2 May 1660, the London shipper gave instructions to "deliver unto Mr. Robert Whithaire or Richard Merret, and in their absence, then unto Mr. Christopher Harris in Queen's Creek in York River, five hogsheads of mault." [4]

William Byrd, one of the more illustrious of early Virginia planters, wrote to England on 11 December 1688, "I fear I shall want also some malt w'ch you or I forgott." [5] This malt was intended for private individuals who evidently had resources for home brewing. The frequent references in Virginia county records to malt houses and malt mills imply that, in addition to such supplies of English malt as entered the

---

* References are made to private brewhouses. Captain John Moon, of Isle of Wight County, for instance, specified in his 1655 will that his brewhouse and land at Jamestown were to be sold for the payment of his debts. A minister near Mockjack Bay (probably Mobjack Bay) wrote to England in 1665, inquiring about "those bals or irons, for heating liquors, for brewing or distilling in barrels," and requested that two or three be sent, since they would be cheaper than copper kettles. ("Isle of Wight County Records," p. 222; "Letter Written by Mr. Moray," p. 157.)

colony, some amount of barley must have been imported from the other colonies, where it was grown in much greater quantities. Malt in itself was certainly considered to have monetary value. It might even be mentioned in a will, as Richard Borden did when he left his wife "twenty bushels of barley malt." [6] And in a James City county court action on 5 February 1691, one Thomas Taylor refused to pay for malt bought of Francis Reeves.*

The author of probably the earliest history of Virginia, written at the turn of the eighteenth century, commented that the Virginia "Small-drink" was either wine and water, beer, milk and water, or water alone.

> Their richer sort generally brew their Small-beer with Malt, which they have from *England,* though they have as good barley of their own, as any in the World; but for want of the convenience of Malt-Houses, the Inhabitants take no care to sow it.

The poorer, we are told, brewed some sort of beer out of molasses and bran, or home-malted maize, or pumpkins, etc. For their "Strong Drink" Virginians enjoyed, besides wine, rum, and brandy, "strong beer, which they have constantly from *England.*" This writer also pointed out a peculiarity of Virginia, which was that it had so few towns. It was a reasonable conjecture that if there had been more towns, there might have been more barley grown, and more malt houses built.[7]

Whereas the taverns of New England and New Netherland had required certain official controls almost from the start, the public-houses of Virginia were relatively free of these until 1658, when the General Assembly took note of "the exorbitant prices of drinke sold by ordinarie-keepers," and therefore took it upon itself to set rates and regulations and, of course, penalties for noncompliance.[8]

The value of beer appears to have increased during the course of the century; its price in 1639 was 12d. per quart and by 1671 it was selling for twice that figure. One commentator attributes the rise in price to the

---

* "That ffr. Reeves, being at his house, did propose to sell to him, forty bushells of good, every way Qualyfyed Malt, which yr ptr having present occasion for, did Agree with the sd Reeves for ye same, & Gave him from under his hand, for the payment thereof. But soe it is, may it please this Court that a little time after the sd Reeves brought to his house a sample of the sd malt, which yr ptr proving, found it to be nothing of malt, but rather Barley spoyled, soe that he refused to accept of the same" (Virginia, *Calendar of State Papers,* vol. 1, p. 28).

fact that brewing was at first local but that later all the better quality beers were imported.[9]

In 1666, the price of Virginia beer was set at 4s. or forty pounds of tobacco per gallon.[10] In 1707, "Virginia & Pensilvania beer" was half a Royal* per quart, while the same amount of English beer was one shilling[11] (a reduction from the 1671 price). Three years later, English beer maintained its price; Pennsylvania beer was 6d. and the home brew was threepence and three farthings.[12] The following year "Rogers's best Virg^a Aile" was listed with Pennsylvania beer at 6d., the English import had risen to four shillings per quart, a noteworthy jump — and "Virginia midling Bear" was still the cheapest drink at its 1710 price.[13] Clearly, the beers brewed in Virginia were the least highly valued: good enough for daily table needs, but hardly a product to be drunk for sociable delectation.

In general, the brewing situation in Virginia differed significantly from that in most of the other colonies. Certainly in some of the New England records, there are many more specific indications of brewing activity. In fact, *too* many people were slapping together some sort of beer; the Company of Massachusetts Bay had to restrict brewing in 1651 to those who had "sufficyent skill and knowledge in the art or mistery of a brewer." It was known that a number of tavern-keepers were brewing their own beer, evidently in contravention of the law and without much experience or discrimination.[14]

From 1647 through 1658 the records are cluttered with references to Martin Stebbin (in various spellings), who was both tavern-keeper and brewer, but one who was frequently in difficulties over his licenses.† The first of the Boston taverns had been established by Samuel Cole in 1633,[15] and he was followed soon after by such tapster-brewers as Isaac Grosse, his son Clement, William Whitwell, Goodwife (or Goody) Upsall, and several others, both male and female, including the ever-present

---

* Or *Ryal* or *Rial*: a gold coin formerly used by the English.

† "Martin Stibbin is forbidden and not allowed to brewe any more bear to sell, save only this week in beinge" [1647]. "Martin Stebbins, being fined five pounds for brewinge without approbation, petitioned for the remittage of his sd fine, which petn was not graunted" [1653]. (Massachusetts, *Records of the Governor and Company*, vol. 3, p. 323; Boston, Record Commissioners, Second Report, p. 91.)

Martin Stebbin. By 1682, there were in Boston six wine taverns, ten inn-holders, and eight "retaylers out of doors." [16]

The Puritan Fathers of Boston kept close track of what was going on in the tavern and the brewery; no doubt they were looked on as meddle-some. In 1651, they specified exactly what quantity of "good barley mault" must go into the brewing of every hogshead of beer and what price could then be asked: 3d. the quart if six bushels were used; 2d. if four bushels were used; and penny beer required the use of only two bushels. They were determined to see to it that taverns were serving good and wholesome beer, because otherwise the population would be put to too much needless expense in wines.[17]

They were also happy enough to acquire funds through taxation of beverages. In the excise act of 1692, it was laid down that 1/6 would be collected for every barrel of perry,* beer, ale and cider. Retailers who might brew their own beer or ale were to make entries with the tax commissioners "from time to time." [18] In a 1702 law, it was decreed that

> every brewer commonly brewing beer or ale for sale, shall pay an ex-cise for each barrel of strong beer or ale by him brewed, the sum of one shilling, and so proportionately for greater or lesser quantities.

These payments were to be made weekly, and "strong beer or ale" was specified to mean beer or ale "usually sold at more than six shillings the barrel." [19]

It appears that private brewing did not come under the provisions of the excise law, as long as the beer prepared in the home was not sold. Various property transactions show the existence of private brewhouses: for example, "Edward Tyng, house, brewhouse, warehouse, with wharf in front, which he sold in 1651, to James Everill." [20]

On the other hand, a really commercial brewing enterprise was con-cerned in the 1678 case of Sarah Frankes, widow, versus Joseph Elyot, Joseph Rock and Timothy Yales, for their failure to operate her brewing establishment as agreed. The inventory of the plant is listed in the ac-tion:

* A fermented beverage made of pears.

16 Beer Barrells at 2s per bb, 6 baggs at 2s, 1 copper ready hung and fix't, 1 mash tubb, 2 great Coolers, 4 troughs, 4 tubbs, 6 Trayes, 2 Brewing tools and one paile, 1 piggin and 1 halfe bushell, 1 large Fatt [vat], 12 quart pots and 1 pint pot, 1 great Funnell with a brass Snout.[21]

This may be taken as representing the typical equipment of a Boston brewery in the latter half of the seventeenth century: sufficient, it would seem, to provide for a tavern and perhaps neighborhood households, but no more.

Boston being a shipping town, local merchants were kept busy (and prosperous) outfitting all sorts of vessels. As of 1638, a little more than a quart of beer was received daily by every member of a New England ship's crew, and this formed a significant part of the provisioning.[22] In the accounts of the general store of John Hull in Boston, the name of Seth Perry appears frequently, between 1685 and 1689, as the brewer who supplied barrels of beer for ships being serviced by the store. Perry, born in 1639,[23] supplied seven barrels of beer at 6s. each for the ketch *Endeavour* in 1685. For the brigantine *Robert*, bound for Virginia, he supplied six barrels at the same price. By 1687, when he supplied seven barrels of beer for the *Endeavour* again, his price had dropped to 5s. Perry also sold the shop barley and malt, and they, in turn, sold malt to a variety of customers: "Mr. Abell Plats, Dr. By 20 Bush[ll] mault at 3/4 . . . Mr. Nathaniel Clark, D. By 20 Bush[ll] of mault." [24] The name of Seth Perry appears in an action brought against him on 23 October 1676 by the Boston merchant Thomas Deane, for having sold "base malt and bad bccr" [25] — a complaint which, in those days of primitive brewing, need not necessarily have implied bad faith.

The prevalence of beer and the ordinary colonist's dependence on it account for the erection of a brewhouse among the earliest concerns of Harvard College, which was founded in Cambridge in 1636. The actual brewhouse, first mentioned in 1674, may not have been built at the very beginning, for the beer required by the students could have been furnished originally by other means — perhaps it was made in some rude fashion in the kitchen. The first and extremely temporary president of Harvard, Nathaniel Eaton, was one of the least successful in the history of the university. By 1639, he was in trouble, and was brought to trial by the college authorities on a number of charges. The precipitating cause had been his mistreatment of the assistant master, Nathaniel Briscoe; but a strong contributing factor in his downfall was the students' dissatisfaction with the rations provided by Eaton's wife. In particular, they complained that they had often had to go without their beer and bread. Mrs. Eaton tried valiantly to deny this charge, but had to admit, eventually, that beer was sometimes "wanting . . . a week or half a week together."

Eaton was dismissed in disgrace, and his place was taken by the first of the admirable Harvard presidents, Henry Dunster, who groaned, in a memorandum of December 1653, that there had been laid "a 3rd burthen upon my shoulders, to bee their steward, and to Direct their brewer, baker, buttler, Cook, how to proportion their commons." [26]

The student at Harvard College in the seventeenth century (there were fewer than one hundred) was provided with two meals a day — called dinner and supper — as well as two bevers (probably from the Latin *bibere*: to drink), in the morning and in the afternoon. The "commons" (provisions served at a common table) referred to by Dunster were eaten at meals, in contrast to the "sizings" which made up the bevers. Bread and beer composed the menu for morning bever — the "sizing" (or portion) of beer being normally a pint, sold to the student at the cost of a farthing.[27]

The brewhouse furnished both single and double ("small" and "strong") beer; among the college rules of 1667 is the instruction that the butler, "receiving his Beer from the Steward, single beer at 2 shill. & double at 4ˢ the barrell shall advance four pence upon the shilling." [28]

The rules and prices were reviewed from time to time. In 1686, Increase Mather drafted a Code of College Laws which included the usual provision for beer supplies:

> The Steward shall deliver in unto the Butler his Bread at 5 shillings per Bushell, and his Beer at 4 per Barrell each Barrell consisting of sixteen gallons of Beer measure allowing thereto two pecks of Barley Malt.[29]

There was a series of brewhouses at Harvard — three, at any rate — the first two presumably being destroyed by fire. In 1762, the brewery then in existence (probably the third) was described as a one-and-a-half-story wooden building "about twenty-five feet long by twenty-four wide." Sometime toward the end of the eighteenth century, the official provision of beer was allowed to lapse, and the brewhouse was used for storage.*

One of the various curiosities about this aspect of Harvard's history is that many of the early students paid for their board with wheat or malt.[30] This was, however, not such an unusual practice in that period. The Boston records, for instance, show the lease in 1657 of two acres of land to William Winburne, for the payment of "a bushel of merchantable barley malt yearely." [31] Barley was one of New England's important crops; most of it was used for malting, but sometimes it was even baked into a fair bread. The author of a study of husbandry in early New England states that "barley and barley-malt figure far more often in the records than wheat — a fact that is scarcely surprising in view of the quantities of beer consumed by the New Englanders." [32] Yet a good deal of malt was imported † (perhaps because of a lack of malt houses and experienced maltsters rather than a shortage of barley). Even though the Puritan authorities sought to encourage the manufacture and drinking of beer, they created hardships for brewers by setting heavy duties on imported malt, and sometimes prohibited importation altogether.[33]

The other New England colonies, though overshadowed by their larger and more powerful neighbor, Massachusetts, continued in their independent ways through the second half of the seventeenth century. New Plymouth expanded with small settlements to the north and south of the original landing, and maintained its separate identity until 1691, when the union with Massachusetts Colony took place. In 1636, Roger Williams, banished from Massachusetts on a charge of heresy, set out into the wilderness and settled on Narragansett Bay, laying the foundation for Rhode Island, a colony dedicated to religious tolerance. Con-

---

* The brewhouse was finally destroyed on 3 August 1814, when some of the student body set it on fire (Bail, p. 71).

† In 1640, the ship *Neptune*, sailing from Bristol, England, for New England carried 40 hogsheads of malt (Adams, *Album of American History*, vol. 1, p. 67).

necticut started as a scattering of settlements in the 'thirties, and received its charter, achieving colony status, in 1662.

All the colonies sooner or later were concerned with the manufacture and consumption of beer, as well as with the conduct of taverns. As early as 1636, New Plymouth passed a law conscribing the sale of beverages to public houses:

> That none be suffered to retale wine or strong water, & suffer the same to be drunk in their howses, except it be at some inne or victualling howse, and there onely to strangers, at their first coming.[34]

Price control was also established: no beer was to be sold in any of those inns or victualling houses "to exceed two pence the Winchester quart." * As the colony expanded, taverns were licensed in the new settlements: Francis Sprague was licensed to "keep victualling on Duxborrow [Duxbury] side" (1638); Thomas Lumbert was licensed in Barnstable (1639); and Richard Paul was victualler in Taunton (1640).[35] As for actual brewers, only the names of John Barnes, in 1648, and Hester Rickard, in 1682, appear in the colony's records.[36] It seems likely, in the absence of any contrary information, that many of the tavern-keepers were their own brewers. But all of it was on so small a scale that one doubts whether the treasury felt much benefit from the excise act passed in 1646, assessing each hogshead of beer at 2s.[37]

Rhode Island must be looked on as a peculiar experiment in the overall history of American colonization: this was the first attempt to establish a colony from scratch with no capital or foreign aid at all. Most of those religious dissenters who followed Williams into exile were farmers, and the colony was hampered by lack of craftsmen, who might have helped to build homes of some sort, repair tools, make shoes and the like. The colonists were so poor that it was ten years before they could set up a grain mill in Providence; prior to that, they had to use a tedious hand device of the Indians to grind their grain. The governor of Plymouth, who visited them during their first year, was so impressed by their poverty that he had supplies sent to them from his own better-established colony.

* A standard of measurement, as formerly recorded at Winchester, England.

Rhode Island was not, however, entirely bereft of the normal beverages of that period.* Williams himself is said to have commented that "the Rhode Island English made good wines of grapes and strawberries, both of which he had often tasted." [38] Williams was the begetter of the first Church of the Baptists in America — a sect which has not been notable in recent history for its toleration of "good wines" or even beer.

The Providence Court of Commissioners, sitting in 1655, was constrained, by experience of Indians' drunkenness, to pass a law prohibiting the sale of liquors to them. This was a reasonable form of self-protection, for the Indians had proven to be most unfriendly, particularly when they had been drinking too generously. At the same time, it was established that each of the four towns that made up the colony (Providence, Portsmouth, Newport and Warwick) should have no more than two innkeepers each. For Providence, the two licensees were Roger Mowry and Richard Pray.[39]

The town of Portsmouth, as far back as 1647, had appointed two innkeepers, one a Mr. Boston, and the other Ralph Earle, who was chosen "to Ceepe an Inne to sell beer & wine & to intertayn strangers." [40] There must have developed some confusion during the following years because in 1650 the licenses were called in and then reissued for a small fee.†

The Town Court also stipulated in 1651 that beer could not be sold for less than 2d. a quart, and directed the "Clark of the Measures" to go once a month to those places in Portsmouth where beer was sold and make sure there were no infractions of the law.[41]

The Rhode Island Land Evidences show two maltsters operating in

---

* Unfortunately, the loss of many early Rhode Island records in 1676, during the hard-fought "Philip's War" with the Pequot Indians, makes it difficult to trace the beginnings of brewing in that colony.

† "At a towne Court march the 4th It is ordered that the Clarke shall Rite the lisences of selling beere victuals and wine and that the ffee for writing such a lisence shalbe 12d for taking bond 12d Mr. William Balston bein lisensed to sell Wine bere & victuals, doe acknowled him selfe according to the tenor of the law to be bound in the some of tenn shillings, to keep good orders in his howse, and Mr. John Porter and Richard Bordin according to the tenor of the law stand bound for Mr Bostons keeping good orders, in his howse" (Portsmouth, R.I., *Records*, p. 48).

William Baulstone, by the way, was "assistant" — i.e., representative — for Portsmouth at the General Assemblies held during this period. Surely Baulstone and Boston are identical.

Portsmouth: Matthew Greenell (1681) and Daniel Greenhill* (1683). And the same source turns up the name of John Headly, brewer in Newport (1671). The latter was the first of a number of brewers who established themselves in that town, which, soon after 1660, began to take prominence over the other Rhode Island towns as a commercial center.

Connecticut began in a most modest fashion. In the year 1635, various settlers from the Boston area, feeling "straitened" for space in which to grow their crops and pasture their livestock, sought and obtained permission to settle certain areas on the Connecticut River which were in dispute between the Dutch and the English. Others came directly from England under separate patents a few years later; and the independent colony of New Haven was settled in 1639.

The Connecticut pioneers were beset from the beginning by famine, by bellicose Indians, and by Dutch harassment. As in Rhode Island, they were woefully short of artisans and craftsmen in the important early stages of settlement. Nevertheless, by sheer determination and grit, they managed to survive, though their life can hardly have been called comfortable in any way until some thirty years or so had passed.

After visiting the settlement of Hartford in 1639, at that time nearly four years old, that voracious journal-keeper David Pieterssen de Vries said: "These English live soberly, drink only three times at a meal, and whoever drinks himself drunk they tie to a post and whip him, as they do thieves in Holland." [42] Somewhat later de Vries found another occasion on which to make the same comment: a ship loaded with wine had sailed to New England in hopes of selling the cargo there, but the captain was unsuccessful "because the English there live soberly." [43] Soberly, of course, in comparison with the Dutch, whose drinking propensities were phenomenal.

Connecticut settlers drank no less than their fellow English emigrants. As early as 1644, ordinaries were set up in the various towns by official order; and by 1647 the General Court had to take cognizance of "that great abuse which is creeping in by excess in wine and strong

---

* In view of the uncertain orthography of that period, these two men may have been related.

waters." Their solution to the problem of intemperance was to prohibit any inhabitant of a town from remaining in any "common victualing house in the same Town where he liveth above half an hour at a time in drinking wine, beer or hot waters." [44]

General regulations for innkeepers who "retail wine, beer and victuals" were laid down in a 1650 Code of Laws, and fines and punishments for drunkenness were stipulated in the same order.[45] In 1703, there were further regulations of taverns, as well as measures taken against "illdisposed and indigent persons . . . [who] presume to sell and retail strong beer, ale, cyder, perry, metheglin,* wine, rum, or other strong liquors," without being licensed to do so.[46]

In the state archives there is no evidence at all of commercial brewing in Connecticut, but there was a great deal of brewing in the home. Inventories of citizens' goods taken after their death include such items as malt, wooden vessels for brewing, barrels, bottles: these were almost universally present.[47]

Still people had to go short sometimes — most likely because malt was momentarily scarce, as a result of a poor harvest or disappointment in supplies expected from Massachusetts. A niece of John Winthrop, Jr.,† wrote to him from Stamford on 23 March 1648 about her being ill. She praised her husband for doing what he could for her: "I am sory he shold sofer soe much for me he drinks water that I might drink bere eats Indian [corn bread] that I might eat whet." [48]

The affairs of Connecticut were much improved by the amalgamation of New Haven in 1664 and the clarification of her boundaries with New York, Rhode Island and Massachusetts. By the end of the century, the citizens of that state as well as the rest of her sister New England states must have faced the future with renewed optimism; they were finally on a firm footing, the hardships of pioneering were for the most part behind them, they had built estimable towns, they were relatively well housed, clothed and fed — and a number of them were beginning to accumulate fortunes in shipbuilding, land and commerce. They were ready to step into a period of considerably more refinement, elegance and sophistication.

* A fermented liquor of honey and herbs.
† See page 17.

ᵏᔐ *FIVE* ᒫᵉ

Brewing in the Middle Atlantic Colonies

PENNSYLVANIA and New Jersey were latecomers among the
American colonies. True enough, there had been in their development a Swedish period and a Dutch period, but the real establishment
of the two colonies had to wait for the time of the English "proprietors."
It was in 1680 that William Penn received his famous grant of land
from Charles II, as payment of a debt owed to Penn's father, the celebrated admiral. By this means Penn became sole proprietor of a colony
which he foresaw as a place of refuge for his fellow Quakers — the nonconformist sect whose faith earned them nothing but contempt and
persecution in England (as well as in most of the established American
colonies). Before he set out in 1682 he sent ahead a government plan
of his own devising, and also a number of representatives to map out a
city to be called Philadelphia. Penn's concept of government was extraordinarily liberal, in many respects tantamount to a genuinely democratic scheme; moreover, he guaranteed complete freedom of worship,
and delegated much more administrative authority than any other of
the colonial governors saw fit to allow.

Penn understood the wisdom of securing friendly relations with the
Indians from the start. In 1683, he established a "Great Treaty" with
them. In exchange for property rights which they were willing to grant
him, he made a practice of giving them a variety of goods — in at least
one instance, a barrel of beer.[1]

Shortly after Penn's arrival, an Assembly was held in Chester, the
former Swedish settlement of Upland. At this meeting his *Frame of*

Government was adopted; and there were also laid down certain laws regulating the licensing of taverns, taxing of beer, sale of alcoholic beverages to Indians, etc. Such laws were sooner or later passed in every one of the American colonies and differ only in the merest details.

Penn himself was enough of a beer-drinker to have a brewhouse constructed at the estate he built in Pennsbury, Bucks County, twenty miles upriver from Philadelphia. At a cost of about £7000 and over a period of many years,[2] the manor-house was erected under Penn's supervision, although he was most of that time back in England. He made a start on the project soon after his arrival in 1682, but he had to return to England in 1684. He commissioned his trusted friend James Harrison as "Steward of the Household at Pennsbury," [3] and from that date until his return, he wrote frequent letters, filled with details about the house's specifications, the gardens, the servants, slaves, etc. "I would have a Kitchen," he wrote from London after he returned there in 1684, "two larders, a wash house & room to iron in, a brew house & in it an oven for bakeing." [4] During the following two years he felt the need to repeat these instructions, which in time were fulfilled.

Penn was not able to see the results at Pennsbury until 1699. At that time, as things turned out, he remained only a year; thus he spent in all only three years in America. Nonetheless, he made good use of Pennsbury while he was there; "Indians almost every morning were waiting in the hall, seated on their haunches." Penn also entertained in that house the governors of Maryland and Virginia, as well as what are usually referred to as "visiting dignitaries." [5]

None of Penn's descendants cared for the house as the proprietor himself had, and it was permitted by sheer neglect to go to ruin. It was finally torn down at the time of the Revolution,[6] but somehow the brewhouse structure managed to survive until 1864. It is described as being 20 by 35 feet, "with solid brick chimney and foundations, 10 inch sills and posts, and weatherboarded with dressed cedar." [7]

That there was beer in the earliest stages of Philadelphia's settlement is attested to by the immigrant Thomas Paschall in 1683: "Here is very good Rye . . . also Barly of 2 sorts, as Winter and Summer, . . . also Oats, and 3 sorts of Indian Corne, (two of which sorts they can Malt and make good beer as Barley)." [8]

In a 1685 account of progress in his colony, Penn wrote:

> Our DRINK has been *Beer* and *Punch*, made of *Rum* and *Water*: Our Beer was mostly made of *Molasses*, which well boyld, with *Sassafras* or *Pine* infused into it, makes very tolerable drink; but now they make *Mault*, and Mault Drink begins to be common, especially at the *Ordinaries* and the Houses of the more substantial People. In our great Town there is an *able Man*, that has set up a large *Brew House*, in order to furnish the People with good Drink, both there and up and down the River.[9]

Farther along in the same document, he identified this "able man" as William Frampton, and to demonstrate the first Philadelphia brewer's prosperity, he added that Frampton had recently built *"a good Brick house, by his Brew House and Bake House,* and let the other for an Ordinary." [10] Frampton — Quaker, merchant, provincial councillor and landowner — originally emigrated to New York and did not arrive in Philadelphia until 1683. If he was as prosperous as Penn makes out, he did not enjoy this state for long: he died in 1686.[11]

In those early days of Philadelphia, many inhabitants are said to have owned their own malt-houses in order to make strong beer at home, and Gabriel Thomas stated in his account of the town (as of 1696) that there were three or four "spacious malt-houses, as many large brewhouses." [12] Thomas, a Welsh pioneer who lived in the colony for fifteen years, also described Philadelphia beer as "equal in strength to that in London," selling for 15s. the barrel — cheaper than in England. In addition, he speaks of Philadelphia beer as having a "better Name, that is, is in more esteem than English Beer in Barbadoes and is sold for a higher Price there." [13] This would be an extremely early, if not the first, instance of American beer being exported outside of the mainland, though there is no indication of the regularity or volume of business thus entailed. In the course of the eighteenth century, Philadelphia beer began to make a resounding reputation for itself: the origins of that fame may lie right here, in this remark of Thomas's comparing the beer favorably with the English product. On the other hand, Thomas's unbridled enthusiasm must not be discounted — he may very well have been trying to paint the prettiest possible picture of conditions in America, and particularly Pennsylvania.

Another brewer of this earliest Philadelphia period was Joshua Carpenter, whose brother, Samuel, had come over from England several years before Penn's arrival. Samuel Carpenter, a Quaker, was responsible for building Philadelphia's first wharf, between Walnut Street and Dock Creek. Joshua, who had followed his brother to Philadelphia some years later and who was himself not a Quaker, did so well out of his brewing enterprise that he was rated as the second richest inhabitant of the town in 1693; his brother was first.[14]

The brewery established by Anthony Morris in 1687, south of Walnut Street, on the riverbank side of Front, was a longer-lasting establishment. Morris (the second of his name) was another Quaker, provincial councillor and second mayor of Philadelphia. He had sailed for America in 1682, and settled first in Burlington, New Jersey. Three years later, however, he went to Philadelphia, and soon set up his brewery there.[15] His son, Anthony, Jr., prepared himself for the business by becoming in 1696 an indentured apprentice to another brewer operating in Philadelphia at that time, Henry Babcock. It was stated in the indenture that he was to spend seven years learning "the art or trade of a Brewer." He undertook to keep the brewing "secrets" of Babcock and his wife Mary, "& from their service he shall not absent himself, nor the art & mystery of brewing he shall not disclose or discover to any person or persons during ye sd term." His father paid the Babcocks the sum of twenty pounds, and they undertook not only to teach him for seven years, but also to lodge and board him, and "mending of his linen & woolen cloaths." They on their side promised not to put him to "slavish work," such as grinding at the handmill and the like.[16]

It must have been this younger Anthony Morris who signed his name, "Morris jun^r," at the bottom of a receipt that read: "Rec^d of Hannah Ring Eighteen Shillings for barrel Ale delivered for funeral of her husband 7mo 4th 1731." [17]

The Morris brewery was conducted as a family business, handed down from generation to generation, until 1836, when ownership of the concern was taken over by outsiders. Through marriage with the Perot family of French Huguenot background, however, the Morrises have maintained an unbroken connection with the brewing industry. In 1823 Francis Perot married the daughter of Thomas Morris, in whose brewery he had spent six years as apprentice. With brothers, sons and then grandsons in charge, the Perot family have been malting in Philadelphia ever since.[18]

Pennsylvania had made an encouraging, even a spectacular, beginning. It had grown like a balloon: within twenty years, by the end of the century, its main city had a population equal to that of New York (4000). And yet, after about twenty-five years, it began to bog down. Penn died in 1718, but a good many years before that he had relinquished personal control of the province, while remaining proprietor. Relations with the Indians deteriorated; boundary conflicts, like sores, kept irritating the relations between Pennsylvania and her neighbors; and the fine promise of commercial prosperity had been disappointed. The bold Philadelphia printer, Andrew Bradford, was hauled before the Council in 1721 for publishing a pamphlet called *Some Remedies proposed for the restoring of the Sunk Credit of the Province of Pennsylvania*. He was reprimanded for so-called libelous statements.[19]

Yet at the same time, the Council, under Governor Sir William Keith, passed laws designed to improve just those conditions which it had called untrue in Bradford's case. Among those was an act "for laying a Duty on Wine, Rum, Brandy and Spirits, Molassoes, Cyder, Hops and Flax, imported, landed or brought into this Province." The self-evident purpose of an act like this was to give aid to home manufactures and, by placing a duty on imported hops, of course, the Council encouraged Pennsylvania farmers to cultivate them locally. Another reason for this act was undoubtedly the wish to cut down supplies of beverages with high alcoholic content, in favor of beer (which did not appear among the list of dutiable items) — but the barn door may have been closed too late, for by the eighteenth century rum was universally available in America, and increasingly popular. Acts of the same kind were passed at intervals by the Provincial Council — in 1738, 1744, etc. — but they appear to have been less than wholly effectual.

A similar law was passed by the New York Provincial Legislature in 1700, called "An act for the Incouraging the Brewing of Beer and making Malt within this province." [20] In view of the fact that the colony's brewing industry had been depressed by the widespread importation of malt liquors from abroad, an extra duty was authorized on the latter.

Ever since the English take-over in 1664, there had been various substantial duties set upon imported rum, brandy, wine and distilled liquors, but beer and cider had been excepted.[21] The same preferential treatment was authorized in the excise laws governing retail sales. All the same, the New York brewing industry had reached a virtual standstill by the end of the century and had to wait some fifty years or more before hopeful changes took place.

In the complicated early history of New Jersey, there is a sort of eventless interim between the Dutch capitulation of 1664 and the arrival in 1675 of John Fenwick (one of the Quaker proprietors) and his party. There existed, indeed, some confusion as to who actually owned and controlled the colony. With the founding of Salem, the first English town on the eastern shore of the Delaware, Fenwick and his group started the basic development of modern New Jersey.

One of the historians of this area writes that when Fenwick's people arrived,

> they straightway busied themselves in erecting breweries for manufacturing beer for common drink. There were four of them in the small township of Elsinborough, John Thompson's, Nicholson's, Morris's, and George Abbott's. There were also several more throughout the county.

The writer continues that "the Friends were among the first who introduced malt and spirituous liquors in this country as a common beverage." [22] Though this statement is not strictly true, it makes a valid reference to the fact that the Quakers were no less likely to include beer in their daily diet than any other of their fellow countrymen.

The situation in the colony as of 1681 was summed up by an anonymous writer in the following way:

> The Husband-Men have good Increase, as well in large Cattle and Hoggs; as also in all sorts of Grain which grow in England; and the same are Sold at Easie and Reasonable Rates; The Increase of their Corn being considerably greater than in England; of which they Make good bread and Brew good Beer and Ale for their Use.[23]

To judge by the relative lack of references in the annals of this period, commercial brewing activities played an unremarkable role. The only mention of an actual brewery as such appears as late as 1752, in a newspaper notice of the sale of Edward Antill's farm, near New Brunswick:

> There is also a large new Brew-house . . . with a new Copper, containing 22 Barrels with all the Utensils proper for Brewing; the Whole contrived for carrying the Liqour from Place to Place with ease, by turning of a cock, or taking out of a Plug; the works are all complete, and the brewing Business is now carried on, and will continue to be carried on by the Owner till sold: the Water is exceeding good, is soft, and washes well, and There is a sufficient Quantity of it; the Farm may be had with, or without the Brew-House.[24]

Similar advertisements appear in the newspapers of 14 March 1757 and 12 July 1759.[25]

The situation in Maryland, in the opening stages of colonization, was quite different. For one thing, Maryland was a relatively sophisticated colony at the time when New Jersey was receiving its first English settlers. The charter was granted in 1632, though for various reasons actual colonization did not take place until the following year. In 1633 corn (probably wheat or rye, rather than maize) was described as being very plentiful and appropriate for brewing.[26] Nevertheless, "adventurers" proposing to emigrate to Maryland were advised to bring malt with them.[27]

In a publication of 1666, we are told that "Common Alehouses . . . in this Province there are none," but the information appears to be somewhat faulty, since there was at least one alehouse or ordinary known to exist then in the main town, St. Mary's.[28]

The Dutch Vice-Governor of New Amstel, as we have seen,* reported in 1663 that the English in Maryland did not brew strong beer; yet the year before, according to the "Assembly Proceedings" of the colony, an act was passed for the encouragement of ordinary-keepers — leading one to the suspicion that some sort of beer, at least, was made

---

* See page 30.

and could be marketed there. An act of the same sort was passed in 1663; and then another, three years later, which specifically mentioned "strong beere or Ale either made within this Province or brought from foreign Parts," leaving no possible doubt of the fact that beer was brewed in Maryland itself.[29]

In 1674, beer prices were given in terms of tobacco, the prime crop of the colony: ten pounds of tobacco per gallon for small beer, and twenty pounds for strong.[30] St. Mary's, in 1681, was enough of a town to boast four licensed ordinary-keepers: Henry Exon, John Baker, Daniel Clocker and Francis Catterson.[31]

Maryland's career was closely tied, for many years, to that of her sometimes helpful, sometimes rapacious neighbor, Virginia. Both were based on agricultural economies, and in both colonies the basic crop was tobacco.

The economy of the Carolinas, on the other hand, after settlement began there in the 1660s, was soon based on another crop entirely: rice, which was enormously successful and determined the development of the colony for a long time.

The production of beer is of hardly any account in the pre-Revolutionary southern colonies, except for Virginia. In Carolina there are evidences of the usual home brewing, but little else. Rum is supposed to have taken over here particularly early and thus reduced the beer requirements. Nevertheless, barley was grown in Carolina; it figured with hops among the various crops that were first experimented with.[32] One of those conventional travelogues, which give so much incidental information, mentioned the barley crop in 1682:

> Mr. Linch [Jonah Lynch], having whilst we were there very good grow- ing [of barley] in his Plantation, of which he intended to make Malt for brewing of English Beer and Ale, having all Utensils and Conveniences for it.

This writer also spoke of a beer made with maize: "a good sound Beer, but it's strong and heady." [33]

On the other hand, in a letter of 1682, Thomas Newe wrote that "the common drink of the Countrey is Molossus and water, I don't hear of any mault that is made hear as yet." [34] He seems to be referring specifically to Charles Town, and it may be true that there were no malting facilities there. It probably would have seemed at the time a fairly academic question, because it was becoming increasingly possible to import beer supplies, especially from Philadelphia, where the whole manufacturing process was easier.

Part Two

SIX

Eighteenth-Century Drinking Habits

FOR THE American colonies, the eighteenth century was a period of superb accomplishment — years of progress and expansion, leaps in population, development of national identity, and political ferment. Paradoxically, it was also a time during which the imperial power of England was being consolidated, and the colonies, left so much to their own devices in the preceding century, were made to feel the rein of British authority. Indeed, colonial freedom versus imperial restriction became the prime focus of political evolution during the second half of the century.

At the beginning of the 1700s, there were some quarter of a million American colonists in all; by the time of the Revolution there were well over a million. While most of the larger number had been born in the colonies, a substantial proportion of them were German, Irish, Scottish and Huguenot French immigrants and Negro slaves — already the makings of a "melting-pot." There could be no doubt that America was a going concern: her ships, in increasing numbers, crossed the oceans and also plied the coast. Soundly built houses were going up in all her towns and on farms, particularly in the South, where a few lavish mansions were erected by those who made fortunes from tobacco, rice and slaves. Newspapers, starting in this century, not only played their part in molding opinion through dissemination of information, but also furnished a means of advertisement for commercial undertakings.

Communications among the colonies were somewhat improved, at least toward the halfway mark of the century. Before that, when Madam Sarah Knight took a journey from Boston to New York in 1704, she was considered an extremely adventurous woman. Fortunately, she kept a detailed journal of this remarkable trip which provides a colorful glimpse into the social life of that era. For instance she writes of an occasion when she visited a farmhouse belonging to a "Gentlewoman" who offered the party "a handsome Entertainment of five or six Dishes and choice Beer and metheglin, Cyder, &c. all which she said was the produce of her farm." [1]

Madam Knight gives a lead toward the changes in drinking habits that were to take place in the course of the new century. Beer had just begun to lose its status as the universal beverage. In the latter half of the seventeenth century, cider (particularly in agricultural areas) had become a substitute. Rum was increasingly prevalent, as the triangular slave-molasses-rum trade developed its profitable pattern. Before the beginning of the eighteenth century, coffee was available; and soon after, tea made its important debut on the American market. Drinking habits began also to take on some subtle social distinctions. Those with means preferred wine at their meals. Madeira was especially favored; to such a degree, in fact, that Cadwallader Colden, writing in 1723 on the trade situation in New York, noted that "The Trade to Madeira is to our Loss this Province consuming more wine from thence, than can be purchased with our commodities." [2] Other wines with social pretensions were Fayal,* Canary, Malaga and sherry (or sack). The most commonly drunk French wine was, following the English taste, the claret from Bordeaux.

Hugh Jones described the drinking habits of Virginians in 1724:

> The common strong malt-drink mostly used, is Bristol beer; of which is consumed vast quantities there yearly; which being well brewed and improved by crossing the sea, drinks exceedingly fine and smooth; but malt liquor is not so much regarded as wine, rack,† brandy, and rum; punch, with drams of rum or brandy for the common sort, when they drink in a hurry.[3]

* Wine from the Azores Islands.
† *Arrack*, distilled from rum and special flavorings.

About fifty years later, the Florentine visitor Filippo Mazzei gave a similar view of American drinking patterns, corroborating the impression that enormous quantities must have been drunk:

> both hot punch and cold before dinner, madeira or Spanish wine, bordeaux in the summer — spruce beer and excellent cider are served before the wine; formerly English porter appeared there exclusively, but it is now replaced by excellent porter made near Philadelphia.[4]

At about the same time, young Philip Vickers Fithian, a Princeton graduate employed as tutor on the Virginia estate of Robert Carter, was gaping at the high life of that immensely rich, aristocratic society and recording his impressions in a diary:

> The Dinner was as elegant as could be expected when so great an Assembly were to be kept for so long a time. For Drink there were several sorts of Wine, good Lemon Punch, Toddy, Cyder, Porter, &c.[5]

Somewhat earlier, in May 1702, Francis Louis Michel, a Swiss who established the first German colony of New Bern in North Carolina in 1710, had dinner at the home of the Virginia governor in Williamsburg. The governor could not be present, and the servants, not being "on good terms" with the French language, which Michel and his friends spoke, apparently performed unsatisfactorily, particularly in the way of beverages:

> They gave us soup with fresh ham and some small beer. But the butler took us into the cellar, filled with all sorts of strange drinks. He gave us some English stout, very strong, afterwards Rhine wine.[6]

The quick rise of tea's popularity is illustrated in the following reminiscence of a traveler from London to Yorktown in 1750:

> So long as our strong beer, wine and brandy lasted we did pretty well, for a bottle of beer, a glass or two of wine . . . would commonly engage the Carpenter, or one or other of the Sailors, by stealth to slip a Tea Kettle full now and then into the cabin.[7]

This Englishman was actually offering his beer and liquors as a bribe in order to obtain tea, a curious reversal from those days at the beginning of the Virginia settlement when thirsty adventurers traded vital tools with the sailors for a tankard of none-too-palatable ship's beer.

It would be easy to conclude that less beer was consumed, less beer imported, less manufactured. But this is not true. In terms of sheer volume, there is every indication that a great deal more beer was drunk in the eighteenth century than in the seventeenth — mainly because of the increase in population. Per capita consumption probably fell, but there were undoubtedly more barrels of beer produced, imported, bought and drunk — to judge by the continued and increasing references to beer in all the available documents and annals of the time, as well as the greater number of commercial brewers who emerged, particularly in the main cities, during the century.

In England, a curious and important revolution took place in the brewing industry at this time. The almost accidental introduction of "porter" * in the 1720s made it possible for, or perhaps caused, the English brewers to revamp their basic manufacturing practices and turn to mechanization some years before other industries did.[8]

It had been for some time the practice of customers in English public houses to ask for a combination of beer, ale, and "twopenny" (a pale small beer) — which meant that the barman had to draw from three different casks. Ralph Harwood, of the Bell Brewhouse in Shoreditch, seems to have been the first, in 1722, to conceive of a brew in which the three elements were already mixed. It was first called "entire butt" or "intire," but eventually became colloquially "porter" because of its popularity with London porters. It was a dark, bitter drink, made of several kinds of malt — black, dark, amber and pale — used in differing proportions that were the distinction of each individual brand. It was a hearty, nutritious beverage, which found a tremendous market in England during the century. According to the most authoritative study of the English brewing industry, porter

seems to have been the first beer technically suited for mass-production at contemporary standards of control, unlike ale which needed "attemperated fermentation" for stability in large-scale brewing. The appearance of the new beer should be seen, therefore, as an event of the first importance, or as an invention exactly equivalent in its own industry

* See page 15.

to coke-smelted iron, mule-spun muslin in textiles or "pressed-ware" in pottery.[9]

Porter was imported into America, though not in impressive quantities, during the latter half of the century, but it was not widely manufactured here until after the Revolution. Certain individuals were partial to this type of beer. George Washington, for example, was one: in September 1760, he paid George William Fairfax £3.5s.3d. for one barrel or small cask of porter.[10] And in the same period he was ordering porter from England.[11] In later years he became extremely dependent on the product of Robert Hare, credited with being the first porter manufacturer in Philadelphia.

Porter, on the whole, never gained popular success in America, either because it was more expensive, to start with, than the local ale and beer, or because drinking tastes in the colonies had diverged from those in England.

In the eighteenth century beer imported from England often arrived either already bottled or else prepared for bottling by the importer.* There was also a certain amount of importing of bottles themselves from England: the Virginia merchant Francis Jerdone, for example, wrote in 1759 to dealers in Bristol for "6 doz: pottle [half gallon] Bottles with flat Sides fill'd with the best Bristol Beer," and the same year he gave instructions to a London ship captain: "50 Groce of cheap Corks for small beer and in case you go to any place where bottles are cheap buy 4 groce for me." [12]

It is extremely difficult to pin down precisely when beer began to be sold or transported at all regularly in bottles. Bottles were indeed used

---

* Beer bottled in England and then transported to the colonies did not always withstand the trip successfully. The important Scottish brewers, Joseph and William Cunningham & Co., included in some of their shipments a printed instruction for preserving bottled beer: "DIRECTIONS for managing STRONG BEER, exported to America, &c. It sometimes happens, that Strong Beer (tho' perfectly fine when bottled) by the effect the different climates it goes through has on it, throws up. If this is the case when it arrives in North America, or the West-Indies; the purchaser will please unpack it, and set the bottles in any warm place on their bottom, and it will fine down in a few days. The warmer the place be, the better. — In cold Climates, Strong Beer will always throw up; and therefore should be kept in warm cellars. From South Carolina to the Northward, all Strong Beer must be kept in cellars, during the Winter, where no Frost can enter. — From that to the Southward, the Beer needs no management, further than the natural heat of the climate." (MS dated 3 March 1767, in Brown Family Papers.)

before the eighteenth century, but they were considered precious and rare, and they were not sold simply as containers. Even in the eighteenth century, bottles "were bequeathed with special mention in wills, and they are the only form of glass vessel named." [13] Charles Carroll of Carrollton, one of the signers of the Declaration of Independence and a rich Roman Catholic landowner in Maryland, included among his bequests "3 Beer glasses" and "18 doz Quart and 2 Doz^n Pint Bottles." [14]

Glasses for drinking purposes simply did not exist before the eighteenth century. Most commonly used instead were heavy black leather jugs, known as "black jacks" — they were waxed, bound and trimmed with silver, and were used mainly for beer.[15] In that early period, the English themselves were inclined to favor stoneware jugs made either in their own country or in Germany.[16] The earliest drinking vessels used by the colonists in America were probably wooden tankards; but pewter is known to have been used in the Massachusetts Bay colony, and in 1640 pewter is listed among the goods sailing from Bristol for New England in the *Neptune*.[17] Pewter tankards were common in all the colonies during the seventeenth century; it was only as conditions improved, and there was some time and money for finery, that silver began to appear, as did gifted silversmiths — Peter Van Dyck, Myer Myers, Edward Winslow and Paul Revere.

Yet bottles and glass as such have a long history which goes much farther back than the European invasion of America. Glass was enough of a manufacture in England and on the Continent prior to 1607 for the first settlers of Virginia to contemplate setting up a glassworks upon their arrival. There is a spot near Jamestown still called Glass House Point and, according to modern students, glass may well have been produced there as early as the fall of 1608.[18] After a number of attempts, all work was abandoned by 1625. As far as can be ascertained, mainly beads were manufactured, for trade with the Indians. Bottles could have been made, but no concrete evidence of them has been found.

In England, bottle-making had become a surprisingly large industry by the end of the seventeenth century. Something like a quarter of a million dozen bottles were probably produced there in 1695 alone, and thirty-nine out of eighty-eight glass factories are supposed to have manufactured bottles.[19] Indeed, bottles made up one of England's many profitable exports, a fact which goes some way toward explaining why the colonies were so slow about making bottles themselves.

In America, glass-making was tried sporadically and with little success during the seventeenth century. After the Virginia experiment collapsed, another was started in Salem, Massachusetts, by Lawrence Southwick and Obadiah Holmes in 1639. That lasted no more than three or four years; supposedly only glass bottles were made there.[20] The Dutch in New Amsterdam had the one relative success in starting the manufacture of glass, which is said to have continued in the same furnaces from 1645 to 1767.

In the following century various glass manufactories did spring up: one in South Jersey, started by Caspar Wistar; another in New York, called the Bamper-Bayard works; and an experiment involving Palatine Germans in a village called Germantown near Braintree, Massachusetts,[21] but the latter plant burned down in 1757. According to one source, the Germantown glassworks turned out bottles exclusively.[22] In 1752, the General Court of Massachusetts passed an act naming Isaac C. Winslow and associates the only glass-makers in that colony; in New York there were two glassworks as of 1732; and during the 'sixties Henry William Stiegel, the one authentic glass artist of the time, was operating in Lancaster County, Pennsylvania.

The true glass-making industry in America, however, began after the Revolution was over. Until then the bottles used for wine, beer or other beverages either were very crude ones made in the ill-fated plants mentioned above or else were imported from England. As an important part of the brewing industry, bottling did not make any noticeable impression until well into the nineteenth century. Yet, in the eighteenth, there is no doubt that bottles were used and valued for beer. Notice this advertisement in the New York *Gazette and Weekly Mercury* of 25 December 1769: "WANTED, any Quantity of QUART BOTTLES, for which a good price will be given by JONATHAN NASH, at Mr. Anthony Rutgers's Brewery, in Maiden Lane." The same newspaper, dated 23 May 1774, ran a similar ad for a competitor:

> Benjamin Williams is remov'd from his store upon Hunter's-Quay, to the house where Mr. Leonard Lispenard lived last, commonly known by the name of the Old Custom-House, in Wall-Street, opposite Mr.

Barclay's, where he intends carrying on the business of bottling beer as usual. Repeated trials have prov'd it will stand the West-Indies. Captains of vessels may be supplied with what quantity they please, on the shortest notice, at ten shillings per dozen; gentlemen in town (for present use) on the same terms, or seven shillings, if they return the bottle.

Bottles could also be provided by the customer, as expressed in this *Virginia Gazette* advertisement of 30 May 1766:

Any person who sends bottles and corks may have them carefully fitted and corked with beer and porter at 6s. or with ale at 4s. the dozen. I expect, in a little time, to have a constant supply of bottles and corks; and if I meet the encouragement I hope for, propose setting up a glass-house for making bottles.

JOHN MERCER

There is no indication how large Mr. Mercer's Marlborough (Virginia) Brewery was or how much beer he could produce in it, although he claimed to have spent £8000 to bring it "to its present state." But we have other clues as to the nature of the size and capacity of the colonial American brewery. One historian gives a "typical" example of a brewery that was 70 by 48 feet, with a malt cellar 70 by 14 feet, and a copper kettle with a capacity of 23 barrels. The works included also a malt mill operated by horsepower, and a storehouse 30 by 21 feet, having a beer cellar with a brick floor.[23]

Some Pennsylvania breweries were twice this size, but in none of them did the process of brewing differ in any essential respect from that used in the household. The utensils were mainly of wood and the operations were performed by hand. Hand pumps were used, malt was ground between stones, steam heating was not practiced, sterilizing, except by boiling, was unknown, and there was no refrigeration. With the exception of strong porters, made for ships' uses and exportation, most beer and ale was consumed immediately. Some country breweries represented an investment of less than $1,000, and what were accounted considerable establishments sold for twice or three times that sum. Usually they were owned by individuals or partners.[24]

From the ledgers and papers of a Philadelphia brewery that functioned between 1733 and 1735, preserved in the manuscript collection of the Historical Society of Pennsylvania, we can obtain a somewhat more detailed impression of a commercial brewing operation in colonial America. This began in 1731, when a partnership of eight men was formed, and there was rented from Mr. John Danby "a certain Messuage or Tenement Brewhouse Wharf Stores and Buildings with the Lot of Ground thereunto belonging," for a term of twenty-one years. The names of the partners were William Allen, Thomas Freame, Patrick (in some papers called Peter) Grame, Robert Charles, Peter Lloyd, Isaac Norris, Jr., Patrick Baird and Peter Cuff.[25] Aside from the last, who appears sometimes to be only manager of the plant and not a real partner, these were all distinguished Philadelphians of their day, and were well placed as to family and position. It would be interesting to know why they joined to engage in "the Brewing and Vending of Beer and Ale in the said City."

It is not clear from the documents what financial arrangements were made at first. On 20 September 1733, the total buildings and stock were evaluated at £2000, and all eight partners laid down £250 apiece. On 26 September, circumstances were such that each agreed on a further advance of £50. The dimensions of the lot were 34½ feet north and south, and 250 feet from the east side of Front Street down to the Delaware River. The width of "the built part" is given as 79½ feet.

The brewery produced "middling" and "double" beer, as well as ale; but from time to time both "small beer" and "stout" make appearances. The prices remained fairly constant over a period of four years or so:

Ale	18/– a barrel
Small (S)	4/6 a barrel
Middling (X)	9/– a Barrel
Strong, or Double (XX)	30/– a Barrel
Stout	36/– a Barrel

In 1735, some pale ale was being sold by the barrel or bottle; it was 4/6 the bottle.

There were of course a good number of steady customers who received the same order week after week or month after month. A typical year's supply came to about £4/10/-. On the other hand, one account shows a sum of £8/2/6, representing beer orders for only three months. A large part of the orders were for ships — always a good means of assuring a certain measure of profit.

Among the regular customers appears the Honorable Thomas Penn, Esq., the proprietor of the colony in 1732, and brother-in-law of one of the partners. His household orders (mainly for "midling beer") from October 1732 to September 1733 amounted to £19/2/6, remarkably higher than the average — but it must be surmised that the proprietor was responsible for a certain amount of entertaining and had a large household as well. The figure quoted would represent deliveries of about six barrels a month — sometimes more, sometimes less — but on special occasions there were single orders of "15 Bls. Strong Beer racked & Casked @ 35/" (15 March 1732) or "12 Bar^ls best midling," evidently for special occasions.

The purchases of the governor, Patrick Gordon, between September 1732 and December 1733 came to £9/7/6: many of these individual orders were for half-barrels of middling or small. There appears in the governor's accounts, incidentally, an occasional charge of 4/- for the cask. The evident practice was to charge for the cask if none was returned at the time of delivery.

There is an account with Benjamin Franklin, from February 1733 to January 1736. Orders are small (half-barrels of ale) and sporadic; a few of them, indeed, appear to be addressed to "Widow Makin," in care of Franklin. In one instance, on 25 March 1734, a barrel of double beer was sent to Carolina and charged to Franklin. The whole account, after three years, came to only £4/9/-.

Another entry, showing export to Carolina, appears on 12 November 1735: "One Bar. XX & Cask sent to Carolina." And the business also had a customer in Trenton, New Jersey, a James Nelson. There are surprisingly few taverns listed among the clients. The "Queen's Head" had steady supplies from the brewery: its annual bill was about £50. Widow Campion, who ran a boardinghouse and inn under the name "Sign of the Tun," bought beer totaling about £63 in the course of six months Aside from beer, "grains" were sold by the bushel, and yeast (i.e., brewers' yeast) by the gallon.*

Five maltsters were used with some regularity, and during the 1735-

---

* Malt after mashing and straining ("spent grains") is extremely nutritious for animals; brewers' yeast derives from fermentation of wort to beer. Both are extremely important by-products of the industry.

1736 season, a woman maltster is mentioned: Elizabeth Griffiths. Both malt and barley were bought. Presumably the barley was then farmed out to the maltsters in question, because there is no evidence of malting being done on the spot. The master brewer, during 1735-1736, was William Cundell, and his salary that year was £60.

Barley was bought during the autumn and winter months from a variety of people, presumably farmers, who would supply 37, 99½, 20½, 24 bushels at a time, at a price ranging from 3/1 to 3/3 per bushel. Hops were furnished mainly by Ob. Johnson, at a price of 1/- a pound.

The partners reckoned that they had bought, between Christmas 1732 and Christmas 1733, 1604 ¼ bushels of barley at a total price of £237/2/10; 1782 ½ bushels of malt at £292/11/10; and 3756 pounds of hops at a cost of £174/11/2. Their total expenses for running the brewery during that same period came to £2904/16/10, including purchases of wood, coals, candles, as well as rent (£55 a year), servants, coopers, freight, and £20 a year for the keeping of the books. Their income in the same period, unfortunately, was only £1122/11/6, and that included about £240 worth of beer stocks on hand.

It was pretty clear that the business was not going to succeed. Perhaps the partners had gone into it with grandiose ideas. Perhaps a reorganization was required. In January of 1734, the copartners sold their shares to Thomas Freame (³⁄₇), Isaac Norris (³⁄₇) and Robert Charles (¹⁄₇). Isaac Norris took over the management from Cuff, but Freame was to all intents and purposes in charge. He took on himself personally all the accumulated debts of the firm — as well as its uncollected assets. He undertook to pay to each of the former partners the sum of £110, and they were then to have no further connection with the business. An accounting at this time listed the "Quick and Dead Stock of the Brewerie" at £1415/13/1.*

---

* This included the following items:
360 bushels of malt valued at 3/8 per bushel
711 bushels of barley in the hands of the maltster
561 pounds of good old hops at 1/– each
815 pounds of ordinary hops at 3d.
199 barrels of Strong Beer
56 barrels of Strong Beer "bad"
32 barrels of ale

Unfortunately, we cannot tell, at this distance from the events, whether Freame ultimately put the brewery on a profitable basis. The ledgers that remain come to an abrupt close at 1735. Chances are, with so discouraging a beginning, that he in turn found himself unable to make the business pay, and that he was forced in the end to sell out to some other optimistic soul or partnership of souls. It was far from easy to succeed in the brewing business in the pre-Revolutionary period.

The same sort of problems as beset the Freame-Norris group may have been responsible for the failure of Timothy Matlack, a Philadelphia brewer of some note, who had the distinction of being one of Benjamin Franklin's many landlords. A merchant originally, he had gone into the brewing business between 1746 and 1750, building a brewhouse and malthouse on Market Street. He vacated his own dwelling in 1750 in order to move nearer to his business, and it was then that Franklin and his wife Deborah leased the Matlack house.[26]

In September 1751, Matlack was forced by his creditors to give a bond and warrant of attorney for £6000 in return for which his long list of creditors agreed to allow him three years in which to repay his debts. Among the creditors were Caspar Wistar (the glass manufacturer) and George Emlen, Jr. (another well-known Philadelphia brewer). Matlack's son-in-law, Reuben Haines, apparently had an interest in the business, and took a share in the responsibility for paying the debts.[27]

When the three-year period was over, another paper was drawn up, indicating for one thing that the debts had not been fully paid, and for

---

28 barrels of small beer
The Indentures of 5 servants, value £32.
A Negro man valued at £27.
30 cords of wood lying at the wharf
An old boat of no value.
Various casks at value of £99/3/9
One large Copper with Copper Back, £183/14/2
One Horse Mill & Stones with Wort and Liquor Pumps, £13.
3 Horses and Harnesses, £30/9/–.
One Dray valued at £11/6/3.
One Malt Screen Bushel & Half Bushel.
"Fixed work consisting of three Working Tuns compleat with a Pump, One cleansing Batch with Scoop Gutters & Schimers [skimmers], two Mashing Tuns compleat with Oars &c., One under Back with Stage & Ladder, three cooling Backs compleat, One Liquor Back compleat and sundry other fixed Work valued in the whole at £422/14/3."

another that, Matlack being by now "late of the said City Brewer deceased," Reuben Haines took over the problem of payment and arranged for another three-year period of grace.[28]

Haines appears to have managed somehow to clear his business of debts and to continue in brewing until well past the Revolution. In a procession that took place in Philadelphia on 4 July 1788, to commemorate the signing of the Declaration of Independence and also to celebrate Pennsylvania's ratification of the proposed Constitution for the United States, he had the distinction of leading the participating brewers.[29]

Haines was known to Washington, who may on one occasion have contemplated selling the brewer the Mount Vernon crop of barley. At any rate, Washington wrote from his homestead on 3 December 1787 to Colonel Clement Biddle:

> You may inform Mr. Haines that my Barley, this year, shared the same fate with my other crops. — The drought during the summer was so excessive that I cannot form any just opinion of what it might produce in a seasonable year; — it yielded about 14 bush[ls] to the acre which was a proportionate crop to any other kind of Grain which I sowed.[30]

The President's household expenses in 1792 show this item: "pd R. Haines & Son for beer rec'd from him in April & May." [31] The "Son" was also called Reuben Haines; he carried on with the brewery after his father's death, but it was eventually sold out of the family — to a German brewer, Frederick Gaul, who turned it into the Gaul Brewery in 1804. Thus it may be looked on as a precursor of the many German breweries that were shortly afterward to be established all over the country.

SEVEN

Brewing in Eighteenth-Century New York and Philadelphia

PERHAPS THE outstanding feature of the colonial brewing industry before the Revolution was the clear emergence of New York and Philadelphia as the leading brewing centers. Both cities were not only the largest producers, but also the most important exporters of beer. A prominent and successful general merchant like Peter Faneuil in Boston would order for his special customers "Six Barrells of your very best Strong beer" from Gulian Verplanck, in New York, a descendant of a family well known in Dutch times. Faneuil reported to Verplanck in 1737 about deliveries, "On the whole the bread & flour proves well in kind as well as the beer." [1]

The listing of Freedmen of New York,[2] between 1695 and 1786, gives seventeen names of brewers and maltsters; the military muster rolls[3] from 1758 to 1762 include seven additional ones.* These were not nec-

* 1695   Harman Rutgerson, Brewer
  1698   John Russell, Brewer
  1700   William Robertson, Brewer
          Richard Sackett, Maltster
  1702   Richard Tobin, Maltster
          Richard Davis, Brewer
          Alexander Mackay, Maltster
          Charles Mansfield, Brewer
  1721   Nicholas Eyre, Brewer
  1724   Peter Mesier, Brewer
          Petrus Rutgers, Brewer
  1727   Jacob Bomper, Brewer
  1732   John Oothout, Brewer
  1733   Rynier Nack, Brewer
  1740   Thomas Carter, Maltster

essarily all men with private establishments; no doubt in many cases they simply worked for established brewers such as the Rutgers brothers and Leonard Lispenard.

Anthony Rutgers, son of Harman, who had moved with his family from Albany to New York and set up a successful brewing enterprise there, had a brewhouse of his own in 1717, on the north side of Stone Street between William and Nassau.* George Clarke, Secretary of the Province of New York, listed among his purchases sometime in the 1720s two barrels of stale beer, to be used for workmen: "Retgers [*sic*] says it is extraordinary good beer and ye taking it off into other Barr[ls] would flatten it and make it Drink Dead." [4]

Rutgers had a daughter who married a Lispenard (thus joining two of the leading brewing families) and a son Peter who continued in the business on Maiden Lane.† Harman II, Anthony's brother, died in 1753, leaving his malthouse, brewhouse, malt mill and other equipment, on Maiden Lane and Rutgers Street, to the widow of his son Harman III. She conducted the affairs of the brewery for a time, but then rented it out to her son, Robert Rutgers.[5]

During the British occupation of New York at the time of the Revolution, the properties of Lispenard and Rutgers were used by the military for the "Provincial Stores" and "Barracks for the Troops." [6]

The Rutgerses' brewery, described as being located "on Brewer's-hill," was destroyed by fire in 1783 and was evidently not rebuilt.[7] The same fate disposed of the Lispenard brewery on Greenwich Street in 1804.[8]

1769   Thomas Horsfield, Brewer
1786   William Grinding, Brewer
From the military muster rolls:
1758   William Depue, 26, born Courtland Manor, Brewer
1759   John Townsend, 32, born Ireland, Brewer
1760   Peter Frasier, 24, born "N. Brittain," Brewer
1761   Matthew Lawrence, 27, born Germany, Brewer.
          Anthony Wear, 38, born Germany, Brewer.
          John Roe, 30, born Ireland, Brewer.
1762   Richard Auldrick, 58, born England, Brewer.

* Anthony Rutgers was responsible for one change in the topographical aspect of New York City: he took it upon himself to start filling in, around 1732, a pond called the Collect, which was located downtown. It was a center for fishing and sociability (and, probably, mosquitoes), but exists no longer, having been reclaimed by Mr. Rutgers, brewer. (Asbury, p. 13.)

† See pages 27-28.

Fire was a constant hazard in breweries, not only in this early period, but up to fairly modern times.

An advertisement in the New York papers of December 1774 gives notice of what must have been a sizable New York brewery, belonging formerly to a partnership of George Harrison, Richard Nicholls and James Leadbetter.* At that time the property, "Very Valuable Brewery and Buildings, situated in the West Ward of the City of New-York, near the Place formerly called Vauxhall," was to be auctioned off. The scope of the business can be surmised from the following details of equipment. There was a brick brewhouse, "allowed by all competent Judges, to be the most commodious and complete of any in America," containing two copper kettles, "the one very large, and the other of smaller Dimension." In addition, a brick malthouse with two cisterns, two kilns, "and every other Convenience for curing, stowing and preserving Malt." The horsemill is described as containing a "sizable Pair of Iron Rollers, by Means of which the Water necessary for the Works may be drawn, and the Malt used in it, ground, without any considerable manual Labour." Adjoining the brewhouse cellar was a "capacious" brick vault; above it a large storehouse. All in all, as the advertisement put it, "The Brewery may vie with any in America, either for Convenience or Pleasantness of Situation." [9] It eventually came into the possession of an English "Porter Brewer," Samuel Atlee, who petitioned for naturalization in April 1795.[10]

Beer was still required in New York during the eighteenth century because the public water supply continued to be unsafe. Even in 1748, a visiting Swede observed:

> There is no good water to be met with in the town itself; but at a little distance there is a large spring of good water, which the inhabitants take for their tea, and for the uses of the kitchen.[11]

Visitors to the city in 1775 were likely to be shown the waterworks, then under construction, with a system of wooden pipes through which the water was distributed to the houses.[12]

---

* See page 129.

This was evidently a well-known business, for it is referred to in a report of 29 October 1779 by Samuel Culper, Jr., one of Washington's spies: "Another Fort is erecting near Harrison's Brewery on the banks of the North River" (Pennypacker, p. 256).

Until the ordinary water was proven to be wholesome and pure, the people of New York would go on drinking manufactured beverages, preferably those with some alcoholic content. A historian of 1756 recorded that the common drinks were "beer, cider, weak punch and Madeira wine." [13] Beer in particular was used in large-scale celebrations. Governor Cosby, for example, after reviewing the militia of the city in 1734, "express'd great Satisfaction at their Order, Discipline, and Appearance, and was pleased to order 12 Barrels of Beer to be distributed among them to drink to their Majesties and Royal Healths." [14] And in 1766, at a meeting held in the city to celebrate open defiance of English repression, "There was a roasted ox, a hogshead of rum, and twenty-five barrels of ale, which were dispensed freely as long as they lasted." [15]

The province of New York was able to supply all ingredients for manufacturing beer except the full amount of hops that could be used. The Collector of New York, in reply to queries of the English Board of Trade, in 1747, included hops among his list of New York imports from "the Northern & Southern parts of this Continent"; an identical answer was given in 1749.[16] On the other hand, barley figures in the list of "Natural produce & Staple Commodities of this Province," drawn up by Governor William Tryon in 1774.[17]

In that same official report, Tryon listed malting and brewing prominently among the manufactures of the province. These industries continued in New York State and also, after the Revolution, it became a leading center of hop-growing, a position it maintained until the second half of the nineteenth century.

The pre-eminence of Philadelphia, where brewing had begun in the 1680s, developed very quickly in the eighteenth century. Thomas Paschall, a pewterer from Bristol, England, who emigrated to Pennsylvania at the time of Penn's arrival, had observed in 1683 that he had "eaten as good bread and drank as good drink as ever I did in England." [18] His son, by the early part of the century, had become the leading maltster of Philadelphia. A Philadelphia citizen wrote to him, on 16 January 1724, the following note (in phonetic spelling):

> Frind Thomas Paskele I deseir of thee two Lat my brothar have three boshals of good moalt that whitch is hy Drayd and good if thee has

any and sand anote by him how much I oe to thee and in so Doin will oblaige thy frind

Thomas Wynne[19]

The younger Thomas Paschall apparently ran a profitable business for the times and was a well-regarded citizen.* Among his customers was the leading Philadelphia brewer of the early eighteenth century, Anthony Morris, who bought fifty bushels of malt at a time (at a price of £10 for that quantity) during 1705. The price for fifty bushels went up to £11/5/0 in the following year, but by 1711 it had been reduced to £8/8/9.

Paschall was sufficiently important in the commercial life of Philadelphia for his name to appear, along with that of George Emlen, on a solemn message from Philadelphia merchants to the merchants of Great Britain, dated 7 November 1765, explaining that the colonials were contemplating a boycott of English goods.[20]

George Emlen† was a well-known Quaker merchant, who owned a brewery on Fifth Street above Chestnut. In the 1730s he was actively providing beer for the outfitting of ships in Philadelphia harbor.[21] This was, in fact, one of the early brewing families, for the first George Emlen, brewer, had arrived in Philadelphia about 1682. His son (1695-1754) was the one who established this Fifth Street brewery, and then George Emlen III continued the business, though its activities seem to have ended at that generation. This last George Emlen was an extremely rich man; he owned a mansion at Whitemarsh Township, twelve miles from Philadelphia, and it was here in Emlen's house that General Washington made his headquarters in November 1777, before moving on to Valley Forge.[22]

Valentine Standley (or Stanley) was a Philadelphian who combined two trades, that of brewer and potter. In the 1769 tax list he is listed as brewer, on other records he appears in his second capacity. His brewery is reported to have stood on "Second street, near the barracks," and in 1772 he was advertising in a newspaper that he made "good Sixpenny beer." [23]

---

* One of his descendants, Benjamin Say, was a Philadelphia brewer in the early nineteenth century.
    † See page 66.

Brewers with more elaborate establishments than Standley's included George Campion, who shipped his beer to Georgia, and Robert Henderson, who had a brewery on Sixth Street between Market and Chestnut. The latter was sold to William Gray in 1772 and became known as Gray's Brewery, in continuous operation until demolished in 1881.[24] When the brewer Edward Crosson died, his "large and commodious Brewery and Distillery situated on Wharton's wharf, next to Swede's Church," was offered for sale in the newspapers.[25] The firm of Clark & Moore were reported to be in a brewhouse on Sixth Street between Arch and Market, just up the street from Henderson.[26]

Philadelphia beer was well known in the other colonies, particularly those to the south. In the course of his early eighteenth-century travels on the American coast, the Swiss settler Francis Louis Michel went to Quiquedam in Virginia to look for a ship that might be sailing to Philadelphia: "There I found a sloop, in accordance with my desire, which had brought beer from Philadelphia." [27] The *Virginia Gazette* reported, from time to time, on imports of beer from Philadelphia: on 9 May 1745, seven barrels at Hampton; on 24 November 1752, six barrels at James River, Lower District; between April 1765 and April 1766 a total of 1288 barrels from Philadelphia; on 20 January 1774, thirty barrels of Philadelphia beer.

One method by which brewers obtained cheap labor and young men learned the art of brewing was the indenture of apprentices. In a 1746 notice, for instance, "*William Cunningham* indents himself servant to Robert Mathews of Philadelphia brewer for three years." The brewers Maurice and Edmund Nihil obtained in this way the services of Hugh Diver. In one case, a man reassigned his own servant to Thomas Brown, brewer of Philadelphia, "for the remainder of his time seven years from August 9th 1745." Oddly enough, this same Thomas Brown had to forego the training of his own son, for "*John Brown* with consent of his father Thomas Brown, brewer, doth bind himself apprentice to David Elwell of Philadelphia house-carpenter for six years from May 16th 1746." [28]

The brewing situation in Pennsylvania outside Philadelphia is not nearly so well documented as that in the main town. It can be taken for granted that home brewing, especially in the large farming areas that

made up pre-Revolutionary Pennsylvania, was most commonly practiced. It is known that the Moravian Brethren, a religious sect who
founded a settlement in Bethlehem about 1740, erected a brewery
there.[29] In the records of the military establishment of Fort Augusta (the
site of Sunbury) in 1757 and 1758, "Mr. Yeates" appears as purveyor of
beer.[30] And in the account books (1765-1767) of the small community of
Fort Pitt, which was to blossom into the great city of Pittsburgh, there
appear the bills of two brewers.[31]

These frontier areas of western Pennsylvania, which were being settled by Germans and Scotch-Irishmen from Ulster, became, during the
second half of the eighteenth century, whiskey-drinking centers. A small
farmer, in those pioneer conditions, found it easier and cheaper to turn
his excess grain into whiskey than beer. Whiskey also kept better,
took up less room, and could be carried more easily in a small receptacle.
Distilling and whiskey-drinking became so common in the frontier area
as to pose a serious problem, and the central government's attempt to
subject whiskey to the excise tax led to the Whiskey Rebellion in 1794.

EIGHT

Brewing in Eighteenth-Century New England

ALTHOUGH Philadelphia and New York may have outdistanced the other colonies — or more particularly the main towns — in the amount of brewing that was undertaken, there were nevertheless a few brewers in the other cities who owned substantial enterprises, with sizable plants and profits.

As far as Massachusetts goes, Samuel Adams must surely be the most illustrious of her citizens who had anything to do with the brewing industry. In spite of what most historians have said, however, it appears that he was exclusively a maltster and not a brewer. It was a traditional trade in the family. Samuel's great-grandfather, Joseph Adams, in his will, dated 18 July 1694, Braintree, made the following bequest: "I do give unto my son Peter Adams* all my dwelling house &c Malt house with all those tools & vessels in my Malt house, commonly used about my malting." [1]

Samuel Adams was born in 1722, graduated from Harvard in 1740, and made tentative efforts to enter the practice of law. He forsook these, however, in 1743, when he entered the counting-house of Thomas Cushing. According to his earliest biographer, W. V. Wells, he wished to start a business of his own, for which purpose his father, who owned a malting establishment, lent him £1000. Samuel gave half of this amount to a friend as a loan but it was never returned. It was then that he went into his father's business, working in the malthouse that stood next to the family dwelling on Purchase Street, Boston.[2]

* Peter Adams was a brother of Captain John Adams, Samuel's grandfather.

Samuel Adams, Sr., died in 1748, leaving the business to his son, who conducted it in person. But his mind was, as it happened, on other things — mainly politics and independence. There is good reason to believe that the malthouse was gone by 1763.* Samuel Adams had by then become an active and dynamic politician.[3]

Nowhere in the sparse pre-1760 records is there any indication that he was a brewer. Even Wells, who makes that mistake in his own text, quotes the poet Green, who called Adams "Sam the maltster." What is clearest about young Adams's career, however, is that he had very little, if any, talent for business; and it is a good thing for the country that he turned to the enterprise to which he was best suited.

A more humdrum member of the brewing business in Boston was Sampson Salter, probably the leading commercial brewer of the pre-1750 period. According to the Boston Record Commission Reports, he was born in Boston on 21 March 1692. He was married in 1715 by Dr. Cotton Mather to Mary (Martha) Robinson. His name appears with great regularity during the years 1731 and 1732 as supplier of beer to those ships outfitted by Peter Faneuil. In March 1731, his beer was placed aboard a new ship built and outfitted for William Le Messurier. In 1732 he provided beer for the brigantine *Lark*, the schooner *Society*, the sloop *Butterfly*, and the brigantine *Amistad*.[4]

In 1760, Salter applied for permission to rebuild his dwelling and brewhouse in Leveretts Lane; this was granted, provided his new brewhouse was made of brick.[5] And his name appeared again some years later in the letter book of Henry Lloyd, Boston "victualler." The latter wrote to Mr. Benjamin Harris in New York on 1 September 1766: "Mr. Sampson Salter demands pay for a bbl the Capt. [Clealand] carried Beer in from hence the price 4/-. if sent back he will receive it." Harris apparently replied to this query and Lloyd sent another letter: "I charg'd the Beer Barrilt to Ship Nelson agreable to your request." [6] In other words, Lloyd paid Salter out of his own pocket, and then charged same to a ship which was in Harris's account.

---

* A fraudulent announcement appeared in the Boston *News-Letter*, August 1758: "To be sold at public Auction at the Exchange Tavern in Boston, Tomorrow at noon. The Dwelling House, Malt-House, and other buildings . . . being part of the estate of the late *Samuel Adams* Esq. deceased." Apparently, Samuel, Jr., managed to forestall the sale.

Another brewer's name which appears in Boston commercial records is that of Robert Whatley, who provided beer in 1765 for the brigantine *Lydia*, outfitted by Thomas Hancock (uncle of John, who eventually inherited the business and its accumulated wealth).[7] In 1753 Thomas Hancock was paying bills to James Gardner for ten tierces* of beer "on board" (3/-) and 47 tierces "from Perkins" (£1/1/11). He dealt also in "velvit [velvet — the best quality of cork bark] corks" and was on at least one occasion involved in the exportation to Philadelphia of two tierces of malt.[8]

Two other commercial brewers in this period were John Carey, who received permission on 6 April 1710 to erect "a Timber building for a Brewhouse of ffifty foot Long Eighteen foot wide" on Cambridge Street, and John Williams, who received similar permission on 17 July 1716 to build the same kind of brewhouse, but of somewhat larger proportions.[9] The prominent Judge Samuel Sewall owned a malthouse;[10] Captain Nathaniel Oliver had a brewhouse in Water street;[11] and Captain James Pitts also owned a brewhouse[12] — but these were probably for private, rather than commercial, use.

The Rhode Island town of Newport, which grew so remarkably in the eighteenth century, was neither as large nor as powerful as Boston, but it was nonetheless an effective commercial rival. The earliest notable brewer in Newport was Daniel Sabeere, who was producing beer during the early part of the century — until his death in 1745. Though he apparently had a good business, he was improvident, left his bills unpaid and eventually failed.[13]

Other names which appear in the Newport brewing business are Anthony Young, John Wright, John Lance, Joseph Belcher and Giles Hosier. Hosier, who has a street in Newport named for him, was active in the second half of the century, and after the Revolution; he died in 1806.[14] For an unspecified period, he entered into some form of partnership with Thomas Robinson, an important local merchant. Robinson wrote, in his capacity as partner, to Moses Brown, who had an ironworks in Providence:

---

* A tierce is one-third of a puncheon, which equaled, at that period, two barrels or 72 gallons — therefore, 24 gallons of beer.

Newport Oct- 8- 1771

Esteemed Friend
Moses Brown

When Governor Hopkins was in Town Giles Hosier had some taulk with him about some Irons we wanted in our Brewery, he has sent up the Dimentions etc. as we stand in great need of them, I shall take it kind of thee if thou woud forward them as soon as possible, we cant go forward with the work without them - - - - - - - - -

I am thy Sincere Friend
THO ROBINSON[15]

In the previous year, these enterprising partners had petitioned the General Assembly then sitting at Newport for permission to rent the cellar of the Colony House (Statehouse) that "has for a long time ben and now is unimproved and bringeth no profit to the Colony when at the same time it may be Rendered Serviceable to your Petitioners and of publick Utility." This was doubtless a cellar in which Hosier and Robinson wished to store their beer. The petition was granted.[16]

On 9 July 1774, however, they presented another petition to the General Assembly, then at East Greenwich:

The Petition and Memorial of Giles Hosier Shewith, That haveing Taken a Lease with Thomas Robinson, sometime past of the Celler under the Colony house in Newport, whereby We were Jointly bound for the Rent, Since which haveing Sold to the Said Robinson my part of the Brewery and agreed that he have the Lease from the Colony in his Own Name, Now your Petitioner Desires that you would please to Order and Regulate the Same.

As far as one can tell, this seems to have been a friendly termination of partnership; at any rate, the petition was granted and Robinson became sole lessee of the cellar under the Colony House.[17]

But Hosier had not abandoned his calling forever. After the Revolution, on 8 June 1795, he was back at the General Assembly with a new petition:

Giles Hosier of Newport Brewer Wishes to inform this Honourable Assembly, haveing some Encouragement of Enlarging his Brewery, so as to make Bottled Beer an Article of Exportation, which is not at Present in his power for want of a Convenient Cellar.

The East half part of the Cellar under the Court House in Newport being unoccupide, He the said Giles Hosier Respectfully ask the favour of this Honourable Assembly that He s^d Hosier may be Permitted to partition off the North East Quarter part more or less of said Cellar in order to try a few Years if he can make the afores^d Business Answer.[18]

This request, too, the agreeable General Assembly granted, and for a number of years, Hosier beer reposed underneath the Newport Court House.

A brewery which functioned in Newport for some years before the Revolution was owned by the Englishman George Rome. He was factor for a number of English businessmen who sent him over to handle unpaid bills due to them. Among other things, he apparently took over the brewhouse in lieu of an unsettled account. It was located on Spring Street, south of the First Baptist Church.[19] Rome was a well-known man about Newport; he evidently did well out of his profession; but in 1775 this "brewhouse and lot" were confiscated. Rome had to go back to England, which was unfortunate because Newport was occupied by the English during most of the war, and he would have been perfectly secure there.[20]

NINE

Supplying Beer to the Southern Colonies

T HE SECOND of the Hanoverian kings was already on the throne
of Great Britain when the colony of Georgia was chartered. There
were several reasons advanced for settling and creating Georgia: the
dominating one was its usefulness as buffer between the Carolinas and
the Spanish colonies to the south. In this role it functioned successfully,
from the time of its first settlement in 1733. But both in its economic
purposes and in the philanthropic ideals of its main trustee, James Edward Oglethorpe, it was a relative failure; only after the charter expired
and it became a royal province in 1753 did Georgia begin to thrive.

One of Oglethorpe's ideas was to prohibit the sale or consumption
of spirits in the colony:

> The Trustees, receiving frequent Information from the Colony, of the
> pernicious Effects of drinking Rum, and other spiritous Liquors . . .
> intituled an Act to prevent the Importation and Use of Rum and
> Brandies in the Province of Georgia, or any kind of Spirits or Strong-
> waters whatsoever. At the same time they endeavored to supply the
> Stores with Strong-beer from England, Melasses for brewing Beer,
> and with Madeira Wines, which the People might purchase at reason-
> able Rates.[1]

Two Carolina gentlemen, who visited Oglethorpe shortly after his arrival, considered that an important enough fact to mention in the account they published in the South Carolina *Gazette* of 22 March 1733:
"He does not allow them Rum, but in lieu gives them *English* beer." [2]

This semiprohibition worked only semisuccessfully. As can always be expected, there was a certain amount of smuggling and bootlegging, and the prohibition against rum was lifted, at royal direction, in 1749. Whatever Oglethorpe and the other trustees may have felt about the "pernicious effects" of rum and brandy, they were typically English and of their period in approving the use of beer. There was an allowance of beer for each emigrant on the journey over and a ration for his maintenance in the colony. An account has been given of a boat trip taken in March 1736 by Oglethorpe and some settlers' families to the town of Frederica from the mouth of the Savannah River:

> As an incentive to unity of movement, he placed all the strong beer on board a fast boat. The rest labored diligently to keep up; for if they were not all at the place of rendezvous each night, the tardy crew lost its ration. Frederica was reached on the 8th and there was general joy among the colonists.[3]

It may well be that Charles Wesley, brother of John and first chaplain of Frederica, was in one of the boats trying to beat the beer up river.

It was difficult to keep a sufficient supply of beer on hand, particularly as there were no means for brewing in the beginning. There is a description, in the journal of the province's secretary, of a sloop just in from New York on 7 October 1738,

> having good Plenty of well brewed Beer aboard, which at this season of the Year was much wished for by most People; more went without any than those few who could find Money to buy and the publick Stores had none.[4]

A similar item of later date (1742) gives some idea of the amounts of beer required by the colonists:

> The New York Sloop having sold most part of her dry provisions, began to Set out for Frederica with what she had else, which being about 150 Barrels of Beer, twas Supposed might Serve there for 3 or 4 days Draught.[5]

One of the colonists, Thomas Jones, wrote from Savannah on 17 September 1740 to John Lynde:

> As to our liquors, we have Wine; chiefly Madeira or Vidonia,* which cost us from 3s. to 3s. 6d. a gallon; Strong Beer 20s. per Barrel of 30

---

* A wine from the Canary Islands, particularly Teneriffe.

Gallons; Cyder 10s. per Barrel. Our Small Beer we brew of Molasses, and is cheap.[6]

The price, at least of the strong beer, does not seem particularly high when compared, for example, with the 30s. a barrel asked by Thomas Freame's Philadelphia brewery in 1733.*

Among the early Georgia settlers was a group of Salzburger peasants from Germany; their pastor was Johann Martin Bolzius from 1734 until he died in 1765. In 1751, he provided written answers to a number of questions sent him by "certain" interested Germans; among them the following:

> At this time bakers and brewers, knitters, clothmakers, glass blowers and so on are not needed in the land. . . . A brewer is not needed for as yet too little barley is grown; and the inhabitants who have the ability cook a healthy beer for themselves out of syrup, Indian corn and hops, or the tops of the white or water firs, which is very cheap. Strong barley beer comes from New York, at times also from England, a quart of which is worth 4d. It is cheaper by the barrel. In these lands little beer is drunk.[7]

At the period of these pioneering activities in Georgia, Virginia, now over a hundred years old, was a settled, highly prosperous, and practically self-governing province. Like Massachusetts, she now had a college of her own, William and Mary, established in 1693 for religious education. Through a variety of misfortunes, the original college buildings burned down three times; as a result the records of its beginnings are woefully meager. It is known, nonetheless, that there was, in the original edifice, provision for brewing.

Writing of the college before the 1705 fire, Robert Beverley explained that the main building

> is to consist of a Quadrangle, two sides of which, are yet only carryed up. In this part are already finished all conveniences for Cooking, Brewing, Baking, &c. and convenient Rooms for the Reception of the President, and Masters, with many more Scholars than are yet come to it.[8]

Rebuilding of the ruined college was not undertaken until about 1716; in that year, the following instruction appeared in the minutes of

* See page 63.

a meeting of the Board of Visitors and Governors of the College: "OR-DERED, That it be referred to the Committie to send to England for Standing furniture for the Colledge Kitchen, Brewhouse, and Laundry." [9] The only regulation giving us a clue to the drinking practices of the college is dated 19 December 1796: "no liquors shall be furnished or used at table except beer, cyder, toddy, or spirits and waters, and these only in a moderate quantity." [10]

There seems to be no doubt, also, that a brewhouse was erected at the governor's residence in Williamsburg. "For rendring the new House Convenient as well as ornamental," it was proposed about 1710 "that all standing Furniture for the Kitchen and Brew house such as a Copper for washing, another for brewing Stove Irons and other things that must necessarily be fixed to the House be bought & furnished at the publick Charge." [11] In Virginia as a whole, beer was increasingly being imported from New York, Philadelphia, and England, or else brewed in the home or plantation. Commercial brewing on any considerable scale did not make headway, though the local brew was less than half the price of the English import.[12] Several commercial brewers did make themselves known in the advertising columns of the *Virginia Gazette.* Mr. John Mercer, who had a brewery in Marlborough, was one;* his lack of success was generally matched by the others.

The partners Joseph Jones and William Woodford, who built a substantial brewery in Fredericksburg in 1771, announced three years later that they would

> dispose of the Lots and Improvements in *Fredericksburg,* where the Brewery now stands. There are three Lots and a Half. On the Lot and Half situate on the River are the Brewhouse, Malthouse, Counting-house, Cooper's Shop, &c. all new, and in good Order for carrying on the Brewing Business. We would also sell the Implements and Stock belonging to the Brewery.[13]

But there were no buyers and in 1778 they advertised again, this time to say that the partnership would be dissolved, and all the property (including Negro cooper) had to be sold.[14] Yet again, the following year, Jones offered his "half part" of the brewery for sale.[15] One hopes that finally some suitable disposition of the property was made.

* See page 62.

Much earlier, in 1736, one Anthony Hoggatt offered for sale his "well-accustomed ordinary, malt-house," etc. in Goochland County.[16] And in 1780 the Westham Brewery was up for sale to the highest bidder.

Although these notices might be thought to convey the impression that commercial brewing was not a promising investment in Virginia, because of the peculiar way that colony was set up, nevertheless a number of advertisements show an opposite trend: individuals anxious to get into the business.

> Manchester, Dec 8, 1777
> Intending to set up a Brewery and Distillery at this Place, I have provided two Stills and three Coppers, one of which contains about 300 Gallons. The Situation and Convenience for carrying on that Business at this Place are equal to any. A Person properly qualified, by Experience, to superintend such Business, may become a Partner, by applying shortly.
>
> JOHN MAYO[17]

Nicholas and Henry Langdon Davies, after stating that they had "laid out a Town on *James* River, below the great Mountains in *Amherst* County, *Virginia*, and near the upper End of Navigation," let it be known that they wished to set up in this "Town" of theirs, called Bethel, a "Linen Factory, a Rope-Walk,* and a Brewhouse; so that all Persons well skilled in said Trades, and who settle in said Town, may expect all reasonable encouragement." [18]

Encouragement was likewise offered by Mr. Bradley at Petersburg to a man, "WANTED immediately," who was acquainted with "the MALTING and BREWING business." [19] These requests continued right into the years of war: in 1778 George Goosley, near Yorktown, advertised for "A MAN acquainted with MALTING and BREWING," promising good wages and "agreeable accommodations." [20]

If these may be called the Help Wanted ads of that period, there were also others that belong in the Positions Wanted category.

> A person just arrived from England, capable of making MALT and conducting a BREWERY, would be glad of Encouragement in the above Branches from any gentleman, or company of Gentlemen. He

---
* A building where ropes are manufactured.

is ready to pledge his All, that he could bring the above Branches to as great Perfection as they are in *Britain*.

JOSEPH KIDD, Williamsburg[21]

Likewise, in the midst of the Revolution, Richard Smaddell advertised for "an overseer's place, or a brewers place, thinking himself capable of either." [22]

Aside from brewers like these, who were presumably more or less professional and properly trained, there are several ads in the Virginia paper for Negro slaves who were able to brew. For sale: "A valuable young Negro woman, very well qualified for all sorts of Housework, as Washing, Ironing, Sewing, Brewing, Baking, &c." [23]

Though there was a coppersmith, James Haldane, at Church Street, Norfolk, who made and sold brewing coppers, and though copper kettles "for mashing and brewing," as well as equipment for malting, were advertised for sale,[24] nevertheless the commercial climate and the social structure of Virginia were not, at that time, propitious for commercial brewing. Virginia farmers had given up, by then, any pretense of growing hops, which were almost entirely imported from London and Boston. Nor was barley grown in quantities sufficient for commercial malting purposes. To be sure, both barley and hops were raised, toward the end of the century, by gentlemen farmers, such as Colonel Landon Carter of Sabine Hill, whose diary records on 20 June 1776, "Barley so full of good wheat that he [Carter] orders the latter to be pulled out before the barley is sheaved. The blooming of some of his hop poles show that the ground is not rich enough." [25] But this was in the nature of experiments that only owners of large plantations could undertake, and they signify no commercial cultivation of the ingredients of beer.

In the columns of the *Virginia Gazette*, there are two tantalizing references to beer imported into Virginia from Maryland, once in 1745 and once in 1774. It is understandable that beer should have been coming in from Philadelphia and New York, but there are no indications of a brewing industry in Maryland elaborate enough to account for exports. Indeed, there was only one possible brewery in Maryland in this period that might have been exporting small quantities of beer to thirsty Virginia, and that was the enterprise of the Barnitz family. The originator, John Leonard Barnitz, had been born in Falkenstein, Germany, in 1677, and emigrated to America probably in the late 1720s. He was a brewer by profession and settled first in York, Pennsylvania, where he established a brewery. Sometime later on he moved to Hanover, Pennsylvania, starting a brewery there; but ended up in Baltimore and, with one of his sons, Elias Daniel, established a brewery which in their lifetimes had a good deal of success. The York brewery remained in the hands of John Leonard's second son, John George Charles, who died in 1796, leaving the business to his two sons. By the beginning of the nineteenth century the family apparently gave up all connection with the brewing business.[26]

Aside from the Barnitzes, brewing was not widespread in Maryland during the first half of the eighteenth century. A British traveler in the 'thirties commented on the shortage of beer brewed from malted grain:

> The beer they brew is excellent, which they make in great Quantities, of Parsimons, &c., of Molasses; for few of them are Come to malting their corn, of any kind, at which I was much surprized; as even the Indian Grain, as I have found experimentally, will produce an wholesome and generous Liquor.

This writer described the "Parsimon" for his English readers as "not unlike a Medlar [pear], tho' somewhat larger," and said that the Maryland planters used it to "sweeten a Beer, which they brew of Caffena and divers Herbs, which is vastly wholesome." [27]

But Maryland struck this traveler as much less developed than Virginia, where he found "more considerable Marks of Opulency." He was impressed, in fact, to find that "English Porter, which is imported generally in Bottles," was available "here and there."

One of the minute details of Virginia history which has obtained credit with very little substantiation is the story that Patrick Henry, the man of impassioned speech known to every schoolboy, was a bartender. According to one of Henry's early biographers, his father-in-law, Shelton, did in fact keep a tavern at Hanover in Virginia.

> Whenever Mr. Shelton was from home, Mr. Henry supplied his place in the tavern, received the guests, and attended to their entertainment. . . . A story has arisen, that in the early part of his life, he was a barkeeper by profession. The fact seems not to have been so.[28]

As for his conduct in later life, he is supposed to have been "very abstemious in his diet, and used no wine or alcoholic stimulants." During his governorship between 1784 and 1786, he wished to offset the apparently harmful effects of distilled spirits, consumed then in great quantity, by bringing into popularity a less alcoholic beverage, and "to effect this object, he ordered from his merchant in Scotland a consignment of barley, and a Scotch brewer and his wife to cultivate the grain and make small beer." His grandson claimed that Henry never drank anything stronger while he lived.[29]

In this practice, or at least in the theory behind his practice, Patrick Henry was very much in line with other prominent Americans who supported, for the welfare of the country, an increase in beer production and consumption after the War of Independence.

৩ৣ TEN ৣৡ

"Buy American"

THE FIRST BOOK printed by Benjamin Franklin, in the year 1725, was by an Englishman, Francis Rawle, who had arrived in Philadelphia in 1686; it was entitled *Ways and Means for the Inhabitants of Delaware to Become Rich*. (By "Delaware," Rawle meant the colonies of Delaware *and* Pennsylvania.) In the course of the book, Rawle speaks of the barley grown in Pennsylvania, describing the three sorts that existed: four-rowed, two-rowed, and a six-rowed kind which he called a "Winter Barley."* He did not think much of the last-named, saying that its only use was in the making of beer. He did not mean that beer was not worth making — but that it was not being made well. Unfortunately, "thro' the Depravity and Viciousness of our Palates and the so frequent use of Spirits, there has not been due Care in the Brewing of beer." This was a common cry in the eighteenth century: that the taste for beer had been debased by the use of spirits. Rawle suggests, however, a conventional solution:

> But not to be wholly without Hopes let the Brewer do his part and the Legislature theirs by laying an Impost on Foreign Liquors and permit the selling of Beer and Cyder free of all Charges. This will further the frequent use of the latter and Disuse of the former, consequently will cause a greater Consumption of the Country-Produce.[1]

Here the twofold purpose was to increase consumption of beer and cider over that of spirits (rum, brandy, etc.) and also to increase con-

* See page 44.

sumption of local over that of imported manufacture. This "Buy American" theme is sounded frequently throughout the century, mainly of course for understandable commercial reasons, but also because Americans were beginning to feel that in a number of fields they could, in fact, compete successfully with the English.

What happened during this period was that, on the one hand, a firm of provisioners like John and Clement Biddle in Philadelphia would be furnishing Mr. John Brown of Providence with Scots ale manufactured by Joseph and William Cunningham & Co. of Glasgow.[2] Or Thomas Hancock, the leading Boston merchant, would keep a running account with the London brewers Lodge & Combrune,[3] and the New York merchant Gerard G. Beekman would be ordering beer from Halifax and Londonderry.[4] On the other hand, a Virginia brewer would advertise in the following terms:

> The severe treatment we have lately received from our Mother Country, would, I should think, be sufficient to recommend my undertaking (tho I should not be able to come up to the English standard, which I do not question constantly to do) yet, as I am satisfied that the goodness of every commodity is the best recommendation, I principally rely upon that for my success.[5]

Or Samuel Adams would use a simple newspaper advertisement for "OLD MALT" as a springboard for patriotic remarks:

> It is to be hoped, that the Gentlemen of the Town will endeavour to bring our own OCTOBER BEER * into Fashion again, by that most prevailing Motive, EXAMPLE, so that we may no longer be beholden to *Foreigners* for a *Credible Liquor*, which may be as successfully manufactured in this Country.[6]

This chauvinistic tack was hardly surprising in a people who, though born in one country, owed allegiance to another. Samuel Adams himself, for example, was a fourth-generation American: it was his great-great-grandfather who had first emigrated in the seventeenth century. What the Americans, in fact, were seeking was not independence from Great Britain (Benjamin Franklin was against independence of the Crown

---

* "Old or strong beer is sometimes called by the cant name of *stingo*; it is moreover designated by the word October, from that month being peculiarly propitious to the brewing of this grateful beverage" (Brande, p. 161*n*).

right up to the start of the war), but treatment as first-class citizens, equal in their rights to their brothers in the home country. It was only the shortsighted denial by the English of this perfectly obvious minimum demand that led to increasing estrangement as well as chauvinism.

In 1763, the Seven Years' War finally ended with the English defeating the French and taking over Canada, but they were somewhat depleted by the victory. The tax burden borne by the English had become so crushing that they naturally looked toward the colonies in America for, at least, financial participation. The years between 1761 and 1769 were a time of financial depression, in both England and the colonies. Farmers, merchants, manufacturers alike found their affairs at lowest ebb; businesses failed; debts piled up while trade languished.[7] The British hoped to ease the effects of depression by taxing the colonies for revenue, whereas the colonists thought of the new taxes as difficult to pay and wrong on principle.

The first moves of the British government at this point were intended to stop up a number of loopholes by which the colonists had been evading the payment of taxes. It also appeared natural, in the home country, for the Americans to help in supporting their own defense. But the very fact that the British had driven the French out of North America made the colonists feel less threatened and therefore less in need of English expeditionary troops.

A series of parliamentary acts and the indignant protests against them led step by step to the Revolution. The Revenue Act of 1764 (called the "Sugar" Act) was designed mainly to put a stop to the smuggling of molasses and sugar from the French West Indies, but it also established duties on a number of other items. The colonial merchants objected strongly to this act and did nothing more. It was the Stamp Act and the Quartering Act, which came within a month of each other in 1765, that roused them to action. Of the various protests undertaken, the embargo on British goods, organized by the so-called Stamp Act Congress, was probably the most effective. Merchants in all the major American ports agreed not to accept British imports until the Stamp Act was repealed. In Philadelphia, Samuel Morris,* of the Morris brewing clan, was

* See page 46.

one of those backing such a move;[8] and there is evidence that colonial brewers in general supported the nonimportation agreement. The English merchants were seriously enough harmed by the boycott to help in lifting the Stamp Act in 1766 — an important victory for the colonists. At the same time, however, Parliament passed the Declaratory Act which established, in effect, its right to tax the colonies for revenue — exactly the point disputed by the Americans.

A new government in 1767 meant additional attempts to regulate colonial affairs. The Townshend Acts received a particularly hostile reaction; they not only included new duties and payment for troops quartered in America, but also provided for a Board of Customs Commissioners, based in Massachusetts, with powers of search and entry, which appeared to many Americans as a new form of oppressive regulation.

The New York legislature, incensed at various provisions of the Townshend Acts, refused to supply the English troops stationed in that colony with salt, vinegar and beer; as a result, Parliament suspended their power.[9] Opposition to the Acts led to the dissolution of the Virginia and Massachusetts assemblies.

The New Jersey administration, under William Franklin, son of Benjamin, was less recalcitrant and on 6 December 1769 passed an act "appointing Commissioners for Supplying the several barracks Erected in the Colony of New Jersey, with Furniture and other Necessaries for Accomodating the Kings Troops. . . ." Among the "Necessaries" was small beer:

> And whereas Difficulties may arrive to the Commissioners in providing and serving Beer to the said Troops, to prevent which and that the Troops may be enabled to supply themselves therewith, BE IT EN-ACTED That . . . in Lieu and Stead of Four Pints of Small Beer hereby Allowed for each Man per day It shall and may be Lawful for the said Commissioners to provide and allow to the said Troops a Quantity of Molasses not exceeding One Gallon to a Barrel of Small Beer.[10]

The American merchants resorted again to the boycott. In Virginia, a nonimportation agreement was signed by George Washington, Patrick

Henry, Peyton Randolph, Robert Carter Nichols and Richard Henry Lee.[11] The agreement was reiterated in 1770 by "the Association in Williamsburg": "That we will not hereafter, directly or indirectly, import, or cause to be imported, from *Great Britain*, any of the goods hereafter enumerated, either for sale or for our own use, . . . beer, ale, porter, malt." [12]

Among the various reports concerning deprivations that might be caused by the boycott is a curious one that South Carolina had a sufficiency of beer and plenty more could be made there. That was not a colony which had shown any other signs of unusual brewing activity, and this announcement was showing perhaps more patriotism than realism. The same newspaper article quotes a letter sent from Charlestown to Bristol, England, in 1769: "I suppose all England has been a good deal astonished at the suddenness of Carolina's coming into resoutions of non importation of goods from England." [13] The Southern colonists, in general, had lagged behind the others in backing the boycott. Except for Virginia, they were less affected by the English taxes than the colonies north of them were, and they were mainly suppliers of raw materials rather than merchants or manufacturers.

Some of the extra-patriotic colonists interpreted the nonimportation agreements as an encouragement to home manufacture. During 1769 and 1770, homespun, though it was less comfortable and stylish than English cloth, was widely sported; "spinning-parties" became a form of sociability. This note was also sounded later, in 1775, when a committee was formed in Virginia for the encouragement of American arts and manufactures. The cultivation of hops and barley was recommended by this group because "brewing malt liquors in this colony would tend to render the consumption of foreign liquors less necessary." [14]

The first test of the boycott undertaken in 1769 — a test of both American solidarity and the English reaction — came over a shipment of malt addressed to Mr. Amos Strettell, a distinguished maltster who emigrated from England and settled in Philadelphia. In July 1769 a vessel with the delightful name *Charming Polly* arrived at the port of Philadelphia from Yarmouth, claiming that Mr. Strettell had ordered her cargo of malt.

The committee of merchants being informed thereof immediately con-
vened. . . . Mr. Strettell attending, laid before the committee the
letter he had received, dated the 5th of May, which he assured them
was all he knew of the matter; that the shipper was an entire stranger
to him, and that the first news he had of such a cargo coming was by
the arrival of the vessel.[15]

The next day a general meeting of the Philadelphia merchants was
called, and it was unanimously resolved that the importing of the malt
from Yarmouth would be "contrary to the spirit" of the nonimportation
agreements, and that it "ought to be discouraged." At this meeting, the
Philadelphia brewers appeared in a body: their names are given as Haines
& Twells, Isaac Howell, Anthony Morris, Jr., Francis Coade, Anthony C.
Morris, Reinard Kreimer, Moore and Chesnutt, Valentine Stanley, and
Woolman and Pusey.[16] They had themselves drawn up and signed a
pledge

wherein they engage that as the load of malt just arrived was contrary to the agreement of the merchants and traders they will not purchase any part of it, nor will they brew the same, or any part thereof,
for any person whatsoever.[17]

Soon after the *Charming Polly* sailed away, without being able to dis-
charge her cargo, another English ship, the *Speedwell* from Liverpool,
came into port. The embargo was so freshly established that the merchants were carefully avoiding any suspicion of seeking to break it;
yet one man was caught trying surreptitiously to buy cheese from the
ship. The merchants of the city upbraided him severely, with the result
that the culprit, much chastened, bought some bread and presented it
along with the cheese to the debtors in jail.[18] The debtors, in a most
curious way, made a good deal of profit out of this particular misadven-
ture: "Two or three more caught in the same way added beer to the
bread and cheese, so that the prisoners had quite a feast of it." [19]

Exemplary patriotism on the part of the Philadelphia merchants —
and not among the least of them, the brewers! Other traders in other
cities were not so honorable as the boycott continued.

The first defector was Rhode Island, whose Newport merchants depended for their livelihood on imports, and to whom smuggling was an

old tradition. Though the other colonies tried to shame her back into a state of virtue, Rhode Island continued on her own sweet, profitable way. The second defection was even more serious; New York began in 1770, first covertly, and then openly, to receive merchandise from abroad. The solidarity for this kind of action was broken, and eventually, at the end of that year, the movement collapsed, but it had by then served its main purpose: the Townshend Acts were repealed.

The idea of nonimportation would not die: at the First Continental Congress in 1774, it was revived. Between 1770 and then had come the East India Company's tea monopoly, the Boston Tea Party, and in response to that the Coercive Acts, including the closing of the port of Boston. The congress was called to decide on what action to take against the Coercive Acts and how to support Massachusetts. Because the colonies had been driven, against their tradition, into closer cooperation, the nonimportation measures had become a clearer gauge of pro-American or pro-English sentiment. Those who would not go along with the embargo were looked on as traitors, and the pressure to conform to the majority was great. By 1774, the political drive was much stronger than it had been in 1769; now the cry of "liberty" was becoming louder than that of "justice."

Recipes for Home Brewers

B Y THE START of 1775, it must have been clear that events in
America had passed the point of no return. Friction between the
rulers and the ruled had begun to produce unmistakable sparks — the
Boston "Massacre" in 1770, the famous Tea Party in December 1773.
Some of the colonists could see plainly what was ahead for them, and
their minds were troubled by the hardships they might suffer when
trade with the English was cut off. On 14 February 1775, for example,
Landon Carter, aware that supplies of imported malt liquors might
dwindle, wrote to the *Virginia Gazette*, offering a family recipe for
making beer out of green corn stalks:

> The stalks, green as they were, as soon as pulled up, were carried to
> a convenient trough, then chopped and pounded so much, that, by
> boiling, all the juice could be extracted out of them; which juice every
> planter almost knows is of as saccharine a quality almost as any thing
> can be, and that any thing of a luxuriant corn stalk is very full of it,
> . . . After this pounding, the stalks and all were put into a large
> copper, there lowered down in its sweetness with water, to an equality
> with common observations in malt wort, and then boiled, till the
> liquor in a glass is seen to break, as the brewers term it; after that it
> is strained, and boiled again with hops. The beer I drank had been
> made above twenty days, and bottled off about four days.

This recipe is, of course, in line with earlier attempts to make beer out
of the native grain, maize. But it follows still another English and
early American tradition, which was to collect, exchange and perhaps

even create recipes for beer — just as cooks have always done with recipes for food.

The most famous of these, simply because of the fame of its owner, is the one which appears in a notebook of George Washington, kept when he was a colonel in 1737, and now in the manuscript collection of the New York Public Library. It need come as no surprise that Washington, being a Virginia gentleman and a beer-lover, should jot down such a recipe:

To Make Small Beer

Take a large Siffer [Sifter] full of Bran Hops to your Taste. — Boil these 3 hours then strain out 30 Gall^{ns} into a Cooler put in 3 Gall^{ns} Molasses while the Beer is Scalding hot or rather draw the Melasses into the Cooler & St[r]ain the Beer on it while boiling Hot. let this stand till it is little more than Blood warm then put in a quart of Yea[s]t if the Weather is very Cold cover it over with a Blank[et] & let it Work in the Cooler 24 hours then put it into the Cask — leave the Bung [Stopper] open till it is almost don[e] Working — Bottle it that day Week it was Brewed.*

A real curiosity in the way of a beer recipe is the one attributed to Major Thomas Fenner of Providence, who "brewed a beer famous throughout the countryside." The date concerned seems to be in the early 1700s:

Receipt to make Bear

One ounce of Sentry Suckery or Sulindine one handful Red Sage or Large 1/4 Pound Shells of Iron Brused fine take 10 quarts of Water Steep it away to Seven and a quart of Molases Wheat Brand Baked Hard. one quart of Malt one handful Sweeat Balm Take it as Soone as it is worked.[1]

So it is reproduced — and probably means something like: "One ounce of senna tree [the dried leaves], chicory or celandine, one handful of red sage, or large quarter-pound shells of iron† crushed into small

---

* Recently a sheet of paper entitled "George Washington Recipe for Ale," and bearing a typewritten recipe, has come to light in the files of the Milwaukee County Historical Society. Completely modern in diction and bearing no evidence of origin, it is obviously highly questionable as to authenticity.

† This could be a number of things: possibly ironwood, *Ostrya virginica*, or the hop hornbeam, with catkins like a hop plant.

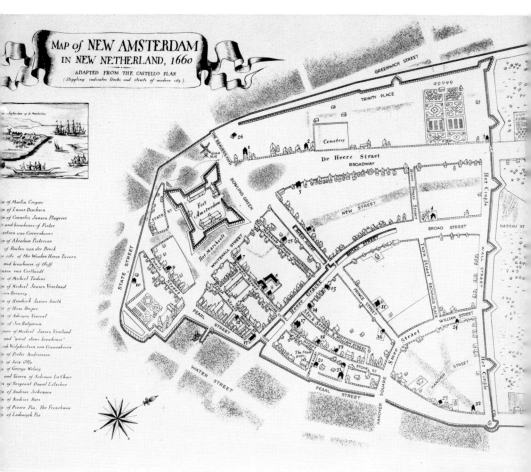

Brewers and taverns in New Amsterdam, 1660

Eighteenth-century fermenting tub

An early cooker

Eighteenth-century mash tub

Primitive English boiler

These four pieces of equipment probably made up the basic
requirements of an eighteenth-century brewery

Brewery built in 1745 at Dock and Pear Streets, Philadelphia,
by Anthony Morris, IV

Receipt signed by Anthony Morris, III

William Penn's house, with his brewhouse at the right

Barnitz Brewhouse in York, Pennsylvania, 1801
Watercolor by York artist, Lewis Miller (1795-1882)

"The old Vater, Johan, George Carle Barnitz starb 1796 alt 74.
"his sons Daniel, Jacob, Carl, John, George, Michael
"names of the hands whose profession is to make beer.
old Bromer hannes, 1800
John Miller, dollen nickname
Jacob Siechrist, 1812

To make Small Beer.

Take a large Sifter full of Bran
Hops to your Taste. — Boil these
3 hours. then strain out 30 Gall.
into a Cooler put in 3 Gall.
Molasses while the Beer is
Scalding hot rather draw the
Molasses into the Cooler & Strain
the Beer on it while boiling Hot
let this stand till it is little more
than Blood warm then put in
a quart of Yeast if the Weather is
very Cold cover it over with a Blankt
& let it work in the Cooler 24 hours
then put it into the Cask — leave
the Bung open till it is almost don
Working — Bottle it that day Week
it was Brewed.

Small beer recipe from a notebook kept by George Washington
while serving as a Colonel in the Virginia Militia

ALE,

Brewed from the beft ENGLISH MALT,
Is now ready to be delivered out for CASH,
as ufual,
At the BREWERY, Maiden
Lane.

YEAST

May alfo be had as above.

Beer & Yeft for the Seafon.

THE fubfcriber refpectfully informs his friends, and the public in general, that he has commenced brewing for the feafon, in the Brew-houfe, known by the name of GORSUCH'S BREWERY, in *Back-ftreet*, near *Griffith's Bridge*; where may be had good wholefome Beer, by the barrel, gallon, or fmaller quantity, at one fhilling per gallon.

Being thoroughly bred to the bufinefs, and wifhing to merit the public's patronage, he has only to recommend a trial thereof for recommendation. CONRAD HOBURG.

N. B. Houfekeepers and others may be fupplied with any quantity of Beer, at any time of the day, at the above price. C. H.

Baltimore, Nov. 26, 1792. eo3t

Beer advertising in the eighteenth century

THE

AMERICAN

PRACTICAL BREWER AND TANNER:

IN WHICH IS EXHIBITED

THE WHOLE PROCESS OF

Brewing without boiling.

Brewing strong Beer with the extract only of the hop, leaving out the substance.

A simple method of giving new Beer all the qualities of age, thereby fitting it for the bottle before it is three weeks old.

A simple method of preventing Beer bursting the bottle.

An economical mode of constructing Vats above ground, possessing the temperature of the best cellars, and thus rendered fireproof.

An economical mode by which every House keeper may brew his own Beer.

A method of brewing good Beer from Bran and Sharts, and of preserving it.

The Bordeaux method of making and preparing Claret Wine for shipping, which may be successfully applied to the wines of this country, particularly those of Kaskaskias.

The best method and season for malting Indian Corn, from which alone good Beer can be made, a process highly important to Brewers.

The best mode of raising Hops.

The best mode of preparing Seed Barley for sowing.

Best construction and aspect of Breweries and Malt Houses in this country.

The French mode of tanning the heaviest Soal Leather in twenty-one days, and Calf Skins in three or four. (Highly important.)

BY JOSEPH COPPINGER,

Practical Brewer.

NEW-YORK:

PRINTED BY VAN WINKLE AND WILEY,

No. 3 Wall-Street.

. . . .

1815.

Title page of a brewer's manual written by
a correspondent of Thomas Jefferson

A letter of Thomas Jefferson's with a reference to
brewing at Monticello

Sir

Monticello Sep. 17. 13.

I lent you some time ago the London & Country brewer and Combrun's book on the same subject. we are this day beginning, under the directions of Capt Millar, the business of brewing Malt liquors, and if these books are no longer useful to you I will thank you for them, as we may perhaps be able to derive some information from them. accept the assurance of my respect & consideration

Th Jefferson

Capt. Meriwether.

An artist's impression of activity around an ale and porter brewery
in New York, 1861

pieces. Take ten quarts of water, steep [boil?] it away to seven; and a quart of molasses. Wheat bran baked hard [into a cake?]. One quart of malt, one handful of sweet barm [yeast]. Drink it as soon as it is fermented."

This Fenner recipe is interesting from a number of viewpoints. It shows, for one thing, the rather haphazard way some beers were made at the end of the seventeenth century: no indication of heats, or how long to boil. It also illustrates the use of herbs, which was common at an earlier age and was then partially supplanted by the use of hops. But the use of herbs went on, in fact, for quite a long time; even in a brewer's handbook of 1852 there are recipes that call for coriander seed, caraway, hartshorn shavings, and the like. The presence of certain flavorings in the recipe indicated a different type of brew: Dorchester ale, for example, contained ginger and cinnamon, "Scurvy grass ale" (thought to be a cure for scurvy) contained Alexandria senna, "hock" had cocculus indicus berry and fabia amora (or bitter bean).[2]

Another contributor to the collection of beer recipes was that great experimenter, Benjamin Franklin. He believed in temperance, abhorred drunkenness: "Eat not to dullness. Drink not to elevation," he said. He drank mainly wine, and apparently some beer. The records of his household expenses for the month of September in 1782, while he was living in Paris, show that he ordered twenty bottles of beer, at weekly intervals — two or three or even seven bottles at a time. During the same period he disposed of forty-one bottles of *vin ordinaire*, bought daily.[3] From that important sojourn in France after the War of Independence, he brought back the following beer recipe (translated from the French):

A Way of making Beer with Essence of Spruce

For a Cask containing 80 Bottles, take one Pot of Essence and 13 Pounds of Molasses. — or the same amount of unrefined Loaf Sugar; mix them well together in 20 Pints of hot Water: Stir together until they make a Foam, then pour it into the Cask you will then fill with Water: add a Pint of good Yeast, stir it well together and let it stand 2 or 3 Days to ferment, after which close the Cask, and after a few days it will be ready to be put into Bottles, that must be tightly corked. Leave them 10 or 12 Days in a cool Cellar, after which the Beer will be good to drink.[4]

Spruce beer was a specially favored brew which had a good deal of popularity in the seventeenth and eighteenth centuries; it was most often made in the home, but was also, in some instances, sold commercially.

A recipe for spruce beer turns up, surprisingly, in the journal of General Jeffrey Amherst, hero of the battle of Louisburg in 1758, governor-general of British North America in 1760.

> Take 7 Pounds of good Spruce & boil it well till the bark peels off, then take the Spruce out & put three Gallons of Molasses to the Liquor & boil it again, scum it well as it boils, then take it out the kettle & put it into a cooler, boil the remained of the water sufficient for a Barrel of thirty Gallons, if the kettle is not large enough to boil it together, when milkwarm in the Cooler put a Pint of Yest into it and mix well. Then put in the Barrel and let it work for two or three days, keep filling it up as it works out. When done working, bung it up with a Tent Peg in the Barrel to give it vent every now and then. It may be used in two or three days after. If wanted to be bottled it should stand a fortnight in the Cask. It will keep a great while.[5]

It is most likely that spruce, in place of hops, served the same purpose of flavoring and preserving the brew.

Among the voluminous papers of the American Philosophical Society, founded in 1743, appears a recipe for ale made of pumpkins; it is dated February 1771, originates in Buckingham County, Virginia, and is signed with the unidentified pseudonym Naso.

Receipt for Pompion Ale

Let the Pompion be beaten in a Trough and pressed as Apples. The expressed Juice is to be boiled in a Copper a considerable Time and carefully skimmed that there may be no Remains of the fibrous Part of the Pulp. After that Intention is answered let the Liquor be hopped cooled fermented &c. as Malt Beer.[6]

The recipe, according to the author's note, was obtained from a person who had made this ale and successfully passed it off as malt ale. The brewer, however, "being no Lover of Malt Beer," did not care for the pumpkin variety for exactly that reason — "their Similitude of Taste & Flavour." The only difference was that a slight "Twang" of the pumpkin remained. "The Novelty of that Taste may displease at first but he believes the Taste of Hops & a hundred Things in daily Use was at first as offensive."

Three dozen bottles of this pumpkin ale had been filled two years previously. It was greatly improved and the "Pompion Twang has acquired something of a Mellowness approaching to Musk which is far more agreeable than before."

Brewing from pumpkins had, of course, been tried from the earliest times in America,* but it had never been popular, possibly because of the "twang," but more likely because malt had been found in all ways to make a more satisfactory beverage. Naso's final suggestion, that "A very palatable Liquor may be made from Peaches in the above Manner with or without Hops," may well have been true, but it did not change the direction of brewing.

A somewhat more professional-sounding recipe has turned up among the letters of Joseph Clarke, general treasurer of Rhode Island colony; its date is prior to 1775.

Directions for Brewing Malt Liquors

You are first to have ready the following Implements, a mash Vat, to put your malt in; a Vessel under this to receive the Wort in; a Copper to boil it in; a Rudder to stir your malt with, and Vessels to cool your Liquor in;

First then fill your Copper with water, take then 6 Bushels of Malt and put into your mash Vat, leaving about a Peck to sprinkle over the Liquor when in, Let your water simper, and be in the next degree of boiling but not boil; lay it on upon the Malt well ground, and when you have laid on such a quantity as you can draw off a Barrel of Wort, stir the malt well together with your Rudder; and then sprinkle the remaining Peck of Malt over all covering it up with Cloths to keep the heat in; for three hours; only when it have stood an hour and half draw off a pail full or two; and lay it on again to clear your tap hole.

This done the next Business is to boil a Copper of Water, to scald your other Vessels with; always taking care to have a Copper of Liquor hot to lay on, upon the malt when you draw off the first Wort, and this will be for small Beer.

The three hours now expired; let go (as the Term is) which is let the first wort run off, putting into the Vessel which receives it a pound of

* See page 16.

Hops; when all drawn off lay on the hot Liquor for your small Beer, clean out your Copper and put the wort, Hops and all into the Copper and boil it for two hours; strain it then off thro: a Sieve into your Vessels to cool it; and put your small Beer into Copper and the same hops that come out of the first Beer and boil it an hour.

When both are almost cool add Yeast to them; to set it to work, breaking the head in every time it rises; till it works itself clear and tun it; Bung it up with Clay and keep it in your Cellar, in three months you may bottle the Strong Beer, the other in a weeks time will be fit to drink.[7]

⊷⧉ TWELVE ⧉⊶

Supplying the Beer Ration

W HEN THE TWO sides finally stumbled into war, as they did
at quiet Concord in April 1775, the Americans, for all their
agitating, were completely unprepared so far as manpower, commanders
and provisions went. Tenacity, naïveté, and a large helping of sheer
good luck combined to make their prosecution of the war possible;
French intervention and mistakes of the British command ultimately
helped them to victory. It was soon after the English attack in Massachusetts that the Second Continental Congress assembled in Philadelphia and named Washington commander of the Continental Army. The
Congress made a multitude of additional pronouncements, among them
a specification of rations to be provided to the soldiers of an army that
did not yet exist. As of November 1775 it was stated that every soldier
was to receive as part of his rations "1 quart of Spruce beer or cyder
per man per day." [1]

The inclusion of beer in the daily military ration appears to have
been common practice at that time. In fact, the soldiers of the Massachusetts militia had been reported in 1757 to be working a "deal" in
connection with this provision:

Orderly Book of John Boyd.

Fort Cumberland, 21 July 1757
Whare as the Solders in Garison belonging to the Province of the
Masechesets Bay have Refused to be at the trifling Expence of two
Pence Per Week Each Man for to have their Molases Brued into
bear and have Insisted upon haveing Molases Deliverd out to tham

Under Protence thay Brew it tham Selues which thay have been
Indulged in Some time that they Might Do So and it a Pearing
now that in Stid of Using the Molases in that way which the Gouer-
nor aford Sd. Desined thay Eat it with thair Vittils to Pregeduce
of Thair Helth Thair fore Nomore Molases is to be Deleverd to
them.[2]

But it is not likely, conditions being as bad as they often were, that
the soldiers received their beer ration with regularity. One of the more
fortunate soldiers, a man from Cambridge, Massachusetts, noted in his
pocket diary on 4 April 1776 while he was serving in New York City,
"Begun to Draw the Allowance of Beer." [3] But it is known that during
that long, freezing winter of 1777-1778, in Pennsylvania at any rate, the
troops went short of practically everything. The ration had to be so
drastically abbreviated that milk and beer and vegetables were omitted.

As the snow and ice kept up a sharp attack, the winter quarters came
so close to mass starvation that General Washington authorized req-
uisitioning of supplies from neighboring farmers. There were also food
markets established at the camp; sometimes the soldiers, by combining
their slim resources, could buy a barrel of hard cider — sometimes even
liquor. And then this practice itself showed signs of giving trouble.

Army officers, fearing the effects of too abundant cheap liquor, then
established a special sutler system for alcoholic drinks. To discour-
age the use of whiskey, rum, and brandy, prices were raised to four
shillings a quart; cider was increased to a shilling a quart; but beer
was reduced in cost. Soldiers could buy "small beer" at the sutlery
for a shilling a quart instead of the old market price of a shilling
tenpence. No other liquor selling was permitted within seven miles
of the camp.[4]

There are unmistakable indications that the commissariat was often
in great difficulties finding the assigned rations. But this was true on the
other side too: beer and food supplies ran short for both rebel and
royalist. As early as August 1775, it was reported that in Boston, under
British control, all stores of cider and malt were exhausted.[5] Earlier in
the year, some supplies had been donated by other towns in the colony:
Sturbridge included a barrel of malt among its contributions in Feb-

ruary 1775, and Marlborough sent one and a half barrels of malt early in April.[6]

Abigail Adams, who lived in Boston through Washington's siege of the city in 1776, wrote to her husband John, then representing Massachusetts at the Continental Congress in Philadelphia, "Their [the British] beef all spent . . . their malt and cider all gone." [7] The British were sufficiently alarmed to draw up contracts with the important London brewers, Felix Calvert and Henry Thrale, to furnish 5000 butts* each of strong beer to be shipped in haste to the troops in Boston.[8]

Those in charge of supplying British troops apparently found it expedient to depend mainly on supplies from home. No doubt even the ingredients for making beer (so much of which had been imported from England) were not easy to come by in wartime America. In November 1775, a ship out of Bristol was boarded by American privateers off Portsmouth and found to be carrying flour, beer and cheese for the troops in Boston.[9] Privateers also brought a ship sailing from Halifax to New York into Marblehead, Massachusetts, and confiscated its cargo of porter, strong beer and barley.[10] In yet another instance, a ship sailing from Liverpool to Halifax and New York was brought into Boston, by then in American hands; it too was carrying beer among other supplies.[11]

What of the American commercial brewers during this period of austerity? Those that were firmly established, such as Rutgers, Lispenard, Morris, and the like, obviously survived. Though probably in smaller quantities, beer continued to be brewed. There is at least one indication that brewers were specifically taxed for war purposes. In a 1779 act of the New Jersey legislature, it is stated that "all brew-houses that brew for sale or hire, shall be rated at the discretion of the Assessors and chosen Freeholders any sum not exceeding one hundred pounds." [12]

In 1778, a Tory schoolmaster and historian, Robert Proud, living in Philadelphia under British occupation, complained that "Strong Beer or Ale is extravagantly high, and much in Demand, tho in this hot country it is more peculiarly adapted for the Winter Season, being much less used in Summer." [13]

---

* A butt is two hogsheads or four barrels or 108 imperial gallons.

John Hancock, in Boston, seemed to find no difficulty in having his beer supplied during the war years by Andrew Johonnot. From December 1778 to April 1783, he was regularly receiving about thirty gallons a month; his aggregate bill came to £129/2/-.[14]

It has even been hinted that some brewers managed to make war profits, though it hardly seems likely to have happened on a large scale. A former soldier in the Continental Army, Thomas Peters, had this to say, many years after the event:

> Seeing that the independence of America was almost a certainty, and that I had from doing my duty in the defence of my country, while many brewers staid at home attending to their own interests and had made fortunes, lost the opportunity, I looked around to see how I could retrieve my lost time as to pecuniary matters. I then formed the plan, which I established in Baltimore, of a Brewery on the most extensive scale of any in America, for the purpose of brewing to serve the American and French troops, for which we had contracted to do, counting that the contest would be determined to the southward and that we could supply them by water. But all things prove the uncertainty of all sublunary things — before I could get to work, happily for my country, peace and independence took place — to the failure of my plans, as the brewery was by far upon too large a scale for the use of Baltimore.[15]

Peters may have overestimated the "fortunes" that brewers accumulated during the war, but there is no doubt that money was to be made in manufacturing beer, at a time of great demand as well as scanty supplies. Even private individuals apparently could make a bit of extra money if they found means of brewing. A Virginian, John Lowry, brought a complaint against Colonel Dabney, who had taken over his plantation, on the grounds that his

> Soldiers has taken and distroy'd a great deal of my barley w'ch I lately bought of Colo. Lewis to Brew Beer. they have deprived me of the opp'ty of Brewing any Beer w'ch is the only way I had to get a little money to enable me to discharge my Taxes. They took my Brewhouse and Break my locks whenever they are opposed.[16]

Beer was certainly being brewed in Massachusetts in 1781, for a present of it was made to Washington by Caleb Davis, Speaker of the Massachusetts House of Representatives, and Washington expressed his thanks in a letter dated 1 August 1781, from Headquarters, Dobbs Ferry:

> Sir: with Pleasure I do myself the Honor to acknowledge the Receipt of your Favor of 5th of June last, with the two Cheese and Cask of Porter which accompanied it. Will you Sir, be pleased to do me the Favor to convey to the Commonwealth of Massa. Bay and to Capt. Sampson, my sincere and respectable thanks for this generous and very acceptable Present.[17]

In view of Washington's evident penchant for porter, this must indeed have been a welcome present.

The account book of a New York brewer, before, during and after the Revolutionary War, now in the possession of the New-York Historical Society, gives us an extraordinarily enlightening view of the situation in that period. The brewer was William D. Faulkner, who is first referred to, before the war, as owning a brewhouse with Rem and Garrett Rapalje at the "Brookland Ferry." In 1709 he married Gerritye Ten Eyck, thus establishing relationship with one of the important New York Dutch families. He had an estate at Mount Hope, near Harlem Heights, where he was able to brew as well as at his New York brewery.[18]

The account book begins with some entries for 1771, when he was selling small beer (5/- per barrel), ale (30/-), ship beer (10/-) and spruce beer (10/-). The records for 1772 show that he had various accounts with ships. One of his customers that year was John Adams, another was the Dutch Churches (North Church and New Church). He sold yeast and occasionally bottled ale; and by 1773 and 1774 he had reduced the price of ale to 24/- a barrel and spruce beer to 6/- a barrel. Business was extremely slow during these prewar years; on the average he took in about one pound a day. On some days his sales amounted to no more than 2/6. He did have a few regular customers, whom he supplied with a half-barrel of beer each week; some of them were Isaac Kip, John Mott, Alexander Moncrief, Doctor van Buren and Joseph Greenwood.

As was common at that time, Faulkner's beer contained a sizable proportion of molasses. He was buying supplies of molasses at frequent intervals during 1774 — about every other day.

A sudden upsurge of business is registered beginning February 1775 and especially in April 1776, when Washington's troops were fortifying Brooklyn Heights. Through Abraham Livingston, Faulkner began to supply the companies of Captain Daniel Denton, Colonel Hutchings (Company of New York Forces), Captain Moses Rawlings, the Morris County Militia, and various others. He had a large account with the company of Colonel Charles Webb, through its quartermaster, John Elderkin, selling half-barrels of beer, ale and ship beer. The accounts were kept in gallons, a half-barrel signifying 16 gallons.

His largest sales to the American forces were made through Quartermaster-General Joseph Trumbull, who ordered for Captain Wolverton's company, Colonel Bond's regiment, for "Pennsylvania Troops," for the 6th Battalion, Major Crane's regiment, Colonel Vernon's regiment, etc. One item dated 17 April 1776 reads: "To 3 Bbl. Beer for Use of General Washington's Guards." The price set down for this sale was £1/4/0. The amount bought by the various companies was between three and four barrels a week.

There are hardly any clues at all in the accounts as to where Faulkner obtained his supplies for brewing. In later years, during the British occupation of New York, he bought some of his brewhouse supplies from the well-known provisioners and importers, Remsen and Couwenhoven, who apparently carried on a successful business while the British held the city. There is only one notation of supplies in 1776: on 7 May, "Bot of Medcaf Eden, 20 lb. Hops @ 2/-."

During the height of that period in 1776 when Washington's troops were being evacuated from Brooklyn and removed to New York before going on up the Hudson, the consumption of beer reached a daily total of 300 barrels, an accomplishment which must have pleased Faulkner and — if he actually received pay — made him feel like a prosperous businessman.

There was a hiatus, however, between the time the American troops were gone from New York, in midsummer 1776, and the time Faulkner began to supply, with equal vigor and success, the British troops. That was in March 1777, and by then Faulkner appears to have moved at least some activities to his Mount Hope estate. The accounts are now headed "Harlem" rather than "New York." There is also in this period

(1778) an interesting note in relation to his work staff: "By Brew House for 6 Mens Board 12 months each, £370/5/8½." It was common practice, at that time and throughout the following century, for brewers to board their bachelor workers on the premises, or in special quarters attached to the brewery.

In 1779, Faulkner had a lucrative contract with the commissary general of British troops in New York, Daniel Wier. He sold beer by the gallon, at 6/- each, and according to his agreement with Wier, he was to use one gallon of molasses in the preparation of twenty gallons of beer. Among the troops and individuals supplied were the 17th Regiment of Foot, Knyphausen's Orderly Dragoons, Royal Artillery, Sir Henry Clinton and servants, General Vaughan, Linsings and Lengerkes Battalion of Grenadiers, Anspach Jäger Corps, General Bose and servants, Hessian Jäger Corps, General Knyphausen's family, etc. The amounts in question were roughly the same as those consumed by the Americans earlier, perhaps slightly more, on the average.

In 1780, Faulkner retired entirely to Mount Hope, where he continued brewing on a noticeably reduced scale. For the next few years, he appears to have coasted along. In 1782, for a brief period, he was evidently operating or working in a brewery in Flushing, Long Island. Then he must have abandoned the brewing business for a time, for on 12 July 1784 he opened a school. What his qualifications for this enterprise were, and how he fared, are not recorded in the account book. Of greater importance, however, is the fact that he moved to Hudson in 1788 and there, with Robert Bell as partner, erected the first brewery in that location.

The expenses he incurred in building a brewery at that period are recorded in detail. The total outlay of money came to £457/7/5, the bulk of this comprising building materials and labor. For the actual brewing operation, he made only the following notations of purchase:

Richard Warner, Noble Town, Copper Kettle	22. 0. 0
Miller, Claverack, for a Brass Cock	2.10. 0
Thos. Escott for fixing it to Kettle &c.	0.18. 0 . . .
Mash Tub	2.12. 0 . . .
Arthur McAuthar, for Pumps	4. 6. 0 . . .
Arthur McArthur, for Pumps	0.16. 0

In other words, the expense of equipment was only a drop in the bucket of payments made for construction of the building.

Of the money laid out by 24 June 1789, when the last details of the brewery were completed (though brewing and sales had gone on since 1788), Faulkner owed £37/14/0 to James Brattle, the same amount to Robert Bell, and £11/12/1½ to Russel Kellogg (a tavern-owner).

The records show the brewery selling mild ale, ship beer, porter, yeast and grains. Porter was 1/- a quart, ship beer 12/- a barrel and mild ale 24/-. Faulkner kept fairly clear records of each brewing, which give a picture of the ingredients he used and their cost. On one day in 1788, for example, he made the following note:

> Mem: This Day Brewed 13¼ Bush¹ Malt 6/3   4. 2.9½
> 8 lbs Hops at   1/–   8.0
> 13 Galls Ms at   2/–   1. 6.0
>   5.16.9½

On the 16th of May he recorded a comparable brew, more highly hopped than the other:

> Mem: This Day Brewed 13½ Malt at 6/3   4. 4.5½
> 12 lbs Hops at 1/–   12.0
> 14 gls M° at   2/–   1. 8.0
>   6. 4.5½

A rather rudimentary method of record, even according to the custom of that time, at least in England. But no doubt, considering the haphazard fashion in which beer was made, such records told Faulkner all he needed to know for future reference: the cost of each brew, and the amounts of the ingredients.

What of Faulkner's political loyalties? They had, of course, no bearing at all on his abilities as a brewer; but the ease with which he shifted from selling to the American troops to selling to the British tempts one to conclude that he was strictly opportunistic. It might also be significant that he discontinued operations in New York after the departure of the British. There is not nearly enough evidence, however, to convict Faulkner of political disloyalty to the rebel cause. He might have been a sympathizer and yet sold to the enemy. There were very few cases of businessmen in the occupied territories who refused to trade with the

British. Among brewers, one case of outstanding patriotism was that of Robert Hare, the porter brewer, who left Philadelphia during the British occupation of that city in 1777-1778 and retired to "Westover," the home in Virginia of his brother-in-law, William Byrd.[19]

It was only the most hotheaded, in any case, who really considered the British as the hated enemy. Most Americans — and probably this includes Faulkner — were caught up in events they could not control, and their private sentiments were not set but wavered as events affected them.

Part Three

Part Three

The President's Beer

THE PROGRESS of the American brewing industry following the War of Independence has been summed up in the following terms by Victor S. Clark in his *History of Manufactures in the United States:*

> When the Constitution was adopted many housewives still brewed small beer for their families, and for fifty years thereafter numerous village breweries continued in operation with an equipment and a volume of business hardly exceeding those of a village bakery. . . . Until 1850, however, America manufactured more spirituous than fermented beverages, and it was not until ten years later that malt liquors gained the definite ascendancy they afterwards maintained.[1]

Various factors were responsible for holding back the growth of the industry. One of these was the general lack of industrial progress in the chaotic years between the end of the war and the ratification of the Constitution, years when the country simply coasted along without any real government in control. But even after the Constitution had been accepted by the states, even after Washington had assumed the Presidency in New York and the Federalist principle had won out, industry was a long time getting started. There was not enough money for large-scale investment; the whole financial system of the country needed overhauling; the pattern of international trade had been distorted by the rupture with Great Britain.

In the course of all this, the question of the manufacture of malt liquors held a curious prominence: statements about its progress, value and future were made by a surprising number of important men of the period.

The President himself, as usual, was indulging his taste for good beer. On the day when New York was finally evacuated in 1783, General Washington had stopped at the old Bull's Head Tavern (located on the street which later became the Bowery) for a draught of ale.[2] His headquarters when he was in New York City had been at the inn kept by Samuel Fraunces, whom he appointed his household steward when he later assumed the Presidency.[3] As a President should, he set the tone for a "Buy American" policy; in a letter from Mount Vernon, on 29 January 1789, he wrote to the Marquis de Lafayette:

> We have already been too long subject to British prejudices. I use no porter or cheese in my family, but such as is made in America: both these articles may now be purchased of an excellent quality.[4]

Once, of course, he had bought his beer from English suppliers,* but no longer. His wife also seemed to have learned the same lesson. In May 1789, en route from Mount Vernon to join the President in New York, Martha Washington stopped off in Philadelphia and entertained some distinguished guests, among them the brewer Robert Hare. A list of what the guests drank follows:

> 10 bottles of Madeira, one bottle of champagne, 2 bottles of claret, 45 bowls of punch, 10 bottles of American porter, one bottle of Taunton Ale, 2 bottles of crab cider.[5]

The "10 bottles of American porter" are reassuring, but what is one to make of the "Taunton ale"? Was there one particularly eccentric guest whose taste had to be propitiated?

In the years preceding his assumption of the Presidency, Washington was a steady customer of Robert Hare. Son of a porter brewer in Limehouse, Hare had emigrated to Philadelphia in 1773 with a gift from his father of £1500. He chose first to do some traveling, in order to get the measure of the colonies, and then sometime in 1774 he started (in partnership with J. Warren, also of London) brewing porter — probably the first ever made in this country.[6] Hare's son, Robert, Jr.,

* See page 59.

took some part in the brewing business, but left it for a career of his own; in fact, he became one of the well-known scientists of the early nineteenth century. The elder Hare died in 1810, and the business was afterward conducted by people unconnected with the family.*

The brewers, as mentioned before,† had their share in the ratification festivities in 1788. The one which took place in Baltimore on 1 May was among the first. "As soon as it was known in town that the constitution for the United States of America was ratified, and our convention dissolved, the joy of the people was extreme." The grand procession included a group of Baltimore brewers and distillers, preceded by Messrs. Peters and Johonnot.[7]

Most of the cities and towns had Fourth of July processions that year, since in many cases that date coincided with ratification. This happened in Portsmouth, New Hampshire, and Winchester, Virginia, among others.[8] Philadelphia managed also to have its procession on that date, and it turned out to be an elaborate, lively affair. As for the brewers, they were

> ten in number, headed by Reuben Haines, with ten ears of barley in their hats, and fashes [fasces] of hop vines, carrying malt shovels and mashing-oars, . . . a standard carried by Luke Morris, decorated with the brewers arms, and the motto, *"Home brew'd is best."* [9]

Because the New York delegates to their state constitutional convention in Poughkeepsie delayed so long in agreeing to ratify, the celebrations there were held up until 28 July. On that day, though, New York had a memorable parade which "exceeded all previous demonstrations in the country." [10]

One of the brewers' flags bore this message: "May he be choaked with the grains, or drowned in hot ale whose business it is to brew mischief." There were twenty brewers and maltsters in all who took part

---

* When the old Gaul Brewery (formerly Reuben Haines's) on Market Street was torn down in 1841, Frederick Gaul moved into the Hare Brewery and his son carried on their business there for some years. This Callowhill Street brewery that Hare had established in 1785 had a longer life than most, for in 1880 it was still functioning, by then belonging to John F. Betz. (Ward, "North Second Street," p. 177.)

† See page 67.

in the procession. The motto of the brewers was "Ale, proper drink for Americans." [11]

"I beg you will send me," Washington wrote to Clement Biddle on 20 July 1788, "a gross of Mr. Hairs best bottled Porter if the price is not much enhanced by the copius droughts you took of it at the late Procession." [12]

Robert Hare's prices apparently did not go up as a result of the Philadelphia procession, and so Washington wrote again to Clement Biddle on 4 August 1788:

> As the price of Porter according to your Account has not been enhanced and is good in quality, I beg if this letter gets to hand in time, that you would add another gross to the one ordered in my former letter.[13]

Even in 1790, when Washington was in residence at Federal Hall in Wall Street, his secretary Tobias Lear was writing to Philadelphia on his behalf:

> Will you be so good as to desire Mr. Hare to have if he continues to make the best Porter in Philadelphia 3 gross of his best put up for Mount Vernon? as the President means to visit that place in the recess of Congress and it is probable there will be a large demand for Porter at that time.[14]

"The best Porter in Philadelphia" — surely a recommendation Hare could have used to good effect, if it had come into his hands. Washington certainly appears to have favored Hare's product; sometime before November 1790 the brewery was destroyed by fire, and Washington wrote from Mount Vernon that he was sorry "on public as well as private accts., to hear of Mr. Hares loss." At the same time he judiciously instructed Tobias Lear, "You wd. do well to lay in a pretty good Stock of his, or some other Porter." [15]

It is interesting to notice that Hare's porter was ordered not directly from his brewery, but through a middleman, Clement Biddle. The latter, an experienced importer and merchant, would have all the facilities for shipping such merchandise out of Philadelphia. Clearly, the brewer at that period, even a successful brewer like Hare, concentrated on producing the beer, and left the delivery or shipment of it to an agent. He probably had his own round of calls to neighborhood customers and taverns; in the nineteenth century, brewers maintained large stables of horses for just this reason. But the shipping of beer outside the city in which it was brewed was almost always undertaken by a commission agent of some sort — a scheme which gradually developed into the modern system of delivery by distributors.

Robert Hare was no longer mentioned by name in 1796 when Washington was making arrangements for leaving the Presidency and returning to his beloved Mount Vernon:

> Before we leave this, we shall send several other matters round, but whenever they are shipped you shall have notice thereof that they may be taken from Alexandria so soon as they arrive there; at which time procure a groce of good Porter to be taken down along with them. In the meantime, have a few Bottles of Porter there, and some wine for particular company, who may be *particularly* recommended to you by myself.[16]

Washington was procuring his porter during the early 1790s from another brewer in Philadelphia, Benjamin Wistar Morris.[17] One of the many brewer descendants of Anthony Morris,* Benjamin advertised as early as June 1788 that he bottled and sold "Philadelphia Porter, Beer and Cyder . . . at the corner of Dock and Pear sts." [18] This must have been the brewery built in 1745 by Anthony Morris IV — the location chosen because of springs which were found on the property.[19]

* See page 46.

FOURTEEN

Encouragement of Brewing

UNDER THE pseudonym Hortensius, George Hay, son-in-law of James Madison, wrote as a shocked correspondent to a Philadelphia newspaper, sounding the theme of the postwar period:

> It appears from pretty accurate calculations, that in the course of the years 1785, 1786, and 1787, TWELVE MILLION OF DOL-LARS have been expended by the United States, in purchasing West-India spirituous liquors. But how much more has been spent in home distilled spirits. . . . The experience of many farmers has already proved, that spirituous liquors are altogether unnecessary for reapers and other labourers. They enjoy more health and better spirits upon beer, cyder, and melasses and water.[1]

The agriculturalist J. B. Bordley evinced the same outraged horror at the abundance of distilled spirits being consumed at that time.

> I cannot express my sense of the ruinous habits in a free use of drinks made from distilled spirits. . . . In country families they are used with a freedom astonishing to strangers, who have been accustomed to more temperate conduct, and are in the habit of drinking mild beer. In our large towns beer is taking place of diluted spirits; which is a reason why there is more sobriety now observed in the towns than formerly, when West India rum abounded at a third of its present price.

Bordley had been farming in Maryland during most of the Revolution, and found it most profitable to give his reapers small beer to drink, for it did not set them "wild, as had been not uncommon under the use of rum." [2]

An English farmer in Delaware agreed that farmhands at harvest time should be given "good beer, or ale," instead of cider and spirits, for beer "would enable them to go through double the labour, with half the fatigue to themselves." [3] And a farmer in New England, in this same period, recommended home-brewing of beer in order to lessen "the use of ardent spirits, which are more costly, and less wholesome than beer." [4]

The manufacture and consumption of spirits had outstripped that of beer, much to the consternation of certain responsible people. Whiskey was a relatively new thing: a convivial and economic means of using up surplus grain in rural areas. It had become fairly common, by the time of the Revolution, in the frontier region of Pennsylvania. In 1804, a description of the Genesee country in upstate New York included the observation that "Whiskey is distilled in considerable quantities, and mostly consumed in the country, and is also exported to Canada and to Susquehanna." [5]

The prevalence of spirits over beer after the Revolutionary War becomes evident in subtle ways. In the account books of a merchant in Massachusetts from 1794 to 1797, for example, there are sales of rum, brandy and wine recorded — but none of beer. [6]

In the minute book, kept between 1805 and 1855, of the Mount Airy plantations in Virginia, there are frequent references to whiskey and brandy, but none to beer. And, curiously enough, one of the Mount Airy plantations, belonging to the Tayloe family, was called "Hopyard," indicating an attempt to grow hops in an earlier period. [7]

Naturally, there were exceptions. In 1789, a farm on the banks of the Mohawk River, sixteen miles from Schenectady, with a brewhouse "in good repair," was offered for sale in a New York newspaper. [8]

Colonel John May, a member of the Ohio Company of Associates (originating in Boston), who helped to set up the town of Marietta in 1788 and became its first storekeeper, wrote in his diary on the second day after his arrival:

> Saturday, June 14th . . . A delightful morning. The river beginning to fall. At 2 o'clock completed my brew-house — and two barrels of beer, and one of vinegar. [9]

Those who were alarmed by the excessive use of spirits advocated, in its place, the adoption of beer and other beverages of low alcoholic content. The prominent Philadelphian George Logan wrote a paper in 1787, attacking the prevalent custom of letting farm workers drink spirits; he recommended the use of beer instead. He was following a line laid down by John Woolman and Anthony Benezet, important Quakers, as well as Benjamin Rush, who was a friend of Logan's.[10]

The distinguished Dr. Rush, signer of the Declaration of Independence and Professor of Medicine at the University of Pennsylvania, made his contribution to the subject in the form of a pamphlet called *An Inquiry into the Effects of Ardent Spirits upon the Human Body and Mind*, first published in 1784. In this document, surprisingly sophisticated for its period, he described the clinical effects of excessive consumption of distilled spirits, and prescribed the use of cider, wine and beer in the interests of temperance.

> MALT LIQUORS. The grain from which these liquors are obtained, is not liable, like the apple, to be affected by frost, and therefore they can be procured, at all times, and at a moderate price. They contain a good deal of nourishment; hence we find many of the poor people in Great Britain endure hard labour with no other food than a quart or three pints of beer, with a few pounds of bread a day.[11]

The General Court of Massachusetts passed an act in 1789 to encourage the manufacture of beer,* among other worthwhile reasons "as an important means of preserving the health of the citizens of this Commonwealth, and of preventing the pernicious effects of spirituous liquors." [12] In the same vein, the administrators of New Hampshire, anxious "to diminish the use of ardent spirits," passed an act in 1792 providing that any person erecting a building for the purpose of brewing in that state was to be "exempted from all taxes of every kind and nature that may be assessed under the authority of this State." [13]

Tench Coxe, an influential Philadelphian who devoted much of his energy and time to promoting the cause of American industry (in spite of having been a royalist neutral during the Revolution), wrote in this period that "the superior virtues, both moral and political, of a country,

* See Appendix Two.

which consumes malt liquors, instead of distilled spirits, need only be mentioned." He also published a scheme for creating a market town on the Susquehanna River; among the industries he included in his project was brewing: "One malt house, $2,000 . . . One brewery, $4,000." [14]

It was sentiment of the same kind that directed the various attempts to stimulate home brewing on a large scale. John Spurrier, in his *The Practical Farmer*, advised farmers not to be deterred by the high price at which beer was being sold by commercial brewers, and showed how inexpensively it could be brewed at home. As to erection of a brewhouse, he suggested that it should be situated on the north side of the establishment "for shade and coolness"; the dimensions should be twenty by fifteen feet; "three sides out of the four should be open, especially of the upper part, to let in the free circulation of air." [15]

In a similar book, Samuel Deane tried to make the setting up of a brewhouse seem much simpler:

> Almost any householder may brew, without putting himself to much, if any, charge for an apparatus. Instead of a large copper, which is necessary in a brew house, a large kettle or two may answer the purposes of heating the water, and boiling the wort: Hogshead or barrel tubs, and other vessels, may serve for mashing tubs, backs, coolers, and tins. [16]

These instructions as to the equipment of a home brewing operation signify no advance at all over similar specifications given as early as 1748.* Brewing methods, except for certain mechanical appurtenances, such as the thermometer, saccharometer, etc., had remained at a complete standstill.

One of the questions that must have been asked by any receptive reader of these books recommending home brewing was: Where are we to buy the malt? "Malt is to be had at country malt-works," Bordley answers, "in the more provident states";

> and maltsters can easily be drawn into the counties of other states, if county gentlemen would in good earnest hold out proper encourage-

---

* A copper: a furnace to the copper; "a Mash-fat [vat] or Tub; a Receiver or Underback; a mashing Oar; a Rudder, Lead, or Pump to pump up the wort out of the receiver into the copper to boil; 2 Jets, one with a long handle, the other with a short handle; Coolers or cool Back; a pump at the back of the copper to fill it with cold water, and to wash the casks" ("The Family Brewer," *Universal Magazine*, Jan.-Apr. 1748, p. 39).

ment. It is better to buy malt, or exchange barley for malt, than to make it.[17]

The truth of the matter is that there were insufficient supplies of malt available to the earnest home brewer. A Massachusetts merchant might be able occasionally to purchase a bushel of malt for six shillings from a neighboring farmer.[18] In the cities, the established brewers malted for themselves, or else used the services of commercial maltsters. And malt, in reduced quantities, was still being imported: between 1789 and 1791, some 5000 bushels came into Virginia from Portugal and England.[19] The widespread importation of malt was deplored by citizens such as Tench Coxe who were trying to promote domestic manufactures.[20]

The same was true of hops. Bordley pointed out that America was favorable to the production of hops, "and they grow wild." The preferred Farnham hop from England had been introduced into Maryland by Governor Sharp, and Bordley had grown some in Pennsylvania.[21] But again, supplies were not abundant — nor had the cultivation of hops been undertaken systematically.

The whole question of manufacturing beer, whether privately or commercially, clearly needed some attention — and from the industrial point of view it was in need of substantial encouragement. This was forthcoming. In his official report on the state of American manufactures in 1791, the first Secretary of the Treasury, Alexander Hamilton, cited, in a list of manufactures which had already made notable success in the United States, not only malt liquors, but also copper and brasswares, "particularly utensils for distillers, sugar refiners, and brewers." His research into the subject had showed him

> that by far the greatest part of the malt liquors consumed in the United States are the produce of domestic breweries. It is desirable, and in all likelihood, attainable, that the whole consumption should be supplied by ourselves.[22]

Unlike certain chauvinistic propagandists, Hamilton stated that the American brew was not up to the best product from abroad, though it was "equal to a great part of those which have been usually imported." He felt, however, that the increase in competition would assure the improvement of American-made beer. "This will be accelerated by measures tending to invite a greater capital into this channel of employment." [23] His recommendation was to increase the import duty to 8d. per gallon. A similar enactment had been effective in Virginia: in 1786, 4d. per gallon "on all ale, beer, porter, or other malt liquor, imported into this commonwealth, and not being the manufacture of any of the United States." And in 1787, the Virginia duty was raised to 9d. per gallon.[24]

This unequivocal adoption of a protective policy was certainly calculated to improve the situation of the American brewing industry. It may, in fact, have succeeded in providing some benefit for the industry. Tench Coxe stated in 1794, "Breweries are multiplying: as their value is becoming manifest." And, in the same document, he mentioned "the success of the Americans in the manufacture of malt liquors." [25] Coxe had also strongly held that porter and ale were among a number of items that should be protected against the competition of imports.[26]

The overall results of protection at that time, however, cannot be accurately gauged, because the earliest official figures are those of 1810, and there are none previous to that with which to make comparisons. The Secretary of the Treasury, Albert Gallatin, cited "malt liquors" as one of the industries "firmly established" in 1810, "supplying in several instances the greater, and in all a considerable part of the consumption of the United States." [27] The total value of the industry was given as $955,791. There were in all 132 breweries, producing annually about 185,000 barrels (31½ gallons each); of these, 48 were in Pennsylvania, 42 in New York and 13 in Ohio. The population at that time was just over seven million.[28] Some impression of the meagerness of this production can be gained by comparison with the output of a *single* London brewery, the Anchor (owned by Thrale, Barclay and Perkins), which produced in 1809 a total of 205,300 barrels, and in the following year 235,100.[29]

The American production was far from impressive in 1810, but by 1820 it appeared to have deteriorated completely. The commercial and industrial outlook in general was apparently not too good; Mathew Carey, another Philadelphian who sought to rouse his countrymen into

supporting indigenous manufactures, contrasted the 1819 situation un-
favorably with that of 1815, when there had evidently been an upgrade.
"We have bought and consumed more than we have sold," he wrote.
"Our imports for five years have been above one hundred millions of
dollars more than our exports." He even made use of a local brewing
situation to illustrate his point: in Pittsburgh and vicinity, the value of
brewery production had dropped from $91,050 in 1815 to $35,000 in
1819.[30]

In the 1820 census, individual breweries were reporting, "Business
diminished in consequence of the increased consumption of whiskey,"
or "Sales diminished," "Dull," "Sales decreased." [31] Except for one or
two individual examples of good sales and profits, the brewing industry
was stagnating, in spite of official and private efforts to stimulate it. It
was on the verge, however, of a spectacular upswing, but this came
somewhat later and was caused by two things which happened toward
the middle of the century: the introduction of a German type of beer
called *lager*, and the wide-scale success of the steam engine and its consequent mechanization of industrial processes.

◆§ FIFTEEN §◆

Brewers at the Turn of the Century

A S THE nineteenth century approached and the country struggled to establish its character and aspirations, three distinct developments were evident in the brewing industry: Philadelphia and New York increased their predominance, brewing in New England declined appreciably, but at the same time new centers and markets for brewers were emerging in other parts of the country along with expansion of the frontier.

Philadelphia's brews were beginning to challenge the supremacy of those traditionally imported from Britain. In 1789, Phineas Bond, the British Consul in Philadelphia, reported to the Foreign Office in London that

> porter might be brewed here to a very large amount; it is now confined to one house which will probably extend its trade as this liquor is in great demand, thro' the Southern States being sold at ½ less than the London porter: the quality is vastly inferior even to Bath or Bristol [porter] — tho' this is imputed to the porter's being used when it is too new. Other malt liquor is brewed here tolerably well. The strong sort is sent in some quantities to the Southern States.[1]

Other (non-British) observers at this time had more generous praise for Philadelphia porter. The Frenchman Brissot de Warville stated without any equivocation that it was "equal to the English: the manufacture of it saves a vast tribute formerly paid to the English industry." [2] That other foreign admirer of America, Mazzei,* echoed this sentiment;

* See page 57.

Philadelphia porter was so much like the English variety, he said, "that even English palates have been deceived by it. This discovery is a real service to America, for by it they are relieved of a tax to English industry." [3]

Aside from their export to the South, Philadelphia beers had a fairly substantial market right in the city itself. According to a traveler in the 'nineties, there were some thirty-five taverns in Philadelphia serving "wine, beer of every sort, grog, liqueurs of different kinds, whiskey . . . There are twenty more places that sell only beer, cider and brandy, and ten others that sell only beer and cider." [4] There was even a street called Brewers Alley.

The well-known Philadelphia brewers of the period between the Revolution and the War of 1812 were those already mentioned: Robert Hare, Reuben Haines and the various Morrises.* Ale was being made as well as the various strengths of beer; the prices, as recorded by one particular brewer in 1811, were as follows:

Table beer	$1.00 a keg, $1.50 a ½ barrel
Middle beer	$2.00 a ½ barrel
Strong beer	$3.00 a ½ barrel
Ale	$2.33 a keg, $3.50 a ½ barrel.[5]

In New York City too there was a multiplicity of brewers.† One of the most prominent, John Murray, Jr., had built his brewery before the Revolutionary War and supposedly supplied Washington and John Hancock with ale while they were in New York. After the war, Murray took in for several years a partner named Cunningham, but eventually he sold his interest to Samuel Milbank, described as a Philadelphia brewer. It became in the end a Milbank family concern, three generations in succession managing it.[6]

* Other names that appear in contemporary Philadelphia advertisements and city directories are Joseph and William Gray, William Dawson, John and George Rehn, Leonard Snowden, Melchior Larer, Conrad Wile, William Innes, Charles Robertson and John Coleman.

A few details of brewers' expenses may be found in the Receipt Book of Philadelphia brewers John and Melchior Larer (1815-1820): e.g., barley bought in September 1818 from five different suppliers came to $243.30, and in the following month to $519.25 (Larer MSS).

† Among the brewers listed in the 1793 city directory were Leonard Lispenard, Janeway & Stringham's, Snyder & Brown, James and Anthony Brown.

For about four years, between 1809 and 1813, John Herring, Sr., father of the John Herring who was somewhat later to become an eminent portrait painter, conducted a brewery in New York City. The unpublished autobiographical notes of the son, now in the manuscript collection of the New-York Historical Society, give some intimate details of this enterprise. "Early in the Spring [of 1809]," he wrote in 1863,

> my father took a lease of some unoccupied ground on 3d. Street; (*Eldridge now*). . . . Here he designed to erect a brewhouse; being satisfied that he could produce ale and porter of quality superior to any sold in New York, at that time.

There is no hint that the father had ever engaged in brewing before; he had made his living in a variety of other ways. But apparently there were few problems to solve when a man in 1809 decided to build himself a brewery: John Herring, Sr., was very soon in business. The son's services

> were now required . . . to open a regular set of books, keep accounts of orders, and deliveries by the draymen; cash accounts &c. &c. — Father was necessarily absent a great part of the time every day, and I had, consequently, too many things to attend to. . . .

The ale produced in the new brewery met with a certain success at once, "not alone in N. York, but specimens, or samples sent to Charleston S.C. sold at auction on the wharf, at an advance of $4. a barrel on the N.Y. price." It was soon necessary to increase the number of drays, horses and draymen in order to keep up with deliveries.

> More help was required in the Brewhouse, and another horse to work in the mill, to grind the malt, &c. The men who at that time could be hired as draymen, or in the brewhouse, were generally unreliable, or lazy tradesmen. Sometimes I had to drive around the city among the customers to collect a drayload of casks, from a 5 gallon keg to a hogshead, because the careless fellows were too indolent to bring them from the cellars, or backrooms, where they were generally kept.

In December of that same year, occurred "a very extraordinary and unexpected circumstance," as Herring calls it: an event so deeply disturbing to the fifteen-year-old boy that he remembered it vividly fifty-four years later.

We had been brewing that day, and the *sweet-wort* was in the copper
boiler over the fire, with the proper quantity of hops . . . The copper
boiler contained 200 gallons, or more; around the upper part of this
boiler there was a square frame work of plank well secured to prevent
the liquid from boiling over when expanded by the heat of the fire beneath. I was up there with a mashing oar in my hands to beat down
the ebulition and the hops: but on this occasion, there was too much
fire beneath, and nobody to slacken it. I used every effort by beating
and stirring, but without avail. The liquor boiled over and run down
the floor; at that moment my father came into the brewery. So soon
as he saw the situation of things, he became very angry and ran across
the yard, into the house for *his horsewhip, to give me a thrashing,
as he called it.* I knew I had exerted myself to prevent the accident, or
abate it, and had no mind to submit.

The boy did not wait for his father's return, but scrambled down
the ladder and out of the brewery. He ran off with some strangers to
Wantage, New Jersey, and acted as schoolmaster there for a year.
When he returned to his family, he worked in his father's business
again, but the business failed around 1813, "in consequence of circumstances connected with our second war with England." Herring then
turned to painting, which became his life's career.[7]

One of the symbols of the worst slums of New York, the Five Points,
in the early part of the nineteenth century, was a derelict building
commonly called the Old Brewery. It was

> the heart of the Five Points, and was the most celebrated tenement
> building in the history of the city. It was called Coulter's Brewery
> when it was erected in 1792 on the banks of the old Collect, and the
> beer brewed there was famous throughout the eastern states. It be-
> came known simply as the Old Brewery after it had been transformed
> into a dwelling in 1837, having become so dilapidated that it could
> no longer be used for its original purpose.[8]

It seems likely that the name of the proprietor of this "famous"
brewery became garbled in some of the records, for he must in fact
have been William Coulthard,* listed as alderman for the 6th Ward in
1815.[9] It was, presumably, no fault of his that the building went to
wrack and ruin after he had gone out of business, but there is no doubt

---

* This brewer may well have been related to Isaac Coulthard, whose brewery was
reported in the New York *Gazette and General Advertiser* of 30 June 1797 to have
been destroyed by fire.

that the Old Brewery, for a long time, conjured up the worst kind of fantasies of debauchery, deprivation and squalor — a place where "the old brewer of all the world's misery" had "dominion." [10]

Although the great concentration of brewers was in New York City, Brooklyn, Albany and Rochester also contributed to the reputation of New York beers. The first brewery of any importance in Brooklyn was built before the Revolution by Israel Horsfield, Jr., and his brother Thomas.* Thomas left the business in 1763 and went into partnership with James Leadbetter;† they announced in the New York *Gazette* of 28 February 1764 that they had opened their brewery in Brooklyn, "where may be had English ale, table, ship, and spruce beer." [11]

Israel evidently failed in 1767, for on 2 November he offered all his property for sale.[12] There are no signs that Thomas made out any better in his partnership; the newspaper reported in 1770 that his malt-kilns at Brooklyn ferry had burned down, entailing a loss of £500.[13] The partnership was soon dissolved, and Thomas continued on his own, advertising that "excellent ship and table beer, from the *Long Island Brewery*," was for sale in a New York store owned by a third Horsfield brother, William.[14]

The beer produced in Albany had always been popular; even in the seventeenth century, Jacob Leisler, leader of the New York insurrection against the English Crown, had been a buyer of "Strong Albany Beer." [15] But the modern period of brewing in that city had its start in 1796, when James Boyd erected on the corner of Arch and Green Streets a brewery which had a capacity of about 4000 barrels a year. Boyd's son, Robert, who succeeded to the business, formed a partnership in 1808 with Hawthorn McCulloch, the firm name becoming Boyd and McCulloch. Under various names — Robert Boyd & Son, Boyd & Brother, Boyd Brothers & Company — this brewery remained in continuous operation for more than a hundred years.[16]

Brewing in Rochester came later, since the settlement there began only in 1812. But, as always happened when new towns were established, a brewer was soon on the scene. Probably the first in Rochester was Nathan Lyman, who began his business about 1819.[17] In the 1827 city

* See note, page 69.
† See page 70.

directory, he was listed as a brewer, and two of his workers were named as boarding with him.

After the Revolution, Boston lost whatever eminence it had achieved as a brewing center during the eighteenth century: in the first city directory (1796) there were just three brewers and one maltster listed. As for the South, only Baltimore appeared to maintain a brewing tradition. The brewery which had been started by the Barnitz family* on Hanover Street was called the Washington Brewery in 1824, at which time it was owned by Peter Glenninger. His main competition came from Eli Claggett, who operated a brewery on King George Street.† In Kentucky there had been at least one brewery prior to 1800,‡ but at the start of the nineteenth century this enterprise evidently lapsed.[18] Though the territory of Louisiana was not strictly in the picture before the purchase of 1803, it has been recorded that in 1788 the establishment of a beer factory in Louisiana was recommended in the Spanish Council of State.[19] There seems some likelihood that a brewhouse was indeed set up at Ste. Genevieve before 1800.§

But the best example of the development of brewing in a new town is Pittsburgh, which long before the Revolution had been part of "Penn's Manor," and later the French Fort Duquesne (after George Washington's failure to build an English fort on that site), eventually destroyed by the English and rebuilt as Fort Pitt. The extraordinary location of this trading and military center, where the confluence of the Monongahela and Allegheny Rivers forms the Ohio, assured its growth as a thriving industrial focus as soon as the frontier was pushed westward. After the war, Pittsburgh began to increase rapidly in population and importance.

Brewing took place there even while it was yet a military outpost. A particular street, which came to be called traditionally Brewhouse Alley

* See pages 85-86.
† This brewery continued for many years to be a family business. In 1845 it was moved to Lombard Street and was listed as Eli Claggett & Sons; in 1864 it was known as William Claggett & Co. (Baltimore City Directory, 1824, 1845, 1864.)
‡ John Nancarrow was reported, as of 19 April 1789, to be setting off for Philadelphia, where he planned to buy brewing equipment. Upon his return he advertised the opening of a "Malting Business" and brewery in "Petersburg on the Kentuckye."
§ See page 171.

or Brewery Alley, had been the site of a small brewhouse. It is recorded
that in May 1782 a petition was drawn up by a group of private citizens,
asking the commander of the fort, General William Irvine, to take note
of the fact that

> several of the officers and soldiers of this town have of late made a
> constant practice of playing at long bullets in the street that goes up
> by the brewhouse, and that a number of children belonging to us, who
> are dwellers on the same street, are in danger of their lives by the said
> evil practice.[20]

This brewing was predominantly for the troops; the first commercial brewery in the town appears to have been the one started in 1795
by Peter Shiras, a Scotsman who emigrated to America in 1765. Upon
arriving in Pittsburgh after the Whiskey Rebellion, Shiras, sixty or more
at the time, looked over the situation and decided to provide the
town with a brewery.

> By means of a brewery of his own he could supply the rapidly increas-
> ing number of taverns with the porter, ale, and beer demanded not
> only by the native population, but by the emigrants swarming west-
> ward, of which as many as two or three thousand at a time could now
> and then be seen milling about the borough.[21]

In partnership with one Robert Smith, Shiras bought the site of old
Fort Pitt, by then in partial ruin. They paid for it the sum of £2500
to John Holker and associates, of Virginia. "The subscribers having
purchased the BREWERY at the Point, in Pittsburgh," their first advertisement states,

> wish to inform the public in general that they intend carrying on the
> Brewing Business, as extensively as the situation of the country will
> permit. Farmers who choose to raise Barley, may depend upon hav-
> ing the price of Five Shillings per bushel, which we now give at the
> Brewery. . . .
>
> SMITH & SHIRAS[22]

Although the population of Pittsburgh at that time was only about
1000, the brewery seemed to be able to make its way. In June 1796,
Shiras bought out his partner's interest for £1750, and the firm name
became Peter Shiras.[23] It now grew increasingly successful, being held
back only by the fact that

while it could ship its products to points along the three rivers, it lacked the profitable duty-free southern trade as far as New Orleans, later made available to American commerce by the opening of the Mississippi after the Louisiana Purchase in 1803.[24]

Shiras seems to have had no local competition except for James Yeaman, who is said to have brewed about 1797 "in a small way." [25]

Peter continued to operate the business, with the help of his son George, until 1802, when he sold it — strangely enough — to his former partner, Robert Smith, with an understanding that young George was to be kept on as manager.[26]

Another man of great interest now entered the scene, James O'Hara, general, merchant, provisioner for the military, Pittsburgh's first "Captain of Industry." It appears that Robert Smith, when he bought the Shiras brewery in 1802, was really acting as O'Hara's agent.[27] O'Hara had previously supplied various forts with alcoholic beverages as well as meats and dry goods; Colonel Strong in Detroit, for example, wrote him in 1797, "if you can make it convenient to send me a little good Wine & Brandy, also a few Bottles of Porter." [28] It was altogether possible that O'Hara bought some of his beer supplies from Peter Shiras. In any case, he had expressed his desire to conduct a brewery of his own while he was still a government contractor in 1798. He brought this plan to fulfillment by buying a property in McKeesport (just across the Monongahela River from Pittsburgh) in partnership with a distiller, John Reed. For four years O'Hara and Reed "brewed and bottled beer and porter, distilled whiskey, and shipped these products down the river to Natchez where they found a ready market." [29]

In 1802, the partnership was dissolved and the brewery apparently discontinued; but at the same time, Joseph Coppinger advertised in the Pittsburgh papers for someone to back him in the brewing business. Coppinger called himself at that time "porter Brewer from Europe." * O'Hara consented to back Coppinger, and it was in this connection that the Shiras brewery was bought. From its physical location it was called the Point Brewery.

* See pages 139-143. Coppinger was also in St. Louis in 1807, apparently selling provisions there, according to a bill paid him by Joseph Hortiz, dated "St. Louis, October 1807," now in the Missouri Historical Society.

For reasons not revealed, the partnership of O'Hara and Coppinger ended in March 1803, and after Coppinger's departure, George Shiras was put in charge of the brewery. Business was evidently growing satisfactorily; by now the New Orleans market was open and ships could deliver from Pittsburgh by way of the Ohio River — one of the town's great strategic advantages.

Prices quoted for Shiras products in 1806 were:

Porter	$7.90 a barrel
Strong beer	6.00 a barrel
Middling	3.50 a barrel

In July 1813, the malthouse, a brick building next to the brewhouse, caught fire and was completely destroyed. The brewhouse, however, was saved, and the brewery's operations were fairly soon brought back to normal. The following year, reductions in price were announced, due to a new money-saving system of malting and brewing, attributed to George Shiras.[30]

Upon O'Hara's death in 1819, the brewery passed entirely into the hands of the three Shiras brothers. By then they were the leading, but not the only, brewers in Pittsburgh. The 1815 city directory offered the names of John Gorman (Second Street in Kensington), Joseph Kenley, George Lewis and Andrew Scott, and stated in a note:

There are three large and extensive Breweries and one upon a smaller scale. They consume from 20 to 30,000 bushels of grain, and manufacture about 10,000 barrels of beer, ale and porter annually.[31]

The population at this time had swelled to about 9000.

In 1819, Thomas Baird & Son was named as a large brewery in operation; the Union Brewery had been founded by Andrew Scott and a partner named Brown; and the Point Brewery continued as the oldest of them all. George Shiras, Jr., took over the management in 1825, when the brewery's value was assessed at $17,000 and its annual capacity (the largest in that city) was 2500 barrels of porter and 1500 barrels of beer. For the following year, an additional brick building was promised, with a capacity of 5000 barrels annually.

The plant was moved away entirely from the Point in 1837, to a new

address at Pitt near Penn Street. At that time, it employed twenty workers, was worth $38,000, and produced 6000 barrels of porter, ale and beer
a year. It had lost ground to a competitive firm, the Pittsburgh Brewery
(owned by Brown and Varner), at 140 Liberty Street, with a plant
valued at $40,000.[32]

The elder George Shiras, who had been responsible for the start of
the whole enterprise, died in 1840; and by then his son, George, Jr.,
had retired from the firm, which was conducted from then on by his
two younger brothers, Oliver and Charles Perry. Oliver was proprietor
until 1844; he was replaced then by Charles; and three years later the
enterprise was abandoned entirely.[33] The Shirases were by then interested in politics, and they apparently had worked themselves up to a
financial position which permitted them to shed the brewery without
any hardship.

The city of Pittsburgh has saluted the Shiras family by naming a
street after them. The same was done, of course, for General O'Hara,
who must be mentioned again in connection with the first Pittsburgh
glassworks which he started in partnership with Isaac Craig in 1797.[34]
It seems quite clear that bottles were manufactured in this factory.[35]
Bottles were generally in such short supply at this period that another
glass factory was founded in Pittsburgh in 1808; it too produced bottles,
in which the cheapest glass (the basic material being mainly lime)
was used.[36] Both of these businesses continued long after their founders
had died.

Thomas Jefferson: Gentleman-Brewer

YOUNG AMERICA was rich in men of genius. Among them all certainly Thomas Jefferson must rank especially high. He was not only the author of one of the most famous of all political documents: he was also an adroit politician, a philosopher, a scientist, a farmer — in short, a man of extraordinary variety, wisdom and attainment.

Like most public men of his period, Jefferson tirelessly kept voluminous records of his correspondence, his activities, his thoughts, his expenses. He had no secretaries, no typewriters — he had to do his own painstaking writing. And in his account books and letters he composed a detailed history of his life and times, often in the most humdrum notation of the routine events of each day.

Since his interests were catholic and his hand was in such a multitude of activities, he has a very special place in the story of beer in America. From all indications he was not particularly a beer-drinker; he was, for himself, more interested in wines — as can be judged by the records he kept of the wines he ordered, and of the length of time each "pipe"* lasted. Late in life, when discussing tariff problems with W. H. Crawford, Monroe's Secretary of the Treasury, he proposed lowering the tariff on wines so that "the midling class" could buy it and thus avoid "the poison of whisky, which is destroying them by wholesale." [1]

The beer he bought during the early days of his political activity was probably for his household. The period when he bought most beer

---

* Two hogsheads or four barrels.

from commercial brewers was after his return from France and during the four years (1789-1793) he spent, mostly in Philadelphia, as Secretary of State in Washington's Cabinet. The likeliest explanation is that, during those years, when he lived at 274 High Street (down the road from Reuben Haines's brewery), he was entertaining more regularly than when in residence at Monticello. From a wine dealer named Farquhar, he bought one dozen bottles of porter for one pound in June of 1790, and the same amount in August. At the end of each quarter, Jefferson made an "Analysis of the expenditures of the last quarter." In the quarter from 9 April to 7 July 1791, he reckoned his brewer's bill had come to $15.00. The brewer who supplied him in 1792 and 1793 (the year of the yellow fever epidemic) was Henry Pepper [Henry Pfeiffer], who had taken over the brewery of Joseph Potts in 1791. Located originally at 2 South Fifth Street, this brewery had been inaugurated about 1774.*

In January 1792, Jefferson paid his bill to Pepper, which came to $39. In January 1793 the bill was only $17; but in July of that year there was an additional payment for six months' supplies at $27.67. It was in January 1794 that Jefferson resigned from the government and retired to his Virginia properties, but in 1797 he came back to Philadelphia, as Vice-President. He was no less meticulous than in the past about keeping track of his household expenses; each day he entered in his account books a record of moneys paid out, even the odd penny to a beggar. There are no entries for beer during these years, but it is possible Jefferson changed his methods and included beer among "provisions," which is the way he was inclined to think of it. On two particular days, 8 June and 22 November 1798, he recorded purchases of hops: the first time a small quantity for 53¢, the second a rather larger amount for $4.15.[2] There is no way to explain these two entries, which do not fit into any of the other patterns, except to conjecture that Jefferson's servants might have been trying to make small beer in the kitchen.

During the years in Washington as President (1801-1809), Jefferson kept in close touch with his farms in Virginia. He supervised his

---

* It continued in operation, with many additions and renovations, until Prohibition in 1919, at which time it was the property of C. Schmidt and Sons. In 1802 the firm was called H. Pepper & Son; George Pepper succeeded; in 1836 David Pepper and Frederick Seckel formed a partnership; and in 1837 Robert Smith, who had been brewing on his own, was admitted into the firm. (Scharf, vol. 3, p. 2279.)

overseers either in person, during vacation breaks, or by streams of letters: there was hardly a seed sown that he was not aware of. His interest in farming machinery, his experiments with all sorts of tools and what we now call labor-saving devices, his plans for making the best use of his land were matters which absorbed a great deal of his time.[3]

At this late-afternoon stage of his career, he was more interested in the serene rural life than the political market place, and so it was with some relief and great anticipation that he finally retired forever from serving his country, and in 1810 went back to Virginia and his busy privacy.

This happened to be a time of farm depression. The war which was to start thundering in two years already hung like an ugly cloud in the sky. The exportation of wheat, on which farms like Jefferson's, devoted predominantly to grain rather than tobacco, depended for their prosperity, had fallen from about five to a little over one million bushels within ten years.[4]

Although Jefferson was constantly improvising schemes for earning greater returns from his farms in order to pay off his incessant debts, it does not seem likely that his venture into the brewing of beer was one of these — simply because there is no evidence whatsover that he ever sold any of the beer that was made at Monticello.

The first mention of his plan to institute brewing is in a letter of 1813 that he wrote at Monticello to Captain W. D. Meriwether, one of his neighbors. "I lent you some time ago," he wrote,

> the London & Country brewer and Combrun's book on the same subject. we are this day beginning, under the directions of Capt Millar, the business of brewing Malt liquors, and if these books are no longer useful to you I will thank you for them, as we may perhaps be able to derive some information from them.[5]

Jefferson and Meriwether had undoubtedly discussed the feasibility of brewing before that day; in fact, there may have been some experiments earlier, because Jefferson noted in his account books that he had sent to "Capt. W. D. Meriwether for malt 2 D [dollars]" on 17 March 1812; a week later, "Capt. Meriwether for 2. more bush. of malt 2 D."; and on 15 April of that year he had paid $1.33 to Daniel Farley for hops.

But the possibility of brewing in earnest depended on the fortunate coincidence of Captain Miller's being confined to Albemarle County as an alien in time of war. He was in a curious position, this Captain Joseph Miller, whose name would probably count for nothing except for his association with Jefferson. In a letter addressed to General Andrew Moore, requesting permission for Miller to go to Norfolk, Jefferson described the man's background: "His father & mother came over about 1768. to Maryland to settle there. he was born there soon after their arrival." The mother returned with her son to England and brought him up there, with the result that he was not considered a citizen of the United States. "He took to the seafaring business which he has followed all his life, except 4 years that he was engaged in a brewery in England." [6]

Miller's reason for coming to the United States was to claim a bequest left to him by a half-brother, Thomas Reed, who had died in Norfolk. Because of Jefferson's intervention, General Moore agreed to allow Miller into the Norfolk area.

It seems to have been the purest of accidents which eventually led the brewing captain to Charlottesville, and there to Jefferson's attention. For years afterward, he was both an aid and a concern to Jefferson, who was diligent in trying to regularize Miller's entangled affairs.

It was characteristic of Jefferson, once he had decided to start brewing, to turn to the authority of books. He was an unquenchable reader and book collector: it was his personal library, after all, which formed the nucleus of the Library of Congress. The two books he had lent to Meriwether and then in 1813 asked back were well-known works on brewing that had appeared in England during the eighteenth century. *The London and Country Brewer*, first published in 1742, written coyly "By a Person concerned in a PUBLICK BREWHOUSE in *London*," described in more than 300 pages "The Whole Art of Brewing all Sorts of Malt-liquors, As practised both in Town and Country; according to Observations made by the Author in Four Years Travels through the several Counties in England." Though this book is written from a professional point of view, inveighing against those "who, if they have but seen, or been concerned in but one Brewing, and that only one Bushel of Malt, assume the name of Brewer," it is nevertheless the epitome of the empirical method, speaking in terms of "blood-warmth" and other homely forms of measurement — which shows that it was written before the wide use of mechanical gauges.[7]

The other book, *The Theory and Practice of Brewing*, published in 1762, was written by Michael Combrune, a practicing commercial brewer, who stated in the preface that his book was "the first attempt, that has been made, to reduce this art [brewing] to rules and principles." Combrune might be called a pioneer of scientific brewing, even though he was quite wrong in his "chemical" analyses.

These books doubtless offered Jefferson some useful clues, but the actual supervision by Miller of the brewing was invaluable. Jefferson was on the trail of yet another book to help with the new enterprise; he wrote to his bookseller in Philadelphia, Nicholas Gouin Dufief:

> In the Aurora of Sep 7. [1813] I see a book advertised as under pub-lication at N. York under the title of "the American brewer & Malster" which, as teaching the method of malting Indian corn I should be very glad to get. could you procure it for me if published or when pub-lished.[8]

Dufief answered quite promptly that the book in question had not yet appeared, but he would send it as soon as it was printed.[9] With a curious persistence, Jefferson continued to make inquiries about the book he had seen advertised. "I am anxious to receive the 'American brewer and malster' as soon as published," he wrote to Dufief on 7 No-vember 1813. "I have both Richardson & Combrune which you men-tion." [10]

Several months later he came back to the same subject: "I must still request you to keep in mind my former unsatisfied commissions. the work on brewing from Indian corn, particularly, if yet published, will be acceptable." [11] Dufief replied without delay that he would write to New York to make sure whether the book had appeared, but about ten days later he had to confess that "The American Brewer & Malster's assistant," as he referred to it, was not even at the printer's.[12]

The book did not reach the public until late in 1815; in the mean-time, the author was probably busily soliciting subscribers in sufficient numbers to make publication practical. Joseph Coppinger, the writer of the book, was a man who deserves some attention in his own right. The first appearance he made on this particular scene was in 1802, when he wrote from New York directly to President Jefferson in Washington, calling himself at that time a farmer from England who had been in the United States only a few months. He expressed the great admiration which many Europeans must have felt for the American experiment; assumed that it was possible in this country, of course, to address the President directly; and ended up by asking how he could obtain a patent for an invention "for preserving animal and vegetable substances. either in their naturel, or a cuit state, and this without the aid of Salt." [13]

Jefferson personally answered this letter and told Coppinger which Act of Congress applied to his request.[14] Coppinger sent a second letter on the same subject from Pittsburgh on 3 January 1803, and then, upon receiving no reply, a follow-up on 18 February, in which he hoped that he had not given offense.[15]

Nothing more was heard from him in Washington until December 1810, when, from New York, he addressed President Madison on a scheme very close to his heart. "Although I am not fortunate enough," he began,

> to have it in my power to interest wealthy and influential characters in the request I am about to make to you. Still I am not without hopes of ultimate success in calling your attention to what I have had long and earnestly at heart, that is the establishment of a Brewing company at Washington as a National object it has in my view the greatest importance as it would unquestionably tend to improve the quality of our Malt liquors in every point of the Union. and serve to counteract the baneful influence of ardent spirits on the health and Morals of our fellow Citizens, considerations in themselves so important as to be well worthy the attention of every wise and good Statesman on the list of whom universal suffrage has given you a distinguished place.

After this well-turned preamble of flattery, he went on to say that a national brewery, such as he envisaged, could be started with a capital of $20,000 — one half to be spent for buildings and utensils, and the other to be "considered as active stock." His scheme was to raise this capital by subscriptions of $500 and $1000 shares.

> I hesitate not to say that under prudent and good management 100% can be securely made on the active Capital of $10,000. on all the

beer & Ale & Porter which may be brewed for this Company and disposed of in the Cask. Whilst that which may be Sold in bottle will leave 200%. this I will pledge myself to prove as clearly as two, and two, make four.

He then drew attention to the revenue England obtained through her breweries, and finally offered his own services in this enterprise. "I have followed the brewing trade nearly twenty years. in that time built two breweries on my own Acct. formed two distinct establishments with success in both." There is appended to the message a list of Coppinger's various inventions through the years.[16]

It would be easy to see in this extraordinary document an effort by an ambitious man to advance himself in the service of the government. Possibly there is some element of self-enhancement in Coppinger's various communications with people in high places, but it is not absolutely unlikely that he did, in fact, wish to offer his services to a government which seemed to afford him great pleasure and expectations.

The letter addressed to Madison clearly reached Jefferson's hands, for the name of Coppinger and date of receipt are methodically written on the document in Jefferson's handwriting. A second, which was also turned over to Jefferson, was dispatched by Coppinger only five days later, reiterating many of the points made the first time, but emphasizing the advantages to the health of the country offered by his scheme. "Those families who are in the custom of using Malt liquor freely as their common drink all summer keep and preserve their health while their less fortunate neighbors who are deprived of it are the victims of fever and disease." [17]

There is no evidence that either Madison or Jefferson replied to these two letters, and for a time Coppinger apparently let this burning idea of a national brewery grow cool. In 1815, however, he was moved to heat it up all over again. On 6 April he addressed a letter to Jefferson with two purposes in mind: one was to present the brewery scheme (in a way which makes it clear that he did not know Jefferson had ever been consulted), and the other was to invite Jefferson to be a subscriber to his book on malting "which I have now in early ready [sic] for the press to be entitled the American brewer." [18] It happened to be a curious coincidence that Coppinger should approach Jefferson, when for a couple of years the latter had independently been trying to get exactly the same book. Jefferson replied quickly:

Monticello Apr 25. 15.

Sir,

I have to acknolege the reciept of your favor of the 6th. I have no doubt, either in a moral or economical view, of the desirableness to introduce a taste for malt liquors instead of that for ardent spirits. the difficulty is in changing the public taste & habit. the business of brewing is now so much introduced in every state, that it appears to me to need no other encouragement than to increase the number of customers. I do not think it a case where a company need form itself on patriotic principles meerly, because there is a sufficiency of private capital which would embark itself in the business if there were a demand, but as to myself particularly I am too old & too fond of quiet to engage in new & distant undertakings. I am lately become a brewer for family use, having had the benefit of instruction to one of my people by an English brewer of the first order. I had noted the advertisement of your book in which the process of malting corn was promised & had engaged a bookseller to send it to me as soon as it should come out. we tried it here the last fall with perfect success, and I shall use it principally hereafter. during the revolutionary war, the brewers on James river used Indian corn almost exclusively of all other. in my family brewing I have used wheat also as we do not raise barley. I shall still desire my bookseller to send me on your book when printed. Accept the assurance of my respect and best wishes for the extension of the use of malt liquors.[19]

For some unexplained reason, Coppinger waited until 15 September to continue the correspondence; at that time he attached a printed prospectus of his "contemplated" work on brewing "which will probably be ready for delivery in three weeks from this day." He undertook to assure Jefferson of receipt of the book if he could have the name of a bookseller in Washington.[20]

The prospectus offers the table of contents of the projected book, and a short statement of its purpose, including the familiar view "that an extensive use of malt liquors is the natural, and perhaps, the only, effectual remedy to the too great consumption of ardent spirits."

It is to be hoped that eventually Jefferson did receive Coppinger's book, but there is no record of his having it. As late as 1821, Jefferson was recommending Combrune's book above all others,[21] so that if indeed he had ever read Coppinger's book it cannot have impressed him especially.

Jefferson's brewing, of course, managed very successfully without the help of Coppinger's book. Miller was clearly extremely efficient in the mystery of brewing, and what was more he was able to teach one of Jefferson's servants, Peter Hemings, so that Monticello was eventually capable of producing beer on its own, without outside assistance. The first brew was started on 17 September 1813,* and by January 1814, Jefferson was on the hunt for bottles. To Richard Randolph he wrote:

> Will you be so good as to send me two gross of your beer jugs; the one gross to be quart jugs, and the other pottle [half-gallon] do. [ditto] they are to be delivered to a mr William Johnson a waterman of Milton, who will apply for them about a week.[22]

But unfortunately there were always minor as well as major problems and delays; Randolph replied that his

> best workman was in New york when I recieved your letter; he returned yesterday, and will make your jugs next week, when they shall be forwarded agreable to your directions.[23]

On at least one other occasion, Jefferson had to have bottles made to order. In September 1814, he wrote to Randolph:

> I am now engaged in brewing a year's supply of malt strong beer, which however I have no chance of saving but by a supply of quart jugs from you. I recieved (I think) 10-1/2 dozen and must ask the favor of 4. gross more for which mr. Gibson will pay your bill. be so good as to inform me when they will be ready. if lodged at mr Gibson; I will direct a waterman on whom I can rely to call for them.[24]

It is always a surprise to find Jefferson spending his time on such small details, but that was the way he conducted all his affairs. Somewhat later it was a matter of finding the best kind of corks. "Not to be too late again in providing corks, as I was last year," he wrote to Miller in 1816, "and fearing I should get bad ones at Richmond, I will ask the favor of you to procure 8. gross for me of the best." [25]

Miller answered, in a mode of spelling entirely his own:

* See page 137.

Norfolk, 6 Dec 1816

Honord Frind I this day have Shiped on Board the Sch Resolution
Capt Coole a Small Bale of Corks which I hope will Come safe to
hand I am a Fraid you will Think me Neglectfull in so long Delay
but Coold not Please myselfe heare I sent to New York for them.[26]

In 1817 Jefferson was back with the same request:

The season calling for corks has come upon me before I had thought
of it, and it being difficult to get them good but from a person who
understands them, I must pray you to send me as many gross of the
best as the inclosed bill of 5. D. will pay for.[27]

And at the same time, Jefferson entered in his account books, "inclosed
5 D to Capt Jos. Millar to buy corks." On that particular day, he was so
anxious about the cork situation that he approached another source simultaneously:

I must ask the favor of you to purchase for me 6 gross of the best
corks to be had in Richmond, and to send them by the stage to Milton
to the address of mr Vest postmaster, the season for using them
being now actually upon us.[28]

This agent replied that he had searched Richmond "for the best
Velvet Corks, & have succeeded in procuring the six Gross wished of
excellent quality." [29].

Then a week later, Captain Miller reported:

This Day I have Shiped on Board of the Slope Hope Capt Lawrence a
Small Baill of Corks which hapen will come Safe and Please you did
[not?] say whether them that I sent in Dec^mr Came or not.[30]

The problem of corks came up year after year, and each time it required a letter written in Jefferson's own hand. In his request to Miller
in 1819, Jefferson commented:

It is so provoking to lose good liquor by bad corks, and so uncertain
to get them good from Richmond that I had rather trespass on your
friendship to get them for me in Norfolk, where I expect better ones
can be got, and selected by your better judgment. I therefore inclose
you a 5. Dollar bill, and I will pray you to send me the amount of it
in good corks.[31]

Miller would have been a most ungrateful wretch if he had not
fulfilled these small commissions for Jefferson, who had been at great

pains to use his influence in settling the captain's problems ever since their first meeting. Their relationship, as far as can be judged from the letters, must have been an odd one, for Miller was always proving to be somewhat relaxed about his obligations, always complaining about the outcome of his projects — and Jefferson was quietly patient, helpful, hopeful.

Jefferson had prevailed upon General Andrew Moore in 1813 to allow Miller to go to Norfolk for a month in order to clear up the details of his legacy. In July of the following year, Jefferson had to write again to Moore because Miller had stayed in Norfolk nine months instead of the one month requested, and in fact was still there. Jefferson wished to make it clear that he was no longer willing to take responsibility for Miller's behavior; and, in view of the approaching invasion of Norfolk, he would raise no objection to Miller's being asked to leave the city.[32] On the same date, he wrote to Miller himself, making exactly the same statement.[33] Jefferson was, in effect, only "covering" himself; no one actually believed that Miller was a spy. As it turned out, Moore did not eject Miller from Norfolk. Miller settled down there, unmolested by the authorities, and no doubt he was considered to be under the protection of Jefferson, no matter how often the latter might deny it.

On the first of September 1815, Miller wrote from Norfolk that he had just shipped "one Cask of X I do not know What we Must Call it: I think Porter Brandy as it was Made from Some Porter Like wine." His letter was mainly intended to announce that he was planning to set out for Monticello, and added an "NB I hope Peter and me will Do Better this year that [sic] last We will let the Wether be Coolder." [34]

While Miller stayed with Jefferson that fall and winter, continuing his brewing instructions with the servant Peter and supervising the brewing for that year, he had many opportunities to discuss with his host the problems which faced him in settling for good in the United States. He had still been unable to secure his half-brother's estate, and the question of his American citizenship remained unsolved. It was in this period that Jefferson drew up a petition to the General Assembly of Virginia on Miller's behalf. But he also wrote to various individuals who might be helpful in forming the General Assembly's decision. In October 1815 he sent a letter to Charles Yancey, discussing the petition of "Capt. Joseph Miller, a resident of Norfolk, but who has staid a great deal in this county, and with me particularly." [35] In his letter to Joseph C. Cabell, Jefferson explained that Miller had set up a brewery in Norfolk

> in partnership with a mr Hays, which he still carries on with great success, being I verily believe the most skilful brewer that has ever come to the country. but during his stay here he has become attached to the neighbors & neighborhood and is looking out for a farm to carry on the business of farming & brewing jointly & on a moderate scale.[36]

In yet another letter to Yancey, he described Miller as "an honest and useful man."

> He is about to settle in our country, and to establish a brewery, in which art I think him as skillful a man as has ever come to America. I wish to see this beverage become common instead of the whiskey which kills one third of our citizens and ruins their families.[37]

As might have been expected, Jefferson's efforts bore fruit: on 17 February 1816 he was able to write Miller that the bill had been passed awarding him his half-brother's property.[38] But there was anything but plain sailing for Miller after that. At about the time his title to the property was settled, his partner Joseph Hays (designated in Jefferson's draft of the petition as one of the executors of Thomas Reed's will) decamped, presumably with some of Miller's money or goods.[39] Miller was also frustrated in his plans to sell his inherited property at advantageous prices; in fact, he was not able to get rid of it at all.

It was brewing season again, just the same, and Miller wrote, "I Could Wish you to Lett Old Peeter Get Sume Grain to work soone   Hops in New York is one Doll^r pr lb by the Bale." [40]

There was a little delay, because Jefferson's affairs kept him at his plantation in Bedford; he was to return there on the 19th of October to stay until the first of December, "yet I shall take measures to enable Peter to go on with his malting and brewing." [41] Miller did not appear that year, however; he complained of "sever pain in my Ancless not Able to Walk for 8 weeks." [42] But the brewing went on nonetheless. Jefferson's comment was, "Peter's brewing of the last season I am in hopes will prove excellent. at least the only cask of it we have tried proved so." [43]

There is no indication that Miller ever did get to Monticello again. Except for the occasional letters concerning the supply of corks for five dollars at a time, he may have had no further contact with Jefferson. Fortunately, Peter Hemings had been well taught and was able to carry on by himself, though doubtless under Jefferson's personal supervision.

In 1820, Jefferson had a request from his good friend James Madison on the subject of private brewing, and he answered in some detail:

> Our brewing for the use of the present year has been some time over. about the last of Oct. or beginning of Nov. we begin for the ensuing year, and malt and brew three sixty gallon casks which will give so many successive lessons to the person you send. . . . on his return he can try his hand with you in order to discover what parts of the processes he will have learnt imperfectly, and come again to our spring brewing of a single cask in order to perfect himself, and go back to you to try his hand again in as much as you will want a house for Malting, which is quickest made by digging into the steep side of a hill, so as to need a roof only, and you will want a hair cloth also of the size of your loft to lay the grain in. This can only be had from Philadelphia or New York. . . . I will give you notice in the fall when we are to commence malting and our malter and brewer is uncommonly intelligent and capable of giving instruction if your pupil is as ready at comprehending it. [44]

Jefferson's beer apparently became well known in that area. He received a flattering inquiry from James Barbour in 1821:

> Some years past I recollect to have drunk some Ale at Monticello which I understood was of your own brewing. The manner of doing which you had obtained by a recipe from some intelligent Briton — Being desirous to introduce that kind of drink and having a facility in preparing the materials of which it is made, you will oblige me much by furnishing me with a copy of the receipt as soon as your convenience will permit. [45]

As usual, though he had just turned seventy-eight and was complaining to old friends like John Adams about the overwhelming extent of his correspondence, he replied to Barbour's request at some length:

> I have no receipt for brewing, & I much doubt if the operations of malting & brewing could be successfully performed from a receipt. if it

could, Combrune's book on the subject would teach the best processes: and perhaps might guide to ultimate success with the sacrifice of 2. or 3. trials a capt Miller, now of Norfolk, but who passes much of his time with Charles Bankhead in Spotsylvania, was during the late war, confined by the Executive to our neighborhood, perhaps indeed by yourself. I took him to my house. he had been a brewer in London, and undertook to teach both processes to a serv^t of mine, which during his stay here & on one or two visits afterwards in the brewing season, he did with entire success. I happened to have a servant of great intelligence and diligence both of which are necessary. we brew 100. gallons of ale in the fall & 100. gallons in the spring, taking 8. gallons only from the bushel of wheat. the public breweries take 15. which makes their liquor meagre and often vapid. We are now finishing our spring brewing. if you have a capable serv^t. and he were to attend our fall brewing, so as to get an idea of the manual operation, Combrune's book with a little of your own attention in the beginning might qualify him.[46]

Presumably, brewing went on at Monticello right up to 1826, when Jefferson died on the Fourth of July. It was only one farm activity out of hundreds, and it was strictly seasonal; but Jefferson brought to it all his characteristic enthusiasm and curiosity. He was, as his own words so clearly illustrate, a real champion of the brewing industry; being a gentleman farmer, he understood its important relationship with agriculture. It is particularly interesting that Jefferson took up brewing at a time when, as an industry, it was at its lowest ebb in the national economy. He symbolizes an influential opinion of that period, which was that the industry could bestow great advantages, both economic and social, on the country, and that it therefore deserved every form of encouragement.

✺§ *SEVENTEEN* ৡ৶

Matthew Vassar: Brewer-Philanthropist

THE NAME VASSAR conjures up for some the idea, and for others the picture, of a college for women situated in the Hudson River town of Poughkeepsie. During most of the nineteenth century, however, Vassar was for many people the name of a brewer who made himself a handsome fortune after modest beginnings. Matthew Vassar's career has many flavors of a Horatio Alger confection in it, not least of all the philanthropic urge which led him to endow an Academy for Young Women in 1860.

He was born in England in 1792, and brought to America when he was four by his parents, James and Anne, who emigrated because, as nonconformist Baptists, they had suffered under religious discrimination in England. In later years, Matthew remembered their arrival from England: "our being met and greeted by English Residents of the City of New York." They stayed for a time with a family named "Withington," * whom Matthew characterized vaguely as "a large Brewer in the upper part of the eastern bounds of the City." [1]

Apparently James Vassar was advised that he would do better outside New York City; in any case, he wanted to farm. And so he sought out a place upriver, finally settling on Wappinger, near the village of Poughkeepsie, where he bought some land.

The brewing of beer was apparently nothing more than a sideline to the general farming, although James Vassar seems to have had a cer-

---

* The Brooklyn Directory for 1796 lists Roger Whitington as a brewer.

tain talent for brewing. One of Matthew's biographers speaks of "the wild hop (*humulus lupulus*), from whose clustering blossoms they might distill the lupuline for home-brewed ale, without which an English family would experience a real privation." It may have been the wild hops that encouraged James Vassar to try to brew enough beer to sell. The crop he wished to raise was barley; there was apparently none in that area, and James's brother Thomas (in what seems a curiously farfetched venture) returned to England and procured there the seed which introduced barley into Dutchess County.[2]

By 1798, Matthew Vassar was "going with Mother to Town on a pleasant Satturday with waggon & horses to Market Butter, Eggs, and a Barrel of home-brew[d] Beer."[3] This is the way the success story started: a barrel sold here, a barrel sold there. The beer caught on, made a reputation for itself — perhaps mainly because it was the only local beer, and would have tasted better than a brew transported some distance. Whatever the reasons, Vassar managed to make enough money out of his beer sales to start up, in partnership with Oliver Holden, a proper brewery in Poughkeepsie itself, and there the family all moved in 1801.

James Vassar sold ale, mild beer, porter, and small beer, as well as malt, grains, yeast and "scimmings." * As early as 1803, the accounts show a number of customers in New York.[4] As the business progressed, Vassar ale became known up and down the river, sold both in bottles and barrels.

In 1806 a family crisis took place, as may happen in even the best-run homes. In order to avoid being apprenticed to a tanner, Matthew ran away.[5] It appears that he was not very far from Poughkeepsie and that he remained in touch with his family, but it was not until 1810 that he came back. His return to Poughkeepsie, he wrote, was

> after an absence of five to six years [*sic*] by the request of my father who wanted me to take charge of his Books & attend to Collections of Ale[s] and Beer[s] Moneys which at that time was quite considerable† having all or most part of the River-towns-trade, from NewBurgh to Hudson.[6]

---

* The fermentation was skimmed off the top of the vat and sold, providing a diluted yeast product.

† Compare these events with the history of John Herring, pages 127-128.

Matthew became the dutiful son, and took over management, in collaboration with his brother, John Guy Vassar, of his father's business. The books show that on the day the two sons assumed reponsibility for the business (15 November 1810), its affairs stood succinctly as follows:

The Stock in Trade

Ale and Beer	$1200.00
Barley Malt Hops etc.	1800.00
The Books accts of James Vassar & Oliver Holden	1500.00
Works and Materials including the Brewery etc. etc. etc.	8000.00
	12500.00[7]

The former partnership, called James Vassar & Co., was dissolved, and John Guy and Matthew Vassar became owners.[8]

The future must have seemed to them completely assured, but fate had a tragedy in store for them. On 10 May 1811 the brewery was destroyed by a fire, representing a loss of about $13,000.[9] But what was worse than that, two days after the fire John Guy, at that time twenty-two years old, went down among the ruins into an emptied beer vat, apparently in an attempt to save some hops that were there, and died of suffocation by carbonic acid gas.[10] This young man, who had married into one of the old Dutch families, Van Kleeck, left two sons, Matthew, Jr., and John Guy, Jr., both of whom were later important in the business.

Matthew Vassar had to start all over again. He did so on the thinnest of shoestrings, operating out of the dye-house of George Booth (whose family became related to the Vassars by marriage), brewing three barrels at a time.[11] The market for Vassar ale had not disappeared with the fire, and Matthew's supply could not keep up with the demand. He soon opened a saloon, situated advantageously in the basement of the new courthouse, and it was here that he is credited with having introduced oysters to Poughkeepsie.[12] His advertisement in the Poughkeepsie *Journal* offered for sale "at Wholesale and retail, London BROWN STOUT, Philadelphia PORTER, Poughkeepsie do. and ALE," as well as bottled cider, wines, "segars," crackers.[13]

The "Poughkeepsie do." must have been what he himself was brewing. There is no doubt that he did brew during this oyster-saloon period, for in the 14 October 1812 issue of the *Journal* he was advertising
for hops and barley. This being wartime, Vassar's type of business made
out extremely well. So well, in fact, that by 1813 he was able to announce that he was "now rebuilding the Brewery in this village"; he had
purchased the beer casks belonging to the former James Vassar brewery
and requested the return of any outstanding barrels.[14]

His partner in this new enterprise was Thomas Purser, a rich Englishman with some experience in the brewing business. Purser stayed with
Vassar until June 1815, and sold his interest at that time to J. M. and
Nathan Conklin, described as well-known merchants of the town.[15] By
1829, Matthew Vassar was able to buy out their part of the business, and
from then on the brewery was controlled entirely by Vassars and
Booths.[16]

Matthew's two nephews came into the business in 1832, and four
years later a new and elaborate building was built directly on the river.[17]
The new and the old breweries were operated together for many years,
but finally it was the river brewery that became famous as the great
Vassar enterprise, producing a well-known ale up until 1895, when the
business was suspended and the building, in 1902, was temporarily used
as a county jail.[18]

Matthew withdrew from active interest in the business in the late
1850s, when he became concerned about establishing his academy for
women, but actually from about 1833, to judge from the journals, Matthew, Jr., was in active control of the company's affairs. He too withdrew from business matters in the late 1860s in order to concentrate
most of his time on his uncle's philanthropic commissions. All the Vassars had, by then, sizable fortunes, though, as one of the local historians
points out, they were "only partly made in the brewing business, most
of them resulting from fortunate investments in outside enterprises." [19]
Among those "fortunate investments" were, appropriately, large pieces
of Wisconsin land, bought even before barley-raising and brewing had
become prime industries in that state.

The diaries of Matthew Vassar, Jr., show how closely a brewer of that
time supervised all activities in his business. He noted on 20 January

1837 that the men were "repairing small copper furnace and kilns." On 30 January a "new Butt" was erected at the brewery on the river. On 6 February he "held consultation about building 2 new Kilns in New M[alt] House, 1 in old M.H." The same day he "Discharged Engineer . . . for leaving without permissions."

In March 1837 he "wrote to Philadelphia, for 200 tons coal," and noted the same day that "our lower small steep this day discharged part of its Water — through negligence men." He had a good deal of difficulty with his employees; he discharged two men, Quin* and Golder, "for misdemeanour," and on the 26th of March 1836 he fired six "out Coopers." They had asked what he considered an outrageous price (4/6 for making a cask) — "direct imposition . . . they cannot at present find any work, if they had worked for reasonable wages, should have kept them — they are willing now to accept our price of 4/ but [we] will not have them."

He also had to keep track of the company's commission agents. He went up to Rhinebeck and Kingston by day boat, on 19 April 1837, to call on an agent there: "to increase sales of Ale raised his Commisn to 6/ p Barrel — he to guarantee as before to use extra exertion in sale of Ale." [20]

The brewing season began each year about mid-August and continued through April. As was the custom among brewers, Vassar kept a detailed record of each brew, noting the following facts: number of brewing, date, bushels of malt, pounds of hops, heat, liquor, extract, gravity, hours boiled, pounds of yeast, when racked, whose malt, etc. He also made general comments:

> The Ales principally the "Brown" was Brewd from Isaac Rose malt . . . a good article — also of malt intended for pale but made into Brown last spring — many bud grains — but a fair article.

Certain brewings were specifically marked "South Shipping" and some were typed as pale, amber, or single. Very little went unremarked: "Hops rather poor too green (Underwood) — inferior liquor"; "Hops inferior (Underwood)"; "Malt all new — not rich malt." Malt was provided

---

* Might this be the Quinn who later became a well-known Albany brewer? See pages 187-188.

either by the Vassar plant itself, or by Alex Proudfoot, several others, and some unnamed maltster in Albany; these would be used in certain combinations, depending on what result was wanted.

He wrote on 29 October 1833, after observing the progress of several brewings, "the Ales from New malt worked much better, altho the malt is nothing to brag off [sic]." "N.B. The fermenting has been rather slack, malt of J. Madden . . . very inferior article — raw and slick mix^d with old malt dried over." His general comment on the November 1833 brewings was:

> The pale Ales were not good and have given general dissatisfaction — our malt this season has been worse than have had in a number years — neither flavour nor richness. . . . If our reputation had not stood fair — should have lost all or most of our customers — have had but little returned — *about 20 Bbls.*

The chanciness had not yet been taken out of brewing, in spite of devices for measuring heat and specific gravity. Vassar sought to place the blame on the malt or the yeast or the weather, but the truth was that he had very little notion what really went on once he put together the ingredients.

The ales of December 1833, he remarked several months after the event, were much better than those of November,

> principal part of which was for Shipping and Amber for N.Y. have had no complaints from JB [J. Beveridge & Co., New York agents for Vassar] is at present out and am now shipping him weekly — he did not dispose of the whole of his stock, which was stored in N.Y. through winter.

In one season, the plant could produce 209 brewings. In going over the records of the 1833-1834 season, Vassar calculated that the average quantity of malt he had used per barrel was $3\frac{1}{8}$ bushels; the average of hops 2 pounds, $7\frac{1}{2}$ ounces. "Have consumed 3 qts. less per Barrel than last year," he remarked in his capacity as good businessman, "making a saving on whole quantity." A similar accounting for the 1837-1838 season shows that he was using a fraction more malt, but had reduced the amount of hops infinitesimally.

When there were two breweries going simultaneously, beginning in the autumn of 1836, the old one was called "Washington" and the new one on the river, "Eagle." From then on records had to be kept of both breweries, which were used either at the same time or interchangeably, the sole distinction being that porter was apparently brewed only at the "Eagle." Capacity was constantly being enlarged, so that by 1841 the combined product was 14,244 barrels. And the 1860 *Gazetteer of New York* lists "M. Vassar & Co's Brewery and Malt Works," with capital of $150,000, employing fifty men, and manufacturing "30,000 barrels of ale per year."

Vassar's journal reflects the serious depression of 1837. "The times are awful! awful!" he wrote in May 1837, "worse than this or any other country ever witnessed." Vassar's business suffered along with the others, but it weathered the crisis nicely. In 1857, there was another financial crisis; money was under great pressure; the New York banks were suspended. Vassar looked on these things from some distance, even though his business depended on the river traffic, on New York customers, and on generally favorable financial conditions. One of the few instances he gives of cooperation with other brewers is an entry on 1 February 1837 that the Vassar company was raising the price of ale from $5.50 to $6.00 a barrel, "in concert with the New York brewers."

Matthew, Jr.'s interest was bought out in May 1866 by his nephew Oliver H. Booth.[21] The brewery's specialty was its export business, particularly to the Caribbean islands, but by the 1880s that was about over.[22] The firm's decline is attributed partly to "complications of ownership, and partly to Mr. Oliver H. Booth's interest in boat-building and other outside matters." [23] Another reason may have been the fact that Vassar persisted in brewing ale and porter exclusively, even after it had been demonstrated that the greatest success was to be achieved with lager beer. At the time when the decision should have been made to shift — as happened in innumerable breweries all over the country — the plant no longer had the dynamic and dominating management which the two Matthew Vassars had apparently exercised.

The plant was finally advertised for sale in 1899:

The Vassar Breweries, including the good will and the right to the use of the name "Vassar" in connection with the same, will be sold

at public auction, at the Court House in the City of Poughkeepsie,
N.Y., on Thursday, the 26th day of October, 1899, at 12 o'clock.

These breweries made the ale which built Vassar College, the foremost
Woman's College of the world, Vassar Old Man's Home and Vassar
Institute, and made the name of Vassar famous among the philan-
thropists of the world.[24]

The history of the Vassar brewery is significant because it was a large-
scale business which predated by some forty or fifty years the famous
breweries of the East and the Midwest. It was directly in the British
tradition, whereas most of those which succeeded later were in the German. No doubt the Vassar enterprise taught later brewers a good many
things — not least of them, how to endow an institution of learning
with over $400,000 (or its much greater modern equivalent).

The Age of Steam Power

THE USES of steam to replace the labor of men and animals had become evident, in a practical way, as early as 1698 in England, when Thomas Savery's rudimentary steam engine was applied to pumping operations in mines. At various stages during the eighteenth century, the steam engine was modified, improved, elaborated; the name best known in this field, perhaps because it was the one best publicized, is James Watt. From 1769 on, Watt applied for patents on a variety of low-pressure steam engines of the piston as well as the "rotative" type. But Watt was something more than the conventional notion of an inventor-dreamer; he had a strong practical bent, which expressed itself in his successful partnership with Matthew Boulton. The firm of Boulton & Watt were the leading manufacturers and suppliers of steam engines in the world at the start of the nineteenth century.

The advantages steam power had to offer to commercial brewing did not go unobserved. Two London porter brewers, Goodwyn and Whitbread, had engines installed by Boulton & Watt in 1784, and other important brewers followed suit shortly afterward. By the year 1800 some seventeen brewers (mainly in London) had installed steam engines varying in horsepower between 3 and 26. An expert on this period in British brewing comments that "the advantages of steam-power were proved immediately. Apart from the most concrete saving in the expense of horses, the uninterrupted, rapid work made possible by the engine added efficiency and convenience to its initial economy." One of the brewers himself wrote, on 1 March 1786, "you may remember our wheel required 6 Horses but we ordered our engine the power of 10, and the work it does we think it equal to 14 horses." [1]

The engines were used in grinding the malt, pumping up the wort, and later a device was worked out making it possible to supplant mechanically the workmen who stirred the mash with oars. "By 1800 . . . thanks to the engine, virtually all the operations of brewing had been mechanized." [2]

The situation in America was quite different at this time. In view of the restrictions which had been placed by the English on colonial manufactures, and the listless rate of advance in industry directly after the Revolutionary War, it is not surprising that the steam engine was introduced slowly in this country. (It must be borne in mind that America was what later came to be called a "backward country," and that Great Britain was the world's industrial giant.) The first date on which there was any inquiry made to Boulton & Watt from an American source was 1797, when a Mr. William Tatham approached their London agent on the question of exporting engines to the United States. [3]

America was generally considered, in 1800, to be some fifty years behind England, in terms of mechanization. Tench Coxe remarked in 1787 that "steam mills have not yet been adopted in America, but we shall probably see them after a short time in New England and other places." [4] In the whole country, there were not more than six engines in operation. [5] The first ever introduced here was brought over from London in 1753 (in the ship *Irene*, which was carrying a group of Moravians to Pennsylvania); it was installed at a copper mine in Belleville, New Jersey. [6] This was doubtless the Schuyler mine,* described elsewhere as being situated on the Passaic River. [7]

During this period of industrial ferment and invention all over the Western world, America did manage to produce at least one indigenous engineering genius, Oliver Evans. A native of Delaware, where he had pioneered the installation of grain mills on the Brandywine, Evans established himself in Philadelphia. He had an extremely difficult time, not

---

* There has been a little confusion about locating this mine. An article by John C. Merriam, entitled "Steam," in *Eighty Years' Progress of the United States* (1864), cites Passaic, N.J., as the location; but it is more reliably reported to have been at Belleville, on the Passaic River.

only as an inventor, but as a businessman. His patents were frequently infringed, and he suffered from the apathy, if not the outright hostility, of the very industrialists who should have been supporting him. He was prominent enough, however, and perhaps aggressive enough to come eventually to the attention of Jefferson, who owned Evans's *Mill-Book* and used some of Evans's inventions in outfitting his mill on the Rivanna River in 1808.

> In said Mill there is Erected Applyed and Now in use, the following Inventions and Improvements Secured to Oliver Evans by Letters from the United States, Viz. One Grain Elevator, one Meal Elevator, one Sett of Conveyors And one Hopper Boy.

The contractors had, in fact, installed this equipment without informing or paying Oliver Evans; when he discovered this, though, Jefferson remitted the amount in question directly to the inventor himself.[8]

Evans had already made some name for himself as a milling expert when he announced in the Philadelphia *Aurora* of February 1803 that he had put his steam engine into practical operation.

> The Engine, in its construction, is so simplified, that it can be easily managed by ordinary mechanics. The Cylinder is only about six inches in diameter. The engine altho in an imperfect state, ground in 12 hours, the other day, no less than one hundred bushels of hard plaster. This immensely powerful agent can, on the new principles, happily applied by Mr. Evans, serve with profit, all the various purposes of machinery; particularly Breweries and Distilleries. It may be made so as to pump the water, grind the malt, and boil the water that is necessary on the largest scale.[9]

One of the main differences between Evans's engine and the one Watt had perfected some years before was that Watt's was based on the low-, and Evans's on the high-pressure principle. It was the latter which was ultimately found to be the more efficient and economical, but when Evans first announced it, Watt had already been selling the low-pressure engine for a good many years. In 1811, the British inventor Richard Trevithick introduced an engine built roughly on the same principle as Evans's: it was this high-pressure noncondensing type of engine that was shortly afterward adapted for locomotives.

In his application for a patent covering his engines and boilers constructed on the principle of high-pressure steam, Evans wrote, "I apply a great part of my steam after it leaves the engine to heat the water to supply my boiler and by these means I mean to perform the boiling in Breweries, Distilleries, Dye Factories, Paper Mills, etc." This offered not only a saving in fuel, but also meant that "the stills and other vessels for boiling may be constructed principally of wood in the simplest & cheapest manner, and all danger of boiling over or burning be avoided." [10]

Evans took every opportunity to emphasize the special usefulness of the steam engine in the various operations of brewing and distilling. He even advertised that "a very small engine" was sufficient "to chop grain and pump for distilleries and Breweries," the implication being that such engines could be acquired for somewhat less than $886.60, the price quoted for the regulation steam engine and boiler.[11]

By 1814 there were twenty-eight of Evans's engines in use or construction — but none of them, apparently, in a brewery.[12] From the experience among English brewers, it was not considered economically practical to install a steam engine when production was under 20,000 barrels a year.[13] Now, in the United States in 1814, although there are no definitive statistics available, it is hardly likely there were any breweries that aspired to a production of that magnitude. Even the Vassar company, which was among the leaders before 1850, produced fewer than 20,000 barrels in 1841 and had reached the prodigious figure of 30,000 in 1860.*

Although Evans's high-pressure engine, for all its advantages, was not installed in any brewery during the first quarter of the nineteenth century, a low-pressure engine, built by Thomas Holloway, was set up in the brewery of Francis Perot on Vine Street, Philadelphia, in 1819.

It is believed to be the oldest stationary steam-engine built in America, and consists of a vertical cylinder forty inches long, which, together with a valve chest, was bolted to a condenser box five feet long, two feet deep and twenty inches wide. This condenser was kept filled with cold water. The piston connected by a shaft with a walking-beam on the floor above. On this revolved a six foot flywheel and the driving

* See page 155.

pulley. The governor, a vast affair, was also rigged upstairs. The engine
. . . developed about ten-horse power.[14]

This was, however, an isolated case, and the engine in question much
less sophisticated than those Evans was making. The general adoption
of steam engines did not come until at least 1850, when an overall expansion began in the industry; when the size of breweries, the number
of employees hired, the markets and the rate of production had all increased. In England, there had already been a full-scale brewing industry in active operation at the advent of steam power; the American
brewing interest had to wait until it was reaching something like the
British level in, say, 1795 before it could afford to change methods and
invest in newfangled devices.

In the meantime, there were minor inventions, of a "tinkering" variety, that turned up occasionally. The agriculturalist Bordley, for instance, devised a "tripartite copper," by means of which water was fil-
tered through perforations over the malt, in much the same way as
water passes through coffee in a drip-method pot. By means of a pump,
the wort, upon reaching the bottom of the device, could be raised again
to the top and dripped through the malt repeatedly.[15]

Something of the same sort was recommended by John Vaughan,
friend of Benjamin Franklin, and treasurer and librarian of the American Philosophical Society:

> Take a wooden Tub, with holes bored in its bottom, & of a size to fit
> your largest Washing Kettle, put your malt in the Tub & on the Top
> put a board full of holes, on which pour the hot water. The Upper
> board is intended merely to divide the Water more equally.[16]

Inventions of this kind, however, while they might make home brewing a bit simpler, were hardly calculated to change the shape and economy of the whole industry, as steam and the later improvements of refrigeration and air-conditioning were to do.

Toward the Mississippi

A S THE Midwest began to open, inviting pioneers, settlers, land speculators and refugees of all sorts into its great uninhabited spaces, trading posts turned into villages, villages into towns, and towns into thriving new cities. In addition to Pittsburgh, the two communities of Cincinnati and Chicago were prime examples of not only potential giants, but also centers of brewing. The earlier of the two was Cincinnati, its date of first settlement on a site that had been bought by a Congressman from New Jersey, John Cleves Symmes, being 1788. Like Pittsburgh it had an extremely advantageous situation, directly on the Ohio River as it flowed ponderously down to the Mississippi. First called Losantiville, it adopted the present name in 1790; it was designated a township in 1791, a village in 1802, and in 1819 it became a city.[1] Its growth was extremely rapid, the population soaring from a mere 960 in 1805 to more than 10,000 fourteen years later.

A visitor, S. S. L'Hommedieu, wrote of it in 1810:

> Cincinnati was then a village, containing about two thousand people.
> . . . It also had its post office, on the corner of Lawrence and Front
> Streets, and its Davis Embree brewery, on the river bank, below Race
> Street.[2]

Embree is generally assumed to have been the first brewer in Cincinnati, even though two (unnamed) brewers and eleven innkeepers were reported there in 1805. Whatever one may care to make of that

earlier pair, Embree is clearly the first to have operated commercially
— forefather of an industry which later attained an important niche
for itself in the city's history. He was a Quaker who took an active
part in the young town's affairs; in 1814 he was town treasurer, and
from 1821 to 1825 president of the Cincinnati Fire Wardens' Association.[3] "Among the most respectable of the manufacturing establishments," wrote the 1816 traveler David Thomas,

> we notice the brewery of D. and J. Embree. The works, though in a
> progressive state, are now sufficiently extensive to produce annually
> five thousand barrels of beer and porter, and the quality is excellent.
> A treadle-mill is attached to these buildings. . . . It is turned by
> horses, and grinds a hundred and twenty bushels of malt a day.[4]

Thomas added, "In the present recess of business, it is employed in
the manufacture of mustard," showing that breweries, even before the
days of Prohibition, had to turn occasionally to some other product in
order to weather a slack period.

Embree's establishment survived a fire in 1815, and was then listed
in the 1819 city directory, address 75 Water Street. At that time, there
were two brewers in the city, the second being Zachariah Ernst. Between him and Embree, there were produced 3100 barrels of porter and
1340 of beer; the figure for ale (no doubt greater than the porter production) is not given, but the total value is quoted as $50,000. The two
breweries employed twenty workmen.[5]

The early explorer Daniel Drake described the two breweries as follows in his 1815 report:

> The first was erected on the river bank, in the lower part of the town,
> four years ago, and uses the river water; the other was established since,
> on a smaller scale, and derives its water from wells and cisterns. The
> two are calculated to consume annually 30,000 bushels of barley. Their
> products are beer, porter and ale, of a quality at least equal to that of
> the Atlantic states. Large quantities have been exported to the Missis-
> sippi, even as far as New-Orleans, the climate of which they are found
> to bear very well.[6]

Embree himself, according to a contemporary of his, "lived well
down to the second half of the nineteenth century." [7] By 1836, how-

ever, his brewery was no longer listed — nor, for that matter, was Ernst's. The names given in that year were Perry and Riley, Dr. Price, Metcalf and Attee, Lofthouse, and C. and J. Schultz (proprietors of the Washington Brewery).[8] The last-named, a more substantial business than any of the others, was located on the riverbank near the waterworks; the ale it produced "was considered by judges to be equal to the imported article." [9]

It is well to remember that Cincinnati was a full-blown town at the time when Chicago-to-be was only an Indian agency. Cook County was organized no earlier than 1831, when the population was under two hundred. The first two licenses for taverns were issued to Elijah Wentworth and Samuel Miller, who sold beer at $6\frac{1}{4}$¢ a pint and $12\frac{1}{2}$¢ a quart.[10]

It is likely that these tavern-keepers brewed their own beer; they could not have depended on regular overland supplies. The first commercial venture, however, had its beginnings in 1833, when William Haas and Andrew Sulzer, recent arrivals from Watertown, New York, established W. Haas & Co. They had brought with them the materials for brewing, a load of malt, and 150 barrels of ale to sell. With a sense of commercial adventure and a capital of $3000, they bought a 100- by 200-foot lot, put up a small building, hired four men, and started to make ale — less than 600 barrels a year at the start.

Sulzer is supposed to have sold his part of the firm in 1836 to William B. Ogden, the man from whom he and Haas had originally bought the lot; and three years later, William Lill came into the business as purchaser of Haas's share.[11]

Ogden, Chicago's first mayor and one of its most important landowners and promoters, was rather like General O'Hara* in the early epoch of Pittsburgh; he had a hand in virtually every commercial scheme of any significance in early Chicago history. He came into the Haas business without brewing experience, and immediately took over the control of the company's financial affairs, leaving the brewing in the apparently capable hands of his partner Lill. In January 1839, he had to send a dunning bill to one Erasmus D. Perry:

* See page 132.

To Wm Haas & Co   dr
1838
Feb. 23. To 1 Bbl Beer   8.00
Mch 17   ”   1 do   do   8.00
Apr 6   ”   1 do   do   8.00
          ”   Bad money returned   7.00
          ”   Balance due on milk   3.00
          _____
                                        $ 34.00

Sent the above a/c to John V. A. Hoes, Ottawa [Illinois] for collection.
wrote him; if Perry paid without Suing he might deduct my a/c Say
$5⁵⁰, but if not He must sue for the whole as my a/c is not legally an
offset. Perry to pay attorney if settled without Suing.[12]

He was active also in procuring supplies for the business. In July he
was approaching a friend in Eaton, New York, about the possibility of
buying hops through him:

> I shall want some 3000 lbs or more this fall probably & should be glad
> to know whether you would like to furnish me that quantity of best
> quality and *perfectly* cured and dry. I want none other than a per-
> fectly certain article for, if after I get them here I should find they
> were musty or bad from any cause I could not replenish my stock
> through the winter & my Brewery would necessarily stop. So you see
> it is of the first importance that I get good hops and get them early
> too before Navigation closes. One year they got frozen in at Detroit
> & we were great sufferers by it.[13]

He had made inquiries about getting hops from Michigan, he writes
in the same letter, but would rather make a deal for the New York crop.

The cultivation of hops in New York State, on a commercial level,
was a relatively new thing. The first hop yard in the state is supposed
to have been set out in the town of Madison in 1808, by James D. Coolidge. Progress was constant but extremely slow. The price paid for New
York hops was at first very low — twelve cents a pound — and there was
great expense involved in hauling them to the Albany market. Besides,
the English hop was still preferred by most brewers and imported in
large quantities.

The industry, such as it was, kept going in spite of the low price
largely because the yield was of a profitable size: 2000 pounds per acre.
Real impetus, however, was given to New York hop growers in 1822 by

a shortage of imports resulting from several failures of the English crop. The demand increased so swiftly from then on that many more farmers became interested in hop cultivation, which then spread out from the original planting in Madison to the counties of Otsego, Oneida, Schoharie, Ontario, and others in that northern region of the state.[14] After 1825, this industry received another boon in the form of the completed Erie Canal, which made it possible to substitute much cheaper shipment by water for the overland trek to Albany, and which also opened up the western market in Ohio, Michigan, Indiana and Illinois.

Ogden's concern with hops for his Chicago brewery was incessant. On 13 August 1839, he remarked in a letter, "Two days since I had occasion to pay A. S. Newberry of Oneida Co. N.Y. a balance due him for hops for my Brewery," [15] and two weeks later, he readdressed his friend in Eaton, Madison County:

E. Townsend Esq.   Chicago Augt 26, 1839
Eaton Madison Co. N.Y.

Dr Edward

I have your favor of the 2nd inst. & have delayed replying until I could hear from Michigan in relation to hops, understanding they could be bought there which would ensure our getting them before the close of navigation. The quality did not suit me and I conclude to order them of you.

Heretofore I have ordered them of Mr Newberry in Sangersfield near you but should be glad to open the trade with you if of any advantage to you.

Mr Newberry writes me that he will buy my hops for the usual commission of 1½ per cent or will deliver me hops on the Chenango Canal at 17 cents or at Chicago at his own risk at 20 cents per lb. . . . Do what you think proper & right, but buy me 3500 lbs hops without delay & see that they are first quality and in good order. . . . Mark them "W. B. Ogden Chicago Ill Care Newberry & Dole, By Steam keep dry."

Write the house you send them to at Buffalo or elsewhere to see that they are forwarded with despatch by the first Steam Boat. . . .

The outlay for Barley, staves, Barrels &c. is heavy at this season & I should be glad to give you drafts for part of it. . . .

Keep me advised of your movements promptly, for delays are dangerous with me after this time of year. . . .[16]

There was indeed a delay which made Ogden even more anxious. He asked for immediate word "as it is getting late in the season & I fear a disappointment in getting the hops for my brewery." [17]

Evidently the hops came through at length; at least, there were no further agitated letters. But it all had to be repeated the following year. "I had made an arrangement for the main part of my stock of Hops in Michigan," Ogden wrote to Townsend on 29 September 1840, very late in the season,

> but owing to the miscarriage of a letter it all fell through.
> I have to day learned that I have to depend upon you for them yet.
> Enclosed is a dft for $800. from our Bank here on Nevins Townsend & Co. I want as many hops as it will buy and want at least 2000 lbs & if the dft wont pay for them if you will advance the difference I will immediately remit it to you on being notified.
> No time can be lost or they will not reach me this fall, dont delay a minute on receipt of this but purchase and ship at once. . . . Be sure they arrive at Buffalo in time for the Boats & before the 1 Nov^r. . . .
> Spare not pains or expense — it is so late it will not do to delay or depend on uncertainties — and send me the hops at any rate. . . .[18]

The hops arrived. "The cost was high but that we expected under the circumstances," Ogden graciously admitted. "Next year we will provide you with means to buy earlier I hope." He expressed his extreme gratitude for Townsend's efforts and added this comment, an odd mixture of glee and sanctimony: "None of the other brewers will I believe be able to get hops at any price & although I wish them no such luck, if it happens it will be all to our advantage." [19]

In 1840, Ogden was concerned with certain financial arrangements in relation to Haas (who had moved to Austin, Texas), indicating that the latter's interest was being paid off gradually. There was a question of $800. "Lill had not got it — times were very hard with me and all others & how to get it I did not know." Because it was "my friend Wm Haas, who had always been so true to me," Ogden determined to find some means of rounding up the money. Unfortunately he had been "taken sick with Billious fevre as last year," and was just back in his office.

So the draft is paid and I have it. The Brewery, Lill & Co, not Lill, have refunded me $400 of the money & the balance I have paid out of my own pocket. I had to pay 10% Exchange between this and New York $80. which I have charged to you as I suppose Mr. Lill was to pay in Illinois money.

The Brewery has done well last year, very, but repairs were heavy and there was no surplus. We bought Barley at 3/- & sold Beer @ $7. & sold all we made & could have sold 300 Barrels more if we had had it. The Brewery is now in fine order, the Beer in good condition, the House moved down in front with good Stone Cellar under it, . . . Barley coming in again at 3/- and if we can sell all the Beer we can make this year at $7. I am sure Mr. Lill will be able to pay up all he owes you next spring certain. . . .

Collections on a/c of Wm Haas & Co. are of course very indifferent in these hard times. Many of your little debts never will be collected probably. . . . I should be very glad to send you more money but don't see how I can get it for you before spring, except Sulzer* pays. he has paid nothing yet, he has fine crops this year and is doing well.

Michael is still with us selling milk & Beer, is as good & faithful as ever. . . .[20]

The Michael mentioned in Ogden's letter was Michael Diversey, an immigrant from Alsace-Lorraine, who had come to Chicago in the early 1830s.[21] He promoted himself from the "good & faithful" milk-seller to partner in the firm Lill & Diversey, an event which must have happened shortly after 1841. At the same time, Ogden apparently relinquished his interest in the business — his commercial involvements, in any case, were numerous.

In 1929, during the Dark Ages of Prohibition, when both Diversey and Lill, long dead, were honored by having Chicago streets named for them, the Chicago *Tribune* published the following item:

Michael Diversey was active when Chicago was enjoying its greatest rate of increase in population [1840 to 1850]. . . . It grew from 4,470 to 29,962 in that period. . . . Mr. Diversey saw the first railroad locomotive arrive here in 1848. He survived the cholera epidemic of 1849. . . . A brewer in Mr. Diversey's day had a business and social rating with bankers, railroad presidents and such.[22]

Lill and Diversey developed their "Chicago Brewery" into what was called in 1857 the largest in the West.[23] They survived the financial

* See page 164.

panic of that year and continued together, successfully brewing and selling ale and porter in the face of strong competition from the German lager-beer brewers of the 1860s, until Diversey's death in 1869. Lill, who lived until 1875, carried on the business himself until the famous fire, caused in 1871 by Mrs. O'Leary's impatient cow, in which Lill's was one of five breweries destroyed.

These were not, of course, the only cities opening up, first gradually and then precipitately, in the hinterland. Detroit, for example, goes back a good deal farther than either Chicago or Cincinnati, claiming as its date of first effectual settlement 1701. A center of French colonization until 1760, it then became a British post and trading center. Detroit was one of the settlements which the British tacitly refused to give up after the Revolutionary War treaties, and it did not become property of the United States until 1796. Once again, in 1812, it was occupied by the British, but only for a year.

The brewing industry was somewhat slow getting started in Detroit. The first sign of any such undertaking comes, curiously enough, from Cleveland, Ohio, where a newspaper in 1829 advertised Detroit beer "just received" for sale.[24]

The date traditionally given for the start of the Detroit brewing industry is 1836, when "a single brewery upon the River road — now Woodbridge street — supplied the demand." [25] This must have been the property of Emerson, Davis and Moore, who advertised that year that 20,000 bushels of barley were wanted "at the Detroit Brewery." [26] This was, at that time, a substantial amount of barley for one brewery to use in a year's operation, and so it is probably a fairly safe assumption that this early Detroit brewery was something more than an insignificant back-shed enterprise.

Cleveland was another late starter as a brewing town, having been first settled in 1796. Since it was a frontier trading village to begin with, it is no surprise to learn that its first business was a distillery, conducted by David Bryant and his son Gilman, who arrived there from Virginia in 1800, all equipped with a still.[27]

Beer, if not made commercially, was certainly produced at home. In August 1831, the local newspaper offered recipes for spruce beer and molasses beer, as well as "a good household beer" of wheat bran and hops, and advice on how to cure "ropy" (glutinous) beer.[28] An early Cleveland resident, J. H. Sargent, remembered that commercial beer was introduced sometime between 1820 and 1840: "Elijah F. Willey, a Baptist clergyman put in operation on the Walworth run near Willey Street a Brewery, so the introduction among us of this wicked beverage cannot be laid at the door of the immigrant Teuton." [29]

Be that as it may, the newspaper in 1832 was advertising the "Cleveland Brewery now in operation," producing ale and table beer, and offering to furnish nearby farms with barley seed and then to buy the harvest.[30] This particular brewery changed its management many times over. It appears at the beginning to have belonged to Joseph and Richard Hawley,[31] but then, in 1837, that partnership was dissolved, Joseph left the business entirely, and Herrick Childs took his place.[32] The firm Hawley & Childs continued until the end of 1840, when John Hawley Cooke and Thomas Hawley (probably a new generation of the same family) leased the brewery.[33] But in 1843, Childs was announced to be "again in the old establishment." [34] The last newspaper mention of the plant is in 1845, when it is called the "celebrated" Cleveland Brewery, now to be leased.[35] There is a possibility that the brewery was leased, or bought, by S. C. Ives, whose name appears in documents of the 'fifties and 'sixties as proprietor of the Cleveland Brewery, 109 Canal Street, and manufacturer of pale and amber ale, brown stout, porter, beer, and a brand picturesquely called "Beeswing Ale." [36]

Concurrently with the Cleveland Brewery, John M. Hughes was successfully engaged in the brewing industry. The most recent biographer of the city states that Hughes, "a brewer in the 'Flats' [the industrial downtown area of Cleveland], was a passenger on the *Dewitt Clinton* [first steam locomotive of the Mohawk and Hudson Railroad, which formed the nucleus of the New York Central] when it made its trial run from Albany to Schenectady, August 9 [1831]." [37]

"Hughes Ale" made a name for itself through the 'forties and 'fifties, and Hughes continued with apparent success in this business until at least 1878.[38]

Yet another town whose beginnings, in this early nineteenth-century period of tentative industrialization, may appropriately be mentioned is St. Louis. This was of course no newcomer, no upstart of a frontier settlement; it had a French background, tied in with New Orleans and early Mississippi River trading, that started in 1764, when the trader Laclede chose its site for his post. Its history was almost exclusively French when, in 1804, it became American territory along with the rest of the Louisiana Purchase.

In the somewhat earlier settlement of Ste. Genevieve, roughly fifty miles downriver from St. Louis, there had been a brewer as early as 1779. The will of one Michel Livernois, dated 28 December 1779, refers to François Colman as master brewer "en ce dit poste." [39]

It was some years later, April 1810, in fact, that Jacques Delassus de St. Vrain (relative of the last lieutenant governor of Spanish Louisiana) began to brew in St. Louis. The *Missouri Gazette* announced that "Mr. St. Vrain, of Bellefontaine [which later became the location of a cemetery], has erected a manufactory and taken into partnership an experienced European brewer." The prices they asked were $10 cash or $12 in produce for strong beer, $5 in cash or $6 in produce for table beer.[40]

This brewery had a short life, burning down in 1812, and eliciting the following newspaper condolence:

> Thus has a worthy and meritorious citizen been crushed, at a moment when he was on the eve of reaping some advantage from a valuable and useful establishment.[41]

One hopes that St. Vrain had some other strings to his bow, for his will of 10 November 1804 shows him to be the parent of a great brood of children and adoring husband of a wife called Félicité.[42]

A contemporary letter, written by Christian Wilt, a trader in St. Louis at that time, makes some comment on St. Vrain's activity and also gives a general picture of the brewer's problems in that area:

> St. Louis, Dec 26, 1813.
>
> Dear Uncle
> . . . I must confess I do not feel myself competent to answer all yr demands in regard to the requisites necess^y for Brewing, but feel confident that the undertaking wld be advantageous (if carried on with

nec^y funds) in many respects — Barley is not an article raised here in common but cld no doubt be had was encouragement given, a good farmer on the N. Hartford land cld raise a deal of it, but know not the quantity ann^lly used in a Brew^y — St. Vrain had one some time Since & got farmers to raise it — I do not think he pd more than $1. the bush. if he pd that — his Brew^y was Burnt it was near Bellefontaine — Luttig is about erecting one with St. Vrain's brewer — but for want of funds will not do much — it is to be up town — hops can be had, they grow wild & only want gathering or cld be raised on an acre of ground — St. Vrain sold his Beer at $10 or 15 [sic] per bbl, & could not make enough — a great deal cld no doubt be sold — there is ann^y sold 50 or 60 bbls bottled porter cont^g 3 dz each from $37\frac{1}{2}$ or 50 [sic] without the bott. & never enough of it — Sells by the bbl (bottles with) at $6 the dz. — the Garrison wld consume considerable & are supplied by Suttlers — we might perhaps get Coopers here Sufficient — I know one very good one, but a trifling Character — I do not think a proper building could be had & it would be better to build one at N. Hartford where Honey tells me there is a pond, which always has the same quantity of water in it & is on an elevated place, which would answer better than wells. . . . The Situation would do to Supply the mines from — Orleans consumes Porter also — there is a building at N.H. very large without cellar that might be had low but is not in a good situation — I do not thk fixtures cld be procured here & if so not of the right kind — I do not consider it So great a disadvantage as you seem to (the time it wld take) since it wld require sometime to get the farmers into the way of rais^g Barley & since we are not overstocked with funds at present — log buildings might answer for malt house & perhaps a brew^y — St. Vrains was log — which costs not a great deal at N. Hartford. . . .[43]

The "experienced European brewer" who worked for St. Vrain was a man named Victor Hab (sometimes spelled Hobb or Haab), possibly a German by origin, who had a variegated career in St. Louis. His naturalization request, in which he stated that he had come to the United States "29 years since," is unfortunately undated, though it would appear to have been submitted prior to 1833.[44] According to the recollections of Mr. Richard Dowling, Hab lived until 1850.[45]

After the St. Vrain brewery burned down in 1812, Hab was presumably out of work. Adversity had landed him in an unpleasant and distressing situation: he used the newspapers to give notice to his creditors that he intended on 22 June 1812 to apply to the Court of Common Pleas, "to take the benefit of the several acts concerning insolvent debtors, and to be released from my imprisonment, when and where they may attend if they think proper." Evidently this affair ended satisfactorily, for by August of the same year he was sufficiently at liberty to advertise for apprentices: "One or two smart boys to learn the coopering business." [46]

By 1817, he was back in the brewing business, this time working for Joseph Philipson, one of the first Jewish businessmen in St. Louis, whose descendants later played an important part in banking. This brewery

> was situated on the west side of Main Street, about where Carr Street now is. It was in a two story frame building, the last house in the north part of the town. Mr. Philipson's brewer was Victor Hab, . . . The first beer was brewed in the fall of 1817, and was cooled in a pirogue, or 'dug-out [canoe],' which lay outside on the north side of the building.[47]

This brewing operation was apparently profitable enough to keep going for a number of years. In 1819, Victor Hab announced that he was running a beer cart through the streets of St. Louis, "for the purpose of selling beer and vinegar by retail." [48] If the presumption is correct that he was still at that time in the employ of Philipson, it seems quite clear that by 1821 he was out. In about 1820, Philipson formed a partnership with Matthew Murphy and James Nagle, under the name Murphy, Nagle & Co.;[49] since Murphy (or Murphey, as it is sometimes spelled), was a practicing brewer, it is not likely Hab's services were required.

The partnership was not an enduring one; in February 1821, a month after the brewery had sustained a fire (it went back into operation "in a few days"), the partners broke up and Philipson was stated to be continuing on his own.[50]

Not long afterward, the brewery, sometimes referred to simply as the St. Louis Brewery, was taken over by John Mullanphy, an Irishman notable as the city's first multimillionaire. The brewer he used was apparently Matthew Murphy,[51] but he also called on the services of "old Victor Hab" to "bore out a pump" for the brewery. Hab, who is cited among other things as the first pump-maker in St. Louis,[52] did the job and charged $7 for it. Mullanphy decided this was excessive, refused to pay, and Hab sued him for the money. It was, of course, a "matter of principle," so when Hab won his case, Mullanphy appealed; the matter was kept in the courts long enough for Hab to be out about $50 in payments for witnesses.[53] A later record of Hab shows that he was not able to make out on "principle" alone; in 1828, all his property was disposed of in a sheriff's sale.[54]

It is just possible that Mullanphy's was the same St. Louis Brewery that was operated some ten years later by Ezra English and Isaac McHose. This brewery had a cave for keeping the beer cool; it became known as "English Cave" and was later an attraction for sightseers in Benton Park.[55] McHose and English operated until the mid-'forties, in competition with Lynch & Co.,[56] the City Brewery (owned by merchants John and William Finney, with John Dorey as brewer),[57] Metcalfe & Son (advertised as having breweries in Cincinnati* and Louisville as well as St. Louis),[58] and the Fulton Brewery of Wainwright & Coutts.[59] Of all those named, only the last endured, through countless vicissitudes, into the next century.

* See page 164.

⋘ *TWENTY* ⋙

"Lager Bier"

JUST AS the introduction of porter changed the history of English brewing, so, a little more than a hundred years later, the same effect was produced in America by the appearance of lager beer. What this beer was, how it originated here, and why it should have created such a distinct revolution, are questions that are curiously difficult to answer.

In most basic terms, let us say that lager beer represented a German process and a German taste, whereas all the rest of what was being brewed in the nineteenth century — porter, stout and the various ales — represented British tastes and techniques. Lager differs from the British beers in a number of chemical and technical ways, but these were not yet known to the men who first ventured to brew it in the United States sometime in the early 1840s. What they knew was first, that lager, as the German word itself implies, was beer that, properly speaking, was stored through the winter in a cool place and was just right for drinking come spring, and second, that it was manufactured with a yeast which, for reasons mysterious and at that time unfathomable, fermented to the *bottom* of the vat rather than the *top*.

Since the properties of yeast were then unknown, it is hard to see how the particular strain which produced lager was isolated and brought to America, except for some happy accident. One explanation, not so farfetched as it may sound, was ventured by a writer of 1882:

> The editor of a prominent American brewers' gazette makes reply that it was necessary first to bring a peculiar living yeast from Germany; that on a long voyage this yeast would lose its strength and be dead

before its arrival; and that it was only when the Baltimore clipper-ships made the voyage in three weeks that the yeast was imported, and thus lager was first produced in America.[1]

(Modern investigations of yeast show that the bottom-fermenting variety can be kept in ice-cold water for thirty days without losing its power.)[2]

There is, as it happens, no unquestionable documentation relating to the introduction of bottom-fermentaton yeast into this country. The most persuasive theory — that a brewer in Philadelphia, John Wagner, brought the yeast with him from a brewery in Bavaria where he had been brewmaster — is based on the memory of Charles C. Wolf, himself one of the pioneer lager-beer brewers of Philadelphia.

Yeast, at that time, was usually procured by skimming a brew in process of fermentation: it was many years before the establishment of zymological laboratories, which play so decisive a role in the modern brewery. In the case of bottom-fermentation yeasts, presumably the brewer obtained the yeast from the residue left in the vat after the fermented wort had been drawn off.

Whatever the circumstances may have been, it has to be taken for granted that somehow a portion of the yeast used in brewing lager beer was transported from Europe to the United States. There is no intrinsic reason to doubt the word of Charles C. Wolf, though he was recalling events that had taken place something like sixty years earlier; and, generally speaking, one would appreciate corroboration from a second source. "The first lager beer brewed in America," according to Mr. Wolf,

> was that of John Wagner in 1840, who had a small brewery in the rear of his house on St. John street, near Poplar, Philadelphia. It was a very primitive plant indeed, the kettle being hung on a crane over an open hearth, and it had a capacity, I remember, of not over eight barrels. The beer was stored in the cellar under the little rear structure which served as the brewery.[3]

This hardly sounds like a commercial undertaking, but a treat made up for convivial friends from "back home" — just as German bakers in America still make *Baumkuchen* at Christmas time, though non-Germans hardly ever taste it. Such was the start of lager in America, perhaps, but it soon became something more than that. George Manger, who worked for Mr. Wolf, was given some of Wagner's yeast and set up a brewery on Second and New Streets. He continued in this operation until at least 1860, at which time his name appears in the city directories. Through his association with the brewer Peter Schemm,[4] Manger indirectly became a forerunner of the modern C. Schmidt and Sons brewery interests, for Schmidt eventually bought the Schemm plant.

It was in 1844 that Wolf himself, in partnership with Charles Engel, a brewer from Germany, abandoned his sugar refining business and established a lager brewery at 352 and 354 Dillwyn Street. Apparently there was a market for this German beer, even though it is quite clear that the market was virtually restricted to German immigrants. The Engel & Wolf brewery

> was for many years the resort of the Germans of Philadelphia, who more than once drank the brewery dry; and often we were compelled to display the placard that beer would again be dispensed after a certain date. At this locality the first vaults built for the storage of lager beer were completed in 1845. With the steady influx of Germans the business grew and additional cellars were rented under the buildings of the Mitchell grindstone works, at York avenue and Wood street, our annual sales at this time approximating 3,500 barrels.[5]

The German engulfment of the American brewing industry, which began here in the 1840s, had a curious analogy in England at least three centuries before, when the brewing of hopped beer in contrast to the traditional unhopped English ale was practically controlled by German and Dutch brewers.[6] The experience in England was, however, an isolated phenomenon not based, as it was in America, on large-scale immigration.

Germans, as mentioned before, had been leaving their native land in favor of America during the whole of the eighteenth century, though their numbers were only a trickle compared with the great tide of German immigration in the nineteenth century. The early Germans had come mainly for religious reasons; the later ones because of economic distress and sometimes to evade military duty; after the 1848 uprisings in Germany, many came for social and political reasons. America was, of course, the land of golden opportunity as well as (by reputation, in any case) tolerance of religious and social individuality. Besides, immigration was encouraged by American agents, particularly for the purpose of populating the newly opened lands in the Midwest.

A good many of the early German immigrants had formed small communities of their own, pockets of German life and culture which did not participate appreciably in the England-oriented fashions and interests of the Atlantic seaboard. Like all new immigrants, they sought one another out, developed neighborhoods of their own within the American cities, nostalgically kept up their national habits as much as possible. In Braintree there was a Germantown;* in Philadelphia there was a neighborhood of the same name; in Brooklyn there was the "Eastern District, irreverently designated as *Dutchtown*";[7] in Cincinnati, by 1844, there was a district called "Over the Rhine," in the Fifth Ward across the Miami Canal;[8] the corresponding area in Chicago was called the "Dutch settlement."

So many German immigrants had settled in Ohio by 1817 that the state constitution and part of the General Laws had to be printed in a German version.[9]

> After 1825, a steady and increasing stream of Germans settled in the State. By 1830, approximately five per cent. of the population of Cincinnati was German; by 1840, twenty-three per cent.; and by 1850, twenty-seven per cent.[10]

Immigrants had, indeed, been turning up in most unexpected places; in New Orleans, for example, Germans had arrived in the early 1700s. This was a group who had been promised land in Arkansas by John Law. When he failed in 1720, the New Orleans administration offered these Germans small allotments in that town, where they remained to form the nucleus of an important German population.

In 1844, a brave group of Germans under the leadership and idealistic patronage of Carl, Prince of Solms-Braunfels, cousin of Queen Victoria, established a settlement near San Antonio — and this before the annexation of Texas to the United States. Solms-Braunfels, who himself spent some time in the Republic of Texas, compared the plight of

* See page 61.

German emigrants with that of American "squatters," a type of pioneer he did not much respect:

> What with the warm climate and the unaccustomed food, life for them is one of privation and hardship. For the American it is normal living. To the American settler, who generally does not own any more than he actually has on his back, it seems strange that the Germans should burden themselves with so much baggage just to be able to live according to the standard of comfort of their own country.

He admired the American pioneer for his skill with a rifle, by means of which he could keep himself supplied with game. The American also had an advantage over the German in knowing how to handle the native beasts of burden, which were not "by any means as tame as those in Germany." [11] In every possible way, he points out how demanding the pioneer life was.

> It is hard for the settler who is used to the European life to shake off the comfort and ease of life in which even the ordinary farmer of Germany grows up, and to supplant it with the difficulties and hardships of prairie life in Texas.

At home, though the farmer worked hard, he could at least go back to a warm house, "and after his evening meal and a glass of beer or wine he can go upstairs to his room and stretch his tired limbs on a bed, even though it be only a mattress of straw." But in Texas, after a day of hard labor, "there is no strengthening drink of beer or wine on the table whereby he could refresh himself." [12]

One has to allow for the fact that this was a patrician princeling speaking about conditions (as far as Germany went) that must have been far outside his ken. However, it was his intention to warn prospective immigrants of the hardships to be faced; he did not want to deceive. Once settled, he wrote, the immigrant could find numerous advantages in Texas: everything was cheap, food was abundant, the land was prodigiously fertile.

> The only thing that is really expensive is wine, beer, and any kind of alcoholic drinks. The beer is imported from the United States, and is very strong. One calls this kind of beer ale. I do not think it can be kept in a good condition during summer.[13]

The settlement did not quite live up to the young prince's expectations, but long after he had returned to Germany, it endured and, in fact, grew, even after Texas was incorporated as a state of the Union. Considering the hardship, expressed by Solms-Braunfels, of doing without real German beer to comfort the farmer after his daily toil, it is no wonder that a superior lager was brewed in San Antonio in about 1855, when the German brewer and cooper William A. Menger set up business there. It was probably the first brewery in San Antonio, though Menger is now remembered rather for the fine hotel he built and operated on Alamo Square. There is one theory that the brewery "attracted so many customers from out of town that Menger had to build the hotel to shelter them." [14] His brewery is supposed to have been so famous that "orders for it came from all over Texas, and his men delivered the golden brew in wagon trains and even ox-carts." [15]

By 1856, it is reported, almost a third of San Antonio's citizens were German-born. They established beer-gardens, a typically German form of sociability, and in 1865 started a German-language newspaper, *Freie Presse*.[16]

This, of course, was what happened in all areas of German concentration: newspapers, beer-gardens, singing societies, and *Turnvereine* (gymnastic clubs). As the lager breweries grew, they themselves installed beer-gardens for the comfort and enjoyment of their customers. This was true, for example, in Staten Island, New York, where the beer-gardens attached to breweries in Castleton and Southfield were visited, mainly on Sundays, by Germans living in Manhattan and neighboring areas.[17]

The Bowery in New York City became particularly famous for a number of beer-gardens that were established on that street in the 1860s.

> We refer to those of the better class, which are patronized chiefly by the German element of the city. These are immense buildings, fitted up in imitation of a garden. . . . They will accommodate from four hundred to twelve hundred guests. Germans carry their families there to spend a day, or an evening.[18]

These beer-gardens are generally spoken of approvingly, because they provided entertainment for simple hard-working families, and offered a wholesome antidote to the corrupt and licentious gin-dives or "dancing parlours" that were also current in New York and other cities. At the beer-gardens, entrance was free:

> Beer and other liquids are served out at a small cost. . . . The music is a great attraction to the Germans. It is exquisite in some places, especially in the Atlantic Garden, which is situated in the Bowery, near Canal Street.[19]

Like all minority groups, however, the Germans were made to feel "different" because of their difficulties with the language, because of their social habits, because they were *foreign*. Even their love of lager was ridiculed in a lithograph, about 1850, called "The Follies of the Age, Vive le Humbug," in which there appears a flag saying "LAGER BEER, allowed to drink 48 glasses," and a German (brutally caricatured) is saying to a policeman: "I trinks Lager, and I have only trunk tirty glasses, so you shust go avay." [20] They were also lumped together with all other immigrants, such as the Irish and Jews, who paid no attention to the Puritan feeling that the Sabbath was a day for solitary meditation, rather than a day for "labor meetings, for excursions, for saloons, beer-gardens, baseball games and carousels." [21]

Such treatment has, as one knows, traditionally been offered to every minority group in its time, and the Germans withstood the taunts or bristled at them, as the case may be, as successfully as any of the others. This treatment, which was not, of course, by any means universal, did have the tendency to give the Germans an even stronger and longer-lasting sense of sentimental clannishness than they might otherwise have had.

A contemporary view of the German situation is given in the manuscript diary kept by George Herancourt (who later became a prominent lager brewer in Cincinnati) upon his arrival in the United States from Germany in 1830.

> New York, 1 September: I went with my Swabian [traveling companion] through the city and looked for a job in a brewery. We visited 7 masters, and were everywhere one month too early, since brewing does not start before October. . . .

4 September: We arrive at 10 o'clock in Philadelphia. There are two brewers here from Baden and another from Weissenburg.

Philadelphia, 5 September: . . . In an inn we had 2 or 3 bottles of porter, in America there is not too much good stuff to drink. . . . Ale and porter are the best kind of the five sorts they have here. . . .

Philadelphia, 8 September: I met a fellow who has already been here 2 years, a brewer from Landau. . . . He has an injured foot and cannot work. If he had the money he would go back to Europe.

24 September: As far as food and the living-standard go, a farmer lives here better than a prince in Germany.

Reading, 27 September: We visited a brewery [possibly George Lauer's, established in 1826]. . . . The brew-master was a German. . . . I went with the farmer's hand to the mill and watched until the malt had swelled.

29 September: Nikolaus Sprenger wanted me to work at his father's brewery 40 miles from Reading, but I preferred to return to Philadelphia.

1 October: I asked at some breweries for a job, but all the places are already promised to others. Five brewers alone are expected from Germany and await a job.

2 October: I was told that there are 20 breweries in Philadelphia, I went to all of them and could not find work anywhere. Here you don't have to be a trained brewer; the main thing is, can you work. Most of the men employed in the breweries are married; they work in the breweries during the winter, and in the summer at sugar-refineries or other factories.

10-16 October: I am promised a job for Tuesday two weeks from now in a brewery with Bartenheimer.

6 November: The job I was promised in the brewery was given to someone else, and I tried in vain to get a job with a cooper. I would not have minded so much, if the brewer had not engaged a fellow who is a miller.

7 November: . . . Zigler told me to see Bartenheimer. His partner asked for me yesterday. When I arrived, he told me that his maltster had fallen ill and if I felt fit, I should come the next morning for work.

14-20 November: On Tuesday afternoon he told me he would pay me 6 dollars a week, but I should sleep there, on Sundays I should work on the malt. . . . But I found out that this is very hard work, much harder than in Germany.

21-27 November: . . . The maltster who had my job is well again and asked the master for work. Since he was paid in advance, and had a family, I was told by the two gentlemen that they had to take the man back. After some hard figuring I got 19 dollars and 20 cents.[22]

TWENTY-ONE

The First Lager Brewers

IN VIEW OF the German love of beer, it is perhaps surprising that lager was not brewed here before 1840. Indeed, the writer of 1882 already referred to tried to make out a case for the existence of lager beer in the eighteenth century; specifically, he conjectured that the New York Palatines and the Barnitz family in York and Baltimore might have brewed lager — simply because they were Germans and *must* have known how.[1] There is no evidence, however, to support this picturesque assumption; and it is clear that, when lager beer did reach the market in the nineteenth century, it was regarded (and for a relatively long time) as something entirely new and original in the beer line.

The manufacture of lager was attempted — on a small scale, to be sure — when there were sufficient numbers of Germans in various urban localities, or even country villages, to make it worthwhile. Large German populations existed, and were being constantly increased, during the 'forties and 'fifties, in Philadelphia, New York, Cincinnati, St. Louis, Chicago, Milwaukee, and certain other fast-growing cities; and it is in exactly these cities that lager, at roughly the same time, was making its debut.

In the decade between 1840 and 1850, when Croton water was introduced into the city, New Yorkers saw tentative moves in the direction of lager brewing being made by George Gillig (whose daughter later married brewer Jacob Ruppert, Sr.) and the Schaefer brothers, Frederick and Maximilian, who were soon afterward to make a phenomenal success of their business.[2]

In St. Louis, it appears to have been Adam Lemp who introduced lager beer. Starting as a grocer, he branched out into the manufacture of beer and vinegar (a not uncommon combination at the time), thus laying the foundation of one of the great St. Louis brewing fortunes.[3]

A German immigrant with a name of various spellings — Herman Riedelschoefer, Reuthlisberger, Reutelshoefer, Reidelschofer — is often credited with being the first to venture into lager brewing in Milwaukee. His operation is virtually undocumented, but writers some years after the event claim to have discovered that the funds for the enterprise were provided by John B. Meyer, and the location of the brewery was the corner of Hanover and Virginia Streets. Herman R. was unable to make the business pay, and so it reverted to Meyer, who in turn sold it to Francis Neukirch (also variously spelled in the city directories) in about 1847.[4] A newspaper account of 1872 takes up the story: "On the death of the latter [Neukirch] the establishment passed into the hands of his son-in-law, C. T. Melms, who for years carried on an extensive business in a new location." [5] It is one of the frequent curiosities to be found in the history of American brewing that this plant was eventually bought in 1870 for $30,000 by Best & Company (originators of the Pabst business),[6] who have since generally come to be considered the earliest brewers of lager in Milwaukee.[7]

In Cincinnati, a new brewery for the production of lager, named Fortmann & Company, was announced in 1844 as one of the recent buildings in the "Over the Rhine" section of the city.[8] The pioneer of lager brewing in St. Paul was a Bavarian, Anton Yoerg, whose business continued until 1952.[9]

A brewery for lager set up in Pittsburgh by Frederick Krauss in 1850 became known in later years as the Kaltenhaeusser Brewery.[10] Detroit was supposedly introduced to lager by a recent arrival from Germany, Frederick Ams, in about 1848.[11] And the Germans in Chicago were first served their favorite beverage by John A. Huck and John Schneider, who began their lager business there in 1847.[12] Even Boston, in 1846, had a large enough German population to make John Roessle consider it a practical idea to start a lager brewery there.[13]

In spite of these, and many other, lager breweries sprouting in various parts of the country, it must not be assumed that lager simply took over the industry from the moment of its introduction. In almost every case, the lager brewers began on an extremely small scale. An expert on Milwaukee history wrote of the firm started by Jacob Best in 1844: "The product and sales of the brewery were necessarily small, being limited to two or three hundred barrels per year, and intended only to meet a local demand." [14] The general reception of lager, according to I. D. Guyler, "was not a welcome one." [15] In fact, lager did not make serious inroads into the popularity of English-style beers until the mid-'fifties.

The really important and successful breweries of the pre-Civil War period were the ale manufacturers — though this was, unknown to them, their swan song.

The leading brewery in Chicago was clearly that of Lill & Diversey, whose ale had established a widespread reputation. It was described in 1861 as "far ahead of any similar establishment in the West." Its capital at that time was given as $300,000; the building occupied two city blocks; its products were sold "as far east as Buffalo, north, to Lake Superior and St. Paul, west, to St. Joseph, Mo., and previous to our National troubles [the Civil War], to New Orleans." [16] In 1860, sales came to 44,780 barrels of ale, stout and porter, a phenomenal figure when compared with the best that Milwaukee was able to manage six years later: 15,159 barrels sold by Valentin Blatz.[17]

Another well-known brewer of ale in Chicago was J. J. Sands, who, in 1855, built the "Columbian Brewery" on the corner of Pine and Pearson Streets.[18] Sands apparently did so well in this venture that four years later he bought the Spring Brewery in Milwaukee.[19] This was probably the brewery started in the early 'forties by Levi Blossom, of New York, and operated by him and his brother Alonzo until about 1853.[20] It appears again in the 1857-1858 directory under the proprietorship of Matthew Middlewood and Pearson Gibson; it was from Middlewood that Sands made his purchase. The local newspaper, pleased to have a new advertiser in town, wrote:

> The Messrs. SANDS, of Chicago, have been eminently successful in manufacturing a beverage combining all the wholesome qualities of English porter, without any of its deleterious characteristics. They have produced an article of ale, which has become a staple of commerce all

over the Union, and is universally acknowledged by good judges to be a healthier and better drink than the imported bottled beers.

The manager of this Spring Brewery, on Eighth, Chestnut and Prairie Streets, was John G. Sands, "one of four brothers," the newspaper added, "all brewers, one living in Lansingburg, one in Troy and one in Chicago." [21]

Sands was not the first ale brewer in Milwaukee: the brewery of Richard G. Owens, William Pallet (or Pawlett) and John Davis, called first the Milwaukee Brewery and then the Lake Brewery, was established in 1840, thus preceding all others. These were three Welshmen who brewed on the traditional British principles, making ale their specialty. The following account of 1881 gives some details of their beginnings:

> The barley used was brought from Michigan City [Ind.] by Mr. Owens in a small sloop called the "Ranger." This was not only the beginning of the business in Milwaukee, but was also the first in the Territory of Wisconsin. . . . [The business] was general in its character, embracing the brewing of ale, porter and beer and the distillation of Scotch whisky, although ale was the principal product. At that time the prices for such goods ranged from $5 per barrel for beer to $7 for ale and $2 per gallon for whisky. The original brew-kettle was constructed of a wooden box lined with copper, which had a capacity of five barrels. In January, 1841, Mr. Owens went to Chicago, with a team, and obtained a copper kettle holding twelve barrels. The trip required four days' time. There was then no coppersmith in Milwaukee, but in 1844 a kettle was made in this place, by which the capacity of the brewery was increased to forty barrels. [22]

In 1845, "in consequence of the great demand for beer," the proprietors had to build a large building in front of the original brewery. [23] Eventually Owens bought out his two partners. In 1864 the plant was rented to M. W. Powell, a brewer from Chicago, and Owen Pritchard; these two men bought the brewery and ran it as M. W. Powell & Co. until 1880, when they abandoned it "because the brewing of ale was less profitable than that of lager beer." [24] By 1867, Powell's was the only ale being brewed in Milwaukee. [25]

The leading brewers of Albany before the Civil War were John Taylor & Sons, Quinn & Nolan, and the Boyd Brothers.* Taylor had started out

* See page 129.

in partnership with Lancelot Fiddler in 1824, producing the then huge amount of 250 barrels a day. By the time he had shed his partner and built a new brewery in 1851, his was claimed (momentarily, of course) to be the largest brewery in the world.[26] James Quinn set up his ale brewery in Albany in 1845, and operated it until 1866, when it came into the proprietorship of Michael N. Nolan and T. J. Quinn.[27] Yet another ale brewer began in Albany in a modest way: Peter Ballantine, who took over the old Robert Dunlop brewery in about 1833 and conducted a business there until 1840, when he moved to Newark, bought a brewery established in 1805 by General John N. Cumming, and thus set the stage for one of the most spectacularly successful of all American breweries.[28]

The city of Utica, New York, with a population of 12,782 in 1840, had at least one sizable brewery, Michael McQuade's Gulf Brewery, which was listed in the 1843-1844 directory and continued — at least as a business name — until Prohibition in 1919. James McIntosh was one of McQuade's brewers, John Myers was his maltster, and the name Thomas Mann appears as "agent for Gulf Brewery." There was also the Oneida Brewery, owned at that time by Stephen Thorn & Co., on State Street; Ralph George is listed as a brewer for this concern. In addition there were a number of independent operators, including three whose occupation is given as "small beer maker." [29]

In Pittsburgh, the Wainwright Brewery was among the leaders, along with the Pittsburgh Brewery and the Shiras family,* all ale brewers. It was in 1818 that the Yorkshireman Joseph Wainwright started his brewery with a capacity of about a hundred barrels a year. It continued in operation, a family business, until 1899, when it was one of the several breweries that merged into the Pittsburgh Brewing Company.[30]

It was a son of Joseph Wainwright, Samuel, who, after serving an apprenticeship under his father, went to St. Louis in 1846 and bought the small Fulton Brewery there, at the corner of Main and Almond Streets.

> In company with his brother, Ellis Wainwright, he conducted the brewing business thus established under the firm name of Ellis &

* See pages 131-134.

Samuel Wainwright until 1849, when Ellis Wainwright died. . . . In 1848, George Busch had established a malt-house and a lager beer brewery at the corner of Third and Plum Streets, and later, had constructed extensive beer-cellars between Ninth and Tenth Streets, on Gratiot and Cerre Streets. In 1854, he erected what was considered in those days a large brewery on the square of ground under which these vaults had been constructed and, a year later, associated Charles A. Fritz with him in business. Samuel Wainwright purchased Mr. Busch's interest in this plant in 1857, and the firm thus formed took the name of Fritz & Wainwright and, abandoning the manufacture of ale and beer by English processes, engaged exclusively in the manufacture of lager beer.[31]

Wainwright is one of the examples of ale and porter manufacturers (and their numbers increased rapidly about that time) who could see the handwriting on the wall, even before the Civil War, a period when manufacturers of lager beer began to swamp all others.

Yet the ale brewers kept on opening new establishments: the Johnson Brewery in Brooklyn, inaugurated in 1850, made ale exclusively until 1897;[32] the firm of Poultney, Collins & Massey, in 1849, took over the old Farmers' Brewery at Tenth and Filbert Streets in Philadelphia,[33] in Syracuse, the Greenway Brewing Company was started in 1853 by the Englishman John Greenway,[34] and by 1859, it had succeeded so well that it was reportedly manufacturing 50,000 barrels a year, 20,000 more than so well-established a firm as Vassar's Brewery in Poughkeepsie.[35] The Detroit City Directory for 1853-1854 carried the advertisements of four ale brewers: Hawley & Co., William C. Duncan ("Central Brewery"), J. Mason, and P. Tregent & Co.

But by the mid-'fifties it became possible to see that lager would eventually outsell ale and porter in the United States. The figures reported for Philadelphia in 1857 were 180,000 barrels of lager manufactured, as contrasted with 170,000 barrels of ale, stout and porter.[36] In Illinois, lager was fast catching up, according to 1861 statistics: 350,000 barrels of ale and 250,000 barrels of lager.[37] Ale had never been able to compete with lager in German-dominated Milwaukee, and in 1866, only 3600 barrels were brewed, while over 68,000 barrels of lager had been sold in the same year.[38]

A general description of the industry, in this period on the brink of the Civil War, is given by the historian Victor S. Clark:

The largest plants now had a capacity approaching 200,000 barrels per annum. Steam was used for heating and sterilizing, as well as for driving pumps and elevators, and refrigeration made it possible to brew a uniform product throughout the year. . . . Technical as well as commercial conditions were already centralizing this manufacture [brewing] and preparing the way for its transfer to the neighborhood of the grain and hop fields of the West.[39]

❧ TWENTY-TWO ☙

The Origins of Prohibition

ALMOST AS a counterpoise to the first signs of growth in the brewing industry, there appeared on the scene a movement destined at length to bring about the industry's temporary ruin. The signal date is 1826: on 13 February of that year was formed in the city of Boston the American Society for the Promotion of Temperance, generally known as the American Temperance Society. This event, spearheaded by Justin Edwards, pastor of the Park Street Church in the same city, was the culmination of scattered temperance activity which had started some years before.[1]

The temperance adherents themselves often give credit to Dr. Benjamin Rush for providing impetus to the movement. "To his labors," writes one of the temperance historians, "the nineteenth-century worldwide temperance movement can be traced by lines of direct influence." [2] The fact that Rush protested the use of ardent spirits and recommended drinking in their place cider, malt liquors and wines* was conveniently disregarded in the years that followed, although at the start of the temperance movement — i.e., before 1826 — ardent spirits were the sole target. The object of the Massachusetts Society for the Suppression of Intemperance, for example, when it drew up its constitution in 1813, was to "discountenance and suppress the too free use of ardent spirits." [3] Even further back, in 1808, when members of the Congregational Church in Moreau, Saratoga County, New York, formed the first rudi-

* See page 120.

mentary organization of this kind, called the Temperance Society of Moreau and Northumberland, they pledged themselves only to use "no rum, gin, whisky, wine or any distilled spirits, or compositions of the same, except by advice of a physician, or in cases of actual disease." [4]

It was thirty years from then, according to the temperance view, when it was discovered (or decided) "that the only logical basis of the temperance movement is entire abstinence from *all* intoxicants." [5] There are two factors here to be noted: the movement intended, in the beginning, only to oppose excess in the use of ardent spirits, and its object was, again in the beginning, exactly what was stated: *temperance*, or moderation. Total abstinence was a later idea, but the word "temperance" went on being used with such insistence that its very meaning came to be a source of confusion.

The original movement was instigated by men of religion: Rev. Lyman Beecher, Rev. Timothy Dwight (president of Yale University), Rev. Francis Wayland (first president of Brown University), Rev. Calvin Chapin, and many others were distinguished figures among its founders. The first permanent paid agent of the American Temperance Society was Rev. Nathaniel Hewitt of Fairfield, Connecticut — called by his admirers "the Luther of the early temperance reform." The society's first newspaper, the *National Philanthropist*, was founded by a Baptist minister, Rev. William Collier.[6]

This was a genuinely religious movement, from which only the Lutheran, Episcopal and Roman Catholic Churches originally kept aloof.* At the outset it obtained its greatest support in New England, where a peculiarly Puritan (in the modern, not the original, sense) strain of social responsibility, abstemiousness, sanctimony, do-goodism and moral severity — all uncomfortably and incompatibly combined — had taken hold. It was also part of the general reform fervor of the nineteenth century, and in case after case its adherents supported abolition and women's rights as well. Its technique was, at this stage, simply "moral suasion." By exhortation, education and example, its members hoped to convince people to stop or not to start drinking.

---

* The only prominent Catholic in the early movement was Father Theobald Mathew, who came to the United States in 1849, after a successful temperance career in Ireland, and proselytized here for two years.

The American Temperance Society, operating along these lines, had an immediate success. By the end of 1829, it claimed 100,000 members. A New York Temperance Society was organized in that city under the sponsorship of Edward C. Delavan in 1828, and in the same year another president of Yale, Rev. Jeremiah Day, headed a Connecticut Temperance Society. There were reported to be more than five thousand temperance societies in the United States at the beginning of 1833, with a membership of a million and a quarter.[7] It was claimed that thousands of distilleries had gone out of business, and a great number of merchants had been persuaded to stop selling spirituous liquors.

That same year, the temperance movement was given a big boost by the formation of the American Congressional Temperance Society, at the behest of Senators Theodore Frelinghuysen of New Jersey, Felix Grundy of Tennessee, Arnold Naudain of Delaware, a number of representatives, and Lewis Cass of Michigan, then the Secretary of War and in 1848 the unsuccessful Presidential candidate of the Democratic Party.[8] Similar societies quickly sprang up in state legislatures; and indeed temperance societies were started in all sorts of places: in colleges, in factories, among Negro groups, women and even children.[9]

At a national convention in Philadelphia in 1833, the national society changed its name to the United States Temperance Union, but at the following convention, which took place in Saratoga in 1836, it became known as the American Temperance Union, in order to be able to include in its organization any country on the North American continent.[10] It was at this 1836 convention that the principle of total abstinence, or "teetotalism," was finally enunciated. It had been in practice previously in many of the local societies, but had not, before this date, been made part of the national society's program. The term "teetotal" is supposed to have been used first* in one of the local societies at Hector, New York, which had two classes of members: those abstaining only from spirits, whose names were marked O.P. (old pledge) on the roll, and those who included wine in their pledge. The latter were identified with the letter T for Total.[11]

---

* Another theory is that the word originated at a temperance meeting in Preston, England, in 1833, when one of the (stammering) members came out for a "t-total" pledge.

The American Temperance Union came out of its Saratoga convention with good reason for feeling confident in its future, but in fact it had merely glossed over a number of disagreements among its ranks which kept it for many years from being as effective and aggressive as it might have been. There were three basic sources of dissension, out of which all the minor disputes grew: (1) Should the Union fight for abstention from all alcoholic beverages or only from spirituous liquors? (2) Should it use political means or continue its reliance on moral suasion? (3) Could Southern members go along with those of New England who were also fierce abolitionists? [12] These questions had to be answered on the local level, by the rank and file, with the result that uniformity of purpose was considerably weakened.

The first skirmish between the temperance forces and the brewing industry took place in 1840, when John Taylor, owner of the important ale-brewing concern in Albany, brought suit for libel against Edward C. Delavan,* retired Albany wine merchant and prominent prohibitionist, who had accused the Taylor brewery of using filthy water in the malting process.

Delavan had made such a statement in 1835 and was challenged to publish it; he did so in the *Evening Journal* of 12 February 1835. His accusation was against the firm of Fiddler and Taylor (who were then in partnership), as well as the malting establishment of Robert Dunlop; and the substance of his accusation was that their malthouses were "being supplied with water for malting from stagnant pools, gutters and ditches . . . water was often taken from puddles in which were dead animals. . . ." [13] Delavan, it might be noted, had made an avocation out of detecting noxious elements in liquor, had published a book on so-called adulterations, and had attributed the characteristic "nutty flavor" of Madeira to a bag of roaches being dissolved in the wine.[14]

For some reason, the trial was delayed for five years. When it finally took place, the evidence on both sides was weakened by the lapse of time; and a reading of the text of the trial also gives one reason to suspect that witnesses on both sides had been bribed. Well-known Albany brewers, such as Garret W. Ryckman, John McKnight and John G.

* See page 193.

White, gave evidence, but there was no consistency in their testimony. Some tried to say that it didn't matter if the water used in malting *was* impure, and others maintained that only pure water could make good malt and beer.[15] Other witnesses claimed that the pools from which water was drawn were not stagnant or putrid; and witnesses for the plaintiff (Taylor) claimed that water used for malting was not, in any case, drawn from those pools. The case was most ineptly prepared on both sides, and most difficult to disentangle. The jury, however, found for Delavan, so that Taylor, who had sued for $300,000, lost not only a good deal of money but also a great part of his reputation, though it did not prevent him from building the (then) "largest brewery in the world." *

The temperance group had good cause to crow over the outcome of this trial; but on the other hand, their movement was bogged down with dissension. Unexpectedly it received a welcome injection of enthusiasm when a group of reformed drunkards in Baltimore established a fraternal organization in 1840, which they called the Washington Temperance Society. The group, which quickly grew in numbers, was called "The Washingtonians" or "The Washington Revival." [16]

This was a movement which began and operated outside church groups; it had, indeed, a wider appeal than any purely religious organization could have. The best way to describe it in modern terms is to call it the Alcoholics Anonymous of its time. It was established by and for reformed drunks: "every-where the reformed men who went about telling their own experience and salvation from the power of liquor found large and attentive audiences." [17] One of the Washingtonians' most effective spellbinders, John B. Gough, wrote of his feelings after taking the pledge in 1842: "Now I was not altogether alone in the world." [18] This expresses with curious exactness what members of A.A. feel when they first join — that there are other alcoholics in the world besides themselves.

This may go a long way toward explaining the great success enjoyed by the Washingtonian movement. This free-wheeling organization, at one time or another, claimed to include among its membership Lincoln,

---

* See pages 187-188.

Grant and Hayes.[19] Whatever significance may be drawn from these claims, there can be no doubt that the Washingtonians exercised a phenomenal appeal in many sections of American society. These were not ministers, reformers, do-gooders talking to "sinners," but "sinners" themselves who, by the simple device of pledging complete abstinence, had reformed themselves. The Washingtonians were particularly fortunate in having in their ranks such zealous and effective speakers as John H. W. Hawkins and the aforementioned Gough, who enjoyed a long and profitable career lecturing up and down America as well as Europe. Gough's power was so great that, in spite of a sordid relapse in 1845, when he turned up in a New York City brothel after nearly a week's disappearance, his somewhat tarnished reputation did not injure his popularity or effectiveness.[20] On the temperance side, the incident was sloughed off in the following words: "John B. Gough is ensnared by a trick of his enemies and becomes intoxicated." [21]

For all the successful ballyhoo, it was clear to members of the original temperance movement that the Washingtonians were not properly organized to bring lasting strength to the cause. It was worrisome that so many of the "reformed" had lapses, and so frequently. There was also resentment among those whose reform impulse was basically religious.[22] These elements particularly criticized the more militant and secret fraternal organizations that had emerged out of the Washingtonian movement: the Sons of Temperance, the Independent Order of Rechabites, the Order of Good Templars.[23] These, however, continued their activities in ways that suited themselves, and in 1843 there was added to the group a women's order, Daughters of Temperance,[24] outgrowth of the 1841 Martha Washington Temperance Society, the first organization of women in a cause which they were later to make practically their own.

The American temperance movement had now encompassed three progressive stages: moderation, abstinence and prohibition. The agitation, in the 1840s, was to prohibit the sale of liquor by law; and this went far enough to introduce in many places that particularly obnoxious legal device, local option. It was especially effective in Massachusetts, in which, by 1842, there was only one county where the sale of spirituous liquor was licensed. The reason it was such an irritating device to the liquor manufacturers is that it was forever changing: one year a county would vote "dry," and the next "wet." Besides, there was some question whether the licensing laws, as practiced, were constitutional, and suits to test them, arising in the New England states, were taken on appeal to the Supreme Court in 1845. In spite of the efforts of Daniel Webster and Rufus Choate as counsel for the liquor industry, the Court upheld the states' right to license the sale of intoxicating beverages, and by implication sustained the principle of local option.[25]

This signal success for the temperance forces was followed up the next year by another and even more telling success: the passage of a prohibition law in the state of Maine. This was brought about through the efforts of the Quaker Neal Dow, later mayor of Portland, Maine, and one of the strongest leaders of the prohibitionists. Dow had participated in the temperance movement since 1829, and from 1833 in various official capacities.[26] It was he who led a radical group out of the Maine State Temperance Society (which refused to embrace total abstinence from all intoxicants) to form the more militant Maine Temperance Union in 1837. He was a thoroughgoing prohibitionist, completely opposed to those who upheld the principle of moral suasion.[27] By hard work, aggressiveness and implacability, he finally managed to get enough prohibitionists elected to the state legislature for a prohibition bill to be passed — in 1846.[28] When this bill was found to be weak in many of its provisions, Dow and his cohorts undertook strictly political means to bring about its revision. As Governor Dana vetoed a bill passed in 1849 that would have added restrictions to the existing bill, the Dow camp set about replacing him at the next election with a more amenable governor. Dow also got himself elected mayor of Portland in order to show how efficiently the prohibition law could be enforced — where there was a will. And in June 1851, the new governor signed what was considered a more workable prohibition law, and it was this law, according to a prohibition apologist, "from which the history of prohibition legislation really dates." [29] Another writer credits this law with changing the whole course of the temperance movement:

> Until then the movement had been a primarily spiritual crusade striving for the millennium of universal personal abstinence; from that point forward it became primarily a political campaign directed toward an ultimate goal of universal legal prohibition.[30]

The "Maine Law" was used as a model for similar prohibition acts which were launched and enacted in various of the states shortly afterward: in 1852 the Territory of Minnesota ratified a "Maine Law," but it lasted only a short time; Rhode Island followed suit in the same year (repealed in 1863); also Massachusetts (repealed in 1868, re-enacted in 1869, repealed again in 1875) and Vermont. Michigan passed a prohibition law in 1853; Connecticut in 1854; New York, New Hampshire, Nebraska Territory, Delaware, Indiana, and Iowa in 1855. Sooner or later, all of these were declared unconstitutional or were repealed.[31] The mere fact, however, that they could be rammed through not-too-unwilling legislatures indicated that the prohibition movement was finding support at a rate that must have alarmed the liquor and brewing industries. The drys seemed to be rolling ahead without opposition, but this was not entirely true, because by 1855 their chariot ran out of fuel and chugged to a halt. The prohibitionists themselves found it difficult to explain this phenomenon.

> It is a remarkable fact that after New Hampshire passed her prohibition law in August 1855, not another state adopted it for over a quarter of a century and most of the states which enacted prohibitory laws in the first half of the fifties went back upon them.[32]

The reason given for the decline of prohibitionism in this period are complex, but boil down to these factors in combination: (1) the problem of abolition took precedence just about now, (2) the prohibition laws, as enacted, had been unenforceable in most of the states, and (3) the prohibition agitators were not yet sophisticated in the ways of political infiltration and influence.[33] Each of these causes in itself would have been enough to put a brake to the movement: in concert, they were ineluctable. The prohibitionists had to regroup, reconsider, re-establish themselves; they were delayed by war; and this delay gave the brewing industry a much-needed breathing space in which to properly develop its production potential.

The Pacific Coast

THE DRIVE toward the West, which characterized the settlement of America practically from its very origin, had never abated, though it was stronger and more persistently implemented in some periods than others. In the years between 1830 and 1860, however, there was a particularly widespread migration ever farther west, and this became formulated politically in the policies of Expansionism and "Manifest Destiny." First the farmlands of Illinois, Indiana and Wisconsin invited the ambitious or the homeless or the foreign; but later, especially after the panic of 1837 and the ensuing depression in the Mississippi Valley, it was the Far West and Texas where the grass began to look a lot greener. Then, in 1848, the discovery of gold on the land of the Sacramento Valley trader John Sutter was like the gunshot at the start of a race: the rush began.

The Oregon Territory, claimed by both the British and American governments, received its first real group of pioneers in 1843, when about a thousand men, women and children made the overland trek (accompanied, no doubt, by the shades of Lewis and Clark) from Independence, Missouri, to Fort Vancouver and the Willamette Valley. The success of this journey, in spite of its immense hardships, encouraged other brave souls to emulate it.

The British, though naturally resentful of this unilateral attempt to settle the ownership dispute by means of peaceful invasion, made a realistic and amicable agreement in 1846, by which the 49th Parallel was established as the border with Canada. There were at that time some 5000 Americans living in Oregon Territory.

Among these settlers were a good many Germans — enough of them, at least by 1852, for a brewing business to be started by Henry Saxer, who had come there from a Swiss town in Illinois called Highland.[1] Mr. Saxer's brewery functioned until 1862, when it was bought by Henry Weinhard, a German immigrant who had come to Portland in 1857 by way of Philadelphia, Cincinnati, St. Louis and California. Weinhard found work, upon his arrival in Oregon, with John Meany, called at that time "the leading brewer of the coast north of San Francisco."[2] The Meany brewery was in Vancouver, across the Columbia River, in what later became the state of Washington. After working here for two years Weinhard bought out Meany's interest, and had a substantial success on his own, before he took over the Portland brewery of Saxer, in partnership with George Bottler, thus instituting a family business which has been in continual operation (except for Prohibition years) ever since.[3]

During the period when he was operating the Vancouver brewery, Weinhard was selling some of his (presumably) lager beer in Astoria and The Dalles, towns which for a time challenged the supremacy of Portland. According to his day books, he charged fifty cents a gallon for his beer, sold in kegs of five, six, eight or ten gallons. He also noted here that Henry Ludwig (who later branched out independently in Portland) worked for him during 1858 and 1859 at a salary of fifty dollars a month.[4]

In 1858 he was buying hops and malt from San Francisco, and his account book for that same year shows that he was dealing with various saloons, had customers in Cascades and Walla Walla, and that he sold some of his hops to his future partner George Bottler, who was probably engaged in some small brewing activity of his own in Portland.[5]

Weinhard's real success began in the 1860s when he finally disposed of the Vancouver brewery and settled down in Portland with the intention of building up an important brewing operation there, and it was in these years that he faced the competition of Henry Ludwig (Liberty Brewery), John Meier (Philadelphia Brewery) and John Philippi, who apparently took over the Liberty Brewery in 1865.[6] The brewing industry made great advances during the second part of the nineteenth century in Portland, as in most other cities; Weinhard, it may be said, was consistently among the leaders.

Brewing had less importance in that area of the Oregon Territory which ultimately became the state of Washington. There is one report of a brewery established as early as 1855 in Walla Walla by Emil Meier, who maintained it until 1871, and then sold out to John H. Stahl.[7] This would appear to have been a minor operation, in view of the fact that Weinhard was also supplying customers in that town.

The date of the first brewery in Seattle is given vaguely as "prior to the spring of 1864"; it was called the Washington Brewery, under the proprietorship of A. B. Rabbeson & Company, and produced porter, beer and cream ale.[8] And in 1858, the little town of Steilacoom, close neighbor to Tacoma and settled two years before the larger city (1850), saw the foundation of a primitive brewery by a German, Martin Schmieg (or Schmeig), an event which was "accepted by the people of Steilacoom as an unusual recognition of the community's growing importance." [9] Not long afterward Schmieg, apparently feeling he had gone as far as was possible in little Steilacoom, sold out and moved on to Seattle, where he established another brewery.

These various efforts to produce and sell beer in the area of Washington were obviously on a restricted scale, probably reflecting its sparsity of population. It was not until the 1870s, when the number of settlers began to rise rapidly, that industries became practicable there.

California, on the other hand, had a much earlier history of settlement and activity, going back to the days of Spanish and then Mexican dominion. Even when that valuable stretch of land was being controlled by missions, *rancheros* and scattered Mexican soldiers, American nationals, between 1825 and 1846, had been establishing toeholds of authority, at least in the northern parts of the province and in the ports on the coast. Thomas A. Larkin, for example, had settled in Monterey in 1832, and Sutter had erected both a fort and a trading empire in the Sacramento Valley, starting in 1839. The United States government had made several unsuccessful attempts to buy California from Mexico, the last in 1845. But a year later, President Polk engaged the country in the generally unpopular war with Mexico, and as a result of that conflict there was no need to buy California; it came to the United States as part of the treaty in 1848.

At the start of the Mexican War, there were 7000 United States citizens in California. Three years later, when the Gold Rush was in full spate, there were 100,000. In 1850, so quick was its progress, California was granted statehood as part of a package compromise which, in its passage, had rocked Congress.

In the years before the Mexican War, beer had been brought into California mainly by ship — possibly by the new clippers on their way to the Orient. There is a record of bottled beer shipped to California in 1843.[10] The first American brewer in the territory may be only a creature of myth popularly called "Billy the Brewer," but the diligent historian Hubert Howe Bancroft claimed to identify him as William McGlove, a sailor, and gave 1837 as the date of his brewing. Bancroft went on, however, to cite the Empire Brewery of William Bull, at Second Street near Mission, in San Francisco, as the first *regular* brewery in California.[11] The fact that this brewery is listed in the 1850 San Francisco directory indicates that it was established at least as early as 1849, since the city directory compilations refer, in general, to the year preceding.*

Certainly beer was available in San Francisco in 1849: Mary Jane Megquier, writing a letter to her daughter on 30 November of that year, described a "nice thanksgiving dinner yesterday." Her friends said "they had no idea there could be so good a dinner got up" — indeed, it was what might be called a "spread," and among its ingredients were porter and ale.[12]

California achieved quick fame as a state of hard-drinking men. Although whiskey formed the main diet, beer must have had its faithful *aficionados*, judging from the great number of breweries that were founded between 1850 and 1860. In 1852, San Francisco is reported to have had 350 barrooms and various other places where drinks could be obtained.

---

* Several additional brewers are listed in the 1850 directory, but it can be taken for granted that they were not important competitors of William Bull. John Neep is cited as proprietor of the California Brewery on Vallejo between Powell and Mason Streets; Ambrose Carner appears as "beer manufacturer," with an address on Sacramento between Stockton and Powell; G. F. Joseph ("Ale and Porter") was on California, between Pacific and Broadway.

With a population of approximately 36,000, San Francisco had one legal saloon for every hundred people, not counting the many additional liquor-dispensing establishments, and it was reputed to have proportionately the greatest number of drinking places of any city in the world.

The same writer, the British traveler J. D. Borthwick, commented on the "second-rate English drinking-shops" where one could "swig his ale." He also referred to the German beer-cellars, but complained of "the noise and smoke which came up from them." [13]

Something of the drinking temper of the place can be judged from the fact that by 1856 there were some fifteen breweries functioning in the city. Many of them were owned by Germans: Adam Schuppert (California Brewery), Jacob Gundlach (Bavarian Brewery), Jacob Specht (San Francisco Brewery), Seidenstrecker and Rathe (Washington Brewery), etc. But there were also the Eagle Brewery of Lyon & Co., which specialized in ale and porter, and the Eureka Brewery, belonging first to J. D. Gibson and then John Mason, which likewise brewed in the British fashion.[14] One of the longer-lasting of the San Francisco brewing enterprises was the Philadelphia Brewery, started by August Hoelscher before 1856 and taken over in 1857 by John Wieland.

One of the names that turns up somewhat surprisingly in the annals of San Francisco brewing is Claus Spreckels, better known as founder of a gigantic sugar refining combine. Born in Germany in 1829, Spreckels had come to the United States in the appropriate year — 1848 — and set up in the grocery trade in Charleston, South Carolina. After some years he sold out, went to New York, and landed finally in San Francisco in 1856. By this time he had married into a family by the name of Mangel, and had a son, John D. Spreckels. In San Francisco he started in groceries with a shop on Pine Street. A newspaper account of 1881 summed up Spreckels's career from then on in the following way:

> His attention was first directed to brewing, almost the only local manufacture of the day, and therefore, in 1857, the *Albany Brewery*, Claus Spreckels & Co., appeared in the field. This brewery is still running, but we believe that none of the Spreckels or Mangel families have any connection with that establishment. While running the brewery, Mr. Spreckels overheard a conversation between some of the employees of the San Francisco Sugar Refinery about the carelessness, extravagance,

and extraordinarily wasteful manner in which that business was conducted.[15]

Thus are great fortunes made! With admirable caution, Spreckels held
on to his brewing interest when he entered the sugar refining business in
1864, but it soon became clear that the money was in the sugar rather
than in the beer (so far as he was concerned) and he disposed of the
brewery.

San Francisco was so precocious in its development that by September 1857 it held an Industrial Exhibition. The brewers' entries were as
follows:

JOHN MASON, San Francisco. Six Bottles of Porter. A very good
article, from the Eureka Brewery, and considered the best exhibited.
A diploma.

LYON & CO. San Francisco. A Half Barrel of Porter. But little inferior to the preceding sample. Bronze medal.

L. DELAFOND, San Francisco. 18 Bottles of Porter.

LYON & CO. San Francisco. 2 Barrels of Ale. From the Empire
Brewery, and superior to any presented. Diploma.

JOHN MASON, San Francisco. One barrel of Ale.

ADAM MEYER, San Francisco. [Cincinnati Brewery.] 2 Kegs and
two dozen bottles of Lager Beer. Best — Diploma.

PHILADELPHIA BREWERY, San Francisco. Barrel of Lager Beer.

E. ANDERSON, San Francisco. Lager Beer.

L. S. FORD, San Francisco. 3 Sacks of Malt.[16]

It would be possible to make too much out of this evidence and jump
to the conclusion that California, in the 1850s, had a rip-roaring brewing
industry out of all proportion to the population. Lithographs and prints
of the breweries at that period prove that most of them were, if not
precisely shacks, one- or two-story buildings of small dimensions; the
inevitable inference is, of course, that their individual output was ex-

tremely small. Even bearing this in mind, however, one has to admit that there was a great deal of brewing activity going on.

Sacramento, a town that vied with San Francisco for pre-eminence and had the advantage of being placed closer to the mining areas, had its first brewery in 1849. Called the Sacramento Brewery, it was established by a German named Peter Kadell. In 1853, Philip Scheld rented the brewery, and the following year Kadell sold it to him.[17]

The population of the city grew from 6000 in 1850 to about twice that in 1855, by which time there were five breweries producing some 7000 gallons (or about 225 barrels) a week, and the Lion Company Brewery of San Francisco maintained an agency there.

In Yreka, Siskiyou County, there was a brewery at least as early as 1853, in which year it was referred to in a letter sent by Bradford Ripley Alden, former aide-de-camp of General Winfield Scott, to his wife from Fort Jones, Scotts Valley:

> I am here in a new land & life is in its elements [*sic*]. The young people slip along very easily, & it rests with me to supply first, absolutely, Bread & water, then a kettle to boil meat, next a kettle to boil clothes, to wash, then a tub scooped out of cedar. Providentially there is a brewery in Yreka, & hops & yeast.[18]

The town of Nicolaus in Sutter County had a brewery in 1850; it was called "the first manufacturing in the county." After two years "the fact became apparent that Nicolaus was not to become a large town," and so the brewer quite sensibly moved on to a more profitable location. This was a risk of the times: prospectors quickly left a nonproductive area, or miners found that a strike was less abundant than they had expected. Those who were set up as provisioners — grocers, merchants, brewers — often found themselves suddenly abandoned by their customers, and a settlement could die just as abruptly as it was born. There were "ghost towns" at all levels: large and small, elaborate and simple.

The Nicolaus brewery faded from sight, but in 1857 another brewery was started in Sutter County, at Yuba City. It was erected at first on the east bank of the Feather River by two brothers named Butler (L. M. and Andrew), originally from Missouri. Because of the danger of floods it had to be moved to the corner of Bridge and Second Streets, where it was still functioning in 1879. The Butler brothers died, but a German, Frederick Klempp, married the widow of L. M. Butler in 1876 and at that time took over the business.[19]

In the early directories, Yuba City and Marysville, though they now exist on opposite sides of the Feather River and in different counties, were treated as one town. On the Marysville side of the river there was a small brewery built by John Rueger in 1852, and the Benicia Lager Beer brewery of Louis Classen, apparently a sizable enterprise, maintained a depot there.[20] In 1855 there were three breweries operating: the Marysville Brewery, the California Brewery (owned by Jacob Geiss), and the Eureka (W. H. Clark, proprietor).[21]

In the important town of Stockton, Philip Niestrath, a Louisianan, started to manufacture beer at the City Brewery in 1851.[22] According to one report the brewery was run by windmill power and was burned down on Christmas Eve of 1857.[23] There was, however, another called the El Dorado Brewery. Its date of origin is somewhat obscure, though there exists a lithograph of Stockton in 1852 which includes the El Dorado as well as the City Brewery.[24] One historian of San Joaquin County claims that it was founded in that year, "near the Asylum," by Philip Umlauff and Peter Totherbush.[25] Another places its origin (wrongly, if the lithograph is to be trusted) in 1855, and gives the names of Bush & Dinkleacker (Denlacker) as its founders.[26] The Stockton City Directory for 1856 lists the brewery as belonging to W. Busch & Co., with the address "Peninsula, opp. Insane Asylum." After 1858, it is generally agreed, this brewery was owned by Daniel Rothenbush (a name enough like the "Totherbush," above, to cast some doubt on the first account), who continued, like his predecessors, to make "steam beer." This form of beer had quickly become a Western specialty, particularly in California, where it enjoyed a long popularity. It originated, apparently, as an invention born out of necessity: on the West Coast it was difficult — often impossible — to obtain the ice necessary to provide the low temperatures at which lager needed to ferment. Steam beer, then, according to an expert writing in 1898,[27] is "bottom fermenting [like lager], and the fermentation proceeds at the high temperature of from 12° to 16° R. [60° to 68° F.]." It had a special advantage, in those fast-moving thirsty times, of being ready to drink in very short order: "Steam beer is allowed from ten to twelve days from the mash tub to glass." None of that long, careful, cool rest required for a mature lager beer!

The "steam" refers to the strong carbonation, "a pressure of fifty to sixty pounds per square inch," caused by the introduction into the beer, when it is already in the barrel, of a portion of new wort at the early stage of fermentation ("green beer") — a process called "kräusening." This is a priming operation, also used by some lager brewers, which leads to after-fermentation in the barrel, thus building up the "steam." Generally speaking, steam beer is not a connoisseur's drink; the writer already referred to had nothing better to say for it than that "it is a pretty fair drink, . . . At any rate, it tastes better than the raw hopped, bitter and turbid ales."

Los Angeles, more Spanish than the California cities of the north and therefore more given to wine-drinking, did not have a brewery until 1854, when Christopher Kuhn established what is referred to as a lager beer brewery there.[28] The same year, a brewery was established in Downieville, Sierra County, by a man named Borge, who sold it after two years to Scammon & Schultz. After several changes of ownership it came into the hands of Ferdinand Busch, who was still running it in the 1880s. A second brewery in that town, the Monte Christo [sic], was operated by an Austrian, L. Nessler, who had started out in California as a miner, then worked in the brewery, and finally bought it.[29]

There were breweries also in the Eldorado County mining towns of Placerville and Greenwood Valley.[30] Placer County, one of the main centers of gold prospecting, with towns called Deadwood, Last Chance, Rattlesnake, had at least six brewers in 1860, all of them with German names.[31] Towns of this sort came and went in the mining area: they were erected almost as quickly as a stage set. One of the prospectors in 1852 wrote back to his wife from Auburn Ravine in Placer County:

> When we came here, about six weeks ago there were only one or two tents in sight, and in one short week our tent is in the centre of a town, with six stores, two blacksmith shops, Drug stores, Taverns, Bakery, Circus etc. Verily, California is a go-ahead country.[32]

He also remarked that a man, in those parts, opened a store before he had even put his roof on, or "a blacksmith will come along, gather a few stones in a heap to put his fire on, and hang up his bellows, and commence hammering away in the open air." [33] No doubt brewers set up their operations just as casually and speedily.

One of the most significant facts about California in its first decade of statehood is, according to a historian of the Pacific Coast, that it

> produced in average years nearly as much barley as wheat, and, in some seasons, even more; but the price being less than that of wheat, it has taken possession of few of the new acres brought into cultivation within the last twenty years [1860 to 1880].[34]

Hops also became an important crop in California agriculture quite soon after statehood. In other words, the materials for making beer were close at hand and did not have to be imported from either the East Coast or the Midwest. Brewing continued to develop favorably in California, though not in many of the mining towns which withered at the end of the rush. San Francisco traditionally remained the brewing center of the state, while the inland areas gradually became the province of the wine industry.

A typical beer garden. The German Winter Garden
at 45 Bowery, New York, around 1850

Beer for German troops on Union side during the Civil War.

Engraving of brilliant and famous Percheron stallion of the 19th century — from a painting by Rosa Bonheur. The Percherons and Clydesdales were the favored brewery horses.

Brewery in Portland, Oregon, 1860. Believed to be
the first in that city (contemporary photograph)

Harvesting ice on the Hudson River

Manufacture of artificial ice by Pictet method, 1878

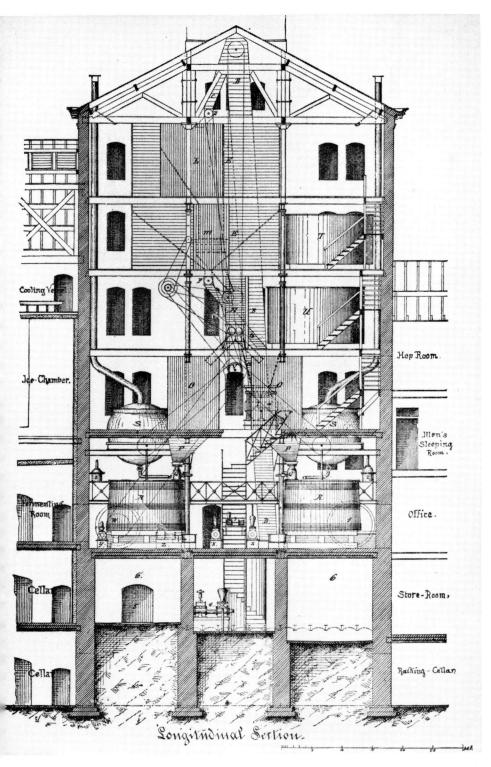

Plan of Rubsam and Horrman's New Brewery, Staten Island,
New York, 1879. Annual capacity: 100,000 barrels

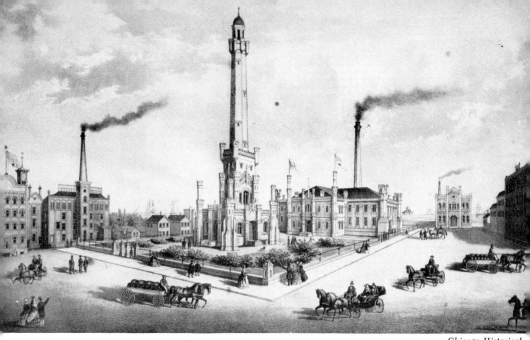

Lill's Chicago Brewery near the water tower and
pumping station, about 1870

Ruins of Lill's brewery after Chicago fire of 1871

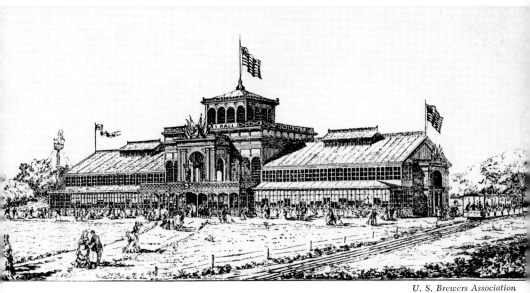

Brewers Hall at the Philadelphia Centennial Exhibition, 1876

Valentine Hoffman's brewery, Buffalo. Built 1842, torn down in 1902

"E. Anheuser Company Brewing Association," St. Louis

REPRESENTATIONS OF NINETEENTH-CENTURY BREWERIES

"Fred Miller Brewing Company," Milwaukee

Part Four

The Brewers Join Forces

AT THE START of a new decade, the disastrous 'sixties, the brewers of the United States must have felt, except for the menacing political situation, enormously optimistic. In 1850 there had been 431 breweries in the country, producing around 750,000 barrels of beer a year.[1] Ten years later the number of active breweries had jumped to 1269 and the annual output to over a million barrels.[2] New York and Pennsylvania still dominated the field, producing something like 85 per cent of the total output — reflecting both their relatively dense urban populations and their large number of immigrants. The overall population of the country, incidentally, had risen between 1850 and 1860 from around 23 million to 31 million.

Particularly for the brewers of German origin, the 'fifties had meant continual expansion and stepped-up production. Several of the firms that were later to forge ahead as industry leaders were founded in that period. The Schlitz brewery in Milwaukee, for example, became firmly established in 1856 when bookkeeper Joseph Schlitz, upon the death of August Krug (founder of the business in 1849), took over control and later married the widow.[3] In the same city, Valentin Blatz, probably in 1851, after working for a few years in the City Brewery, founded by John Braun in 1846,* bought it and immediately began to increase its production.[4] And the Menomonee Valley Brewery, also called the "Plank-Road Brewery," set up in 1848 by Charles Best (of the large

---

* He also married Braun's widow.

brewing family already represented in Milwaukee), was bought in 1855 by an eager young brewer fresh from Germany, Frederick Miller.[5]

The story was similar in St. Louis, where, in 1857, a soap manufacturer, Eberhard Anheuser, found himself the unexpected owner of a small brewery started in about 1850 by an obscure brewer named Schneider.* Anheuser had the good fortune to obtain Adolphus Busch, a young man then in the brewers' supply business, for his son-in-law; between them they laid the basis for one of the most famous and successful of modern American breweries.[6]

In Cincinnati the important firm of Christian Moerlein was started in 1853; that of J. H. Sandman and Herman Lackman in 1855.[7] Brooklyn, New York, saw the establishment of at least three lager beer manufacturers during the 'fifties: the only one that has triumphantly survived is that which Samuel Liebmann originated in 1855.[8] But in the newer towns, also, this period witnessed a great rise in brewing activities. Christian Stahlman set up his brewery in St. Paul in 1855,[9] and in about 1857 Andrew Keller engaged in business at the Pittsburg Brewery on Trout Creek near Stillwater Road, an establishment that was taken over with profitable results in 1864 by Theodor Hamm, a German immigrant who had started out as a butcher and then became a tavern-keeper.[10] In the neighboring town of Minneapolis, not yet the significant place it became, the 1859-1860 directory lists the brewery of John Orth, and in the same neighborhood the establishment of John Rank and "Godaliep Cluyke" (obviously Gottlieb Gluek) — which has lasted for over a hundred years as the Gluek Brewing Company.

In Chicago, Boston, Albany, Baltimore — in fact, all over the country — new breweries were established year after year. Some of them were not properly financed, or their product never became sufficiently popular, or, all too frequently, they simply burned down. But the bulk of them must have managed fairly well, as long as their location was within a beer-drinking market. A good many, of course, made successes even beyond their expectations, had to enlarge their facilities to meet growing demand, and realized great profits out of their business. The manifest prosperity of the brewers at the time war broke out made it inevitable

---

* Possibly George Schneider, listed in the 1852 St. Louis City Directory as a brewer at Third and Elm Streets.

that the Treasury Department should appraise them with eager eyes, particularly after the short-lived but sharp depression of 1861.

After General Beauregard's attack on Fort Sumter had precipitated civil war, both sides hastily set about the problems of supplying the fighting men. In this war, the brewers did not have any direct responsibility; there was no military ration of beer, as there had been in the Revolution. Evidently the beer ration had lapsed sometime early in the nineteenth century and was replaced by a liquor ration, for in 1832 the prohibitionist Secretary of War, Lewis Cass, had officially canceled that ration and prohibited the introduction of liquors into "any camp, fort, or garrison of the United States." [11] The troops who fought in the Civil War were supposed to be "dry." *

Apparently, though, this was a case of wishful thinking, to judge from a speech made by Senator Henry Wilson of Massachusetts in June 1862, in which he said: "Since this war opened we have lost thousands of lives by rum." [12] Due allowance must be made for the fact that Wilson (Vice President during Grant's second term) was a prohibitionist; all the same, the introduction of rum into the army, even though not official, can hardly be doubted.

To some degree, beer also was unofficially used by the troops. *Harper's Weekly* carried an illustration showing "The Lager Bier Wagon," which was presumably used to supply the regiments made up of German immigrants.[13]

Another indication appeared in the New York *Herald* of 23 August 1862, in which there was a bitter reference to "new people, who have interests in some kinds of government transactions . . . the noble army of shoddy contractors." These war-profiteers, the newspaper claimed, "drink the best champagne . . . and they began [beget?] upon the army ale and porter."

The main contribution of the brewers to the war effort was not, however, their supplying the troops but helping to finance the government. This was brought about by the passage on 1 July 1862 of an Internal Revenue Act which specified a tax of one dollar a barrel on all beer sold

---

* In 1862, the Confederate states passed prohibition laws as a grain-saving measure. In spite of bans against importation of alcoholic beverages, smuggling through the blockade was apparently widespread. (Eaton, pp. 141, 241.)

and also a license fee for individual brewers. The institution of this Act was an important event. One commentator points out that "The internal revenue system of the United States, during the Civil War period, was essentially a new creation." [14] Something of the sort had been attempted twice before, from 1791 to 1802 and from 1813 to 1817. But when the need had ended, these taxes had been dropped. The government had usually been able to pay its way without internal taxation, through proceeds from customs duties and the selling of public lands. The national debt had never been a pressing problem.

From all indications, the brewers, by then mainly German, showed an exemplary sense of patriotism to their adopted country; even some of those in the South were loyal to the Union cause.[15] Many of them saw active service at the battlefield or, like William Lemp of St. Louis, served with the City Guards and bore responsibility for the protection of their cities.[16]

When the Internal Revenue Act was passed, it became evident to certain brewers that the industry as a whole was involved and that the individuals would have to get together and speak with one voice. The first step toward organizing was taken in New York City, where an association of lager brewers was formed on 21 August 1862 at a meeting held at Pythagoras Hall, 134 Canal Street. John N. Katzenmayer was the driving force behind the association; James Speyers (of the firm Speyers & Bernheimer) was chosen president, and Katzenmayer was secretary. Among the first acts of this organization, which represented thirty-seven New York brewers, was the calling of a national convention of brewers for 12 November of that year. This duly took place. Thirty-four brewers in all attended, every one of them from the Eastern states, and elected Fred Lauer of Reading as president, Katzenmayer and Otto Johns as secretaries. They did not, it might be noted, settle on any name for themselves, but referred to the organization as the Lager-beer Brewers' Association or the National Brewers' Association or Congress. It was not until the fourth convention in 1864 that the permanent title was affirmed: United States Brewers' Association.[17]

The first convention concentrated on the formulation of certain grievances the brewers felt as a result of the Internal Revenue Act. They objected specifically to these provisions: (1) the bond required from brewers to guarantee their payment of taxes, (2) the excessive power granted to minor officials of the tax department, and (3) the government's intention to collect taxes on beer brewed before the Act went into effect.[18] A committee was appointed to draw up amendments to the Act as it stood, and among the members of that committee appeared (hopefully) the names of certain Midwestern brewers who had not even been represented at the convention. It gives some indication of how tenuous communications were at that time to see that the names of Michael Diversey (Chicago) and Joseph Uhrig (St. Louis) were misspelled in the published proceedings.[19]

At the second national convention, which took place in Philadelphia on 4 February 1863, many more delegates attended, some this time from as far as Chicago, Cincinnati, Davenport (Iowa) and Pittsburgh. The Wisconsin brewers were represented by Otto Johns of New York. All the brewing centers had been circularized since the first convention, and there had been time for most of them to form local associations. From the start, the national association had tended toward a "representative system" — that is, it was to be an association of associations rather than of individuals. This produced a good many problems in future years, and eventually, since it was seen to be impractical, the association shifted its point of view and became an organization of individual brewers or firms.[20]

The most important action taken at this second convention was the appointment of a special committee to proceed directly to Washington and confer with the Internal Revenue Office. They were advised, at the beginning, by a friendly Representative, J. W. Killinger, that they would always do better if they pleaded their own case rather than using a lawyer for that purpose; they followed this method for many years with excellent effect.[21] In fact, shortly after this first attempt, the brewers became the "teacher's pet" of the Internal Revenue officers: they were cooperative and did not try to evade taxes as other industries — among them the distillers — were said to be doing. Indeed, the brewers were sensible enough, in the years that followed, not to make outrageous demands or to balk at strictures which were sensible and unavoidable.

Their first negotiations in Washington were successful, and for a time the tax was reduced from one dollar to sixty cents a barrel, but by 1863 the tax was raised again to its original figure. Step by step the brewers' representatives managed to straighten out inequities in the law — many of which had been caused simply by inexperience of the tax officials and unfamiliarity with the peculiar problems of the brewing industry — except for the claims relating to taxes on beer brewed before September 1862, and those were not settled until 1869.[22]

The association, as first organized, was composed of German brewers of lager beer, and proceedings were carried on entirely in the German language. For a long time, any attempt to change this practice was stoutly resisted. Proceedings were at least published in both German and English from the third convention (October 1863) on; but English was not officially used at the conventions themselves until the fifteenth in 1875. Because of this, the American ale brewers were disinclined or unable to join, but starting with the second convention, a handful of their representatives were always present, and individual ale brewers took an active part in negotiations from time to time. It is Frederick Collins, of the ale-brewing firm Collins, Massey & Co. in Philadelphia, who gets the credit for the proposal to send a committee abroad to study the various forms of tax collection followed in the European countries and to draw up, on the basis of this study, a proposal for changes in the American form of collection as it then existed. And when the committee was finally designated, it consisted of not only himself and the lager brewer Fred Lauer, but another ale brewer, M. P. Read of New York. The Secretary of the Treasury approved of this idea, and the three-man committee sailed on 19 April 1865, ten days after Lee's surrender.

Their findings were presented at the fifth convention of the association, held in Baltimore on 18 October 1865 and attended by the new Special Revenue Commissioner, D. A. Wells. Three possible forms of taxing brewers had been examined: a tax on malt, a tax on the wort during fermentation, and a stamp tax on the barrels that left the brewery. The recommendation of the committee was the stamp tax, and this was accepted, mostly in the form presented by the brewers, by the Office of Internal Revenue, which issued the new stamp regulations on 31 August 1866.[23] Though there were certain details of this new system which had to be argued occasionally, and changed or modified, on the whole it worked extremely well and continued in effect until the modern report system.*

The curious effect of the introduction of a tax on spirits and on beer, as both "wet" and "dry" commentators agree, was to strengthen the distilling and brewing industries, to increase their efficiency and profits. A spokesman for the brewers wrote as follows in 1896:

> Between 1842 and 1863 brewing had developed so rapidly and became so firmly established that it could, doubtless, have held its own ground successfully, even without discriminating legislation; but, on the other hand, it is quite certain that without such legislation it would never have become a national beverage, nor would its progress during the past thirty-five years have been what it actually is. Hence, the introduction of the internal-revenue system really proved a blessing to the trade, not only on this account, but also because it called into existence the *United States Brewers' Association.*[24]

The prohibitionist writer was more explicit. According to him, the introduction of the 1862 tax made it difficult for small manufacturers with limited capital to stay in business. Many had to quit.

> The rest proceeded to enlarge the business. First, more capital became necessary, and with it a more intelligent organization and management of the business. A larger investment of capital, in turn, required a larger income; which required larger sales, which made necessary the extension of the trade.[25]

These factors led to increased competition: "The supply was made to create a demand." The drinking places had to be refurbished — "light, screens, mirrors, music, pictures, games, free lunch, family entrance" — all to attract additional customers. That bane of the prohibitionist, the saloon, came into full flower.[26]

The other important effect of the tax was, as already noted, to impel the brewers together into a united front. This in itself was a source of strength and power which had been lacking before that. This early trade

---

* The stamp was pasted over the bunghole so that, in opening the keg, the stamp would be torn (as happens to a cigarette tax stamp).

association of the American brewing industry has remained in uninterrupted operation longer than any other in the country. It shares with
the prohibition movement (and that is all they ever did share) the distinction of being a pioneer in the profession of lobbying.

TWENTY-FIVE

Coming of Age

THOUGH IT was specifically the Internal Revenue Act that brought about the formation of the United States Brewers' Association, that organization served another very important function, which may not have been foreseen by its original founders. That was the fight against the prohibition movement.

The prohibitionists, as noted before, had a serious loss of momentum around 1855 and thereupon entered a period of relative quiescence. The atmosphere of the war years was not sympathetic to prohibition agitators. The war itself had depleted their ranks. "All the temperance organizations in the South had suffered immeasurable evils during the war," according to a prohibitionist writer, "and at its close only here and there a division of The Sons of Temperance could be found." [1]

There were, however, enough flickers of life left for a National Temperance Convention to be held right after the war, in the summer of 1865, at Saratoga. Out of this convention grew the National Temperance Society and Publication-house,[2] and though this revival was extremely modest, with more vague hopes than real prospects, its leaders worked and propagandized so diligently that the movement quickly regained its pre-1855 drive and was able to organize a national prohibition convention in 1869 that impressed both pros and antis.

The prohibition problem did not enter into the early considerations of the United States Brewers' Association; in 1866, for the first time, it was evoked as a reason for more brewers to join the association.[3] In his address to the sixth convention held that year in St. Louis, secretary John Katzenmayer said:

> Just now a note of war is heard coming against us by fanatics, who, in pretending to support Sunday and temperance laws, are in fact trying to annihilate the self-respect and independence of mankind, and liberty of conscience and trade.[4]

The following year, at the seventh convention in Chicago, an explicitly militant stand was taken:

> *Resolved,* That we will use all means to stay the progress of this fanatical party, and to secure our individual rights as citizens, and that we will sustain no candidate, of whatever party, in any election, who is in any way disposed toward the total abstinence cause.[5]

There was no mincing of words here: it was outright war against the prohibitionists. The brewers were feeling united and strong; Henry Clausen, Jr., the president of the Principal Association, had been able to declare, in his opening address to the same convention, "The Association, since its organization, has always been successful." [6]

This sense of confidence was bolstered by the failure of prohibition efforts in Iowa and New York during 1867, and also by the "liberal" (*i.e.,* anti-prohibition) findings of Massachusetts Governor John A. Andrew, published as *The Errors of Prohibition.* Another cause for self-satisfaction was the rise in production of beer: between 1863 and 1867 the annual figure had gone from about 2½ million to nearly 6 million barrels. In 1867 there were also breweries in every state and territory of the country.[7] The number of brewers in America had reached the astonishing total of about 3700, a peak from which there was a sharp drop the following year, after which there was a second rise.[8]

Another element in the brewer-prohibitionist struggle that must not be overlooked was the anti-German propaganda which had emerged into politics during the era of the American Party, unaffectionately called the "Know-Nothings" — from 1852 to about 1856. The German population of America (and certainly among them the lager brewers) undoubtedly smarted under that kind of attack, and also in later years when the prohibitionists accused them of keeping America "wet" by means of bloc voting.

The Germans in America thought of themselves as models of true temperance; they were always pointed out by the "liberal" side as living proof of the assertion that beer-drinking was a guarantee of sobriety, sturdiness and sanity. The brewers, of course, tried to make as much of that view as possible, and this necessarily entailed their complete disassociation from the distillers. Whether they were wise to disassociate themselves as thoroughly as they did might, in the light of later events, be questioned. As early as 1865, when the committee that had examined the tax systems of Europe prepared a "Brewers' Memorial to Congress" on their conclusions, there was a denunciation of the use of spirits as violent as any the prohibitionists had offered:

> The fearful consequences of the excessive use of ardent spirits the most florid declamation cannot too highly color. Its hideous statistics have been collected from prisons, almshouses and hospitals; from the dwellings of the rich, where domestic misery was mocked by the luxury and splendor which surrounded it; from the dwellings of the poor, where, alas! it imposes still heavier burdens upon the gaunt shoulders of poverty. . . . Humanity has wept over it.[9]

There is no reason to impugn their sincerity in holding this viewpoint; obviously they believed passionately that the problem of drunkenness had nothing whatsoever to do with beer. But the very vehemence of the above statement and others like it repeatedly gives the impression that the brewers sought to protect their interests at the expense of the distillers, and with the conviction that if prohibition were ever to come it would involve only spirits and not beer. If indeed this was their hope, it was sadly frustrated, for the prohibition forces, before long, actually turned their main wrath and their biggest guns against the brewing industry.

The prohibition writers themselves attribute the founding of the Prohibition Party directly to the passage of the Internal Revenue Act of 1862 and the organization of the United States Brewers' Association.[10] In June 1867, the Grand Lodge of Good Templars of Pennsylvania took note of the resolution of the brewers to withhold their votes from political candidates with prohibitionist leanings* and followed suit: "We do accept the issue thus made, and declare that we will not vote for men who countenance the liquor traffic, or degrade their official positions by the use of intoxicating liquors." [11]

The issue was by these means brought squarely into the political arena, and it was there that the long conflict took place. The first proposal to form a political prohibitionist party was made in 1868 at a meeting of the Right Worthy Grand Lodge of Good Templars in Richmond, Indiana: "We recommend to the temperance people of the country, as soon as practicable," the resolution read, "the organization of a national political party, which shall embrace, in its platform of principles, prohibition of the manufacture, importation, and sale of intoxicating liquors to be used as a beverage." And then in 1869 the Good Templars, meeting at Oswego, New York, issued a call for a national convention to establish "a distinct political party, with prohibition of the traffic in intoxicating drinks as the most prominent feature." [12]

The first presidential election in which the prohibition question may be said to have played a part was in 1872, when the opposing candidates were Horace Greeley, editor of the New York *Tribune* (Democrat), and General Grant, running for a second term (Republican). Greeley was an out-and-out prohibitionist; the whole body of German-American opinion was against him. The Republican convention went through the motions of adopting a mild plank on prohibitionism — a firmer one was not absolutely required, since the bulk of German-Americans were traditionally Republican in any case.[13] It seems likely that Grant would have won, whatever the issues, but it is important to notice that his party went as far as it did toward wooing the German-American vote (though Henry Wilson as Vice-President must have been hard for them to tolerate). The prohibitionist James Black, running on the ticket of the hastily established "Temperance" party, was awarded a total of 5608 votes.

As the brewers fell slightly from their 1867 peak, there was a growing sense of disappointment in the efforts of their association's Washington

* See page 220.

Committee. Attempts to obtain a reduction of duty on barley imported from Canada were futile. Nor were the brewers able to solve satisfactorily the question of the amount of tax rebate to be allowed for leakage or spoilage.[14] In subtle ways, their relations with members of Congress appeared to be shifting; and whereas they had been able in the beginning to draft amendments or discuss implementation of certain regulations with the expectation of success, gradually they had to work hard simply to hold their ground against efforts by inimical legislators to increase the beer tax, reduce the rebate and generally harass the industry.

The association, however, continued to function and follow up these problems. There was now an official German-language organ, *Der Amerikanische Bierbrauer* (*The American Brewer*), which had started monthly publication in January 1868. At the tenth convention in Davenport, Iowa, in 1870, the association finally adopted a constitution: the official title was given then as "Principal Association of the Brewers of the United States." One of the provisions of the constitution was that hop-growers and maltsters (since their interests were so closely meshed with the brewers') would be admitted as members of the association as long as they were persons of "unblemished character."[15]

In 1872, the patient agitation of the association finally resulted in passage of a new revenue law which, while it did not meet all the brewers' requests or anticipations, did go a long way toward eliminating unfairnesses and petty harassment. What pleased the brewers most about the bill was that it drew a distinction between the distilling and brewing industries. The brewers' historian wrote that this gave "the association a legal basis and sanction for the missionary work which they were about to inaugurate upon a larger scale than had hitherto been the case."[16] They were going all the way in their effort to make for themselves a public image separate from that of the distillers. A second magazine began in 1871 to represent the association: its original title was the *American Brewers' Gazette and Distillers' Journal*. The latter half of the title, however, was quickly dropped with the statement that "the interests of the brewers and distillers were not only *not* identical, but, on the contrary, decidedly inimical."[17] This sense of enmity was generally sustained through the successes and failures that both industries were later to experience.

The association felt that the distinction made in the 1872 revenue act was the greatest victory it had won, a victory underlined by the presence of C. A. Bates as an official representative of the federal government at the twelfth convention, held in New York City in 1872. In his speech Bates had nothing but praise for his hosts, the brewers, and disdain for the distillers. "Your moderation has won the esteem of the law-makers," he told them, and ended with this remarkable statement:

> Yes, you have begun well. Let us take no backward step. I say us, for I am with you. The Commissioner of Internal Revenue is with you. The President is with you. Every patriotic citizen is with you, if you will hold to your course.[18]

Perhaps because of the extremely laudatory character of this speech, and the very clear implications it gave of Administration sanction, the prohibitionists concentrated their attack now on beer, as the real source of all evil.

In spite of unflagging propaganda, they had not been able to conduct much more than a sniping operation since the end of the war. In 1873, however, the movement gathered new strength from the founding of the Woman's Crusade by Dr. Dio (Dioclesian) Lewis, a minister from Boston whose father had been a drunkard.[19] It was Dr. Lewis's notion to persuade the women of America to go in bands to barrooms, saloons and beer-gardens, and there to seduce from evil the owners, barkeepers, and patrons with prayer and hymns.[20] This quaintly original form of peaceful agitation had a curious appeal to the country at large; and the picture of pince-nezed, bonneted women on the warpath is the one ever afterward most closely identified with the prohibition movement. The writer for the brewers commented, "The craze spread like an infectious disease through the whole country." [21]

What was more significant, however, was the development of the Crusade into the Woman's Christian Temperance Union in 1874. This was a different matter: a well-supported, highly organized body of women, driven from the center by a gifted spinster, Frances E. Willard, and dedicated to a long hard struggle.[22]

At the fourteenth convention of the Brewers' Association in Boston (1874), an "Address to the People of the United States" was drawn up by Henry Pfaff (Boston), Frank Jones (the distinguished New Hampshire brewer and Congressman from that state) and William Massey (the Philadelphia ale brewer). This document, presumably part of the "missionary work" referred to before,* was based on an entirely new argument in support of the brewers, and this was an economic and financial one. In 1873 there had been yet another of those recurring panics, when banks had failed, factories had closed down, and once again the cities and towns were filled with the unemployed. At a time like this, the "Address" said, the prohibition forces wanted to cut off one of the main sources of the federal government's revenue, and "ultimately deal a deathly blow to the finances of the country." The statistics showed that in the fiscal year of 1873, taxes paid by the brewers (and distillers) of America accounted for 55% of the "entire Internal Revenue Tax collected from all sources subject to it throughout the country!" [23] And in the whole federal revenue picture, the manufacturers of "stimulating beverages" (the term the authors of the "Address" used to hide their embarrassment at having to include the distillers in their statistical analysis) accounted for 20% of the total income.

This financial contribution that the brewers made to the government, and the political power it could not help giving them, were not lost on the prohibitionists. Their point of view was expressed in the following way by one of their more eloquent spokesmen: "The American citizen sanctions and sustains the public drink trade, not that it is good, but because he thinks it pays him well. It is Ruskin who observes that the condemnation resting on the world is not that men do not believe in their Lord, *but that they sell Him!*" [24] That last line, calculated to make one's heart beat faster, was necessary to the prohibition attitude, for it could only base its argument on "morality." When these writers shifted their attack, as they frequently did, and tried to show that, in *addition* to what they called the immorality of drinking alcoholic beverages, the "havoc" it wreaked was more expensive than any profit the government could gain from it through taxation, they were on less secure ground and failed to provide authoritative statistics as evidence for their case.[25]

* See page 223.

When the brewers met in congress in 1875 at Cincinnati, Henry H. Rueter at that time replacing the ailing Clausen as the association's president, they must have felt somewhat less encouraged than the previous year. The depression continued, and with it the danger of increased taxes. The sensational exposure of the Whiskey Ring and its machinations among Internal Revenue officials could not help making the brewers uneasy, even though they came out of the sorry mess of fraud and corruption with clean hands. The prohibitionists were maintaining their pinprick annoyances and had managed, in several states, to reduce the number of breweries in operation.[26] From a record figure of 4131 (the most ever recorded in this country) in 1873, the number of brewers had dropped in two years to under 3000.[27] The production of barrels annually had fallen from almost 9,000,000 to 8,743,747.[28] These figures could not cause any grave alarm to the industry as a whole, except insofar as any decrease at all in industrial progress is a source of, at least, anxiety. However, there was one prospect which obviously engendered a good deal of optimism and excitement — the Centennial Exhibition planned for 1876 in Philadelphia. From the start, the brewers had every intention of exhibiting there.

In many ways the brewers' show at the Centennial Exhibition marked the coming-of-age of the industry. Unwittingly the prohibitionists helped them to create a really conspicuous exhibit. By pressing to keep the brewers out of Agricultural Hall, where they would ordinarily have been represented, the prohibition forces made it possible for them to erect a building of their own in Fairmount Park, which was called an "annex" to Agricultural Hall.[29] The two-story building itself, with the inevitable statue of King Gambrinus over the entrance,* cost $20,000 to put up. On display were principally the new machines that had been created to take care of the increased market for beer and the modernized methods of malting and brewing. But, for a contrast, the exhibitors showed a model brewery of a hundred years before, when all the labor was done by hand. A New York brewer, Charles Stoll, set up a modern working brewery, called the "Centennial Brewery," with a capacity of

---

* In Germany, the patron saint of brewers and sometimes called "inventor" of brewing. A legendary figure, probably based on Jan Primus, thirteenth-century Duke of Brabant.

150 barrels at each brewing. The most popular part of the exhibit turned out to be an icehouse for the storage of beer, where draught samples of American and European brews were always available.[30] In the interests of propaganda and education, the brewers also prepared a pamphlet called *Essays on the Malt Liquor Question*, in which the industry's viewpoint was fully expressed with an air of great confidence:

> That a brewer is just as necessary to the commonweal as a butcher, a baker, a tailor, a builder, or any other economic industry, is proven by the present position of the trade in the United States.[31]

As far as the awards for products went, the brewers came under "Group IV, Animal and Vegetable Products, and the Machinery for their preparation." The report was written by Ryland T. Brown, who paid tribute to "the activity and energy with which the brewing interests of the United States have developed their branch of industry into one of the leading ones of the country." [32] All the brewing machinery shown had been manufactured in the United States, which had in this field gone beyond the Europeans. The exhibition was claimed to have "proved that American brewing had reached the highest plane attainable by means of every scientific and technical improvement applicable to the industry at that time." [33] It might have seemed, indeed, during that summer when crowds milled in and out of Brewers Hall in the park, that the industry had reached the pinnacle of success. Later events were to prove that this was only one of the plateaus, and that success, techniques, range and fame beyond imagining in 1876 still lay ahead.

✠§ *TWENTY-SIX* §❧

The Brewmaster as Mechanic and Engineer

BY THE 1870s the American drinking public had made a clear choice for lager beer over ale, porter and the other English beers. What was more, the Americans preferred a lager closer to the Pilsen than the Munich type: *i.e.*, a pale, light-bodied, clear and effervescent beer, relatively low in alcoholic content. A scientific writer has described the earlier pre-lager beers as "half sour, muddy and intoxicating." Whatever else those beers may have lacked they

> made up in alcoholic strength. In the light of our present knowledge, we can see that this excessive quantity of alcohol was essential to their stability; and was, in fact, the only means that could guard them against decomposition or undue acidity.[1]

The course that the American brewing industry took during the second half of the nineteenth century was dictated in great part by this declared difference in taste. Of course, there were other factors involved, one of the most important being the phenomenal increase in demand that must have resulted from something more than the mere increase in population. One explanation is that the type of lager developed in America was well adapted to the prevailing meat diet of Americans.[2] Another may be that the temperance agitation did have this effect: by dwelling on the dire results of drinking spirits, it had induced an appreciable number of people to switch to beer.

Whatever the cause, the increased market for beer meant that the brewers had to step up production, enlarge their capacity, serve more extended markets — and this meant that techniques had to be improved, mechanization had to be adopted wherever possible, organization had to be streamlined.

The ingredients themselves of the beer that most Americans seemed to want had to be reconsidered. It was gradually discovered that barleys containing less albumen than starch made a more popular beer. The barley most easily available, however, was heavy on the albumen side, and so the deficiency began to be made up by the use of additional starch in the form of rice or, less often, corn. It was found, incidentally, that the use of raw grain adjuncts also brought down the cost of production, something no brewer was going to overlook.

Steam power, in its modest beginnings, had shown that labor costs could be saved in many parts of the brewery. As steam became more generally applied to the processes of brewing, it was demonstrated that greater efficiency and uniformity also resulted. A New Orleans newspaper of 1865, in describing the new Old Canal Brewery of George Merz, gives the following examples of the use of steam power:

> The engine is sixteen horse power. It can, at the same time, grind the malt, sift it, throw it into the mash tub, let in boiling water that it has made to boil, stir up the malt and water, draw it off, pump it up stairs and throw it into the kettle, heat the kettle of liquid until it boils, throw it out into the coolers, cool it, force and carry it off into vats, ferment it, chafe it, and draw it off beer. With a little practice the engine could be taught to drink the beer.

Steam served an especially useful function in providing heat for the boiling of the wort. Formerly the heat had been supplied to the kettles by open fire from below, "precisely as we boil potatoes"; but now steam introduced into pipes under the kettles offered a more reliable and economical form of heat.[3]

Mechanical ingenuity showed up in countless new forms. There were elevators of all kinds, hoists, pumps; there were automatic grain separators and graders; there were machines for stirring the mash, pitching the kegs, keg scrubbers, bunghole augers, bung extractors. Various inventions had become available for cooling down the wort after its boiling: the Baudelot method of horizontal pipes filled with cold water and ice was the most popular.

One of the problems faced by the early brewers of lager in the United States was the necessity of "lagering" or storing the beer in a cool, undisturbed place for several months after brewing. The usual solution was the use of underground caves, where such were available or could be made. The Schaefer brothers in New York City built caves for their lagering as early as 1849. There was solid rock under the site at Fiftieth Street and Fourth (now Park) Avenue, which they had bought for a new enlarged plant on the basis of their initial success farther downtown.[4]

In the Mohawk section of Cincinnati, where nine breweries were located during the nineteenth century, an old "aging cellar" once used by the Felsenbrau Brewery and later the Red Top concern came to light in 1960.[5] In Pittsburgh, the abandoned caves or "vaults," as they were called, of brewers who had started to make lager there in the early 1850s were still considered curiosities — not quite so romantic, of course as the catacombs of Rome — in 1911.[6]

In Franklin, Pennsylvania, center of oil-prospecting as far back as 1860, a well being drilled at Point Bluff in December 1881 provided an uncommon accident:

> At a depth of a few hundred feet unexpectedly found what was supposed to be oil; the bailer was run several times and brought up a liquid resembling oil in color, but which was discovered to be beer; it was soon ascertained that the well had been located directly over the storage vault of [Philip] Grossman's brewery, and that the drill had penetrated the vault filled with beer; the vault had been dug out of the solid rock and extended back into the hill for over 100 feet, the brewery being on the opposite side of French creek, at the foot of South Park street.[7]

The brewery established in 1855 in St. Paul by Christian Stahlman was actually called the "Cave Brewery"; its caves covered an area of one mile and were three stories deep.[8] When William Menger began brewing beer in San Antonio, he had his cellar "so near an *acequia* [irrigating trench] that the flow of the water kept the brew cold." [9]

It is not surprising to learn that the ground below Milwaukee provided space for a number of elaborate brewers' cave-systems. A newspaper reporter in 1864 was moved to great flights of atmospheric description after a visit through one of them:

We recently spent an hour in the Mammoth Cave connected with the Brewery of Gen. Philip Best, on 9th street, near Winnebago. The party consisted of some half dozen persons, Mr. Pabst, a son-in-law of Gen. Best, and formerly a lake captain, acting as *cicerone*. All carried torches, which were necessary to properly illuminate the dark recesses, and to enable one to find his way out into daylight, should he chance to stray away from the others. After passing through several long cellars, with floors flagged with stone and roofs arched with brick, and lined on either side with rows of huge puncheons, we plunged still deeper into the bowels of the earth, only to find still longer and more numerous arched passages, all lined with the same enormous puncheons, and the puncheons all filled with foaming "lager." . . . A prominent traveler and political writer who was one of our party, informed us that it very much resembled the Bastile.[10]

The caves belonging to the Miller Brewing Co. in Milwaukee have been preserved and transformed into a museum. Started by Charles Best (brother of Phillip Best, mentioned above), who built the Plank Road Brewery in 1850, they were much enlarged by Frederick Miller when the business came into his hands. Their dimensions were 15 feet in width and 12 to 15 feet in height, built of brick and totaling 600 feet of tunnel. With a capacity of 12,000 barrels, the caves were used until 1906, when their function was taken over by refrigerator buildings.[11]

The temperature of these caves was not always cold enough and in many cases ice had to be used, particularly during the summer months, to assure the proper level for the beer being stored. This was easy enough to provide in Milwaukee, where ice could be cut from Pewaukee Lake during the winter and kept for summer needs; but in other parts of the country the providing of ice was both a big problem and a big business. It had particular reference to the way lager beer was manufactured as well as the way it was aged and carbonated.

Among various factors which helped Milwaukee to gain prominence in the brewing industry, the availability of natural ice was certainly an important one.* A writer on the industry as it developed in Cincinnati attributes Milwaukee's ascendancy over the older Ohio city mainly to this one advantage.[12]

---

* In later years, when refrigeration was perfected and the cost of fuel began to make the greater difference, Cincinnati appeared to have the advantage, but that proved to be only momentary.

An article in an Arizona newspaper dated 1875 gave some data on the ice industry for the enlightenment of readers in a climate where ice had to be imported from the North:

> Those who live in southern latitudes, where the altitude is not as high as in Prescott, where they never see ice formed more than an inch thick, can hardly form an idea of the immense amount of capital invested or the large numbers of men, animals and machinery employed in cutting and storing ice during the winter in the northern and eastern States, . . . From Nova Scotia to New Jersey, on every navigable river and at every fresh water pond of any size within easy distance of every seaport, the winter season is one of great activity in harvesting the ice crop.

The reporter adds that, north of New York, the Hudson River, its tributaries and the canals would freeze during the winter; the men thus put out of work would then be hired by the ice industry. The ice, once cut, would be stored in icehouses built all along the banks of the river. Some of the larger-scale ice companies could pack away as much as two and a half million tons to be sold in warmer weather. Certain large enterprises in New England were said to concentrate their entire trade on export supplies of ice for Baltimore, Washington, New Orleans, Havana, etc. "The principal consumers of ice are brewers, packers, hotels, restaurants and saloons in all large cities." [13]

The use of ice in the United States goes back at least as far as the days of Williamsburg, when the governor had an icehouse for the use of his palace. George Washington supposedly harvested ice on his estate, Thomas Jefferson had two icehouses of his own design at Monticello, and Madison had an icehouse on his property in Virginia. The commercial exploitation of ice began, mainly in the Boston area, after 1800; about three thousand tons a year were exported from there in the 1820s. The harvesting was facilitated and made cheaper by the invention of an ice cutter, patented by Nathaniel Jarvis Wyeth in 1825. Soon after this important advance, exports of ice increased enormously, particularly to the West Indies and to centers like New Orleans, Atlanta and Charleston in the southern United States. During the 'forties and 'fifties, the Boston companies involved in this industry erected a chain of ice-depots in their customer territories, where great cubes of ice could be stored and sold all through the summer months.[14]

Although Boston dominated the industry until after the Civil War, other northern cities exported on a smaller scale. In the city of Detroit, for example, the industry had its start about 1834, when a Mr. Gavin offered ice for sale. At that time the ice on the river was cut by hand with crosscut saws and hauled into an icehouse, where it would be cut again into smaller pieces as wanted. By 1866, there were four large ice concerns there, putting up among them some 20,000 tons, mainly for local use. The following year the figure had risen to 27,000 tons. Detroit's export business, however, was not a certain one, depending almost entirely on the kind of winter there might have been farther south. In some years, Detroit ice packers would ship to Cincinnati and Chicago; but in a year like 1866, for instance, none at all would be shipped south because a severe winter had insured local supplies of ice as far as St. Louis.[15]

This, in fact, was one of the principal problems relating to natural ice in the minds of both suppliers and customers. The market could not be entirely depended on, but neither could the production. One mild winter in the North and ice supplies became dangerously short. One of the reasons Boston lost its pre-eminence as a supplier was that Maine, with its colder winters, was more reliable.[16] A scarcity developed during the 1868-1869 season, with consequently high prices;[17] and in the year 1875 there was a particularly difficult crisis in ice supplies.[18]

Brewers needed the ice not only for the "lagering" process itself, but also in order to meet the great increase in demand and sales by brewing all year round, not just during the winter. The ice-room or icehouse, which soon became a regular feature of lager breweries, is spoken of as an independent development of the American brewing industry.[19] The ice, thus stored, was always available for year-round fermentation which, in the case of lager, had to take place at low temperatures. Not only did the fermentation of lager-yeast prove most effective in a cold atmosphere, but the cold also prevented the growth of bacteria which so often ruined the beer.

The brewers of Milwaukee were reported in 1872 to be storing about

20,000 tons of ice, 14,000 of that amount by Best, Blatz and Schlitz.[20] The Phillip Best Brewing Co. required 60,000 tons of ice itself by 1880, when production had substantially increased.[21] It owned, besides, a large icehouse in Chicago. Valentin Blatz built his icehouses between 1868 and 1870, and used 30,000 tons a year; and Frederick Miller, in 1881, was supposed to own two icehouses in Milwaukee, one in Waukesha and one in Chicago.[22]

The important Lill and Diversey brewery in Chicago had two ice-houses in 1861, described as follows:

> The ice is in the middle of the ice house, in two bodies, one measuring sixty by thirty and twenty-five feet high, and the other sixty by sixty, and twenty-five feet high, packed in tanbark, and encased in wood, by which means a temperature of forty degrees is kept up during the year. The absence of cellars has been the greatest drawback to Chicago as a brewing point, but these ice houses overcame all that.[23]

Any town which had its own ice was considered to have an immediate advantage: even Leadville, Colorado, where Henry W. Gaw started a brewery in February 1878 on a property which had ice on it.[24]

It became evident, however, that somehow or other ice would have to be manufactured by artificial means, and inventions along these lines were patented in England, France, Germany and the United States starting in the 1860s. The earliest efforts were based on the demonstrable theory that solid bodies in solution (such as salt in water) absorb heat and are therefore instrumental in reducing the surrounding temperature. But a second line of experimentation, using the evaporation of volatile liquids such as ether and ammonia, proved more fruitful in the end.[25] Siegfried Giedion, one of the important historians of modern technology, gives Oliver Evans credit for foretelling the principle of producing cold by mechanical means with the use of ether.[26]

Among the pioneers in refrigeration was the Florida physician John Gorrie, called the "Father of Air Conditioning," who perfected an ice-making machine in 1850, which was not, however, taken up for industrial purposes.[27] The credit for the ice-making machine most widely adopted by brewers is usually given to a French inventor, Ferdinand P. A. Carré, who used liquid ammonia in his compression machine.[28] At the

London Exhibition of 1862, Carré demonstrated a machine that manufactured blocks of ice. Among the unsung American inventors might be included Samuel David Lount, whose first patent for an ice-producing machine was taken out in 1869. Lount transferred his operations from Virginia to Phoenix, Arizona, where he intended to "make ice in a desert." With ammonia and the compression method he did indeed make ice, which was being sold in Phoenix in 1890.[29]

The various inventors already mentioned, plus the German Franz Windhausen, realized quite soon after the compression principle had been established that the machinery developed from it could not only make ice, but could also be made to refrigerate rooms without ice — the first hint of modern air-conditioning. But this was a notion that most ice-users could not assimilate before a long time had passed, and they were pleased enough to have artificial ice. "Mechanical refrigeration," according to one scholarly study of the subject, "was earliest adopted on a large scale by the brewing industry because of its inherent advantages. It freed brewers from dependence on natural ice with its uncertainties of supply and price." [30] Eventually it also proved its worth by reducing labor costs and leading to a more economical use of space.

Among the early users of these various mechanical refrigerating devices was S. Liebmann's Sons Brewing Company in Brooklyn, New York, where a Carré machine was installed in 1870. In 1869 George Merz, the first New Orleans lager brewer, tried a device invented by Charles Tellier. The well-known brewer of Alexandria, Virginia, Robert Portner, is reported to have formed an early interest in the possibilities of artificial refrigeration. At the Centennial Exhibition in 1876, he became acquainted with a machine for that purpose invented by Thomas Cook. According to report, he bought this, rebuilt it and installed it successfully in his brewery in 1878. Emil Schandein, of the Phillip Best Brewing Co. in Milwaukee, saw this machine in operation and wrote favorably of it in 1880 to his brother-in-law, Frederick Pabst: "So far the Cook system seems to be the best for it serves its purpose and keeps the cellars as dry as a room. With Portner's improvements it can't be surpassed." [31] In general, this is considered to have been the first such machine to operate in a brewery with complete success.[32] Another which developed into a useful piece of equipment was manufactured by

Daniel Boyle; the first of these was tried out in the large brewery of Bemis and McAvoy in Chicago.[33]

The one which finally took over the field, however, was the ammonia compression machine of John C. DeLaVergne, which in the 'eighties and 'nineties was installed in many of the leading breweries in the country. There were even others which had good success, but all were used at this time mainly to make ice. Not only brewers but ice-making companies took advantage of these inventions. In Houston, for example, a city which, because of its climate, was peculiarly suited to the manufacture of artificial ice, such a plant was organized in 1880: the Central Ice Company. Another in that city, the American Brewing Company (beer and ice were both sold) was formed in 1894, Adolphus Busch of St. Louis being the principal owner.[34] The ice business, in fact, came to be, in many cases, an adjunct of the brewing industry.

A brewery architect, Fred. Baumann, conjectured in 1876 about the brewery of the future. What he predicted was that cold air, not ice, would be the answer for the brewer; and he believed that only a "brief span of time" would give it to him. His second prediction was that eventually the fermenting stage in brewing would take place in a vacuum. In both cases he turned out to be right.

> If with this knowledge we view the brewery of the future we find it without ice-house and Baudelot coolers. Instead, we find a large and splendid engine room with at least three different cold-air machines; a machine shop is therewith in connection, to facilitate repairs, which become unavoidable where there is so much machinery. We also find a gasometer for the storing of carbonic acid generated by the fermenting process and necessary for the cooling of the wort.[35]

The modern brewery was virtually a reality in the year of the Centennial Exhibition!

By the changes just described, the brewmaster* or the brewery superin-

---

* Indeed, in this period the brewmaster was the man in control of the brewery. This was such a vital position that the brewmasters all over the country formed an organization of their own in 1887. It was called the United States Brewmasters' Association and was founded, according to its manifesto, "to make the interests of the brewing industry its own." The national organization grew out of brewmaster societies already formed in New York, Cleveland, Cincinnati and a few other brewing centers. When it was incorporated in 1912, the title "Master Brewers' Association of the United States" was adopted; in 1933, however, the name was changed to "Master Brewers Association of America."

tendent, who at one time had been little more than a superior cook, had been transformed into a mechanic and an engineer. After the discoveries made by Pasteur and Hansen from their studies of yeast, the brewmaster had to enlarge his *expertise* even more: now he had to become chemist and biologist as well.

The Brewmaster as Chemist and Biologist

FOR REASONS that might not be easy to identify, Louis Pasteur, once an obscure research chemist, has become in recent times one of the world's best-known scientists. His name, of course, has the distinction of being the root of a household word; and no doubt, through the pasteurizing of milk, he is popularly (and properly) thought of as one of the great benefactors of mankind. Biographers by the hundreds have embraced him; the movies gave him their supreme accolade; Pasteur is one of the immortals.

What is less commonly known about him is that a good part of his research centered around fermentation problems in the manufacture of beer, and that the pasteurization process was originally proposed as a means of preserving wines and beer.

Pasteur first began his research into fermentation in 1857, when he made an examination of distilling problems, and at that time worked out the formula that "life must be derived from life," and that infinitesimal bacteria were responsible for deleterious effects which had formerly been blamed on "spontaneous generation." [1] He went on from there to study the properties of yeast, as illustrated in the making of vinegar and finally of beer. He came to the examination of beer, as he states in the preface to his book, *Etudes sur la Bière*, as a direct consequence of the 1870 outbreak of war with Prussia[2] — which he refers to as "*nos malheurs*," as one ironically speaks of "the late unpleasantness." He wished to place the French brewing industry on a level with the German, which had always been superior; and he believed, by the discoveries evolving out of his experiments with yeast and the fermentation of beer, he had achieved a system which would greatly benefit the French brewers.

The nature of yeast, while it might still at that time have been a dark mystery to most brewers, was not entirely unknown to chemists who, as early as 1835, had recognized that it was simply a form of plant life.[3] The genus was called *Saccharomyces* ("sugar fungus"), and the credit for proving that it was not just present at, but essential for, fermentation is given to Mitcherlich, who made this finding in 1841.[4] Pasteur's main contribution was to prove that the so-called "diseases" of fermented liquids were caused by bacteria, and that a yeast free of bacteria produced a fermentation free of disease.[5] The practical result of his research into bacteria was the process which was at first called "steaming" and then "pasteurizing": that is, the heating of the finished product at temperatures high enough to kill all harmful microorganisms or bacteria that might still exist in it. This is only another form of sterilization, which had stemmed from Pasteur's original establishment of bacteria as the cause of disease.

A necessary step beyond was taken in the early 1880s by the Danish biochemist Emil Christian Hansen; backed by Carl Jacobsen, the owner of the Carlsberg Breweries in Copenhagen, he was able to prove that certain yeasts, once identified and differentiated, were harmful in the fermentation process while others worked exactly as desired. Another scientist, writing on Hansen's work, put the problem as follows:

> *Pasteur's* object was to free the yeast from bacteria. He did not ask at all whether the yeast thus purified consisted of one or more species. *Hansen,* on the other hand, took up the problem from quite a different standpoint, and he introduced an entirely novel principle: the absolutely pure culture of a methodically selected species or race — namely, the one proved to be the best suited to the brewery concerned.[6]

Through the experiments of Hansen, two favorable brewing yeast strains were isolated: *Saccharomyces cerevisiae* (top-fermenting) and *Saccharomyces carlsbergensis* (bottom-fermenting). There are numerous other varieties, all of which are called "wild" yeasts, in contrast with the two named above, which are "culture" yeasts.[7] It was in November 1883 that Hansen introduced at the Carlsberg Brewery the first absolute pure culture, as it was called: a yeast, that is, which had been propagated from a single selected cell. Hansen then followed this signal discovery through with a practical apparatus designed for the culture of pure yeast strains[8] — the rearing, as it might be called, of a pedigreed family of yeast.

Thus, within a space of twenty years or so, great strides had been made, in terms of pure science, across the gulf of ignorance toward a system which took the prevailing chanciness out of brewing. Through the absence of bacteria in the yeast and in the finished product, brewing failures were virtually banished. Through the use of pure culture yeast, the nature and quality of the resulting brew could be planned and counted on.

The findings of Hansen were much slower to make their impact on American brewers than those of Pasteur. It has been remarked that "in comparison with European developments, the process had made but little progress in America up to the time of Prohibition." This is attributed to first, characteristic American brewing methods which had developed a *natural* pure culture yeast through empirical means rather than in the laboratory, and second, the use of unmalted cereals (such as rice or corn-grit) in brewing, an American practice which reduced certain dangers of failure that were present when only malt was used, as in Europe, and which also improved the reproduction of yeast during fermentation. Besides, the drinking public prior to Prohibition has been described by the same author as somewhat undiscriminating: "The slight deficiencies resulting from the use of inferior types of yeast escaped notice." [9]

But certain progressive and ambitious American brewers — those who were competing on a national scale and wished to establish their label as one of superior quality — were quick to see that Hansen's pure culture strain of yeast could assure them uniformity of product. William J. Uihlein, one of the six brothers who had inherited Joseph Schlitz's brewery in Milwaukee, reportedly brought a pure culture yeast back to America from Copenhagen in 1883 (the year Hansen first used it at the Carlsberg plant).[10] The Pabst brewery adopted the use of pure culture yeast in 1887, and also installed a research chemist.[11] In the same year Max Henius, cofounder of the Wahl-Henius "Brewing Station" in Chicago and himself a disciple of Hansen, was instrumental in introducing pure culture yeast into the F. J. Dewes Brewery in the same city.[12]

It is clear, however, that the use of pure culture yeast was far from universal until much more recent times. Pasteurization, on the other hand, was swiftly adopted in this country; perhaps as early as 1873, when Adolphus Busch is generally considered to have begun the bottling of beer for shipment on a large scale.[13] An article written in 1877 mentions "the steaming process, to which all good bottlers now subject their beer, on the theory of Pasteur that it improves its quality and renders it better for shipment." [14] A British writer, professing surprise in 1879 that pasteurization had not been taken up by the British brewers, stated that "the method has been adopted with success by some Continental and American brewers." [15] And Professor J. E. Siebel, writing on the preservation of beers in 1880, commented that pasteurizing "is now generally applied for bottled goods." Of the process itself, Siebel said that it

> consists in subjecting the beer in the bottles, well corked, to a temperature of about 150 degrees Fahrenheit, which is done by placing them in a water-bath, which is gradually heated to about 160 to 170 degrees.[16]

In the earliest stages, pasteurizers or "steaming tanks" were simply fairly large vessels fitted with steam injectors at certain points; "The bottles were placed on trays or in baskets, then submerged by filling the tank with cool water, warmed up by steam, and cooled with fresh, cold water." As the demand for bottled beer grew during the 'eighties and 'nineties these primitive devices were quickly outmoded; and a new system, the "basket-type pasteurizer," was instituted. By these means, bottles in baskets were suspended from chains and moved *through* the steam bath, thus providing a continuous process.[17] All improvements since then have tended toward the maximum mechanization of pasteurizing: the bottles (or cans, at a later stage) were to be moved on a conveyor belt into and out of the pasteurizer, and no handling by workmen would thus be required. At the Pabst Brewing Company, as described in an 1895 article, the then latest type of pasteurization method was used — a conveyor mechanism, to be sure, but one that still required the bottles to be placed into a receptacle and then taken out of it again.[18]

The selling of beer in bottles was, of course, nothing new; it went back at least as far as the eighteenth century.* The novelty of bottling in the 1870s, as inaugurated by Adolphus Busch and other rapidly expanding brewing interests like his, lay in its volume and in the stability of the beer sold this way. The stability was assured by pasteurization, as well as by rigorous cleanliness in the brewery and improved methods of production. The volume, on the other hand, depended on two interweaving factors: the enormously increased market for beer and the imaginative drive with which the larger brewers competed for it.

Bottled beer had, in the past, found a good part of its market in areas where breweries did not exist. In Mobile, Alabama, for example, there was a bottling establishment set up in 1838, which announced its intention of "keeping on hand a supply of porter, Ale & Cider." [19] Bottling in itself was a sufficiently widespread business for an association of bottlers to exist even before the 'eighties. Under the name of "The Bottlers' and Soda Manufacturers' Association," such an organization was formed locally in Boston in 1866; its main concern was setting up price regulations for the bottling of beer. In 1872 and 1873, however, because of the bottlers' close tie-in with the brewing industry, their association took up the struggle against prohibition. On 24 April 1872 they were concerned with a vote coming up on prohibition in Massachusetts, and in May 1873 they agreed to pay a lawyer "for his services to defend each and every one of the Undersigned that may be complained of under the Prohibitory Law." [20]

Bottle manufacturers all over the country, of course, were directly affected by the increase in sales of bottled beer. The brewers' periodicals at that time were full of advertisements for glass works which specialized in beer bottles. The Pittsburgh City Glass Works claimed, "We are the pioneers in the manufacture of BEER BOTTLES for shipping purposes. A process, only known to us, assures to the trade a bottle that will stand the steaming of Beer." [21] This firm was reported to be one of the

* See page 59.

suppliers for the Anheuser Brewing Association (as it was called at that time) in St. Louis, and to have "shipped as many as three thousand gross to Milwaukee in one order." [22]

A firm called the Mississippi Glass Co. in St. Louis advertised beer bottles as its specialty in 1878, and in La Salle, Illinois, the De Steiger Glass Company made the same claim for itself.[23] But it was not only the bottle makers who profited from the upswing in this aspect of the brewing industry: there were also the cork suppliers, the label makers, the manufacturers of special machinery, such as bottle washers, bottle fillers, etc. The search for a foolproof and economical means of stoppering the bottles went on for a long time, and patents were issued year after year for hopeful solutions. Corks themselves were expensive, required special skills in their use, and were not altogether reliable. By the 1890s, the most widely used stoppers were the "Bottle Seal," or one of the ceramic and/or rubber types which were attached to the bottle or wired down. These were, on the whole, satisfactory, and could be used repeatedly; but they still required the human agency, and what the brewers wanted was a stopper that could be applied by machine. The "crown," which was patented in 1892 by William Painter, turned out to be the complete and enduring answer to the stopper problem, though bottlers did not see it all at once.[24]

This stopper, named because of its vague resemblance to a royal crown, was, in effect, a bottle *cover* rather than a stopper: a circle of tin plate, molded to fit over the mouth of the bottle, its sides corrugated and its edge skirted in order to lock under the rim of the bottle. According to the authoritative history of the crown:

> When crowns first came into use, the bottles were all hand made and the lip diameters and lip shapes varied considerably. Such variations could be accommodated in the early crowners which were foot operated. However, with the introduction of high speed automatic crowners, more uniform bottles became necessary. The glass industry had to adopt a standard bottle for the standard crown.[25]

Affixed to the inside of the crown was a thin disc of cork; the extreme pressure of the crown's locking around the bottle top made the cork gastight, and thus the high carbonation of lager beer was not lost in the bottle. The cork also kept the liquid from touching the metal. From about 1907 on, however, composition cork replaced natural cork — first because it was more economical, and later because it was found to have unexpected advantages of its own. Composition cork is not, in fact, an accurate description, since the product is made mainly of cork waste: it is manufactured "by binding together small cork granules with an adhesive binder in a manner very similar to the way the cork cells are held together by the resins in natural cork." With composition cork crowns, there were fewer "leakers," as they are called in the trade: they have generally been guaranteed on the basis of no more than one leaker in a thousand bottles.[26]

By 1893, the Crown Cork and Seal Co., Baltimore, was proudly advertising its product as "The Most Perfect System of Bottle Stoppering Ever Invented." [27] It was "far superior to patent stoppers or corks, in tightness, keeping qualities, security, cleanliness and purity of goods, ease of opening, and handsome, elegant appearance." It would stand an internal pressure of over 150 pounds to the square inch, "and in steaming Beer requires no wires or extraneous appliances." The system, as the advertisement points out, is cheap, "although there is no suggestion of 'cheapness' in its appearance." An additional attraction of the crown to its users (though this was not stated in the advertisement) was the fact that brand names could be lithographed on it.

In a short time, beer-bottling itself, as an adjunct to the brewing business, became an important and thriving industry. The curious thing about it, from the contemporary point of view, is that at first, generally speaking, brewers did not do their own bottling, but set up concessions for those who were willing to engage in that particular trade. There was a newspaper announcement in 1877, for instance, to the effect that "Messrs. Sam Rindskopf and P. O'Dyke will open their beer-bottling department in connection with Blatz's Brewery [Valentin Blatz in Milwaukee]." [28] The beer of the Lion Brewery, owned by Windisch, Mulhauser & Co., in Cincinnati, was bottled in 1882 by the Lion Bottling Co., Haskill & Thornton, proprietors.[29] The bottling department established by the Schlitz company in 1877 was conducted in an exclusive arrangement by Voechting, Shape & Co.[30] The Pabst brewers, when they started bottling in 1875, set up a department of their own, but by the following year they found it to their advantage to turn it over to the firm of Stamm & Meyer, who operated what is described as "a small one-story building." [31] The brewery of F. Borcherdt & Sons in Milwaukee announced in the 1877 newspapers that, on 22 April of that year, they had "disposed of our beer-bottling department to Messrs. Sidebotham & Witt." [32] Those who ran their own bottling shops began to call themselves "brewers and bottlers." Lemp of St. Louis advertised that his beer was "bottled in the brewery," [33] as, in another industry, wine is described as "bottled in the château." Anheuser-Busch, from the beginning, took care of its own bottling in St. Louis, although when the Budweiser brand was introduced in 1875, it was bottled by C. Conrad & Co.[34] Busch considered the bottling of beer a major aspect of the industry:

> Before the Anheuser-Busch Brewing Association introduced the Pasteurizing process for the preservation of bottled beer, the bottle beer trade was solely carried on by European Brewers. Whole cargoes of bottled beer, from Bremen and other European ports, were imported to New Orleans, Galveston and other ports. This association can therefore point with honest pride to the marvelous change wrought by it in a few short years by virtually creating a new and important industry, a source of national wealth, giving employment to many thousand citizens, and proving the main factor in stimulating and developing the manufacture of bottles, corks, labels, wire, etc., to such extensive dimensions as the most sanguine and hopeful never dreamed of, since the Anheuser-Busch bottle beer has proved so superior to any imported German or English brands.[35]

By the law which existed at the time when bottling shops were being established by breweries all over the country, the bottling could not take place

> in the brewery or warehouse or anywhere on the brewery or warehouse premises. This rule also prohibits washing or storing of bottles, steaming, and all operations connected with bottling. Bottling must be done in a building entirely distinct and separate from, and having no communication with, the brewery or warehouse. This means that the location and arrangement of the brewery or warehouse and the bottlery must be such that it is a physical impossibility to take beer from the former to the latter without carrying the beer over the surface of a street or road which is a public highway and actually and commonly used by the public as a thoroughfare.[36]

The absurd routine, then, was to fill the kegs as usual. When they were bunged and the tax stamp fixed "upon the spigot-hole in the head of the package," they were taken out into the street and transported to the bottling department.[37] Only then could the beer be drawn from them in order to fill the bottles. The separation of bottling department from brewery or warehouse, and this laborious, time-losing process of first racking and then bottling the beer, were both factors obviously governed by the tax laws, which had been devised before bottled beer was produced in significant quantities.

The ridiculous aspect of these strictures is shown by the example of the Pabst company, which "was filling about 75,000 barrels a year in the racking room simply to take them across the street to the bottling house where they were emptied." Captain Frederick Pabst, then in charge of the firm, decided to seek amelioration for this situation, and it was through his efforts that the Internal Revenue Act was changed on 18 June 1890 to allow "the construction of pipe lines from storage cellars to bottling houses." [38]

This did not cancel the requirement that the brewery and its bottling department must remain separated, but it certainly facilitated the operation in most respects. The pipe line could not be used unless a revenue officer was present, and all the time beer was running through the pipe the officer had to remain on hand. The amount of beer run through was measured by gauge; the brewer was then required to hand the inspector the appropriate number of canceled stamps.[39] This method continued right through to Prohibition, and it was only with Repeal in 1933 that the method of tax collection was more or less rationalized.

TWENTY-EIGHT

Beer in the Western Mining Territories

T HE DRIVE toward the Oregon Territory and to California had, as it were, leaped over some of the intervening terrain. The bulk of the states forming a wide strip between the Minnesota-Louisiana line on the east and the California-Oregon line on the west developed late and achieved statehood relatively slowly. Utah, to be sure, had been populated by the Mormon emigration in 1848, but it did not become a state until 1890.

The years of Colorado's first settlement were 1857-1858, and the Gold Rush in 1859 naturally attracted settlers, prospectors, opportunists of all kinds, in great numbers. In the development of Denver, a village called Montana, completed in October 1858, was the first stage, even though it was deserted the following spring and some of the houses removed to a new town called Auraria (later West Denver). St. Charles, on the site of present-day Denver, was established in October 1859 and the following month it was named Denver City in honor of Governor Denver of Kansas. After a year or so of pointless competition over status, Auraria and Denver City were united in March 1860, the population then being 1000. By 1866, in spite of the intervening war, the population had grown fourfold.[1]

The first brewing of beer in the territory is supposed to have taken place on 10 November 1859, in Auraria, when a lager beer brewery was established by Salomon,* Tascher & Co. According to one who

---

* Fred Z. Salomon is listed elsewhere as a "merchant."

claimed to remember, "That beer, though quite drinkable, was as inno-
cent of hops as our early whiskey was of wheat or old rye." [2]

A more formal and serious brewery — one which has, in fact, survived
as the Tivoli Brewing Co. of modern times — was noted in an 1861
newspaper:

> Those capital brewers — Messrs. Endlich & Good of Highland [North
> Denver] this morning rolled into our office, a keg of the first Buck
> Beer* ever brewed in the Pike's Peak County, and their wagons have
> since been delivering that delicious beverage to customers throughout
> the city.[3]

According to one report, this brewery had been started in December
1859 by James Endlich. John Good, an immigrant from Alsace-Lorraine,
who started out in early Denver as a merchant and unsuccessful pros-
pector, settled finally for what appeared to be a safer business and
bought into Endlich's concern.[4] The first manager of the brewery was
Philip Zang, who eventually went off and started on his own a business
that prospered until Prohibition, which came to Colorado in 1914.

Morris (or Moritz) Sigi, proprietor of the Colorado Brewery, was
among the pioneers of the Denver industry. He was killed in an accident in 1874, and the business on Larimer Street was eventually taken
over by Max Melsheimer, who conducted it under his own name until
about the turn of the century.[5] There was also, in the 1860s, an establishment called the One Horse Brewery, originally owned by Henry
Graff and bought in 1866 by Louis Hessemer.[6] This did not fare as well
as some of the others, in spite of its picturesque name; by 1873 it was
run by Leonhard Summer as a cooper shop as well as brewery, but
Summer soon abandoned this enterprise and set up one of his own in
the town of Fair Play, where he operated into the 1890s.[7]

One of the important Denver breweries of the late nineteenth century was started in 1892 by the Neef brothers, Frederick and Max.
These German immigrants, after spending a year in St. Louis during
1871, were lured on to Colorado by rumors of the Del Norte gold strike.
But they learned in Denver that the strike had turned out to be disap-

---

* *Bock beer:* a dark beer of German origin, identified with early spring. The origin
of the term is in dispute.

pointing, and so, changing their minds, they opened a saloon instead. According to a newspaper report, in 1892

> they bought the old Western Brewing Company, at what is now W. 12th and Quivas St. The brewery was known as the Neef Brothers Brewing Co. and its Gold Belt Beer was nationally famous. . . . They operated the brewery with the help of their sons, Emil, son of Frederick, who held the job of secretary, and Rudolph, son of Max, who was assistant treasurer and assistant secretary.[8]

This plant finally had to close in 1916, after trying in vain for two years of Colorado prohibition to carry on with near beer.

Outside of Denver, wherever there was a mining town there were saloons and a brewery. As early as 1862 a German called Melanger reportedly set up a small brewery in Laporte, Larimer County.[9] A brewery of some importance was established in Boulder by Frank Weisenhorn and Charles Voegtle in 1875; it lasted into the 'nineties.[10] In the Bonanza mining district, in the northeast segment of the state, the town of Sedgwick, during the 1880s,

> had the distinction of having the only brewery in this part of the country. It was located in a little gulch north of town, through which runs a little stream that flows into Kerber Creek. This gulch and creek are known as Brewery Gulch and Brewery Creek.[11]

The town of Howardsville in the southwestern part of the state had a brewery in the 'eighties that had been established by Charles Fischer. He started out, according to reports from that area, in a "washboiler," but he soon ran a regular brewery, "first at Howardsville and later at Silverton where in 1889 he built a stone brewery." The extraordinary thirst of the local population continually taxed his resources, "for the saloons always had to ship in additional beer." [12]

One of the most colorful and successful of Western breweries, the Adolph Coors Company, had its beginning in late 1873, when Adolph Coors, in partnership with Jacob Schuler, opened an establishment in the town of Golden, some fifteen miles west of Denver. A German by birth, Coors had been a brewer's apprentice at Dortmund. He worked there until 1867; after that in breweries in Kassel, Berlin and Uelzen. Upon making the decision to emigrate to America, he came to New

York and then to Chicago on 30 May 1868. For a year he worked in a brewery there; then found a job in the brewery of John Stenger at Naperville, Illinois, where he stayed until 1872. The West evidently proved an irresistible attraction, or at least offered less-trodden paths, and so he moved on to Denver, where in May 1872 he set up a bottling business in partnership with John Staderman. The partnership lasted only until November of that year, when Coors took over the business himself: in the 1873 Denver City Directory he advertised as "dealer in Bottled Beer, Ale, Porter & Cider — imported and domestic wines, seltzer water, etc. Tappan Block, Holladay St. between E and F."

But it appears that he was only biding his time, and looking out for a suitable brewing situation. This he must have found to his satisfaction in 1873, when the brewery in Golden was built and the business in Denver sold. According to a local historian writing in 1880:

> They began by erecting a small building. Since that time, however, they have enlarged their business and built additional buildings, as their business increased from year to year, until, at present, the brewery is one of the best equipped in the State, and known as the Golden Brewery.[18]

Only a year after its establishment, the local paper reported that "Messrs. Schuler and Coors have leaped to the front rank of brewers in a remarkably short time, and their beer is regularly sold in Denver and the mountain and valley towns." [14] Schuler was bought out in 1880, and from then on the brewery has been a Coors family affair.

It was in the 1880s that the number of breweries in the state of Colorado hit a peak — twenty-three.[15] These were considered to be among the state's industrial leaders; but soon afterward their numbers were depleted through failures, even floods and fires, as well as the inevitable prohibitionist pressures.

The other states in this central western band had, on the whole, fewer established breweries than Colorado. There was a sudden rash of brewers in Nevada during the silver-mining period: the Pacific Coast Business Directory for 1871 lists at least twenty-one in such towns as Carson City, Empire City, Eureka, Gold Hill, Washoe, etc. Virginia City had a great but momentary success, and by 1871 its population was on the decline. Nevertheless, there were still four fair-sized breweries there at that time: Union (Baker & Duttenhoffer), California (John P. Deininger), Eagle (D. W. Osborn), Pacific (Jacob Riem), as well as several on a smaller scale.

In Idaho Territory there were only four breweries: one each in Boise City, Lewiston, Silver City and Pioneerville. W. A. Nunally, in Pioneerville, was listed as "postmaster, saloon, brewery" [16] — a multiplicity of trades which gives some clue to life in those small, isolated communities. Utah Territory, because of its nondrinking Mormons, was largely dry; Salt Lake City, with a population of 25,000 in 1871, had no brewers. In Corinne, however, listed as a "Gentile [non-Mormon]" town, there were two breweries, one owned by F. P. Winschell and the other by Toland & Campbell; and in Ogden, William D. Williams had a brewery. By 1884, some eighteen breweries were listed for the territory as a whole (including three in Salt Lake City itself), but in the 1890 directory the figure had declined to nine.[17] The production of beer in the territory was at its height in the year 1883, when a total of 22,270 barrels was reported; the following year, however, there was a sharp drop to 3705 barrels, and from then on, during the nineties, production was so meager that Utah and Montana were reported together.[18]

As for Montana Territory, the 1871 directory lists breweries in Blackfoot City, Bozeman (population 168), Diamond City (population 46), Missoula (population 119); as well as three in Virginia City, once a large settlement but in 1871 reduced to 867 souls, and four in Helena, the largest town in the territory with a population of over 3000. Of those in Helena, only two were of any size: the one owned by Horsky and a variety of changing partners, and the one which belonged to Nicholas Kessler. Kessler, who established a brewery that stayed in operation until the 1950s, came to America from Luxembourg in 1854, and spent his first ten years in this country in New York; Sandusky, Ohio; Detroit; Chicago; mining in Colorado; and finally searching for gold in Montana. He was persuaded by a man named Charles Beehrer to give up what was proving to be a fruitless quest for gold and settle down with a brewery. Kessler began to build one in Blackfoot City, but learned that the digging was about exhausted and that the population of that place would soon be moving on. He consequently abandoned his work there and returned to Helena, where he undertook to help Beehrer set up a brewery on a site a couple of miles outside of town, where there was access to a mountain spring. In 1865 the brewery began operation, and in May of that same year, Kessler bought out Beehrer's interest. For about twenty years, Keesler managed successfully, in spite of necessarily haphazard conditions; and in 1886, he installed what is considered to be the first ice-making machine that operated between Chicago and the Pacific Coast. From then on, the Kessler business continued to grow, new improvements and expansions took place, and two sons, Charles and Frederick, inherited when their father died in 1901.[19]

Another illustrious brewer who began in Montana, though his name became more closely associated with another state, was Leopold F. Schmidt, a German who started out in youth as a seaman, came to the United States in 1866, there engaged in carpentering in various cities, and eventually found his way to Butte, where, in partnership with Daniel Gamer, he founded the Centennial Brewery, named for the year of its establishment, 1876. According to the recollections of one of his sons, Frederick, Leopold came into the brewing business almost by accident. He had come to know a brewer in Deer Lodge called Peter Vallaton; during a period when the latter went back to Europe for a visit to Baden-Baden, Schmidt was invited to manage the business for him. After starting his own business in Butte, Schmidt went back to Germany himself to attend a brewing school in Worms; there he met the woman he married.

Schmidt became a prominent enough member of his community to be elected to the Montana constitutional convention, as well as the state legislature. In 1804, while serving on the Capitol Commission of the state, he went with a party of officials to inspect the capitol buildings in Salem, Sacramento and Carson City that had been designed by the famous architect Stanford White. The one in Olympia, Washington, was just being started, and during his visit there Schmidt was so struck by a river site at the nearby town of Tumwater, as well as the artesian spring water there, that he bought the property and within two years had finished off his affairs in Montana, brought his family to the Pacific Coast, and established in October 1896 (after issuing about $125000 in capital stock) the Capital Brewing Company, nucleus of what has since become the highly successful and still Schmidt-managed Olympia Brewing Co. of Tumwater.[20]

Arizona Territory, where the amount of brewing before 1900 remained well below that of all the other territories or states in that region, reported five brewers in 1871: in Prescott, Jackson & Co. and Raible & Sheerer; in Tucson, Sales & Smith and Levin & Co.; in Wickenburg, where there was a flourishing mine, A. H. Peoples.[21]

According to reminiscences of an Arizona pioneer, James M. Barney, the last-named brewer was "Abe Peeples," owner of the Magnolia Brewery and Saloon at Wickenburg, and first producer of beer in that area.[22] Phoenix, as a town, barely existed in 1871. Prescott preceded it as territorial capital, and even in 1868 had two breweries: the Pacific and the Arizona. But by April 1872, fast-growing Phoenix was reported to contain "four stores owned by Mennasse & Co., Dennis & Murphy, Bichard & Co, and —— [sic] Smith; two saloons by John Roach and G. A. Carpenter; a good hotel by J. J. Gardner; a brewery by M. Cavuness [sic]." [23] According to Barney, again, Roach was "the pioneer Saloon man in Phoenix," but the one a little later owned by "Cavaness and Cosgrove on East Washington Street" was more fashionable. Those two gentlemen took over a saloon, situated in what was called the Old Brewery, that had been operated in early 1872 by Cromwell A. Carpenter. Matt Cavaness, who had hauled ore from the Silver King Mine, aside from brewing and saloonkeeping also conducted, with his partner Frank Cosgrove, a wagon and blacksmith shop behind their saloon, and engaged in a host of other activities.

Quite soon after this, German brewers began to operate in Phoenix: the United States Brewery was started in 1878 by Gustav Becher and A. H. Sales (or Sayles), making "a superior article of beer, ale and porter";[24] and C. A. Luke and J. Thalheimer ran the Arcade Brewery, called "the only brick brewery in the Territory, and the coolest place in town." [25] The Arcade was first announced in April 1879, when Luke and Thalheimer contracted for the construction of a brick building 24 by 60 feet to be occupied as a brewery and saloon. The newspaper comment was: "We are pleased to see the gentlemen adopt the brick instead of the abominable adobe." [26] The newspaper followed up with a report in May, saying that the building was "getting into shape" and would be ready in two weeks. The building to house the saloon was one thing; behind it was to be put up "a brewing shed twenty-two by twenty-four" [27] — which gives some idea of how informal and conscribed such a brewing operation was in that time and place. In September, when all was in order and functioning, the reporter called it "the largest brewery in Arizona." It was lager beer that Luke and Thalheimer made, and

> From the outset their beer found favor in the eyes of the beer imbibing portion of the inhabitants of Phoenix, so that they were forced to turn out over one hundred gallons daily, and continue doing so till date, all of this beer being brewed from malt received from San Francisco.

This latter practice had turned out to be so expensive, that the proprietors built a malthouse, "the largest and most complete in the Territory," which promised to make their business that much more profitable.[28] At any rate, it was still there in 1884, but by 1890, it and all other Phoenix breweries were out of business.

One of Phoenix's specialties would drive one to the conclusion that bottled beer was once particularly popular in that town: a sidewalk which was built there out of empty beer bottles. In 1911,

> workmen who were digging a trench for a gas main along Goldberg Bros. store yesterday thought they had discovered something prehistoric, and the foreman of the gang, who is something of an antiquarian, believed that he had found proof that the forgotten people who had inhabited this valley and left no other traces of themselves than mounds, pottery and stone axes, knew something about glassworking. There was dug up a lot of old bottles which seemed to have been planted in the ground, neck down and so close to each other as to form a causeway. But inquiry among the antediluvians remaining in Phoenix brought out that the bottles were not prehistoric. Those bottles once formed a pavement along the First Street side of that store building, extending to the alley almost. Just when the pavement was constructed could not be recalled, though it was probably some time in the '80s, for in the early '90s it showed considerable wear. Where the small heel of the cowboy had struck with some force directly on a single bottle, the bottom had given away [sic], but as late as '92 most of the bottles were still intact.[29]

One of the old-timers claimed that the walk had been laid back in 1885. "People from all parts of town contributed bottles," he recalled,

". . . and they made a fancy walk, believe me!" This man said he used to go two or three blocks out of his way to walk on the bottle sidewalk.[30]

There was some disagreement as to whether the bottles made a good or a perfectly terrible walk. An account of 1898 stated: "After all these years of use as a pavement not more than one-fourth of the bottles were broken, showing that glass makes a good and durable walk." [31] But another newspaper wrote that "the walk was so uneven a person felt as if afflicted with the blind staggers when walking over it." [32] Though one may no longer be able to ascertain the quality of the sidewalk, one is permitted to say, until proven wrong, that it was unique.

Bisbee, one of those towns that sprouted wherever there were miners, reportedly had an adobe brewery in about 1880, started by Al Sieber. The camp at Bisbee numbered only a few hundred at that time, but Sieber also drew his customers from the mining camp of Tombstone and the garrison at Fort Huachuca. Sieber's brewery was in a gulch, and thereby created the name "Brewery Gulch" for one of Bisbee's streets. Bisbee's current newspaper, the *Brewery Gulch Gazette*, has recapitulated some of the town's early history, particularly with reference to the brewery:

> The Fort had been established a few years earlier for the military forces that protected southern Arizona from Indian raids, and the soldiers preferred beer to hard liquor. . . . Al Sieber soon sold his little brewery to the Dubacher brothers, Henry and Frank, and they continued to make beer until in later years it could be brought into the camp by railroad.[33]

The quality of beer brewed in this establishment was apparently not the best: "not even up to the grade of the home brew of prohibition days." One of the main problems, of course, was keeping the brew cool. This was done by primitive means: "The huge copper container of one day's output was wrapped in sacks which were kept wet, and evaporation in the warm weather cooled the brew somewhat."

The adobe brewery ended operations when the railroad came to Bisbee in the 'nineties, carrying Midwestern beer to the many taverns there. One of these was called simply The Brewery, and was owned by a relation of the Dubachers, Joseph M. Muheim. Its main attraction, for a time, was a pet bear which became a great consumer of beer; but its sense of fun was evidently a bit rough, and eventually it had to be disposed of in order to keep the customers happy and, what was more, safe.[34]

◄§ TWENTY-NINE ℬ►

The National Brewers

I N THOSE PALMY days of the brewing industry between about
1880 and 1910, the number of brewers was steadily decreasing
whereas the production of beer constantly — and at a quicker pace —
increased. Improved methods of production and distribution meant
that fewer breweries could manufacture more beer. Withdrawals* rose
from slightly over 13 million barrels in 1880 to just about 59½ million
in 1910, and in the same period the total population of the country almost doubled.[1]

Though the bulk of the breweries at that time (and in 1910 there
were still over 1500) were small, local enterprises, making all their own
deliveries by horse-drawn wagons, it was the few large, highly mechanized factories, with merchandising chains extending beyond their own
neighborhoods or towns, that controlled the major part of the market.
Formerly, each brewer had known the exact confines of his market and
been able to maintain it with relatively little competition: the consumer
simply was not offered so many choices. But the development of a national web of railroads — improved communications in general — had
drawn the whole country closer together; and the great technological
advances within the brewing industry itself had made it feasible for individual brewers to look for customers farther afield. This era was
marked, then, by the emergence of the national brewer — a new concept in the industry, which, with its technical paraphernalia and merchandising innovations, constituted an immense step forward.

* Term used for amount of beer on which tax is paid — a measure of sales.

An extremely successful local brewer could continue, in this period, to increase his sales appreciably, but not at the rate available to the national brewer. George Ehret, for example, largest brewer in the country in 1877 and operating entirely in New York, reported production of 138,449 barrels for the year. Phillip Best of Milwaukee, ranking second, was credited with 121,634 barrels.[2] In 1890, Ehret had pushed sales to 412,851 barrels, a very profitable figure "attained to without any forced efforts to open new channels outside of the limits of the State of New York."[3] Best, on the other hand, under the new name of Pabst Brewing Co., had reached a million-barrel annual sales figure, with the help of national distribution and absorption of another Milwaukee brewery, by 1893.[4] Another of the national brewers, Schlitz, arrived at the magic million-barrel figure after the turn of the century,[5] and a third national giant, Anheuser-Busch of St. Louis, sold just under a million in 1900.[6]

With the possible exception of the Jacob Ruppert Brewery in New York, which managed to spurt ahead of its nearest competitors and was reported in 1916 to be manufacturing over a million barrels a year,[7] none of the local brewers was able to approach that level before Prohibition. It took an amalgamation of some twenty-one breweries, under the name of the Pittsburgh Brewing Co., to sell a phenomenal 700,000 barrels in 1913;[8] it was unlikely that the ordinary brewery, operating on its own and without national outlets, could create so large a market under prevailing conditions at that time. Even an important plant like P. Ballantine & Sons in Newark proudly announced around 1900 that its annual sales had reached half a million barrels[9] — a good way from the national brewers' accomplishment.

The decision of a brewer to "go national" posed a number of problems which the local brewer entirely avoided. The basic requirement for a national brewer was, of course, a reliable and well-conducted distribution system, consisting usually of "agencies" in the leading cities. The St. Louis firm of William J. Lemp, for instance, maintained branch offices in Birmingham, Los Angeles, San Francisco, Leadville and Pueblo in Colorado, Atlanta, Wichita, Atchison, Joplin, Memphis, El Paso, Galveston, Salt Lake City, and many more towns and cities in all parts of the country.[10] Some of these were nothing more than small icehouses situated near the railroad depots, but others were substantial offices and warehouses, equipped to take orders, keep stock on hand, and make local deliveries.

Agencies of this kind had been maintained by a number of brewers even before the era of national distribution. In New Orleans there existed in 1864 an agency for the Lowell Ale Brewery of St. Louis.[11] The Vassar company in Poughkeepsie had maintained representatives in New York City and along the Hudson River even before 1850.* The leading Albany firm, John Taylor & Sons, established important depots in New York City and Boston in 1851.[12] In 1876, Anheuser's "St. Louis Lager Beer" was advertised as being sold by first-class grocers and liquor dealers in Denver.[13] But these were barely comparable to the elaborate network of distributing agencies set up in the 'eighties and 'nineties by Anheuser-Busch, Pabst, Schlitz, Lemp and a few others. Between 1878 and 1893, Pabst established forty branches throughout the country.[14] By 1884, Anheuser-Busch had thirteen agencies in Texas alone.[15] The Christian Moerlein Brewing Company of Cincinnati had agencies for its beer in New Orleans and Americus, Georgia, thus competing with firms that were larger than itself.[16]

Among the technological improvements that made it feasible to step up the "export" of beer to distant parts of the country were the refrigerated freight cars. Anheuser & Co. had made an early investment in these after they were shown at the 1876 Centennial Exhibition in Philadelphia. In 1877 that company was reportedly using forty refrigerator cars, and was about to shift to a new invention, the "Ayer Rubber Car," which was of much lighter weight than its predecessors.[17]

Overloading of cars with a superfluity of ice to make sure the shipment would not spoil had created friction between the brewers and the railroad managements.[18] There were various other causes for occasional conflict between the railroads and the brewers, such as price discrimination — a practice which caused the Jos. Schlitz Brewing Co. to bring suit against the Southern Pacific Railway in 1893. (Schlitz won the case.[19]) In order to avoid such headaches, the large national brewers sought control of the railroad facilities they used. Anheuser-Busch, for one, helped to set up the Manufacturer's Railway Company;[20] and

* See pages 153, 154.

Joseph Uihlein, of the Schlitz management, was the real owner of the Union Refrigerator Transit Corporation, a fact which found its way into state politics when, in 1904, Robert LaFollette accused Emanuel Lorenz Philipp (later governor of Wisconsin), as president of that corporation, of receiving rebates from certain Milwaukee brewers.* (Philipp afterward successfully sued the press which had repeated these charges.[21])

The national brewers competed strenuously with one another, but they were also in a position to take business away from the local brewers who had been accustomed to a safe and stable market. The large brewers had, of course, superior facilities for getting new customers and keeping old ones; they also had sufficient capital to exploit such means as advertising to gain national ascendance.

Advertising of one sort or another went back at least as far as the eighteenth century, when the pages of the newspapers gave over a good many columns to business "announcements," real estate notices, and the like. This kind of "notice" advertising went on into the nineteenth century, by which time there were advertising "agents," who handled the placement of these newspaper announcements for their clients. In 1832, for instance, the Boston advertising firm of Adams & Hudson handled, among other accounts, that of Meldrum & Co., brewers, for whom they placed advertisements for "Pale Porter" and ale.[22] A similar firm in Boston, Homer & Palmer, had an account in July 1833, with George Odin, Meldrum & Co. (presumably the same brewery), for the advertising of porter and ale; and they also undertook to place newspaper announcements for the proprietors of the South Boston Brewery.[23]

Advertisements for breweries also appeared frequently in the pages of local city directories. These were inclined to be somewhat more elaborate than those in the newspapers, part of the advertisement generally being a print of the brewery itself, with some conventional device

---

* It was reported in the American Brewer (v. 28, p. 20) that in 1895 the Pabst and Jos. Schlitz Brewing Companies of Milwaukee "have just completed the organization of the Mississippi and Northern Railroad Co. The officers are Gustav G. Pabst, president; Alfred Uihlein, vice-president; E. L. Phillips [sic], secretary. The last named gentleman was formerly connected with the Chicago and North Western Railroad Co."

of barley stalks and hops. Show cards were another well-used form of advertising. These were placed in the windows and on the walls of beer parlors and such places. Produced to begin with of paper, they were eventually made more durable by means of printing on glass and iron: specimens of these were shown in Brewers Hall at the Centennial Exhibition.[24] Show cards did at least impress on the drinking public the names of the brewers who supplied their beer, though very few of them would be suitable today. The artwork was generally quaint, arch or saccharine; by modern standards they were fearsomely overloaded with copy; yet one must presume that they reflected the tastes of their time.

It was not until the great growth of the beer market following the Civil War that brewers, on a large scale, developed trade names and trade marks — what we would today call their distinctive "labels." At earlier stages, various beers had been identified with a place: Albany ale or Philadelphia porter, for example — and then, when the lagers came, "Erlanger," "Vienna," "Pilsener," "Culmbacher," "Budweiser," and the like, describing the *type* of beer rather than just giving it a name. A trade mark such as the three interlocking rings of the Ballantine company in Newark (adopted in 1879) came a bit later. The length of time that many of the trade marks have lasted attests to the selling importance they must have had. The Anheuser-Busch trade mark of "A and Eagle" is claimed to have started in 1872,[25] though its actual form has been changed occasionally since then. The Jos. Schlitz Brewing Co. has long been identified by a globe of the world incorporated in its label. The trade name "Knickerbocker" was first used in November 1892 by the Bartholomay Brewery Co. in Rochester, New York.[26] "Rheingold" was so popular and likely a name for a light golden beer that it was used before Prohibition by at least three brewers: S. Liebmann's Sons in Brooklyn (who were eventually able to make it their exclusive symbol), the small Weisbrod & Hess concern in Philadelphia, and the United States Brewing Co. of Chicago, which used a charming "Rheingold Girl" * in an advertisement published in 1911.[27] Another girl used for advertising purposes is the one who has been perched on a crescent moon in the labels and posters of the Miller Brewing Company in Mil-

---

* No relation to that most successful and widely known beer salesgirl of them all: "Miss Rheingold."

waukee since 1903. The Pabst "Blue Ribbon" label has lasted since the 'nineties;[28] the company put so much store in it that in 1904 they brought suit against the Storz Brewing Co. of Omaha for alleged infringement of the "Blue Ribbon" copyright.[29]

In some instances, a label has been considered important enough to buy from a defunct firm: Falstaff Brewing Corp.'s characteristic shield, for instance, was originally the property of the William J. Lemp Brewing Co., which had used it since March 1896 and registered it on 25 August 1903.[30] The Sicks' organization, which began brewing operations after Repeal in Seattle, Washington, under the name Seattle Brewing & Malting Co., paid a million dollars in 1940 for full rights to the trade name "Rainier," and thereupon changed the firm name to Sicks' Rainier Brewing Co.[31] On at least one occasion, an international sale of a trade name took place: in 1886 the San Antonio Brewing Association (now the Pearl Brewing Co.) bought the formula and name for "Pearl" beer from the Kaiser-Beck brewery at Bremen, Germany.[32]

Another form of advertisement was presented in the guise of exhibitions at the various international fairs that took place after the triumph of the Crystal Palace, London, exposition in 1851, and the Centennial Exhibition, 1876, in Philadelphia. The brewers were eager to follow up their success in Philadelphia with an exhibit at the 1878 Paris Exposition; among those represented were the Ph. Best Brewing Co., Lemp and Anheuser from St. Louis, Henry Clausen & Son from New York, and Bergner & Engel from Philadelphia. The Anheuser display was obviously the most elaborate, "as Mr. Adolphus Busch has been over personally to look after the arrangement." The Grand Prize was awarded to Bergner & Engel, but E. Anheuser & Co. and the Ph. Best Brewing Co. both took off Gold Medals.[33]

The World's Exposition at New Orleans, which took place in 1884-1885, was on a smaller scale, but nevertheless attracted a number of brewers, including Valentin Blatz of Milwaukee, the Continental Brewing Co. (John Gardiner) of Philadelphia, and the Anheuser-Busch Brewing Association. The Chicago Fair of 1893, officially called the World's Columbian Exhibition, was considered much more important and included exhibits by some twenty-four brewers. The major competition was between Pabst and Anheuser-Busch, who came out practically neck-

and-neck as far as awards went.[34] But the importance of the brewers' participation consisted not so much in the number of medals won (though the individual winners took as great advantage of these as possible) as the fact that the industry as a whole was well represented. There was one momentary flurry before the fair actually began, when Mrs. Potter Palmer, head of the Woman's Commission, voiced some objection to her photograph's being used to decorate brewers' advertising calendars, but the brewers sententiously pointed out:

> As an official of the World's Columbian Exposition of so distinguished merit and accomplishment, she has become also a distinguished individual, and her face and fame a public possession. Greatness is death to privacy, and a distinguished success pays the penalty in publicity.[35]

Even at fairs of a more local interest, brewers found it advantageous to show their product. At Leadville, Colorado, an "Ice Palace" was built in 1896: the Pabst company was represented as well as the Colorado breweries of Phil Zang, the Neef Brothers and Adolph Coors. The latter had sent from Golden six barrels of bottled beer which were to be frozen into ice blocks. In case anything went wrong, he also sent several dozen extra bottles. The extras were too tempting for the workmen to resist, but only six were opened: the workmen found to their dismay that Coors had filled the bottles with colored salt water so that they would not break when frozen.[36]

Brewers from the East also displayed their products at the 1905 Lewis and Clark Centennial Exposition in Portland, Oregon, though that was mainly a Pacific Coast affair, with the Henry Weinhard firm prominently represented and the Olympia Brewing Co. running a Swiss chalet on the fairgrounds.[37]

The culmination of all these activities was clearly the Louisiana Purchase Exposition which took place in 1904 in St. Louis. In every way, this was the largest, grandest, most popular and successful of all international fairs held in the United States up to that time. Being a prominent and rich citizen of St. Louis, Adolphus Busch was naturally intimately involved with arrangements for the fair. He was both adviser and backer (as well as exhibitor, of course); and one of his special efforts was to see that the German nation was well represented, an activity for which the German Emperor awarded him the Order of the Crown, second class, in 1905.[38] In 1902, he wrote from his German home, Villa Lilly, to ex-Governor David R. Francis of Missouri, who was in charge of the Exposition Company:

> There is no doubt in my mind but that the German Empire will exhibit with us, as I have this promise from the Secretary of State and others, but they will probably limit their exhibit to art and education. . . . But what I am after is industrial exhibits from this and other countries, and we must gain our point through the zealous work of our consuls, our ministers and special commercial people that are sent here to solicit such exhibits.[39]

The response was eventually much better than Busch had foreseen and the fair was a rousing success. He himself resigned as a director toward the end of the season, giving as his reason alleged discrimination by the management toward one of the concessions in which he was interested.[40]

The brewing interests of the country made good use of the fair that summer: not only did the annual convention of the United States Brewers' Association meet in St. Louis in June, but the Brewmasters National Convention also took place there, and the Pure Food Congress (which many brewers attended). The brewers of St. Louis combined to set up a "Tyrolean Alps" concession, which included a "grand, picturesque Tyrolean castle"; various other structures designed to give an impression of life in the Austrian mountains; and of course a huge restaurant pavilion. During the course of the exposition, a Gold Medal was awarded to the Zymotechnic Institute of J. E. Siebel (established in 1872) and the Brewing Academy attached to it. The grand prize for an individual beer was awarded to the Indianapolis Brewing Company for their "Gold Medal Duesseldorfer." The company celebrated by closing the plant for a day and "all employes took part in a magnificent industrial parade, which was one of the finest ever seen in Indianapolis." [41]

Consolidations and Syndicates

I N A SITUATION of tooth-and-nail competition, it is quite clear that one of the various means (though often an expensive one) of insuring a free field is to buy the competitor's plant and either operate it or close it down. One of the paradoxes of an economy based on free competition is exactly this trend toward swallowing up competition.

The early cases in which one brewer bought the plant of another appear to have been predicated basically on the need for expansion. When the Ph. Best Brewing Co. bought in 1870 the brewery that had belonged to the late Charles T. Melms, and named it the South Side Brewery, the point was to acquire a property with first-class equipment, which would help to increase the quantity of beer that Best could put on the market.[1] This must also have been the consideration leading to the purchase of the brewery of Peter Ahles in New York by Henry Clausen & Son, who in 1877 needed the extra space in which to set up a bottling establishment.[2] One would assume that S. Liebmann's Sons of Brooklyn, in 1878, bought the plant of J. P. Schoenewald, which had been out of operation for a year, for similar reasons.[3] In these cases, an additional plant was bought for use — an alternative to having new buildings erected.

In many instances, such plants were simply absorbed; their names and custom were not considered to have any commercial advantage. Sometimes, however, the local situation was such that the buyer, though himself a successful brewer, wished to continue the firm name or brand name. When Edward Schmidt, of the Philadelphia C. Schmidt & Sons Brewing Co., bought the venerable establishment of Robert Smith, ale brewer, the well-known Smith name was retained; and this policy was matched when Schmidt bought the Peter Schemm plant in the same city.[4]

Adolphus Busch, probably more than any other of the large brewers, had a stake in multiple plants. Perhaps the first brewery outside of the home factory in St. Louis in which he had a financial interest was the Lone Star Brewing Co. in San Antonio. This was established in 1883 with Busch as president; the manager was Otto Koehler, who some years later moved over to the competitive brewery in the same city that eventually became the Pearl Brewing Co.[5] Busch was reported, in 1895, to have bought the Alamo Brewery in San Antonio for $70,000, with the intention of closing it and transferring its trade to the Lone Star Brewing Co.[6]

He was also back of the American Brewing Association in Houston, chartered in 1895, and was supposed to have holdings in the Texas Brewing Co. at Fort Worth, chartered in 1890.[7] At least one other Busch brewery in the South was the Shreveport Ice & Brewing Co., at Shreveport, Louisiana.[8] In 1902, it was reported that the Anheuser-Busch Brewing Association was "chief promoter and owner" of a company that had bought land in Oklahoma City with the object of building a brewery there.[9] And in 1904, plans were reported for yet another branch at Grand Rapids, Michigan.[10]

These plants were not established to produce Budweiser and the other Busch products; they manufactured under labels of their own. It must be assumed that Busch simply saw good investments in this practice of backing breweries other than his own. The same may be said of Frank Fehr, one of the leading brewers in Louisville, Ky., who was chief promoter of the Louisiana Brewing Co., established in New Orleans in 1885.[11] An important Chicago brewer, Michael Keeley, had an interest in the Dallas Brewing Association;[12] William J. Lemp of St. Louis was president of the Little Rock Brewing & Ice Co.;[13] the Columbia Brewing Co. of St. Louis acquired the Algiers Brewing Co. in Louisiana in 1894, when the latter was in receivership;[14] and no doubt there were others throughout the country, silent or otherwise — investors and officers in breweries other than their own.

It was not just the industry leaders who became acquisitive in this period of consolidation. In the state of Washington, the Hemrich family represented widespread brewing interests, even though they were not precisely aspiring to make their products world-famous. Andrew Hemrich, son of a brewer, first appeared in Seattle in 1881. He began his career there with the Bay View Brewery, and was soon joined by his brothers Alvin and Louis. In 1893, a consolidation took place of this and two other Seattle breweries, forming the Seattle Brewing & Malting Co., of which Alvin Hemrich was president.[15]

Several years later, however, Alvin and Louis Hemrich founded a new enterprise, the Hemrich Bros. Brewing Co.[16] But their control of other breweries multiplied, until, at the time of Prohibition (1916 in Washington), Alvin Hemrich was president of not only the firm begun by him and Louis, but also the Aberdeen Brewing Company in Aberdeen, Washington, and the Claussen Brewing Association in Seattle.[17]

The Olympia Brewing Company also decided to branch out from Tumwater, building first a brewery in Bellingham, Washington, in 1901, then going out of the state to Salem, Oregon, and establishing a brewery there. The Schmidts of Olympia also bought out the Port Townsend Brewing Co. of Jacob Duttenhoefer, and when Prohibition struck in 1916 they transferred their activities temporarily to San Francisco, where they operated in the Acme Brewery, converting their agency building next door into their bottling plant.[18]

Consolidations were increasingly the order of the day: the *Western Brewer*, taking note of the phenomenon in 1899, called it "an almost insane craze." [19] The pressure of competition was so great that every brewer had to find some way to augment his productive capacity as well as his distributing structure. One of the results of sharp competition most harmful to the small brewer was the cutting of prices in the rough battle for customers. The so-called "price wars" could only be survived by the larger organizations. Besides, in a business based on penny profits, there was no doubt that a number of firms in consolidation could shave off costs in many areas, particularly in the ordering and delivery of raw materials. A leading Detroit brewer, E. W. Voigt, was quoted on this subject as follows in 1893:

> There are too many breweries in Detroit; not a brewery in the city is being run to its full capacity, and at the present prices there is no money in the business. . . . There is no doubt but a big saving can be made by combining and closing out the small concerns.[20]

The first consolidation or merger of this kind was bruited in Cincinnati around 1876. Nothing came of that, however, and in 1879 the scheme was revived, the local brewers, according to the *Western Brewer*, "feeling the necessity of reducing local competition, and getting a better price for beer." [21] The plan received a great deal of publicity, but in the end failed to be implemented because of lack of agreement about various financial settlements.

A merger successfully brought off was that between the two Milwaukee firms, Franz Falk Brewing Co. and Jung & Borchert, who joined forces in 1888 and used the name "Falk, Jung & Borchert Brewing Co." [22] After four years under this form of management, the firm was taken over by the Pabst Brewing Co.[23]

The impetus toward consolidation came from a surprising source: in the late 1880s, a widespread industrial depression in Great Britain caused British financiers to become increasingly interested in foreign investments. Syndicates formed in Britain were known to be investing in cattle-raising companies;[24] they were also reported to be buying into the Pillsbury and Washburn Flour Mills and the Otis Steel Works.[25] Their attitude toward brewery shares was described by an American journalist in London:

> [The British] are tired of investments in oriental bonds, African mining stock, colonical [sic] promotions organizations, etc. There is no money in those affairs, and they are quite risky. Hence American securities attract large attention. But British speculators will not invest in American railroad stocks. . . . Nor will they invest in mining stock. . . . American brewery stock is a more stable commodity.[26]

The first British syndicate to buy into the American brewing industry took the name New York Breweries Co., and was comprised of H. Clausen & Son Brewing Co. and Flanagan, Nay & Co. This was in 1888, and at the same time another British syndicate had bought the John F.

Betz & Son concern in Philadelphia for $1,250,000. The press assumed that this was the beginning of a huge beer trust which would spread over the nation, but these were actually two unrelated speculative moves.[27]

Nevertheless, within the next few years, the syndicates had raised some ninety million dollars and bought approximately eighty substantial breweries and two malthouses. A general comment was made on the situation in 1895 by a brewers' magazine:

> In most cases the former owners had sold under the most favorable circumstances, although it cannot be said that they have deceived the Englishmen. Still they took advantage of the English craze for buying and demanded high prices which, in many cases, they secured without much ado.[28]

The British buyers were thwarted in their hopes of landing the really big fish. In 1889 a plan was proposed for a consolidation of the three leading Milwaukee brewers: Schlitz, Pabst and Blatz. A purchase price of $16,500,000 was offered. Another group spoke of even larger figures, and requested Captain Pabst to see if he couldn't round up all the Milwaukee brewers into one large merger. But both Pabst and the Uihleins of the Schlitz company, whose businesses were booming in any case, chose to have no part of the British scheme, and only Blatz eventually capitulated and sold a share in his brewery to the Milwaukee and Chicago Breweries, Ltd., in Chicago.[29]

The British speculators, even though their offers were frequently outlandishly generous, consistently missed out on the large, flourishing concerns. In St. Louis, for example, they obtained eighteen breweries for twelve million dollars, but were unable to tempt the two leaders, Lemp and Busch, even though they offered the latter eight million.[30] There never was any sizable penetration in New York City, though some of the Newark and Albany brewers were bought. During the height of the syndicate movement, breweries were controlled in the following cities: Baltimore, Rochester (N.Y.), Philadelphia, Chicago, Cincinnati, Denver, Detroit, Indianapolis, Boston, Milwaukee, St. Louis, San Francisco, and several smaller towns.[31]

The decade of the 'nineties, unfortunately for the British investors, was not marked by the same swift rise in beer sales as the former decade had been. In 1889, sales stood at about 25,000,000 barrels; in 1892 there was an increase of roughly seven million; but between then and 1896 the rise was only four million. In addition, there was a drop in 1894 and 1895 (years of industrial depression) from the 1893 figure.[32] The Spanish-American War (1898-1899), during which the barrel tax was raised to $2, also helped to diminish beer sales. For these and other reasons, the British did not receive the huge, easy profits they had expected; they began indeed to grumble about being "cheated by the Yankees." [33]

The British syndicates were also responsible for a number of disagreeable and unprofitable "price wars" that took place in the 'nineties. One was reported from Chicago early in 1892, when prices were forced down from $6 a barrel, which was considered a reasonable price (in some towns a barrel had sold as high as $8), to $4 and even $3.50.[34] Peace was not established until September of that year:

> The terms . . . are based on a deposit of a sum in a trustee's hands, to be held as a forfeit, which in case of violation of the agreements entered into will be lost by the transgressor and inure to the benefit of other members of the association. This sum is so large that any single brewer will hesitate a long time before inaugurating another war which will, besides the indirect losses, involve also the loss of his deposit . . .

The cost of the price war to the Chicago breweries, both syndicate and non-syndicate, was estimated at $4,000,000.[35]

Another such price war took place in St. Louis a year later; here a number of non-syndicate small brewers, backed by Anheuser-Busch and Lemp, formed an association to fight the syndicate breweries.[36] The public were the only gainers, as saloon prices were forced lower and lower.

One of the results of the British move into American brewing was the formation of combines among local brewers in opposition to those gobbled up by the syndicates. In New Orleans, six breweries had been in negotiation with an English syndicate all during the early part of 1890. British representatives came to New Orleans to look over the plants; New Orleans representatives went to London to pursue the bargaining. By June it was known that the deal had fallen through. The brewers, however, were determined to do something about price competition and sought to form an association of their own. This quickly led to a merger of the six firms: Southern Brewery, Louisiana, Weckerling, Pelican, Lafayette, and Crescent City. This combine operated as the New Orleans Brewing Co., but it did not fare particularly well; by 1913, four of the constituent breweries had been closed down, and only the Louisiana and Weckerling plants were still operating.[37]

In Pittsburgh, twenty-one brewers decided in 1899 to effect a consolidation and call themselves the Pittsburgh Brewing Company. About six of these were substantial enterprises: Iron City Brewing Co., Z. Wainwright & Co., Eberhardt & Ober, Winter Bros. Brewery, Phoenix Brewery and the Straub Brewing Co. The others were small concerns, many of them without bottling facilities or modern machinery. One, the Latrobe Brewery,* was worth about $8000 altogether. Within a year two of them, the Phillip Lauer and J. Seiferth plants, were liquidated; and gradually all have been dismantled and sold except the Iron City Brewery (operating as the Pittsburgh Brewing Co.), which remains, in effect, as the synthesis of the whole combine.[38]

In 1905, fifteen other Pittsburgh breweries joined to form the Independent Brewing Company; they were liquidated during the years of Prohibition, except for the Duquesne Brewing Co., which has been the sole survival.[39]

When six San Francisco breweries announced their consolidation in 1917, it was stated that they were joining "on a co-operative basis in buying and selling." This combine was to have no paid-in capital stock and profits were to be divided on the basis of business prior to consolidation. "By buying and selling in bulk it is expected to reduce expenses very materially."[40]

Up until the advent of Prohibition, mergers of this kind continued to be formed in all parts of the country. Though self-protection against the British syndicates may have furnished the first impulse for this trend, there was patently something more behind it, for it continued even after it had become clear that the syndicates, far from mopping up,

---

* This was neither the small brewery of the Benedictine Society, which was started in 1844, nor the current Latrobe Brewing Company that belongs to the Tito family (James B. Tito, president) and produces "Rolling Rock Beer."

were having an uneasy time of it themselves. On one side, it might be said that this frantic formation of mergers reflected an anxiety within the industry, the smaller brewers' fear of being engulfed by the industry leaders. Another consideration, however, is that consolidation was taking place in many other industries: in the railroads, mines, steel and the like. Expansion had, in many cases, been hasty, and as a result, individual firms were deeply in debt or else were operating on reduced profits.

In the particular case of the brewing industry, there had been a huge outlay of capital between 1880 and 1890 for new equipment, new buildings, new processes, new personnel. Only the most soundly based firms could survive this investment so long as price cutting was not restrainable. And only a firm with large reserves could afford to buy a sufficient number of "corner saloons," which seemed to be a fine method of keeping up sales. *Fortune* describes this aspect of the pre-Prohibition industry as follows:

> Few will deny that the saloon deal laid the foundation for most of the great brewing fortunes in America. A brewer simply went out and captured as many corner locations as he could, then rented or deputized the premises to a saloonkeeper who sold the owner-brewer's beer exclusively.[41]

Schlitz was reported, in 1887, to own something like fifty retail outlets in Milwaukee. Pabst was somewhat slower about moving into this field, starting out tentatively in 1880 by investing "small sums averaging about $20,000 a year in properties in the Milwaukee area that might be useful for retailing purposes." [42]

Such outlets were not, of course, restricted to saloons, but also included beer-gardens, restaurants, taverns, and even hotels. The Schlitz Hotel and Palm Garden in Milwaukee was built in 1889.[43] Pabst at one time controlled nine hotels or restaurants in New York, Chicago, Minneapolis and San Francisco, as well as his home town.[44] The Excelsior Brewing Co. of Brooklyn, owned by John Reisenweber, had a restaurant during the World War I years at Columbus Circle in New York City, where a table d'hote dinner was served for one dollar, and a cabaret called "Merry Moments" came along with the dinner.[45] Busch owned the Adolphus Hotel in Dallas, which was named for him, and had interests in at least two St. Louis restaurants, Tony Faust's and Carl Conrad's.

The practice of owning outlets appears to have been universal among brewers throughout the country, as it was and still is, for that matter, in Great Britain and Germany. The two British syndicates in Chicago decided in 1892 that they would be well advised to raise money in order to buy or lease "for long periods desirable locations for saloons which shall be controlled exclusively by these companies, each to have its own exclusive premises." [46] They spoke of this as a system of "tied houses," an expression still used by the British, and which appears in America only in legal documents.

The corner saloon was one of the important economic props of the brewing industry before Prohibition, but it also may have been the industry's undoing in 1919, for it was exactly at the saloon that the prohibition pressure groups finally aimed the attack which won them a temporary victory.

◆§ *THIRTY-ONE* ℰ◈

Organization of Labor

LABOR AS SUCH had never been a force in the brewing industry until the increase in mechanization and the widespread growth of the factory system brought about a greater concentration of workers in individual plants. The brewer of the eighteenth century and the first half of the nineteenth could make out with a crew of two to fifteen men, with each of whom he was in constant touch. They worked, so to speak, side by side, and the workmen felt a kind of kinship with the owners. This continued to be true (or perhaps was even more to the point) when the lager brewers from Germany began their operations in various parts of the country.

This situation was described officially by the brewers as follows:

> Before the organization of labor unions the employing brewers in the smaller cities maintained a sort of patriarchal relation toward their workmen, eating with them at the same table and otherwise treating them as members of their household. In the larger cities the relation between employer and employed was not quite so close and intimate; but the friendly feeling between them was no less sincere.[1]

But this intimacy, these "friendly feelings," gradually changed as the plants were expanded, as ice machinery was installed (requiring a crew of engineers), as steam took over so many hand operations, as teamsters became involved in deliveries, as the separation between employer and employee became more clearly defined. The brewery workers participated in a general labor movement that originated wherever there were factory conditions, wherever conspicuous profits were going into the hands of the few.

The organization of the Philadelphia shoemakers in 1792 is generally cited as the original spark of the American labor movement. This was a strictly local group with a local problem; in its first form it lasted only a year. It was reorganized, however, in 1794, and gathered sufficient strength to muster the first American labor strike in 1799; but by 1806 the organization was dissolved.

Not until 1827 did another rudimentary attempt at labor organization take place: that was the Mechanics' Union of Trade Associations, formed in Philadelphia, which led to the Working Men's Party — the world's first labor party.[2] But depressions in 1828-1829 and 1837 held back any progress along these lines. According to the standard history of American labor by John R. Commons, "Modern trade unionism may be said to begin with the first half of the decade of the fifties." [3] Even that date may be a little optimistic because only local organizations, at most, made any attempts at "unionism" until after the Civil War.

The first local organization of brewery workers, founded in Cincinnati in 1852, was a mutual aid society.[4] Apparently discussions toward the same end took place in 1850 among the German brewery workers of St. Louis but there is no evidence that anything ever came of them. But in New York, in 1867, another mutual aid association came into being — hardly a "union" in the modern sense, since employers belonged to it as well as employees.[5]

In other industries, organization had developed more rapidly, and by 1866 there were enough local trade unions to make a national group seem possible. A meeting was called in Baltimore that year, and the National Labor Union, which may properly be considered the first national labor organization in this country, was formed.[6] Its major purpose, as stated at the time, was to bring about the eight-hour day, but by the time it vanished in the 'seventies its achievements were few.[7]

An organization destined to have a much stronger effect on the labor movement was the Order of the Knights of Labor, formed in Philadelphia on 28 December 1869. For ten years, under the leadership of Uriah S. Stephens, it operated clandestinely, gradually gathering strength for the overt struggle. In 1879, when Terence V. Powderly became "Grand Master Workman" in Stephens's place, the organization came out into the open; its height of power was reached in the mid-'eighties; within ten years after that, its efficacy had begun to wither. A partisan of labor wrote of this organization as follows:

> The Order of the Knights of Labor emphasized the general demands of the working class. It took vigorous action in favor of the eight-hour day, agitated against child labor, and in general taught the solidarity of the working class.[8]

By general consensus, the one really important contribution of this organization was its emphasis on solidarity. It also represented an advance far beyond the National Labor Union in calling for union recognition, in using the strike and boycott as weapons, and in fighting for the principle of collective bargaining. Its concrete results may not have been spectacular, but it served a useful historical purpose.[9]

In 1881, some 107 delegates representing 262,000 organized workers met in Pittsburgh and laid the foundations for the American Federation of Labor — a name which did not come into effect until five years later. It was at the second convention, which took place in Cleveland in 1882, that Samuel Gompers, the man whose name became inextricably associated with the A.F. of L., was elected permanent presiding officer. Largely through his efforts, but also because of manifest weaknesses in the organization of the Knights of Labor, it was the A.F. of L. which consolidated and synthesized all the various labor groups in the country.

What of the brewery workers? What were their working conditions? What did they fight for?

The spokesman for the union paints a dismally black picture of the brewery workman's plight before union organization:

> The condition of the brewery workmen in America before their organization was as bad as can be imagined. It was not only that the wages paid were the smallest possible and that the working time was confined only by the natural limits of human endurance, but besides this the treatment of the workmen was of such a kind that it seems impossible today [1910] to understand how they could submit to it.[10]

It is hard to tell whether this offers an accurate picture of conditions as they were or, in the interests of special pleading, a highly colored distortion of the facts. Unfortunately, the period in question is a difficult one from which to glean satisfactory statistical evidence. One would need first to establish what the average wages and working hours of brewery workmen were before, say, 1870, and then compare them with similar figures in other occupations. Even more difficult, one would have to make some kind of analogy between the value of the dollar then and in later periods. Such statistics are not complete, and the best one can do is to make some reasonable assumptions on the basis of figures that do come to hand.

For example, the account book of the Sandman & Lackman Brewery in Cincinnati for the years 1855 to 1858 shows that various workmen received between $15 and $18 a month, plus board, but gives no indication of the number of hours worked each day.[11] In 1860, the Ph. Best Brewing Co. of Milwaukee was paying its workers an average of $25 a month, a figure which is alleged to compare favorably with wages paid in other Milwaukee industries.[12]

In the account books of Henry Weinhard, when he was running the Vancouver [Washington] Brewery in 1858, the workman Henry Ludwig is down for $50 a month, which seems an extremely high figure for those days except that his work was seasonal — during the summer months he was laid off.[13]

Frederick Miller wrote a letter from Milwaukee back to members of his family in 1879, in the course of which he gave the salaries of his twenty-five employees. The first clerk or bookkeeper had started in 1869 at a salary of between $200 and $300 a year. "Today he has a responsible position with a salary of $1,200." The first foreman of brewers, "a cousin of my wife," was receiving $1300 plus "free living quarters, wood and light." The men under him were paid $700, $650, $480; six drivers received between $480 and $540; and the maltsters $600. "In addition to the salaries are all the meals," and all but the foreman paid $15 a year for bed and lodging.

In connection with these figures it is important to consider prices that Miller quotes for the same period: eggs at 8¢ a dozen, butter 7¢ to 8¢

a pound, porterhouse steak 10¢ a pound, potatoes 60¢ to 80¢ per hundred pounds, a "good man's suit" $15 to $20, etc.[14]

Hard as it may be to judge these relative values, it does not seem as if Miller (who may or may not represent the majority of brewers) was paying starvation wages. The average farm worker in the same year was making only about $480 a year with board[15] — and that was Miller's minimum wage, for the least skilled and experienced of his laborers. The union writer, without citing any authority, gives $40 to $55 a month as the average wage for brewery workmen in New York "shortly before 1880" (and only $35 to $40 in other parts of the country) but adds that "the brewery boss deducted $5 a week for board and the remaining $20 or $25 [sic] was paid over to the workman." [16] Even so, the brewery wage rate would seem to be somewhat above the average for all industries: the earliest figures, for 1890, show that the average annual earnings in all industries, including farm labor, were $438.[17]

What cannot be denied is that the work day, in the brewing as well as most other industries, was unbelievably long. Even Miller, in the letter already referred to, wrote that he woke every day no later than 4 A.M., toured the brewery "energetically," and then had his breakfast at 7. Fred Pabst himself was quoted as follows:

> I dare say there are many of our old timers who remember very well when the men started at four o'clock in the morning and worked until half past six, when they stopped for breakfast. At seven o'clock they went back to work and worked until twelve and then worked in the afternoon from one to six.[18]

Not only was a working day of fourteen to eighteen hours considered normal in breweries, but a certain amount of work time on Sundays was also expected of the workmen. Though the eight-hour day was the rallying cry of the unions, it was considered a great victory in the 'eighties when, here and there, some factory would be prevailed upon to reduce the working hours from thirteen to ten and a half.[19]

The first brewery workers' strike ever attempted took place in an unorganized fashion in New York City in 1872. Though most of the workers came out and there was a certain amount of violence, the brewery owners were apparently not the slightest bit intimidated. "Thus," wrote

Hermann Schlüter (in tones of doom) for the brewery workers' union, "was the first wave of the brewery workmen's movement dashed to pieces against the power of the brewery capitalists." [20] In 1877, the brewers generally raised wages, a move which can hardly be attributed to an unsuccessful strike five years earlier, though Schlüter tries to make just such a connection.

The important labor agitation in 1877, a strike of the railroad workers, was lost in spite of pitched battles and mob scenes that caused President Hayes to call out federal troops.[21] The largest effect of the railroad strike was to increase the workers' fervor for reform. Among various unions that developed in the wake of the railroad disaster was one of the Cincinnati brewery workmen in 1879, called the "Brauer Gesellen Union." After joining the Central Trades Assembly — the central labor organization in that city — the brewery workmen, in 1881, drew up a number of demands to be presented to the brewers. These were: (1) a reduction of the work day from thirteen to ten and a half hours, (2) a reduction of Sunday work from eight to four hours, (3) a minimum wage of $60 a month, and (4) freedom for the worker to seek board and lodging wherever he liked.[22] The smaller and weaker brewers were willing to accede to these demands, but the large interests stood firm and, in spite of using the usually effective device of boycotting non-union beer, the union lost, and in consequence also lost the confidence of its members.

In the same year, an accident that caused four deaths at the plant of Peter Doelger in New York City led directly to the formation of the "Brewery Workmens' Union of New York and Vicinity." The breweries countered this move by firing the ringleaders of the new organization. But this was followed by a boycott of the beer produced in these breweries, which, since the workers enforcing the boycott were the breweries' best customers, proved so effective that the owners gave in and rehired the men.

The organized workers were so carried away with this victory that they presented demands to the owners: a twelve-hour work day including two hours for meals, and on Sundays a two-hour day at fifty cents an hour. The owners refused these demands and, inevitably, a strike was called. After five weeks of idleness and agitation, during which their jobs were often taken by others, the brewery workmen had to admit defeat.[23]

The brewery workers' union shriveled and died as a result of this blow, and no reorganization took place until August 1884, when the Brewers' Union No. 1 of New York was formed, as a local assembly of the Knights of Labor. Though its membership was tiny and its influence restricted, it was given an unintended boost in 1885, again by the Peter Doelger management, who fired several of the organized workers in that plant. This led the Central Labor Union of New York to order a boycott on Doelger beer, a move which this time met with surprising success. Doelger finally reinstated the discharged men, recognized the union, and even paid $1000 in costs.[24]

Organization of workers in other breweries then proceeded at a quickened pace, and on 16 April 1886 a contract was worked out with the United States Brewers' Association, the terms of which called for a monthly wage of $60 to $72 a month, the work day reduced to ten hours and Sunday work completely eliminated.[25]

The United States Brewers' Association recognized the labor question for the first time at its twenty-sixth convention, which was at Niagara Falls in September 1886. In his opening address, the president, William A. Miles, New York brewer, said:

> During the past year a question, which our Association has never before been called upon to consider, has grown into great prominence and has engaged the attention not only of our trade, but of all classes of manufacturers throughout the land. I refer, of course, to the labor question; a question which for the good of all parties concerned should be settled as promptly as possible, and upon such a basis of justice and equity as shall make that settlement lasting.[26]

Miles was somewhat aggrieved that his industry should be having labor problems "for the reason that the average wages of the employees of breweries are higher than those of almost any other industry."

It is no wonder that Miles should call attention to the labor movement at that particular moment, because 1886 was a year of tremendous development in the progress of unionization. Brewery workers were organized in that year at Baltimore, Chicago, Newark, St. Louis, Philadelphia, Detroit — in short, almost every city which had a concentration of brewing activities.²⁷ Several strikes were undertaken, a good many of them with success; of these the United States Brewers' Association later remarked:

> The friendly relations were suddenly torn asunder by the violently aggressive methods of labor leaders of avowed anarchical tendencies — among them men who subsequently betrayed the confidence of their constituents. These men wantonly provoked the great struggle of 1886.²⁸

The cry of "anarchism" was current as a result of the Haymarket Square riot in Chicago that had shocked the public earlier that year, as well as the even bloodier steel strike at Homestead, Pennsylvania — both of these names are hallowed in labor movement annals.²⁹

The 1886 surge of organization among brewery workers culminated in August, when the "National Union of the Brewers of the United States" was established, with a national executive to be located in New York, and an official craft paper to be called the *Brauer-Zeitung*. Four months after its formation, this organization had more than four thousand members. At its second convention in Detroit, in September 1887, the important decision was taken to include in the national union's ranks such allied workers as brewery engineers, firemen, maltsters and beer-drivers. The name consequently was changed to "National Union of United Brewery Workmen of the United States." A move was also made at this meeting to dislodge certain local unions which still adhered to the Knights of Labor, for its leader, T. V. Powderly, had taken a stand in favor of prohibition. Application for a charter was made to the American Federation of Labor, and this was granted in March 1887.³⁰

When the maltsters joined the national union, they brought with them a grievance which shortly thereafter broke out in a strike. Their wage demand of $60 a month had been refused by the malting concerns in Milwaukee, while the brewers in that town who did their own malting had already granted their maltsters a wage of $75. Upon striking, the union sought to persuade brewery owners not to handle malt produced at the non-union malting concerns, but this was considered by the owners to be interference and the strike spread, along with a nationwide boycott of Milwaukee beer.[31] The brewers' official viewpoint on this was expressed at the twenty-eighth convention of the United States Brewers' Association in St. Paul in May 1888:

> The attempt to dictate to Milwaukee brewers where they should or should not buy their material, was but the beginning of a preconcerted plan, by which it was intended to so hamper and harass the employers as to make it impossible for them to conduct their business in the usual legitimate way.[32]

The only way the brewers could counteract the union's main weapon was to agree individually not to move in on competitors' markets and cash in quickly at a time of boycott: this was called "the St. Louis resolution," and worked fairly well on the whole. One example of its *not* working was the attempt of the Banner Brewing Co. of Cincinnati, in July 1889, to market Banner beer in St. Louis, at a time when the Brewers' and Maltsters' Union of that city was boycotting the beer of the St. Louis Brewing Association. The St. Louis *Republic* called it "The Beer War":

> Mr. Albert Fuldner is the St. Louis agent of the Banner Brewing Co. of Cincinnati, and he received the first car-load of this brew last night. . . . He stated to a REPUBLIC reporter yesterday that beginning to-day he would supply 22 saloons in the northern and southern part of the city with Banner beer.[33]

The United States Brewers' Association castigated this action, but in any case Banner made little headway.

A backward step was taken in 1887 when the New York brewers, alarmed at the progress made by the brewery workers' union, formed a "pool," reaffirmed the St. Louis resolution of noninterference, and announced that they would not enter into any new agreements at the end of current contracts — thus virtually turning their backs on union recognition. "We brewery proprietors," they stated, "are . . . fully determined to . . . return to the independent control and management of our business affairs, the adjustment of which we consider the right of the employer toward his employees." [34]

A lockout of employees of the New York breweries proved to be the opening maneuver in a nation-wide struggle of the brewery owners against the union leaders, in the course of which many jobs were lost, profits doubtless suffered, hard feelings were engendered — and in the end, though in some cases it took over ten years, union recognition was won in all breweries just the same. The outbreak of a strike or a boycott call came to be considered part of a day's work. In a survey of the brewing business in 1888, the *Western Brewer* commented:

> The business was slightly interrupted in the early part of the year by strikes of the brewers' employes at New York, Chicago, Milwaukee and other points. The strike in Chicago collapsed in the course of a few days. In New York it took somewhat longer to convince the employes that they could not dictate to their employers, but they finally had to surrender. The employing brewers acted throughout with admirable spirit and discretion.[35]

The union view was, naturally, somewhat different:

> The hand of the powerful brewery capitalists lay heavily upon the workingmen who had taken their fate into their hands in order to protect their interests from the brewery princes. They were refused work everywhere. And if by mistake they did get work in some place, they were driven out with scorn and derision when the mistake was discovered. The capitalists now revenged themselves upon the leaders of the workingmen for having caused them two unpleasant years and curtailed their profits.[36]

Gradually, however, during the twenty years from 1890 to 1910, the unions managed to achieve the major portion of their aims: the closed shop, reduced working hours and a minimum wage. An agreement drawn up (in both German and English) on 5 February 1891, between the Brewery Proprietors of Portland, Oregon, and the United Brewery Workmen's Union of the Pacific Coast, specifies that "only Union men, *i.e.* members of the United Brewery Workmen's Union of the Pacific Coast, shall be employed in all Brewery and Malt-house departments." As for working hours, nine hours were to constitute a full day's work, and the working week was to consist of six days. Wages ranged from $15 a week (for employees in the wash-houses) up to $18 (for first maltster and coopers).* Every man was to be free to lodge and board wherever he pleased.[37]

---

* Certain individual brewers paid even higher wages. Account books belonging to the Pittsburgh Brewing Co. show that the firm of Eberhardt & Ober, in Pittsburgh, was paying $21 a week to brewers, $25 to engineers and $17 to $19 to drivers in 1911.

These conditions were a good deal better than the average:* according to official figures, in the year 1891 the average number of hours worked a week in all industry was 58.2, and the average annual earnings in all industries (excluding farm labor) was only $487, or just over $9 a week.[38]

The labor problem in the brewing industry came up in a curious way during Senate hearings late in 1918 on the subject of brewery interests and German propaganda: the secretary of the United States Brewers' Association at that time, Hugh F. Fox, stated: "The brewers were, I think, perhaps the first great industry to become, and perhaps they are to-day the only industry to be, 100 per cent unionized." [39] The United States District Attorney for the western district of Pennsylvania, Major E. Lowry Humes, leading the questioning of Fox, said:

> Is it not a fact that the attitude of the brewing industry toward organized labor was a subject of much agitation and much discussion, and that it was finally decided for political reasons that in order to secure or endeavor to secure the help and cooperation of organized labor in political contests it was expedient to unionize the industry? Is not that a fact? [40]

Fox replied that he did not think the political argument was in question, but that more likely "the determining consideration was the fact that probably 90 per cent of the product is consumed by workingmen."

> Maj. HUMES. Is it not a fact that the United States Brewers' Association utilized or created a labor department in its political activities for the purpose of trying to dominate as far as possible the labor vote in its political contests?

> Mr. FOX. Not to my knowledge. It might have been to some extent the case without my knowing it.

> Senator WOLCOTT. Mr. Fox, how long has the industry been 100 per cent unionized?

> Mr. FOX. I do not know. I have been associated with it for 11 years, and I should say before that time.

* Generally speaking, average wages for brewery workers have stayed ahead of wages in most other industries. In 1960, the average weekly earning of $120.56 for workers in the malt beverage industry was well above the comparable figure for workers in all manufacturing industries, $90.91 (Brewers Almanac, 1961, p. 49).

Since this investigation was determined to find all sorts of shady practices going on among the brewers, even this attempt was made to show that, somehow, the labor question had been manipulated for political purposes; but in fact, there was no evidence whatsoever for the charge, and it was not pursued.

In the second half of the 'nineties, the major problem of the brewery workers' union became an internal one. The coopers, maltsters, teamsters, firemen and engineers had all gone along with the development of the union and been members of it, but then they were gradually being organized on a national trade, rather than industrial, basis — and this naturally led to jurisdictional disputes. The coopers were the first to broach this problem when, at the brewery workers' convention in Cincinnati in 1896, they raised the demand for an independent coopers' union. The engineers and firemen were next: they received charters from the American Federation of Labor in 1896 and 1898 to organize their own national unions, and of course they expected those engineers and firemen who worked in breweries to leave the brewery workers' union and join them. These were difficult questions to solve; the Federation at its 1900 convention in Louisville decided, by and large, in favor of the United Brewery Workmen. But this did not settle the issue; in fact, so many moves and countermoves were made that finally, in 1907, the executive of the A.F. of L. revoked the charter of the United Brewery Workmen. The charter was restored, however, in February 1908, with the declaration that the United Brewery Workmen "were to have jurisdiction over all workingmen employed in the brewing industry." [41]

This was a controversy (and one that existed in a number of other industries) which continued to rage well into current times. In the case of the brewery workers, however, the struggle reached an abrupt and somewhat unexpected end when the whole business of brewing became something of an academic issue with Prohibition.

THIRTY-TWO

The Brewing Dynasties and Their Enemies

The Anti-Saloon League is not, strictly speaking, an organization. It is what its name indicates — a League. It is a league of organizations. It is the federated church in action against the saloon. Its agents are of the church, and under all circumstances loyal to the church. It has no interest apart from the church. It goes just as fast and just as far as public sentiment of the church will permit. It has not come to the Kingdom simply to build a little local sentiment, or to secure the passage of a few laws, nor yet to vote the saloons from a few hundred towns. These are mere incidents in its progress. It has come to solve the liquor problem.[1]

THOSE ARE the words of Rev. Purley A. Baker, General Superintendent of the Anti-Saloon League of America. They underline the fact that this latest and most effective of the historical prohibition movements was based to begin with (just as the original temperance movement was*) on principles of religion. Indeed, the man generally conceded to be founder of the league, Rev. Howard Hyde Russell, considered himself to be divinely inspired to lead this movement.[2]

Though the W.C.T.U. had recharged the prohibition drive in the 'seventies and 'eighties, increasing the number of states in which local option laws existed and bringing about prohibition in eight states by 1890, there was then an ebb in prohibition sentiment.[3] The brewers, meeting in 1889, felt somewhat encouraged; the vice-president of the United States Brewers' Association, Thies J. Lefens, said in his opening address to the convention at Niagara Falls, "New hope has come to all

* See page 192.

who a year ago looked upon the future as darker than ever." [4] The brewers went on being encouraged, right up to the outbreak of World War I and even longer, although the forces of prohibition were bristling around them. In some ways, the statistics helped them to overlook the latent danger of the prohibition movement: tax-paid withdrawals of beer rose from nearly 63 million barrels in 1890 to 66 million in 1914[5] — a slowing down in the rate of gain from the previous twenty years, to be sure, but a gain nonetheless. Another reason why the brewers may have underestimated the power they were up against is that by 1900 a good many of them had become extremely rich, themselves wielding great power — both political and economic — founders of brewing dynasties with international connections. That was, after all, the era of the "beer barons."

In these brewing dynasties the adherence to succession was very strong. When Phillip Best retired from business in 1864, control was passed on to his two sons-in-law, Captain Fred Pabst and Emil Schandein.[6] Next in line was Fred's son, Gustav, who became president in 1904[7] and remained in that position until Prohibition. The latter was one of those who married into another dynasty: his wife was Hilda Lemp, daughter of the St. Louis brewer, William J. Lemp.[8] Gustav's brother, Fred, followed that same tradition by marrying Ida Uihlein, a member of the family that operated Schlitz, Pabst's great competitor in Milwaukee.[9]

Direct succession took place in the case of the F. and M. Schaefer Brewing Co.: Rudolph J. Schaefer, son of one of the original founders, Maximilian, took over in 1912, and in 1923 control passed to his son, Rudolph, Jr.[10] The Jackson Brewing Co., which was founded in 1890 by Lawrence Fabacher, was passed on to Lawrence, Jr., in 1923.[11] Three sons and a son-in-law took over when Frederick Miller, founder of the Fred Miller Brewing Co. in Milwaukee, died in 1888. The eldest, Ernest, was in control of the business, and upon his death in 1922 his brother, Frederick A. Miller, became president. The latter's nephew, Frederick C. Miller, who succeeded in 1947, died in a plane crash in 1954, and the man who became president at that time, Norman Klug, is not related to the Millers, but Lorraine John Muhlberger, a grandchild of the founder, still keeps an interest in the company.[12] Samuel Liebmann, founder of the firm in Brooklyn that bore his name, left his business to three sons, Joseph, Charles (or Carl) and Henry, who were to rotate the office of top executive among themselves at regular intervals. This rather original practice continued in the following generation — this time involving six young Liebmanns[13] — but after Repeal in 1933, it was mainly Julius and Alfred (sons of Charles) who assumed control. In recent years, Alfred's son, Philip, has been appointed president of the firm, representing the fourth generation.[14]

It was also common among brewers for a son-in-law to inherit the business. Fred Pabst and Adolphus Busch have already been mentioned. The brewery founded in 1856 by George Schweickhart became the property of his son-in-law, Adam Gettelman, in 1876, and ten years later the firm name, A. Gettelman Brewing Co., was adopted; two generations ran the plant after that.[15] The Portland, Oregon, brewery of Henry Weinhard passed to Paul Wessinger, husband of Weinhard's daughter, in 1904.[16] In Newport, Kentucky, George Wiedemann started a brewery in 1870; it was taken over by his son, Charles, in 1890, and after that by a grandson, H. Tracy Balcom, Jr.[17]

The succession in the Schlitz company has been somewhat more complicated. The original brewery, founded by August Krug, came into Joseph Schlitz's possession when Krug died and Schlitz married his widow.* Eight-year-old August Uihlein, a nephew of Krug's, came with grandfather George Krug to America in 1850 "to visit his uncle August who was childless." [18] Eventually six Uihlein boys in all came to Milwaukee, and learned the business; when Joseph Schlitz and his wife (also childless) were drowned in the ship *Schiller*, while on their way to Germany, the firm was left to the Uihlein brothers — specifically Henry, Edward, Alfred and August. August's son, Erwin C., was head of the plant from 1933, and in 1961 his nephew, Robert A. Uihlein, Jr., took over control.[19]

The epitome of the dynastic brewer was St. Louis's Adolphus Busch, a man with great zest for life, habits of ostentation unfamiliar to puritan American society, and a regal attitude toward the world. He had not only a lavish home near the plant called No. 1 Busch Place, but also a

* See page 211.

great country estate, "Grant's Farm"; two homes in Pasadena — "Ivy Wall" for himself and his wife, Lilly, and "The Blossoms," for the children and visitors; a property and hop farm at Cooperstown, New York, birthplace of baseball; two villas at Langenschwalbach, Germany (one for himself and Lilly, one for the children and visitors); and a private railroad car called "Adolphus." In a book about the family, granddaughter Alice Busch Tilton remarked that when her father, Adolphus, Jr., was born, "a salute of guns were fired off the Brewery. There was great rejoicing, and well there should have been. The Crown Prince was born!" At all the estates, there were fabulous grounds, and Busch had a fancy for furnishing his gardens and woods with carvings of the characters in Grimm's Fairy Tales. "Our gardens in California," Mrs. Tilton recalled, "were really like a scene from 'Midsummer Night's Dream.' We employed 40 to 50 gardeners." [20]

The golden anniversary of Adolphus's marriage to Lilly Anheuser, celebrated 7 March 1911, was a world event. There were those, of course, who disapproved of all this splendor and fame: on 2 May 1911 President William H. Taft's office received a note from Cedar Rapids, Iowa, enclosing this newspaper clipping:

> The Busches of St. Louis, had a pleasant golden wedding in California the other day. The ways of beer have been pleasant ways for them. The husband crowned the wife with a $200,000 diadem. The president of the United States sent a $20 gold piece. Col. Roosevelt sent a solid gold loving-cup and the emperor of Germany sent a like gift. Presidents, ex-presidents and emperors paid tribute to the man who made beer and made it pay. It pays to succeed and to get rich. In the meantime, every man who drank a glass of the Busch beer contributed his mite to the happiness in California.

The accompanying note, written by Mrs. Sue F. Armstrong, said: "I enclose this newspaper clipping and wish to know if the statement in regard to the president is true. Here in Iowa where we are trying to put out the saloons we should be glad to say that this report is untrue." [21]

Mrs. Armstrong was evidently one of the great army of the Anti-Saloon League, that determined prohibition organization that had been founded, first in Ohio in 1893, and then on a national scale at a meeting in Washington, D.C., in December 1895. At that time, its official aim was "the suppression of the saloon." [22] By 1907, however, a significant expansion had taken place: "The object of the League is the largest present repression and the speediest ultimate suppression of the beverage liquor traffic." [23]

The Anti-Saloon League had certain factors immediately in its favor: for one thing, it was in a position to combine all prohibition forces as well as all churches (though in practice its major strength always came from the Methodist and Baptist Churches). It had no political party affiliation, and so could not be branded for one side or the other (but could play one against the other). In starting out to abolish the saloon, it had a campaign assured of wide support.

There seems to be no doubt that the saloon was an easy target for the drys. Even the brewers had become alarmed by the conditions of saloons; in 1909 the yearbook of the United States Brewers' Association devoted a whole section to the saloon problem, and the "cleanup movement." [24] The Anti-Saloon League, through the instrument of relentless propaganda, made the saloon out to be the very focus of all evil: drunkenness, political chicanery, corruption of all kinds, seducer of the young.[25]

The men who are given the credit for first projecting the Anti-Saloon League and then forging it into a weapon of extraordinary power were H. H. Russell; Rev. Hiram Price, the League's first president; Bishop Luther B. Wilson; the General Superintendent, Rev. Purley A. Baker; Ernest H. Cherrington, who managed the league's publishing activities; and Rev. E. C. Dinwiddie, the league's first lobbyist in Washington. But, as its activities developed, it was Ohioan teetotaler Wayne B. Wheeler, with his pince-nez, sparse hair and sandy mustache, who became its primary spokesman, symbol and controller.

From 1888 on, when the Supreme Court upheld the principle of federal control of interstate commerce by ruling that it was legal to ship alcoholic beverages into a dry state, the drys had struggled to redefine the law and find some way to keep alcohol out of prohibition states. The Wilson Act of 1890 was designed for just this purpose, declaring that upon arrival in a dry state, alcoholic beverages became subject to local law. The Anti-Saloon League took over this particular fight, and sought to push through a law that would eliminate the loopholes that began to show in the Wilson Act and subject liquor to "local jurisdiction upon its arrival within the state, both before and after delivery to the consignee." [26] By gradual steps, such as the Hepburn-Dolliver Bill (1903), the Littlefield Bill (1908) and the Webb-Kenyon Bill (1913), the league was advancing its campaign toward national prohibition, which was to be the apogee of its activities.

The brewers, in the meantime, were concerned with attack from other quarters; namely, the question of adulteration of beer. The drys managed to engender agitation about "poisons" or "impurities" in beer from time to time during the second half of the nineteenth century, and the brewers were called upon to educate the public in the way beer was manufactured and what ingredients went into it. As early as 1861, a Milwaukee newspaper raised this subject, saying that England had "a great deal to answer for."

> A few years ago a hew [sic] and cry was raised that the ale contained *coculus indicus* and *aloes*; that porter was made of strychnine, and beer of lobelia and bootlegs; that certain brewers did not scruple to put tobacco and liquorice in their stock, and others used arsenic to keep it. Ridiculous as these things were, thousands believed them, and the brewers in England employed the services of five of the best chemists in the kingdom to analyze and examine their products, and publish the statement. In that statement first appeared the announcement of the celebrated *Dr. Ure*, since verified by chemists in this country and France, that strychnine or *nux vomica* cannot be introduced into any liquor brewed with hops, because it is entirely precipitated by infusions of that wholesome herb.[27]

Suspicions cropped up periodically, particularly when it was learned that various types of lager beer were made (as had been found advantageous) with unmalted grain adjuncts such as corn and/or rice. At the 1888 United States Brewers' Association convention, for instance, attention was drawn by Louis Schade, the association's attorney, to a publication of the Agriculture Department, headed "Food Adulterations," in which an analysis of twenty-eight beer samples had proved charges of adulteration or "sophistication" to be ungrounded.[28] Again, in 1890, the Advisory Committee of the association mentioned "Absurd Statements Concerning Adulterations." [29] In that same year a series of bills was proposed by Congressman E. J. Turner of Kansas, which would have forced brewers using "glucose or grape-sugar, starch, corn, rice, soda, bicarbonate of soda, aloes, or any other substitute for hops" to designate their product "adulterated lager beer" and also to pay special taxes.[30] This bill, backed by the drys, was based on a complete misunderstanding of brewing methods; Professor Francis Wyatt, William A. Miles and A. Schwarz, director of the U. S. Brewers' Academy, gave expert testimony for the brewers and, incidentally, a future United States President, William McKinley, was in the chair during these hearings.

The brewers were eager to help in settling this problem, feeling perfectly secure in their ability to counter the adulteration charge. The Department of Agriculture, and particularly its chief chemist, Dr. Harvey W. Wiley, were trying to work out a Pure Food Act which would cover standards of all foods, including beer. The brewers were represented at the first Pure Food Congress, held in 1898 in Washington for the purpose of studying the Pure Food Bill introduced by Representative Brosius of Pennsylvania.[31] Two years later, a Senate Committee on Manufactures, assisted by Wiley, conducted an extensive investigation of malt liquors, and gave the brewers a clean slate:

> The Committee, then, is of the opinion that the present system in America is fairest and more nearly just to the manufacturer and consumer to permit the brewer to be the judge himself of what wholesome and healthy products he desires to put into his beer.[32]

The "Brosius bill" was introduced in Congress several times, but never passed. After 1902, however, it became less essential, since in that year, as noted in the Advisory Committee's report to the United States Brewers' Association convention in 1903,

> the Department of Agriculture secured the necessary authority (by the incorporation of a suitable clause into the appropriation act of 1902) to establish standards of the purity of food products and to determine what are adulterations for the guidance of the various States and of the courts of justice.[33]

The brewers faced yet another problem that deflected their attention from the main issue of prohibition. One of the results of the Spanish-American War in 1898 was a doubling of the beer tax from $1 to $2 a barrel.* As might be expected, it was most unpopular with the brewers, who had successfully campaigned against a rise in the tax at various times since 1873.[34] A war-tax could not, however, be fought with any hope of amelioration, simply because such an action, particularly in the jingoistic atmosphere of 1898, would be branded antipatriotic. All the brewers could do was urge as strongly as possible that the tax last only "for the duration." The trustees of the United States Brewers' Association sought to reassure the brewers in these terms:

> If both the manufacturer and the dealer keep in view the indisputable fact that all excises of this character are taxes upon consumption, and that this particular beer-tax is, according to an explicit avowal on the part of the lawmakers, designed to be borne by the consumer — as in fact neither the maker nor the seller could possibly bear it — an arrangement should and can be effected by which the evil results that usually attend such unwarranted interferences with industrial interests can easily be minimized.[35]

The *Western Brewer* pointed out optimistically that the consumer could best assume payment of the tax, because it would only come to about one-fifth of a cent a glass; and besides, "As the extra tax is purely for the purpose of raising money to carry on the war, and as the war was undertaken in the interest, not of any class, but of all, all ought to assist in paying it." [36]

According to figures adduced by the brewers, they contributed, between 1 July and 30 November 1898, forty per cent of the entire war tax (some $15,00,000 out of almost $38,000,000).[37] If in fact it was the consumer who eventually paid the bill, he did so reluctantly, for sales dropped by almost a million barrels in 1899.[38] The *Western Brewer* gave this analysis of the situation:

> A little less beer in each glass, a little smaller allowance in the amount tapped into the poor man's pail or pitcher, makes in the aggregate a large decrease in the total consumption and a considerably lessened demand on the manufacturer. . . . The beer the brewer makes costs him a dollar a barrel more to produce and he sells fewer barrels. The supposition that he could shift the burden of the added tax upon the dealer and the dealer in turn shift it upon the customer proved to be erroneous. In practice it would not work.[39]

* See pages 213-214, 215-216.

The treasury was naturally not a bit anxious to let go of such a potent source of revenue, and the tax went on until 1901. Business conditions in general, however, were so good after the war that beer sales rose by nearly three million barrels in 1900.[40] The brewers continued their pressure in Congress and finally, in July 1901, the tax was reduced to $1.60 a barrel and exactly a year later to the original rate, $1. The brewers were far from completely satisfied since the reduction, they felt, was

> offset by the increased prices for barley, hops, labor, and in fact on almost every element that enters into the cost of beer production; so that the brewer will still have to struggle as before under the unequal and unfair burden of a war tax which was supposed to be only an emergency matter, and temporary.[41]

As for the government, Theodore Roosevelt began by 1905 to regret the relief given to the brewers; he wrote privately:

> We never ought to have taken off all the war taxes. But Hanna, Aldrich and the others were resolute about it, and McKinley had committed himself to it. It may be that a reimposition of fifty cents instead of a dollar on the beer business will enable us to raise enough revenue; but of course in such case we have to count just how much dissatisfaction will be felt among those who think the tariff ought to be revised and how much the Germans, that is, the brewers, will resent our action.[42]

All the same, within eighteen years of 1901, the brewers would be looking back to a year like that, in spite of all its problems, with nostalgia and envy.

THIRTY-THREE

Victory of the Drys

I T WAS EVIDENT, fairly early in the second wave of the prohibition movement, that the final outcome of the anti-alcohol struggle would have to be a political one; and the Anti-Saloon League was only too happy to test its strength in the political field. The day had been reached when the prohibition question was alive in practically every election — local and national; candidates too sure of themselves began to fall by taking the wrong stand or giving the wrong answers. "Are you on our side or not?" was the ticklish query of the prohibitionists, frequently making politicians cynical in their allegiances and public utterances.

As early as 1867, William McKinley, a Methodist, had identified himself with the temperance movement. In her biography of him, Margaret Leech remarks that for some years McKinley "was the leading speaker in Stark County [Ohio] on behalf of total abstinence." He served one term in his county as prosecuting attorney, during which he kept up a "war on the illicit sale of liquor." [1] At the time of his election to the Presidency in 1896, prohibition was not a dominating issue of the campaign, but his own temperance background obviously did him no harm, for he cut the Prohibition Party's vote to about half of what it had been in the previous national election.

In 1887, President Cleveland could still say:

I drink beer and light wines myself, and I think I feel all the better for them, but I do not recommend their use to others, because I believe every man should be a law unto himself in this matter. [2]

As the Anti-Saloon League extended its power after 1896, Presidents and candidates had to be even more careful, more equivocal, in their statements.

Theodore Roosevelt, who started out with a hearty dislike and distrust of prohibitionists, gave this practical advice to William H. Taft, Republican candidate in 1908:

> If ever there was a wicked attitude it is that of those fantastic extremists who advocate a law so drastic that it cannot be enforced, knowing perfectly well that lawlessness and contempt of the law follow. But as a mere matter of precaution I would be careful to put in your hearty sympathy with every effort to do away with the drink evil. You will hardly suspect me of being a prohibitionist crank; but such hideous misery does come from drink that I cordially sympathize with any successful effort to do away with it or minimize its effects. . . . My experience with prohibitionists, however, is that the best way to deal with them is to ignore them.[3]

Roosevelt was sufficiently sophisticated as a politician to realize that he was not satisfactory to either the prohibitionists or the brewers. As president of the Police Commissioners of New York City during 1895 he had alienated the brewers by his strict enforcement of the Sunday Excise Law, the so-called "Raines Law," which forebade the sale of alcoholic beverages in New York during Sundays. Tammany administrations in the city had traditionally winked an eye at the law, but Roosevelt, appointed by a reform-fusion mayor, had a different conception of his responsibilities. "I have now run up against an ugly snag," he wrote to Anna Roosevelt, "the Sunday Excise Law."

> It is altogether too strict; but I have no honorable alternative save to enforce it, and I *am* enforcing it, to the furious rage of the saloon keepers, and of many good people too; for which I am sorry.[4]

The brewers, for their part, through the *American Brewer*, spoke of Roosevelt's "unparalleled severity and inconsiderateness, which has turned nearly all of his law-abiding friends into bitter enemies." Roosevelt had, in addition, heaped abuse on the brewers by calling them "the richest and most powerful organization that there is in this city," [5] a description they vehemently protested. The Raines Law came up for a vote in the autumn 1895 elections. The *American Brewer* stated before the vote "that henceforth no megalomaniac à la *Roosevelt* shall cripple a part of the business and drive it from the city by his tyrannical effrontery and caprice." [6] But in fact the election outcome was not favorable to the "liberal" cause.

Roosevelt wrote to Taft in 1901: "The fanatical temperance people have always opposed me, while the saloon element has recognized in me an infinitely more dreaded foe than any prohibitionists." [7] Though he expressed repeatedly his abhorrence of the professional prohibitionist, his career shows a gradual opportunistic tendency toward the anti-alcohol camp.

He wrote to George Bruce Cortelyou (who later became his Secretary of the Treasury) in August 1901:

> Of course, in the future I shall be, as in the past I have been, against any legislation in Congress against the brewers. With state legislation I do not interfere; but in national legislation I am unqualifiedly against any such legislation — which from the standpoint of morals even more than of business I regard as utterly mischievous. [8]

And even in July 1914 he predicted that national prohibition "would merely mean free rum and utter lawlessness in our big cities." [9] Yet a year later, when Roosevelt was asked by Raymond Robins what the chances were of his trying to make another attempt at the Presidency, his lengthy yes/no reply showed that he was much more willing to go along with the prohibitionist forces than ever before. [10]

The first important triumph of the Anti-Saloon League in the political field was a local one: in 1904 the league, spearheaded by Wayne Wheeler, managed to prevent the re-election of Governor M. T. Herrick of Ohio, who had put himself out of favor by vetoing a local option bill during his term of office. [11] In this instance, the Anti-Saloon League turned against a Republican, backed a Democrat in a predominantly Republican state, and produced a victory. Wheeler's public secretary wrote of this event many years later:

> The character of the campaign waged by Wheeler may be gathered from the fact that he reported to the Ohio Board of Directors that in the year he had arranged 3,000 public meetings and had distributed 75,000,000 book pages of literature. He won. Roosevelt had carried

the state by 255,000 in 1904. Herrick had been elected for his first term by 113,000. Pattison [the Democratic candidate] defeated him by 43,000.

Strutting with victory, Wheeler reported to his directors, "Never again will any political party ignore the protests of the church and moral forces of the state." [12]

President Taft was a frequent target of the Anti-Saloon League and its satellites: one particular occasion was the announced attendance of Secretary of Agriculture James Wilson at the Second International Brewers' Congress in Chicago, October 1911. The President's office was deluged with protests. Early in September he received the following letter from Homer C. Stunts, First Assistant Corresponding Secretary of the Board of Foreign Missions of the New York Methodist Episcopal Church:

> I feel very strongly on this matter of the prospective relation of Secretary Wilson to the International Brewers Congress. I hope you will find it in your power to induce him to refrain from relating his name, in any official relationship, to that liquor organization. Such a relationship would carry with it an implied approval by the government of the liquor business in so far as it is represented by this body of brewers and their friends. As I see it, such a step would be giving an entirely needless amount of comfort to the brewing interests and it would be construed by millions of our best people as a sanction of their program of making and vending liquors in this nation. Just now, when the temperance sentiment is so very strong throughout the nation, an acknowledgement like the one mentioned would seem to me to be out of harmony with sound political policy.[13]

The leaders of the Anti-Saloon League had arrived at the stage where they were "suggesting" to government officials what statements they should make and how they should behave. The superintendent of the New York Anti-Saloon League, Ferd. C. Iglehart, addressed Charles Hillis, the President's secretary:

> I write this letter to you personally because our relationships have been very close and our moral and intellectual affinities have been as nearly alike as our political opinions. Wilson might get a stomach ache about that date or might have some business in Washington, instead of Chicago at that time.

In passing this letter on to the President, a note was attached:

We are getting about fifty to sixty of these a day; they are being sent to the Agriculture Department without acknowledgment. . . . The clerk [in Secretary Wilson's office] stated that they are getting somewhat alarmed at the proportions the protest was assuming.[14]

Even Dr. Purley A. Baker called in person to make a protest against Wilson's appearance at the Brewers' Congress. Taft was vacationing in Beverly, Massachusetts, at the time, but Baker's message was relayed to him there. The official reply, dated 8 September 1911, was: "The President feels that he can not interfere in it at all." What Taft had actually written on the memo in his own handwriting was: "I can not & will not interfere — I think the societies might be about more useful business than clearing such phantoms." [15]

Wilson, though slightly perturbed, made his appearance at the congress as honorary president, and reported to Taft afterward:

I attended the International Brewers Congress at Chicago. Delegates were there from nearly all the countries of Europe. There has been, as you doubtless have observed, considerable criticism of me for going there at all, but of course there was nothing else to do. The prohibitionists have been threatening that they will take away votes from you in the coming campaign. The brewing people assure me that they will make good everything of that kind, and I think it would have been a great mistake if I had not gone there. It would have been regarded as an insult to those people, and that would have been resented by our own people.

I merely drop you this note to let you know that my judgment is that the best has been done that could be done, and there where a friend to you may have been lost I am well satisfied one, if not more, has been gained. There is a little side thought that comes in here and that is that a very large percent of the people who have been making so much noise about welcoming strangers here, do not vote the Republican ticket anyway, and some do not vote the Democratic ticket. They vote the Prohibition ticket. These people are the noisiest.[16]

The protests continued after the Brewers' Congress was over, their implication being that Taft would suffer in the Presidential election the following year. The fact that Taft lost in 1912 can hardly be attributed to his lack of cooperation with the Anti-Saloon League; Theodore Roosevelt and the Progressive Party intervened and upset the balance of votes.

One of the last things Taft did before relinquishing office was to veto the Webb-Kenyon bill, designed to prohibit interstate shipments of alcoholic beverages into dry states. But Congress passed the bill over his veto, thus giving Wheeler and the Anti-Saloon League their biggest triumph up to that time.

It was not surprising that they should launch their campaign for national prohibition at that year's convention. The first move was a dramatic march on the Capitol in December 1913 by four thousand men and women carrying a resolution for the submission of a constitutional amendment to prohibit liquor in the United States. This was only a symbolic gesture, to whip up enthusiasm and publicity. Although the Anti-Saloon League controlled a good many Senators and Congressmen, having helped to put them in office, it still lacked a sufficient number to secure passage of a constitutional amendment bill: the House vote in December 1914 was 197 for and 190 against, a majority but not the required two-thirds.[17]

The league managers were delivering their well-prepared attack from various angles. Most important, perhaps, was the extension of their control of Congress: in every state, county, city and national election they backed certain candidates, opposed others. They also increased the number of states with prohibition laws: by 1912 nine states were dry, and in 1914 alone, five more states entered the prohibition ranks. By the end of 1916, there were twenty-three states in all, with dry laws, that could be depended on to ratify a constitutional amendment if Congress could be prevailed upon to submit one.

It was another victory for the league when Secretary of the Navy Josephus Daniels issued in 1914 an order prohibiting alcoholic beverages of any kind in naval vessels, or in any naval installation on shore.[18] An even more significant success was the league's ability to ram through a prohibition law for the District of Columbia, first presented in 1915 and finally passed in February 1917.[19] In the 1916 national elections, although the league was realistic enough not to try to buck Woodrow Wilson, it managed to secure a predominantly dry Congress. "Many hours before the country knew whether Hughes or Wilson had triumphed," Wheeler said, "the dry workers throughout the nation were celebrating our victory. We knew that the Prohibition Amendment would be submitted to the states by the Congress just elected." [20]

Members of the brewing industry had apparently begun waking up to the necessity for making a strong presentation of their case. As early as 1912, when their annual convention met in Boston, the beloved, extroverted and anti-dry mayor of that city, John F. Fitzgerald, exhorted the brewers to make it their policy

> to take care that the law-makers of State and Nation are correctly informed as to your business, the character of the men engaged in it, the amount of capital involved, the kind of men who are in organizations like this, having as its object to see that the business is properly conducted.[21]

A propaganda war of publications and statistics was being grimly waged with the Anti-Saloon League, but the brewers could not, from the nature of things, muster the same backing of mass appeal, of religious fanaticism, of moral indignation. They could only continually deny the flagrant inaccuracies of the prohibition propaganda, and were not able, on the other hand, to get across a valid picture of their aims and activities. In discussing the United States Brewers' Association's propaganda campaign, that organization's president said at the 1915 convention:

> Our previous efforts had been limited largely to putting the facts before those men and women whose position and influence qualified them to take the lead in molding public sentiment. There is no doubt of the soundness of this method, but, unfortunately, everything relating to the use of alcohol is the subject of such bitter controversy that the mass of the people find themselves involved in such a maze of contradictions that the truth is obscured. . . . We have, therefore, to face the task of putting the facts directly before the mass of the people.[22]

The brewers could not find the proper means to counteract the prohibitionist-instigated impression that they were more concerned about protecting their investments than they were in the commonweal. Even in the political field, they were much less adroit than Wheeler and his league. The league was able to campaign openly and blatantly against or for candidates in all parts of the country; it could exercise a species of political blackmail over individual candidates by threatening to keep them out of office unless they went down the line with the league's demands. But if the brewers tried tactics of this sort, they were almost always in trouble. In 1915, for example, the attorney general of Texas filed suit against seven brewers in that state on two counts: violation of antitrust laws and interference in politics. The major charge was that the brewers had joined in the Texas Brewers' Association to fight against prohibition.[23]

The evidence, offered in rich detail, showed only that the brewers were doing exactly what the prohibition forces were doing; but the league's means were not available to the brewers. They had no other recourse than to contribute financially to political campaigns if they hoped to sway them. Besides, their funds for propaganda and agitation were based on their own contributions to their association, whereas the league's finances were supposed to be provided by its multitude of supporters, "the little people," though no one had any doubt that John D. Rockefeller, S. S. Kresge and other dry-minded millionaires were backing the league to the hilt.[24]

The charge in the Texas court, however, was that the brewers had used "funds to influence legislation in favor of the brewery interests of the state"; as pointed out by the *Western Brewer*, this seemed "to challenge an inherent right guaranteed the people by the constitution of the United States and that of the state of Texas to petition the legislature and to combat hostile legislation."[25] Yet the Texas brewers were advised, because of the technical aspects of the case, to plead guilty. They paid fines amounting to $280,000, and this evidence of a technical violation was widely disseminated and misconstrued.[26]

The declaration of war with Germany and the final push for a prohibition constitutional amendment came almost simultaneously, a concurrence of events which may not have been entirely accidental. One of President Wilson's early wartime measures was a food control bill; during the 1917 debates on this bill, attempts were made by the dry forces to shape it into a statute outlawing the manufacture of all alcoholic beverages — in other words, a national prohibition bill.[27] Here the full extent of Wheeler's power was vividly illustrated. Since amendments had been attached to the original bill which would have made it illegal to use any food materials for the manufacture of alcoholic beverages, some of the wet Senators had threatened to filibuster the bill out of Congress. In this impasse, Wilson appealed to the leaders of the league, through the agency of Senator Thomas S. Martin of Virginia, a dry, to withdraw some of their demands so that the bill might go through in time to be effective before the autumn harvest. The compromise effected was to take the beer and wine provisions out of the bill, but not to alter the provision concerning distilled liquors.

Before agreeing, the league insisted that Wilson put his request in writing, which — so effectual was their pressure — he did, not once but twice.[28] The bill as passed carried an amendment providing for the complete cessation of production of distilled spirits as of 8 September 1917, while the President was given discretion to limit or prohibit the manufacture of beer and wine as he saw fit. Wilson did, in fact, exercise this discretion on 11 December 1917[29] by reducing the food materials allowed for the manufacture of beer by thirty per cent, and at the same time reducing the legal alcoholic content of beer to 2¾% by weight.*

The league had written a peculiarly sanctimonious letter to the President after extracting the written request from him at the end of June 1917:

> We are aware of the threats made by the friends of beer and wine in the Senate, of an indefinite and protracted filibuster against these provisions of the bill. We beg to advise you that as patriotic Americans, determined to uphold you as commander-in-chief of the army and navy in the present war, we will not, for our constituency, offer any obstruction to the prompt passage of the Food Control Bill.
>
> Of course we cannot presume to indicate to members of Congress what action they should take in view of this request from the President of the United States. They will doubtless act in accordance with their convictions of duty.[30]

---

* It is customary to express alcoholic content of beverages that have small amounts in terms of weight or volume (rather than proof). The percent in volume is somewhat higher than the percent in weight, because a given amount of alcohol weighs $\frac{79}{100}$ of the corresponding amount of water. Hence a beer specified as containing 3.2% alcohol by weight might also be called a beer containing 4.05% of alcohol by volume. The general practice among brewers in the United States is to use the percent-by-weight formula.

In fact, the majority of Congress voted the way Wheeler and his associates advised them it was politically expedient for them to vote. And as for the league itself — anyone studying its activities in this period must come to the conclusion that it was clearly more interested in pushing through the prohibition bill than in the successful prosecution of the war.

Had the league agreed to the Food Control Bill compromise because the Congressional leaders offered them a deal? That bill, as finally redrafted, passed on 10 August 1917; the resolution for a prohibition constitutional amendment was passed in the Senate on 1 August. Among the various frantic maneuvers that took place at the last minute was the one which placed a limit on the amount of time in which the states would be allowed to ratify. Senator Harding suggested five years; Wheeler, after consulting his figures, held out for six — and in those terms the bill passed. As it turned out, ratification took just over one year from the time the House passed the resolution in December 1917, after yet another deal was made: in exchange for a year's grace for the liquor industry to clear up its business and dispose of its bonded stocks, the league demanded another year for ratification, thus making seven in all.[31]

The brewers cannot have felt very optimistic at this point, but yet another sideswipe was in store for them: a Senate investigation into relations between the German brewers of America and German war propaganda. It appears to be true that, up to the time of the American involvement in the war, many of the Germans living in the United States supported the Central Powers against the Allies. In a German-language publication, the *Jahrbuch der Deutschamerikaner für das Jahr 1918*, the editor Michael Singer wrote a long article citing British "atrocities." The British, he charged, unable to beat Germany with arms, had begun starving her babies by means of the naval blockade.[32] It also comes as a surprise to read an announcement that George Ehret, the New York brewer, was in Germany in 1916 and had decided to stay on indefinitely,[33] though in fact he left for Switzerland as soon as diplomatic relations between Germany and the United States were broken off.

But statements and activities of this kind need not be taken as subversive: the United States was maintaining a strict neutrality and there

Example of nineteenth-century brewery architecture:
B. Stroh Brewery, Detroit, 1885

THE BERNARDIN WORLD RENOWNED BOTTLE CAP.

No need of tin foil, when these caps are used. They will retain the cork perfectly while steaming the beer. They are used throughout the U·S and in many foreign countries. send for SAMPLES AND TESTIMONIALS

Our **CYCLONE BEER STOPPERS** have been on the market for the past three years and are pronounced superior by all who use them. We make all standard sizes, eccentrics, bails and neck wires. ⁓ Any of the parts shown in above cuts are furnished as wanted. ⁓ SEND FOR SAMPLES AND PRICES

Various beer bottle stoppers before the invention of the crown cap

Bottle shop, Pabst Brewing Company, around 1910

Bottle shop, G. Heileman Brewing Company, La Crosse, Wisconsin, around 1911

Two different methods of delivering beer in 1910

Advertising in 1908: The sociable aspect of beer

Advertising: Fine ladies and beer in 1911 and 1949.
The Rheingold Girl and Miss Rheingold

Carling Plant at Natick, Massachusetts, completed 1956

Schlitz Plant at Van Nuys, California, completed 1954

Brewhouse, Falstaff Brewing Company, New Orleans, Louisiana

Bottle shop, August Wagner Breweries, Columbus, Ohio

was no legal reason why individuals had to support one side or the other. There is plenty of evidence that, once Wilson was driven to ask for a declaration of war, the majority of German-Americans proved to be completely patriotic citizens. Among brewers' families, Joseph E. Magnus, grandson of Adolphus Busch, enlisted in the Army in May 1917, soon after the declaration of war. Gustav Pabst's son, Henry, enlisted in the Marines. Many more could be cited. As for contributions to the war effort, S. Liebmann's Sons Brewing Co. bought a $50,000 Liberty Bond at the outset, the Busch family contributed $500,000, the brewers of Milwaukee and their employees bought $2,000,000 worth of Liberty Bonds.[34]

But the Anti-Saloon League was determined to give the public a picture of German-Americans plotting secretly to undermine the nation. It was mainly Wayne Wheeler who appreciated the explosive propaganda value of this issue. During an investigation of possible connection between German-American brewers and German propaganda, which took place in 1916 in Pittsburgh, the files of the United States Brewers' Association had been seized but not made public because the brewers of Western Pennsylvania decided to plead guilty to the charges and pay fines. It was these files which Wheeler wanted to expose at just the right time, and the time he chose was 3 May 1918, when he wrote to A. Mitchell Palmer, Custodian of Alien Property:

> Dear Mr. Palmer:
>   I am informed that there are a number of breweries in this country which are owned in part by alien enemies. It is reported to me that the Annhauser [sic] Busch Company and some of the Milwaukee Companies are largely controlled by alien Germans. I assume that you have the right to investigate the books of these companies to ascertain who owns and controls them. Have you made any investigation? If not would you be willing to do so if we could give you any clue that would justify your taking such action? [35]

Eventually Palmer turned out to be willing — for which his payoff was appointment as Attorney General. At the hearing which began on 27 September 1918, a multitude of confused charges were made against the brewers, including their support of a Washington newspaper owned by Arthur Brisbane, their partial subsidizing of the National German-

American Alliance, their attempts to influence political candidates, their boycott against manufacturers of prohibitionist tendencies, and various other instances of what obviously appeared to most brewers as self-protection.[36] In those feverish anti-German days, when symphony orchestras were not playing the music of Beethoven and Brahms, and sauerkraut was being called "liberty cabbage," the hearings could not help coming out strongly against the brewers, almost all of whom did happen to be of German descent; but the attempt to link them to subversive activities was in itself far more sinister than successful. The technique used against the individual brewers concerned and the industry as a whole came to be called, somewhat later, the "smear."

The Eighteenth Amendment to the United States Constitution was ratified by the required thirty-six states on 16 January 1919, which meant that national prohibition would take effect one year from that date. The amendment is short enough to be quoted in full:

> After one year from the ratification of this article, the manufacture, sale, or transportation of intoxicating liquors within, the importation thereof into, or the exportation thereof from the United States and all territory subject to the jurisdiction thereof for beverage purposes is hereby prohibited.
>
> The Congress and the several States shall have concurrent power to enforce this article by appropriate legislation.
>
> This article shall be inoperative unless it shall have been ratified as an amendment to the Constitution by the legislatures of the several States, as provided in the Constitution, within seven years from the date of the submission hereof to the States by Congress.

There was something academic about various of the provisions, because in fact national prohibition was already effective in September 1918. The distilleries had been closed down in August 1917 by the Food Control Law, and the following year, partially because of crop failures and labor shortage, supplies to breweries were cut off by Presidential decree.[37]

Nor was this all: in that same month, September 1918, Congress passed a "wartime" national prohibition amendment, as a rider to the so-called Food Stimulation Act. It became law on 21 November 1918, ironically ten days after the Armistice. The provision that affected the brewers was:

After May first, nineteen hundred and nineteen, until the conclusion of the present war and thereafter until the termination of demobilization, the date of which shall be determined and proclaimed by the President of the United States, no grains, cereals, fruit, or other food product shall be used in the manufacture or production of beer, wine, or other intoxicating malt or vinous liquor for beverage purposes.[38]

Strangely enough, beer could be manufactured for export.

The New York *World* commented on this act in an editorial on 5 November 1918:

[The Anti-Saloon League's] present efforts to club Congress into action indicate their abandonment of pretense. What they want is Prohibition regardless of war conditions or military efficiency or constitutional processes, and their present attitude toward the pending legislation exhibits their animus. . . . Prohibition to win the war was one thing. But Prohibition saddled on the country by political intimidation in advance of the action of the States on the constitutional amendment and against the wishes of the majority is intolerable.

But the League's drive continued unabated. It was like a poker-player with countless aces up his sleeve: Prohibition had arrived in a number of disguises — in the shape of the Food Control Bill, masquerading as a wartime measure, and ultimately as a constitutional amendment. And then in May 1919, Representative Volstead of Minnesota presented a bill (H.R. 6810), which bore his name but which Wayne Wheeler claimed to have written, establishing the apparatus for the enforcement of prohibition, in both its wartime and constitutional amendment guises. The feeble protests of the wets were overridden, and Congress passed the bill on 10 October 1919.[39] President Wilson vetoed it on 27 October, on the grounds that the war was over and therefore the provisions for enforcing "wartime prohibition" did not properly belong in the bill. But such fine points were hardly enough to act as a brake: Congress passed the bill over the veto with almost indecent haste. Prohibition was to be had at all costs.

Part Five

The Unpopular Law

H OW WAS IT possible for Prohibition to happen? Why was the opposing propaganda so ineffective? Charles Merz, in his study of the first ten years of Prohibition, sought to answer these questions by saying that the opposition lacked an organization as effective as that of the Anti-Saloon League:

> In fact, they were not organized at all. The only organized opposition to ratification [of the Eighteenth Amendment] came from the brewers and distillers. The brewers were under fire as pro-German. The distillers had been outlawed for the duration of the war. Ordinary people who were neither brewers nor distillers, but who were opposed to prohibition on principle or as a matter of personal taste, had no organization to represent them at the state capitols, no lobby and no leaders.[1]

There is also another and less demonstrable theory — that prohibition was inevitable, that it was inherent in the growth of the industrial system. John Allen Krout tries to make this point:

> As workers were slowly but steadily concentrated under one management in larger enterprises, the relation of intemperance to labour efficiency became a problem of more than passing interest to the factory-owner. Arguments which lacked force when addressed to farmers employing a few labourers, were more influential with manufacturers who regarded unnecessary labour-turnover from the point of view of diminished profits. The industrial enterpriser was beginning to see in the liquor business a potential menace, a menace not at all lessened by the constant infiltration of foreigners into the United States. By the

middle of the nineteenth century the prohibitory movement enrolled
in its ranks some of the rising "captains of industry," who were not
unaware of the economic implications of the trade in intoxicants.[2]

What cannot be denied, in looking over the whole situation, is that
the Anti-Saloon League was tougher, more ruthless and realistic than the
forces arrayed against it. The brewers were so anxious to see the bright
side of things that, as late as October 1917, with the world falling over
their heads, they could still read in the *Western Brewer*, an official
publication of the industry, that "Virginia and Maine Turn Tide
Against Prohibition":

> The signs of the times are encouraging. They indicate that the tide
> has turned against prohibition. The Philadelphia *Sunday Dispatch* says
> the long-looked-for reaction has set in; fanaticism and social regenera-
> tion has run its course; there are signs on all sides of a return to na-
> tional sanity.[3]

The brewers were also surprisingly maladroit in their public relations.
For example, they had used for many years as an argument proving
their value to the national economy the fact that they bought such a
great amount of the country's agricultural product; then, in 1917, when
they were threatened with extinction in order to conserve the national
grain supply, they brought forth statistics and graphs to show that in
fact they required the tiniest fraction of the nation's grain output.[4]
This type of shifting argument worked admirably for the Anti-Saloon
League: there it was nourished by virtually hysterical emotion. The
brewers, backed by no such blinding device, could not get by with what
looked like opportunism.

But Prohibition came, and for the brewers it meant either liquida-
tion of property without compensation, or manufacture of some product
other than alcoholic beer. While they studied their possibilities for the
future, certain legal maneuvers were continuing in the courts. The
main contention by which the brewers thought they might yet save
something out of the wreckage was the question of what constituted an
intoxicating beverage. Various suits were undertaken in 1919, on behalf
of the Jacob Hoffman Brewing Co., Jacob Ruppert, Inc. (both of New

York), and a number of other breweries in different cities, to establish that the beer containing 2.75% alcohol by weight manufactured during the war did not come under the heading of "intoxicating beverages." [5] According to testimony given by the brewers' attorney, Samuel Untermyer, at Senate hearings in July 1919 relating to the Prohibition enforcement act, prewar beer had contained 4% and sometimes as much as 6% alcohol by weight. The brewers had accumulated a great deal of clinical evidence to demonstrate that 2.75% alcohol by weight did not lead to drunkenness, and therefore could not be called "intoxicating." The theory was that in order to get drunk one would have to drink more liquid with that amount of alcohol in it than the human system could take. Wheeler countered with his own statistics, experts and case histories which, to the layman, were just as effective, if not more so.[6] It was the Volstead Act that defined ½ of 1% by volume as the outside limit for a nonintoxicating beverage,[7] and it was that figure which the Supreme Court upheld in its finding in the Ruppert v. Caffey case, 5 January 1920.[8]

Brewing on a national scale came to an end at this point; only certain firms were licensed to manufacture a beer containing more than ½ of 1% by volume for medicinal purposes. But this was brought to a halt by the Willis-Campbell bill, passed on 23 November 1921.

As early as 1917, Carl A. Nowak, secretary of the Master Brewers' Association of the United States, had written and published a book called *New Fields for Brewers*, which outlined means of adapting breweries to the production of low alcoholic (or near) beers, non-malt beverages and fruit juices, yeast products, vinegar, malt extract, breakfast foods, commercial feeding stuffs, dairy products, industrial alcohol and mechanical appliances.[9] This was a case of not only preparing for the future, but also facing the facts of the present; by 1917, twenty-five of the states were dry. This cut deeply into the market of the national brewers, who felt the pinch much more than, say, the New York City or Baltimore or Detroit local brewers. "Near beers" or "cereal beverages" were already on the market; Anheuser-Busch had built a plant described as "colossal" expressly for the production of its non-alcoholic beverage called "Bevo";[10] a great flood of near beer trade names were being registered during 1917.* Many of the breweries were, therefore, fairly well prepared to shift gears when real beer was finally outlawed. In any case, the best way to make near beer was to make real beer and then de-alcoholize it,[11] though some brewers used the check-fermentation method, which had the disadvantage of being less stable.[12]

The breweries began to reincorporate for the manufacture of cereal beverages, and changed their corporate names: for example, the Krantz Brewing Co. in Findlay, Ohio, became Franz Products Co., the Billings Brewing Co. in Billings, Montana, became Advance Manufacturing Co., the Jackson Brewing Co. in New Orleans became the Jackson Pure Products Co. Some brewers actually expanded their holdings: Christian Feigenspan, the brewer of Newark, N. J., bought a controlling interest in the Dobler Brewery in Albany and also controlled the Yale Brewery in New Haven. This was in 1919, when he apparently still believed that 2.75% beer would be allowed.[13]

At first, the producers of near beer had reason for optimism. Production for the year 1921 was almost 300,000,000 gallons (compared with over 1,000,000,000 gallons of real beer produced as late as 1918), but the figure dropped steadily from that year on: by 1932, only some 85,750,000 gallons were recorded as produced.[14] The comment of the *American Brewer* on the industry picture in 1921 was: "Brewers who entered the field of cereal beverages or soft drink manufacture were disappointed by the poor demand for their product." [15] Their greatest competitor, of course, was the supplier of bootleg beer or whiskey.

Various alternatives were tried. Many found it profitable to manufacture ice cream, malt syrup and malt extract. The Schlitz management built the "Eline" plant for the manufacture of chocolates and candies.[16] Anheuser-Busch announced that it was going to use part of the plant to manufacture "high grade packing house products." [17] The Valentin Blatz company was manufacturing industrial alcohol; the David Stevenson Brewing Co. in New York City was using a part

---

* Some of them were YIP, ONA, PABLO (Pabst Brewing Co.), CHRISMO (Christian Moerlein Brewing Co.), FAMO (Jos. Schlitz Brewing Co.), LUX-O (Stroh Brewing Co.), LUXO (Henry Weinhard Brewery), QUIZZ (Geo. Wiedemann Brewing Co.), VIVO (Fred Miller Brewing Co.) and HOPPY (another Pabst label). (*Brewers' Journal*, vol. 41, pp. 180, 266, 304, 344, 386, 427.)

of the plant for the storage of furs; the Fortune Brothers Brewing Co. in Chicago manufactured spaghetti and macaroni.[18] What most of the breweries were doing, however, was closing down. The trade publications were full of statements like the following:

Adolph F. Haffenreffer, manager of the Old Colony Products Co., Fall River, Mass., announces that the company will probably discontinue business, as it is impossible to compete against the real beer flooding that section.[19]

In the course of 1922 alone, the Anthony & Kuhn Brewery (a branch of the British-owned St. Louis Brewing Association) was sold to a laundry company; the old Fitzgerald Bros. Brewing Co. of Troy, New York, closed down; the once-flourishing Wm. J. Lemp Brewery of St. Louis was sold at auction, at a loss of over 90% on the investment; the property of the Henry Elias Brewing Co. at 411 E. 54th Street, New York City, was bought by Bloomingdale Bros.; United Breweries Co. of Chicago (another syndicate-owned business) was liquidated; the Connecticut Breweries Co., Bridgeport, was in the hands of receivers.[20] And yet, in that same year, the brewers (unjustifiably) felt new stirrings of hope. Notorious drys like Volstead in Minnesota and Senator Frelinghuysen in New Jersey were trounced at the elections. Colonel Jacob Ruppert was quoted as stating, "The leading New York brewers expect the return of beer and are ready to turn out the real stuff. They look to the Congress which assembles next year to speedily modify the Volstead law." [21] Was the baseball colonel whistling in the dark or did he really believe this?

There might have been some small excuse for this optimism, because the first two years of Prohibition had shown that enforcement was in danger of becoming a farce. One of Wayne Wheeler's infrequent mistakes was his calculation that five million dollars a year would be enough to support the Prohibition Bureau. In fact the appropriations granted by Congress rose steadily from just over six million in 1921 to sixteen million in 1932.[22] And even so, this was not enough to pay for a reliable staff of investigators and agents who could eliminate the big-city speakeasies, the rum-runners, the illicit stills, the smuggling from Canada and Mexico, the bootleggers, gangsters and racketeers. The first Federal Prohibition Commissioner, John F. Kramer, after a year at his job, woke to the conclusion that Prohibition had been "to some extent forced upon whole states and especially upon large cities in which people had no sympathy whatever with the idea." [23]

The Volstead Act is a classic example of a law so unpopular with the general public that it cannot be enforced except at huge expense and by measures that come close to abrogating constitutional rights. Even though all the Congresses during the Prohibition period had comfortable dry majorities, even though Wayne Wheeler reached the height of his power and control before his death in 1927, it appeared impossible to kindle enough ardor to get the really substantial appropriations that might have made enforcement somewhat less of a failure and frustration. Both the Harding and Coolidge administrations were proud of running the government economically; Congress went along with this; the country as a whole was experiencing a fantastic postwar boom. And so that whole era, on which the passage of time has bestowed a retrospective and specious glamour, of the hip-flask and "Joe-sent-me" and bathtub gin and poisonous denatured alcohol and set-ups and spiked coffee and gangster warfare, was allowed to run its merry course.

From time to time, to be sure, some token measure was adopted, as if a magic formula would make everything all right — particularly after there had been one of frequent scandalous disclosures. In 1922, for instance, a bill was proposed that provided for the deportation of aliens flaunting the Volstead Act; this passed the House but not the Senate.[24] In October of that year the Attorney General ruled that American ships on the high seas came under Prohibition laws.[25] In 1927, a plan for a government-controlled corporation to manufacture and distribute medicinal whiskey was proposed and defeated.[26] In that same year, the Prohibition Bureau was finally separated from the Commissioner of Internal Revenue's office and brought under Civil Service regulations, thus making it somewhat easier to overcome the widespread corruption of enforcement officers themselves. In March 1929, Coolidge signed the Jones-Stalker bill, by which the maximum penalties under the Volstead Act were raised to $10,000 fine, five years' imprisonment or both.

Besides passing or killing such bills as these and others, Congress occasionally bestirred itself to conduct long-winded hearings on the whole business of enforcement. In 1926 a House Committee held such hearings on Civil Service and Prohibition; from 5 to 24 April of the same year, there were hearings on bills to amend the Volstead Act before a subcommittee of the Senate Committee on the Judiciary; the 71st Congress in 1930 had hearings on modifications of the Volstead Act and also "Investigation of Prohibition Enforcement." [27] And the year before, President Hoover, fresh in office, called on George W. Wickersham to head a commission on law enforcement and observance, which concentrated on problems of the Volstead Act.[28]

What appears to one now as the simple truth, though it may have been much less obvious at the time, is that enforcement of the Eighteenth Amendment in terms of the Volstead Act went against the will of the people. Every attempt to rouse public opinion against the bootleggers and the speakeasies met eventual failure, for Prohibition fed corruption and Prohibition was not popular with the majority of the country. It had never been subjected to a national referendum, and one of the factors in favor of its passage in the state legislatures was the advantage given to rural (and mainly dry) areas in the establishment of voting districts. As early as 1919, the state of Rhode Island brought a suit in the Supreme Court to declare the Eighteenth Amendment void. New Jersey took an identical trial step in 1920. After some experience with the failure of Prohibition, Montana voted to repeal the state enforcement law in 1926, and similar votes took place by referendum in Colorado, California and Missouri.[29] Except in those states which had traditionally been dry even in the nineteenth century, public opinion was predominantly against the results of Prohibition and the Volstead Act, and by 1930 a strong movement for modification or, even better, repeal had gathered force. Wheeler and, after him, other dry leaders fought hard and successfully against a national referendum;[30] an unofficial one, such as that conducted by the *Literary Digest* in 1922, found a majority of the public in favor of either modification or repeal of the Volstead Act.[31]

The wet campaign, as shown before, had never been a successful one, perhaps because it was conducted almost entirely by the beer and liquor industries themselves. It was only after Prohibition had arrived and the obvious antisocial effects of the Volstead Act became clear that those citizens not involved in the production of alcoholic beverages who considered national prohibition socially and morally wrong began to organize against the overweening forces of the Anti-Saloon League, the W.C.T.U., the Prohibition Party and all their satellites. The first such organization was started in Washington in 1920 by William H. Stayton and was called the Association Against the Prohibition Amendment.[32] In 1926, this Association's activities were enormously strengthened by backing from the du Pont family. Another organization of this kind, the Moderation League, was incorporated in 1923; at first, considering repeal unattainable, its members "favored modification of the Volstead Act as a practicable compromise." By 1932, it favored outright repeal of the Eighteenth Amendment.[33] There was also a Women's Organization for National Prohibition Reform, started in 1929; the Voluntary Committee of Lawyers, organized in the same year; and the Crusaders, started in 1930. The American Federation of Labor was consistently antagonistic to Prohibition;[34] in 1931, the American Legion voted for a referendum on national prohibition;[35] and from the start of Prohibition on, certain influential private citizens such as Nicholas Murray Butler and William Randolph Hearst expressed themselves as being squarely on the side of repeal. A number of important newspapers throughout the country, appalled by the disregard for law that seemed to them to stem from Prohibition, used all their power to support the cause of modification or repeal; the New York World, in particular, was boisterously outspoken and also contributed the conception by cartoonist Rollin Kirby of Mr. Prohibition as a tall, gaunt, red-nosed, stovepipe-hatted hypocrite.

A scholarly analysis of the whole field of prohibition stated in 1932: "Not even the most confirmed prohibitionist will deny that the movement against prohibition is rapidly gaining ground." The writer went on:

> Official state referendums prior to and since prohibition, as well as unofficial straw votes, while by no means conclusive, all show a marked shift in public sentiment against the attempt to enforce "universal total abstinence by law." [36]

The defeat of Al Smith in the 1928 elections was a blow for those who had hoped to move swiftly for repeal. H. L. Mencken, consistently on the wet side, wrote of the election:

> If Dr. Hoover was elected, then so was the Anti-Saloon League elected. Its exultant claim that it shared his triumph and is entitled to its share of his power is well grounded in the facts.[37]

Nevertheless, forces were working for the repeal advocates. In 1930, Governor Dwight W. Morrow of New Jersey came out against Prohibition.[38] And then, as a writer totally committed to the Prohibition side has put it:

> In the weeks preceding the 1932 national conventions of the two major parties the nation was treated by the wets to an unparalleled display of fireworks. It began with a rocket which General Pershing sent up from Paris, declaring his disapproval of Prohibition. This was followed by another from Mr. [Walter] Chrysler. Then came the glare of the Rockefeller Roman candle, a pin-wheel from Dr. John R. Mott, two more rockets from Mr. Sloan of General Motors and Mr. Firestone.[39]

The startling announcement of John D. Rockefeller, Jr., in the form of a letter to Nicholas Murray Butler in 1932, was that he could no longer support Prohibition. Rockefeller financed a study of liquor control practices in Europe, published under the title *Toward Liquor Control,* and wrote in the foreword:

> I was born a teetotaler and I have been a teetotaler on principle all my life. Neither my father nor his father ever tasted a drop of intoxicating liquor. I could hope that the same might be true of my children and their children. It is my earnest conviction that total abstinence is the wisest, best, and safest position for both the individual and society. But the regrettable failure of the Eighteenth Amendment has demonstrated the fact that the majority of this country are not yet ready for total abstinence, at least when it is attempted through legal coercion. The next best thing — many people think it a better thing — is temperance. Therefore, as I sought to support total abstinence when its achievement seemed possible, so now, and with equal vigor, I would support temperance.[40]

The great hope of the repeal advocates was the election of a President in 1932 sympathetic to their side. Mencken, not always astute on political issues, editorialized early in that year:

> If the Democrats could go before the country in November with a
> tried and implacable wet leading them, and on a platform damning
> Prohibition from hell to breakfast, there is little doubt the Lord
> Hoover's first (and last) term would end on March 4, 1933, and
> with what, on lower levels, would be called a bum's rush.[41]

But, Mencken went on, the Democrats lacked the courage; hadn't they
in 1928 wedded "wet" Al Smith to a Vice-Presidential candidate,
Joseph T. Robinson, who was acceptable to the Anti-Saloon League?

Franklin Roosevelt may not have fitted Mencken's conception of "a
tried and implacable wet," but he certainly campaigned on a strong
repeal-of-Prohibition platform. Soon after the election, on 7 December
1932, hearings started before the House Ways and Means Committee
on modifications of the Volstead Act along lines supported by the
President-elect. Under consideration was a bill "to provide revenue by
the taxation of certain nonintoxicating liquor." [42] Though Roosevelt
had advocated and practically assured the country that the Eighteenth
Amendment would be repealed, this "beer bill" was an independent
matter. In his statement at the hearings, Congressman Fiorello La
Guardia made the issue quite clear:

> [This bill] is before us, first, by reason of the great need of additional
> revenue; second, owing to the complete failure of prohibition en-
> forcement; third, by reason of the changed attitude on the part of the
> American public.[43]

There is no doubt that the depression, in full flood by 1932, played
some part in the favorable reception by Congress of this bill. A good deal
of the testimony given at the hearings was on the subject of jobs which
would be created by re-establishing the brewing industry: coopers,
bottlers, maltsters, hop-growers, and all the other industries whose interests touch upon those of the brewers.

The greatest discussion centered on the percentage of alcohol to be
allowed in beer brewed under these new provisions. The very reason
beer could be brought back before the country had yet acted on a repeal
amendment was that the Volstead Act left it up to Congress to establish what an "intoxicating beverage" was. At the start of Prohibition enforcement, the figure of ½ of 1% by volume had been insisted on by
the Anti-Saloon League; by the end of the 1932 hearings 3.2% by

weight was the figure accepted. In his letter read before the Ways and Means Committee, T. C. Haffenreffer of Haffenreffer & Company in Boston wrote:

> An alcoholic content of 3.2 per cent is preferable to 2.75 per cent in both beer as well as ale and porter, as all brews improve in taste, flavor and aroma directly in ratio with the increased alcoholic content. The improvement in palatability does not come from the alcohol itself, which is tasteless and only incidental to fermentation, but from the aromatic properties produced in the process of fermentation. Hops used in all brews, primarily for flavoring purposes, contain resinous substances soluble in alcohol. The higher the alcoholic strength, the greater the solubility of aromatic resinous substances. This is one of our prime reasons for desiring the maximum permissible alcoholic strength of our products.[44]

There was some uneasiness among the brewers as to the speed with which the beer bill would be passed. It was seen safely through the House on 21 December 1932, and awaited action in the Senate.[45] Roosevelt, true to his campaign promises, sent a message to Congress on 13 March 1933, shortly after his inauguration, recommending passage of legislation "for the immediate modification of the Volstead Act." The measure finally passed by both houses of Congress, the Cullen bill (H.R. 3341), was similar in most of its provisions to the one which the House had passed earlier: it permitted the production and sale of 3.2% beer in states which did not have state prohibition laws; it provided for a tax of $5 a barrel and a brewers' tax of $1000 a year; and it prohibited shipments of such beer into states where it was illegal.[46]

The sentiment of the brewers of America was expressed by the *American Brewer*: "Victory at last, and a beer bill which will make it possible to produce a good, wholesome, palatable beer! We are grateful that the will of the people finally has prevailed." [47]

THIRTY-FIVE

After Repeal

THE DEVELOPMENT of brewing since 1933 can be divided into two parts: the first period starting with Repeal and ending with the conclusion of World War II, the second comprising what has happened since 1945. Both periods were tumultuous ones, in which far-reaching and generally unpredictable changes took place, but the tendency has been consistent — to take every possible advantage of improved merchandising and production techniques; to make large budget allocations for promotion; and to bring the public idea of beer into focus as the beverage of moderation.

Passage of the beer bill meant at first just one thing: to get as much 3.2% beer on the market by 7 April 1933 as could be made. BEER FLOWS IN 19 STATES AT MIDNIGHT, was the headline of the New York *Times* on that date.* The brewers had been so sure of the bill's passage that many of them had begun to produce 3.2% beer on advance permits before they could legally sell it, in order not to put "green" beer on the market. Alvin Griesedieck, who became president of the Falstaff Brewing Corporation in 1938, has described this process:

> Naturally, we were prepared in advance of that [7 April 1933], that is to the extent of our ability to produce. Bear in mind again, that under our permit to sell near beer, we first had to make a normal

---

* In fact, twenty states plus the District of Columbia sold beer legally on 7 April 1933. The other states gradually repealed restrictions on the state level, Kansas being the last. Beer was re-legalized there in 1937.

alcoholic beer — then de-alcoholize it. So all we had to do was turn off the de-alcoholizing unit.[1]

Those breweries which had managed somehow to keep going with near beer were better off, when it came to reviving their beer trade, than those which had adapted to other products. But in all cases, a significant amount of re-equipping and refurbishing was necessary. Bottling machinery, used increasingly during Prohibition by soft-drink manufacturers, had made enormous advances since 1920, rendering machines bought before then virtually obsolete. The complete acceptance of automobiles by the end of the war made it necessary for breweries of any size to invest in whole fleets of delivery trucks. These problems faced each individual brewer who decided to take up his business again or build a new plant.

By June 1933, some 31 brewers were back in operation; a year later 756.[2] In the beginning, there was an expectable scramble to get on what seemed to be a beer bandwagon. In fact, however, results that first year were somewhat disappointing. At the first post-Repeal convention of the United States Brewers' Association, in February 1934 (by which time the Twenty-first Amendment had been handily ratified and all federal restrictions on alcoholic beverages lifted), its president spoke of "the unfavorable conditions under which the legitimate sale of beer in our country has started." [3] Colonel Jacob Ruppert was referring, of course, to the devastating depression the country was undergoing. There was no way to overcome the fact that the consumer's purchasing power was severely curtailed. Because beer was still looked on at that time as a workingman's drink, the brewers were anxious to secure a reduction in the $5 a barrel federal tax and so get back to the "five-cent glass." As a consequence of the higher price, as well as a noticeable slowness in winning back the beer-drinkers and some degree of bootlegging that persisted through 1933, tax-paid withdrawals for the year came to only about twenty and a half million barrels, well below the pre-Prohibition figure, which had been around 60 million between 1910 and 1917.[4]

There was, besides, strong competition from a new quarter — the soft-drink industry. In 1917, the attitude of those who claimed to speak

for the brewers was that soft drinks should be classified under "amuse-
ments."

> Aside from wholesomeness, which is equally desirable in tooth-paste,
> teething rings and everything else that enters the mouth, the qualities
> which are essential in foods are not particularly required in these
> drinks.[5]

The brewers, soon after Repeal, were forced to take the soft-drink business more seriously: it was like a youngster who was beginning to grow
up. The value of that industry had only risen from about $135,000,000
in 1919 to over $175,000,000 in 1931,[6] but this turned out to be just the
beginning of a sustained increase in the consumption of root beer,
ginger ale, fruit pops, the various colas, and the like. Their value in
terms of shipments was estimated as almost $750,000,000 in 1947 and
about a billion and a half in 1958[7] (a year when the comparable figure
for the brewing industry was nearly two billion).*

As Colonel Ruppert expressed it in yet another statement, the brewers had an additional handicap in those early days of re-legalized brewing: "the presence in the industry of many men inexperienced in
brewing and many breweries improperly financed."

> When beer was legalized many people felt that a new industry would
> offer an excellent opportunity for profit and employment. Breweries
> were erected as the result of stock market operations, without regard to
> the necessities of the locality or the possibilities of sound business.
> . . . Many such breweries are being placed in stronger hands or are
> being closed.[8]

It had been obvious, even before Repeal, that there would have to
be some dependable regulation of the trade in alcoholic beverages. In
January 1933, Walter Lippmann had stated the prevailing view: "The
chief advantage of the beer bill, to my mind, would lie in its power to
awaken the people to the need of preparing a regulating of the liquor
traffic to take the place of prohibition. . . . Repeal does not solve the
liquor problem." [9]

Regulations were needed, to start with, at the local and, particularly,
state level. In January 1933 a sample regulation bill was proposed for

---

* Comparable figures have always put the brewing industry in the lead, but,
recently, by somewhat smaller margins.

the District of Columbia, which provided for a tax of $2.50 per barrel, a $100 license fee for all establishments selling beer by the glass (on-premise consumption), a $20 license fee if sales were only by bottle (off-premise consumption), no sales to minors and no "tied houses." These features appeared in most of the local regulation measures adopted throughout the country, but the $2.50 barrel tax was considered excessive and was, in general, reduced. In Maine, for example, a tax of $1.25 a barrel was set in April 1933; in Iowa it was $1.24, in New York $1.00, in Tennessee $1.20.[10] The local brewers and their associations participated, wherever possible, in setting these regulations.

On the industry level, a whole new concept of regulation was introduced with the Fair Competition Codes that were worked out under the terms of the National Industrial Recovery Act and the Federal Alcohol Control Administration. On this subject, Colonel Ruppert made the following comments early in 1934:

> The same unsound economic conditions responsible for the lessened purchasing power, and for the increased taxes to which I have referred, is [sic] also responsible for the establishment of a Code for the Brewing Industry, as for the other industries of our country. This I feel we may well regard as a blessing and an opportunity.
>
> From the time it became probable that the National Recovery Act would be enacted and Codes for the various industries established, the officers and directors of your Association have been most helpfully active in the creation and development of a proper Code for the Brewing Industry.[11]

The importance of the operation of the Code, which was concerned mainly with pricing, labeling and wholesale practices, was that it helped to stimulate the concept of self-regulation — one of the most important advances the industry made after Repeal. The brewer William Piel, particularly concerned with the success of the Code and at that time chairman of the Third Regional Board for the Brewing Industry, stated in an article in January 1935 that it was left to industry, "in virtue of self-regulation, itself to invoke the sanctions of the codes — the government willing to prosecute and punish code violators only at industry's own command." [12]

Though the NRA was declared unconstitutional, and these codes themselves (once the honeymoon with Franklin D. Roosevelt was more or less over) began irresponsibly to be called "socialistic" in design, they served a most useful function for the brewers in those early days of trying to rebuild the industry: they helped in the weeding out of those who were in brewing to stay from those who had jumped in for a quick kill; they created the legal and practical framework by which the modern brewing industry was able to function; and they made possible a solidarity among brewers which until then had been distinctly sporadic.

Many members of the industry felt that the loss of the Code after the NRA's extinction was, as expressed by the general manager of the Tivoli Union Co. in Denver, D. W. McLaughlin,

> a matter of regret from many aspects. Undoubtedly there were a number of highly advantageous points to it, and with that thought in mind, the leaders of the industry are, today, making plans to supplement it with a voluntary code.[13]

To replace the Federal Alcohol Control Administration that had to be dissolved along with the NRA, Congress passed in 1935 the Federal Alcohol Administration Act, creating the Federal Alcohol Administration (FAA) as a division in the Treasury Department.[14] The regulations by which the FAA (and, after 1940, the Alcohol Tax Unit of the Bureau of Internal Revenue, which took over those functions*) controlled the alcoholic beverage industry quite clearly evolved from the Code worked out in cooperation with government agencies in 1933 by devoted members of the brewing industry.†

Changes in the conduct of brewing were of course to be expected: it could not simply resume where it had left off. One of the changes which came fairly gradually was the incease in sales of packaged beer (bottles and cans) in relation to draught (barrels or kegs). In 1934, the first normal year after Repeal, the ratio of sales was 75% in favor of draught. Packaged sales rose year by year until, in 1941, they actually overtook the sales of draught, 51.7% to 48.3%;[15] and they have increased annually ever since. Draught beer had outsold packaged for a number of reasons. The saloon was one of these: draught beer was sold there over

---

* The responsible agency, as of 1961, is the Alcohol and Tobacco Tax Division of the Internal Revenue Commission.

† The text of the Code as approved by President Roosevelt on 4 December 1933 was published in the *Western Brewer*, December 1933, pp. 49-53.

the counter, at tables and in cans or pitchers for consumption at home. The taverns and barrooms and so-called "cocktail lounges," which took the place of saloons after Repeal, maintained the tradition of draught at first, but they too began to stock bottles, hitherto considered the exclusive province of the "export" trade. Many beer-drinkers had lost the tavern habit during Prohibition and, because of the rise in private ownership of refrigerators, it became easier to keep beer at home — naturally in bottles. Tavern-keepers also found it simpler to sell bottled beer. Draught beer, which is not pasteurized, requires special handling, and has to be sold fast. The draught equipment has to be maintained; there is inevitable leakage and spoilage; it is harder to keep a check on employees when only draught beer is sold.

Another boost in the sales of packaged beer came from the introduction of canned beer, which took place commercially in Richmond, Virginia, on 24 January 1935, as a result of co-operative pioneering by the American Can Company and the Krueger Brewing Co. of Newark.[16] The advantages of the so-called "Keglined" canned beer were supposed to be many. For one thing, the can was used only once, was not returnable, and therefore required no deposit. Consumers were thought to like the idea that no one else had ever drunk from the same receptacle. It weighed less than a bottle and took up less space. As far as the brewer was concerned, it had the dual advantage of being impervious to light (which is unfriendly to beer) and requiring shorter pasteurization. Though the American Can Company scored something of a "scoop" it was only by a couple of months: supplies were soon on the way from the National Can Company and the Continental Can Company. The latter and Crown Cork and Seal Co., Inc., were responsible for a slight variation in the cone-top "cap sealed" can that had a special vogue for a time. In July 1935 it was announced that Pabst Export Beer would be going into cans, and only a month later plans for canning their beer were publicized by G. Heilemann Brewing Co. of La Crosse, Wisconsin, Berghoff Brewing Corp. of Fort Wayne, Indiana, and Bridgeport Brewing Co., Inc., of Albany.[17]

At about the same time, the glass bottle manufacturers brought out what they called a "one-trip" beer bottle: shorter and lighter in weight than the standard bottle, and having one particular advantage over the can — it did not require new machinery. A writer for *Brewery Age*, taking note of these developments, commented:

> Those who prefer to drink their beer in taverns will always find that source open to them. But this new form of merchandising — whether it is "canned beer" or the "stubby bottle" — reaching the low income homes and bringing in its development increased beer consumption, increased moderation and temperance, should be encouraged in every possible way.[18]

In any case, the trend was to bring beer into the home. This was done in terms of advertising, which tended to show beer consumers not in taverns but at ordinary social events: listening to the radio, entertaining friends, at the tennis court or swimming pool. The increased distribution of packaged beer in grocery shops and supermarkets also made it easier for the consumer to keep a stock at home.

Much of the credit for the progress made in the first few years after Repeal must be given to the United States Brewers' Association, which had kept a small flickering light glowing all through Prohibition. In that period, the Association had maintained an extensive library and the secretary, Hugh F. Fox, had periodically issued a publication called *Periscope*, which was a compilation of notes, press clippings and arguments for the return of beer. In his opening address to the 1934 convention, the president said, "It was a small but loyal and intrepid band of brewers that made up the active membership of this Association during the days of Prohibition" [19] — there were no regular meetings during those idle years, no regular collection of dues. It was mainly a few Eastern brewers who supported Fox's office and work. When the Association started up again after Repeal, there were about sixteen active members and $7000 in the treasury.[20] At the end of 1933, however, membership had increased to 120. Most of the large brewers in the country re-joined: Sol E. Abrams represented Schlitz, Fred Pabst was an officer, R. A. Huber attended as representative of Anheuser-Busch, and there were others from as far as Texas and California.[21] There appeared, however, some dissatisfaction with the Association's basic attitudes as reflected mainly by Colonel Ruppert and his Eastern supporters. According to Cochran's history of the Pabst Brewing Company:

Harris Perlstein [whose Premier Malt Products Co. merged with Pabst in 1932] shared the conviction of some of the more forward-thinking brewers that not enough was being done to protect the industry from a renewal of dry activity, and that a positive program must be undertaken. Failing to secure action in that respect and indignant over the failure of the U.S.B.A. representatives on the code authority to protect the right of Pabst to a hearing before certifying an alleged code violation to the Department of Justice, Pabst withdrew from the association in 1934. Anheuser-Busch subsequently followed suit and as a result, by 1936, two of the three largest brewers were outside the association.[22]

It was at the October 1936 convention of the Association that William Piel announced what he called "a momentous message of good news to every brewer in America": the formation of a separate organization, the United Brewers' Industrial Foundation, Inc., with the following aims:

1. Public education on the economic importance of the brewing industry to the welfare of the country;
2. Public education to stimulate the wide use of beer by the American people;
3. Ultimate realization of separate governmental control for beer; and
4. Education of licensees to promote a merited pride in a socially and economically sound operation of their business.[23]

In other words, the Association was creating the sort of public relations apparatus that the Western dissidents had apparently been favoring at the time of their resignations. They, earlier in 1936, had organized some of the independent brewers into a new trade association, called Brewing Industry, Inc., with headquarters in Chicago. August A. Busch, Jr., was president and Harris Perlstein treasurer.[24]

There was also a third brewers' organization, the American Brewers' Association, originally founded in 1930 by a group of near beer producers, which was headed in 1935 by William L. Goetz, the St. Joseph, Missouri, brewer, with John C. Bruckmann as director, M. J. Sommers as secretary and George P. McCabe as counsel.[25] At this period, it remained independent from the other two associations, but without public expressions of rancor.

Alvin Griesedieck, who became an active member of Brewing Industry, Inc., agreed with a number of his fellow brewers that the launching of the United Brewers' Industrial Foundation, Inc., in April 1937 was "ill-advised and not in the best interest of industry public relations." [26] (One might note incidentally that relations between Griesedieck's group and the United States Brewers' Association were far from cozy at that point; at the time of the schism Colonel Ruppert and the founders of Brewing Industry, Inc. had made public an exchange of somewhat angry letters.[27]) The leaders of Brewing Industry, Inc., decided to work out the industry's public relations problem through other methods, and employed Bernard Lichtenberg, head of the Institute of Public Relations, to help in this project.[28] Lichtenberg and an associate, T. Howard Kelly, came up with a plan which Griesedieck described as "almost diametrically opposite to that launched by the United Brewers Foundation [sic]." [29]

The plan was presented by Lichtenberg in August 1938 to a joint meeting of Brewing Industry, Inc., United States Brewers' Association, American Brewers' Association and United Brewers' Industrial Foundation, Inc., representatives: its main principle was to "substitute ACTION in place of PROPAGANDA, that it must swiftly translate its promises into performance." [30] Beforehand, during that summer, the plan had been tested in Nebraska, where action against offending taverns and the organization of responsible state and district committees had succeeded in thwarting a proposed drive by the dry forces.

Lichtenberg's contribution came to be known as the Nebraska Plan and rapidly developed into the self-regulatory apparatus which became an integral part of the brewers' trade association.* Reporting on this subject in 1940, Carl W. Badenhausen, president of the post-Prohibition P. Ballantine & Sons brewery and at that time chairman of the United Brewers' Industrial Foundation, wrote that

---

* It should be noted that the Nebraska Plan was not absolutely new in conception, though perhaps unusually elaborate and well organized in its operation. As early as 1882 the United States Brewers' Association had established a Vigilance Committee which took over, generally speaking, what would nowadays be called the Association's public relations responsibility. The state associations, doubtless following this lead, began Vigilance Bureaus on the state level; the one begun in Ohio in October 1907, for example, investigated saloons, reported "obnoxious" ones, and took legal steps to have them closed.

state committees have conducted 18,002 investigations which have resulted not only in 2,158 warnings to retailers to correct certain conditions, but also in 23 probations, 38 license suspensions, 71 injunctions, 125 prosecutions of bootleggers, and 459 license revocations by enforcement authorities.[31]

Adoption of the Nebraska Plan on an industry scale helped in healing the rift between the United States Brewers' Association and Brewing Industry, Inc. In the fall of 1938, the two organizations, in the words of *Business Week,* "buried the hatchet, [Brewing Industry, Inc.] joined U. S. Brewers in the management of United Brewers Industrial Foundation." [32] The death of Jacob Ruppert on 13 January 1939, after the tributes and expressions of regret, eventually led to an easier rapprochement between the two organizations. In January 1941, all the brewers' trade associations joined under the title of United States Brewers' Association, although the public relations corporation (which changed its title in 1942 to Brewing Industry Foundation) remained separate until 1944.

By 1940, sales of beer had reached approximately the level of the pre-Prohibition years, although the number of brewers was not even half of what it had been in 1910. This meant, clearly, that individual breweries were producing and selling much greater quantities of beer. In 1940, there were six breweries each selling over 1,000,000 barrels annually: they were Anheuser-Busch, Schlitz, Pabst, Ballantine, Schaefer and Ruppert.[33] Fifty-two brewers were considered the industry's leaders, and the lowest sales figure among these was about 225,000 barrels.

Though it was gratifying to have returned to a high level of sales, these figures represented a reduction in per capita consumption, since the population of the country had increased at the same time. The reason most frequently given by the brewers for not being able to push sales higher at that time was the tax burden, which not only cut down profits but also made the price to the consumer higher. In July 1940, the federal barrel tax was raised from $5 to $6. This was called the "Defense Tax," not altogether surprising in view of the war being waged in Europe; its effect on certain small brewers was decidedly unfavorable, since they could not absorb the tax as the large producers could and therefore had a hard time competing with the national or regional brands.[34]

The industry was naturally in an anxious state because of the threat of war. At the start of 1941, R. J. Schaefer, president of the United States Brewers' Association, stated, "We must, perhaps, first of all recognize that we are definitely in a military economy and shall continue to be for many years irrespective of the fortunes and the progress of the war." [35] The brewers not only had nightmare memories of the previous war, but knew that the drys, hot for a reversal of events, were ready to use a wartime emergency to try once again to inflict prohibition on the nation under the disguise of patriotism. Bills were already being proposed to prohibit or to curtail the sales of alcoholic beverages in Army and Navy installations or to military personnel.[36] The specter of Mr. Prohibition was revived by a number of newspaper cartoonists.

Fortunately, the industry was united at the outbreak of war, the various associations having combined in January 1941. The brewers faced many of the problems suffered by all industry in wartime, but also several that were characteristic only of the brewing industry itself. There was, of course, a manpower problem; the problem of dwindling supplies; means of actively supporting the war effort; regulation of licensees, particularly near military and naval installations; countering the virulent dry propaganda — and along with all this, trying to make and extend profits out of the industry.

Even before Pearl Harbor, as president of the association, R. J. Schaefer set up a Defense Liaison Committee, with Alvin Griesedieck at its head.[37] Early in 1942, Edward V. Lahey, treasurer of the Association, took over the chairmanship of the Defense Liaison Committee and pledged the industry's complete cooperation with the government.[38]

Since conscription had begun in 1940, the question of whether beer would be allowed in military and naval establishments demanded attention before the United States was actually in the war. The drys naturally mounted a strong campaign, based on all their familiar clichés, to force prohibition on the serviceman, but the evil results of Prohibition in practice were still too well remembered and a number of bills presented to Congress during 1941 with the purpose of prohibiting sales of beer to servicemen were killed in committee or defeated. The association secretary, C. D. Williams, clarified a degree of confusion about the legality of beer in military installations by reviewing the appropriate statutes and concluding "3.2% beer is legal at Army Posts, and is so recognized by the military services of the United States." [39]

The characteristic attitude of the military leaders was expressed in 1941 by General George C. Marshall, Chief of Staff:

> It would be harmful to the men in the service to direct a prohibition against them that did not apply to other citizens. To do so would inevitably lead to intemperance.[40]

An editorial in the New York *Times* on 3 June 1941 commended the government's anti-Prohibition stand:

> Common sense supports the opposition by Secretaries Stimson and Knox to Congressional imposition of dry areas around Army and Navy camps. House and Senate bills which they condemn would make it possible to re-establish Federal prohibition in and around fifteen of our largest cities, with more than a third of the country's population.

What emerged quite early in the course of the war was the fact that beer constituted an important morale factor for the serviceman; and after the experiences of the recent past this was rather like a return to the official ration of beer which was ordered for the soldier in the Revolutionary War.* In order to make sure that the drys' arguments might have minimum validity, the self-regulation program of the Brewing Industry Foundation was strengthened and extended. This was one of the major themes at a Foundation meeting which took place in Chicago in January 1943. Chairman Alvin Griesedieck stated in his opening address:

> While our State Directors and their staffs have by no means been entirely successful in their attempts to clean up or close up all of the objectionable outlets . . . much progress has been made. The principle on which our self-regulation program is founded is basically correct.[41]

One of the important speakers at that meeting, Colonel Joseph V. Dillon, commanding the Provost Marshal General's Training Center, spoke of the favorable conclusions of a report on army camp drinking by the

*See page 101.

Office of War Information. "This is a high tribute," he said, "to the foresight of the Brewing Industry Foundation, which contributed more to limiting the indulgence by soldiers than any other single factor or agency in this entire matter." [42] One statement in the OWI report had been: "The sale of 3.2 beer in the post exchanges in training camps is a positive factor in Army sobriety." [43] Indeed, certain War Food orders issued from 1943 on required brewers to set aside a specified proportion of their production of 3.2% beer for military use. Order 66 of 28 July 1943 specified 15 per cent; on 1 December 1945 that was amended to 7½ per cent; on 1 January 1946 to 4 per cent; on 1 September 1946 to 3; and finally in March 1947 the requirement of beer for military use was entirely rescinded.

The importance of beer for wartime morale was again firmly underlined in January 1945 when the War Labor Board, in ruling that a strike by the Teamsters' Union against certain Minneapolis breweries had to stop, gave as its reason that brewing was an essential industry.[44] It fitted this category for two reasons: one being its morale value, and the other, the amount of revenue collected from the industry in taxes. In 1944, the barrel tax was up to $8;* withdrawals in that calendar year came to almost 80,000,000 barrels; taxes paid during the fiscal year ending 30 June 1944 totaled over $567,000,000.[45] This was a sum that a wartime government could hardly forego; in addition, brewers were paying a variety of state and local taxes which were enormously beneficial to an extended economy.

Increasingly the American brewers had to deal with the questions of transportation, labor supply and raw materials at a time of total industrial mobilization. The earliest shortage was that of crowns: first it was the cork that was hard to supply, later it was the tin plate itself. In mid-1942, fears were expressed that the War Production Board might prohibit the sale of bottled beer in outlets that had draught beer equipment.[46]

Because of tin scarcity the beer can (except for military orders) was an immediate casualty. Up to spring 1942, bottled beer was in good supply, but then tin plate for crowns was prohibited. Suppliers used

---

* On 1 November 1951, during the Korean War, the tax was raised to $9.

blackplate after that, but could only produce 60 to 70% of their former tonnage.[47] Ultimately, supplies were eked out by collecting used crowns and making them up again for reuse. Another solution was the increased production of quart and half-gallon bottles, offering more beer for fewer crowns.[48]

As for manpower, certain key inside brewery workers were deferrable, at the discretion of local draft boards. But the industry suffered from worker shortages in other categories, and began in 1943 to take on women,[49] particularly in bottle shops.* Supplies of malt and hops were rationed on 28 February 1943 under War Food Order 66 and quotas were revised thereafter by various amendments. Many brewers were forced to make temporary alterations in their formulas because certain ingredients were often lacking.

Though production continued at top speed, occasional crises did occur, of course; conflicting government orders as to supplies were issued and then canceled. Shortages were unavoidable, and stocks could not be maintained at satisfactory levels. On 1 August 1943, the New York *Times* took note of a typical crisis in beer supplies:

> In March [1943] the WPB said that malt was needed to make alcohol for munition; that brewers must cut their use of it 7 per cent under the 1942 figures. To make up the deficiency brewers turned to corn and rice. Now breweries are feeling the pinch of the nation-wide corn shortage. . . . On top of corn and transportation shortages there was a lack of bottles and barrels.

In spite of these multifarious problems, the production and sales of beer showed a spectacular rise, from about 53,000,000 barrels in 1940 to almost 80,000,000 five years later at the end of the war. That last figure went well over the former record year, 1914, when slightly more than 66,000,000 barrels were sold.[50]

The theme of the 1946 convention of the United States Brewers Foundation (the new name assumed with the merger of the United States Brewers' Association and the Brewing Industry Foundation in 1944) was that the industry started 1946 in "a greatly improved financial position." [51] On the public relations level, the situation was much

* Before World War I, women had sometimes worked as bottle-washers, but not between the wars.

better than it had often been in the past. The general business outlook was favorable, especially for such industries as brewing which had not needed to alter equipment for war purposes. In terms of the United States Brewers Foundation, the industry was operating from a united front, having made a good many new friends — and new customers.

THIRTY-SIX

New Directions

IT IS TRUE that a few new breweries have been built from the ground up since the end of World War II, but the typical modern brewery is a conglomeration of good solid buildings erected at various times in the past, some as long ago as the 1880s but most of them in the first fifteen years of the twentieth century. Perhaps more than in any other industry, it has been possible for brewery plants to be remodeled from time to time to fit most modern requirements and standards, rather than being demolished. This is only one of many aspects in which the brewing industry combines the new with the old, the traditional with the experimental.

The process of brewing itself, except for the standards of uniformity made possible by yeast culture and pasteurization, has changed very little; the great changes have concerned what happens to the beer *after* it has been manufactured. Once the construction of the modern brewhouse and bottling plant was set at the beginning of the twentieth century, progress, though extensive, has concerned mechanical details, always aimed at reducing costs simultaneously with the increase of production. This is a continuous process, to which engineering ingenuity is contributing all the time. But the larger changes and the greater progress in the industry since the end of World War II have been in the fields of promotion, advertising, organization and distribution.

The rise in sales after all wartime and postwar restrictions were lifted in 1948 was slightly disappointing to the industry, even though the figure, every year, has been well over 80,000,000 barrels. The amount of tax-paid withdrawals in fiscal year 1960, as it happened, set an all-time record of 88,928,882 barrels.[1] The industry as a whole, however, in spite of the fact that there have been fewer individual breweries operating than at any other time, except Prohibition, since the Civil War (and probably even before then), has geared itself to produce a good deal more than it was selling in the 1950s. Hence the concentration of effort toward sales and distribution improvement, as well as market expansion.

The difference between the small and large brewer has become more pronounced. This was the basis of a fairly typical comment at a United States Brewers Foundation meeting in 1946:

> All individuals do not achieve the same stature, mental or physical. That is equally true in business. It is not necessary nor possible for each brewer to be the largest in order to achieve success, but every brewer can be a successful brewer if he will. It rests with the individual. Size is not the only hallmark of success.[2]

Though breweries in the middle range of production and sales have suffered a good deal from strong competition, a few of the local breweries with a capacity under 100,000 barrels still appear to command a sure and faithful market for their product. Such breweries function best in predominantly beer-drinking areas such as Wisconsin and Illinois, but there are a few even in other parts of the country. Probably the smallest of all commercial breweries in the United States is the Ernest Fleckenstein Brewing Co. of Faribault, Minnesota, with a capacity of around 20,000 barrels a year.

But the dominant trend, from Repeal on, has been to increase production capacity and expand markets. A plant like the Theo. Hamm Brewing Co. of St. Paul, having reached a capacity of about 600,000 barrels a year when Prohibition came, started a million-dollar expansion program directly after Repeal which increased its capacity to a million barrels.[3] In 1937, the Stegmaier Brewing Co. of Wilkes-Barre was spending $250,000 to double its bottling capacity; G. Krueger Brewing Co. in Newark planned in 1936 to increase its brewing and storage capacity by 50% at a cost of half a million dollars; Anheuser-Busch, in September 1936, started new construction to increase its capacity by 50,000 barrels.[4] Indeed, virtually any brewery that had seriously resumed operations at Repeal was forced to devote the following seven or eight years to raising its production potential.

But these expansions seem extremely small when compared with those that took place after World War II. According to official statistics for the year 1939, the amount of money spent by breweries on plant and equipment was roughly $20,000,000. This is to be compared with the same category of expenditure in 1947, when the total had risen about fivefold to approximately $110,000,000.[5] The only other industries listed as spending comparable amounts for the same purpose in that year are sawmills and planing mills, paper and board mills, and certain key industries coming under the categories of chemicals, petroleum products, metals and transportation equipment.[6] The postwar expansion of brewery plants was, in other words, extraordinary. The figure of a million barrels capacity had once seemed phenomenal; but by 1938 sales over two million barrels were registered by Anheuser-Busch, and four years after that both Pabst and Schlitz saw their sales climb above two million while Anheuser-Busch was pushing up to three and a half million.[7] It was hard to see why such increases should ever stop.

At an earlier stage, it had been possible simply to enlarge a brewery, to install additional bottle lines, to buy more trucks and add space to already existing buildings. But now there were certain plants which could not be expanded by these means; if they wanted to increase their capacities, they had to think in terms of branching out into additional factories, either in the same city or farther away — depending on what became available for lease or purchase, and what advantages could be derived from such deals. When Falstaff leased the Krug Brewing Company in Omaha in 1935, the Griesediecks were not intending to start a trend that would affect the industry as a whole. Alvin Griesedieck wrote of that event:

> I realized that if we could take over the Krug Brewery on a lease basis we could substantially increase our business in the Omaha Territory, and at the same time the Krug stockholders would receive an equitable return on their investment which otherwise would be a total loss.[8]

The Omaha operation went so well for Falstaff that in 1937 the company, going farther afield, bought the National Brewery in New Orleans for $543,700.[9] What was novel, in both these cases, was that the Griesediecks immediately began to brew their St. Louis Falstaff beer in the newly acquired plants. They were one of the earliest companies, in other words, to create a *chain* of breweries. This happened quite naturally in the history of Falstaff; it suited the market it had developed since its post-Repeal incorporation and was economically more advisable than buying land in St. Louis and adding to the existing capacity there.

In a similar way, the Pabst company, through its merger with the Premier Malt Products Co. in 1932, acquired a plant in Peoria Heights, Ill., which in 1934 was licensed to function as a brewery. In December 1945, however, Pabst extended its brewing operations into the important New York area, buying the Hoffman Beverage Co. in Newark, and adapting a part of its plant to the production of Pabst's own Blue Ribbon beer.[10]

These moves were not like the consolidations and mergers that took place before the First World War.* In those days it had not been considered feasible to manufacture the same brand in various parts of the country. For one thing, the label was associated with a particular location; and besides, the chemical processing of water to be used for brewing had not reached a sufficiently sophisticated stage to ensure identity of product. But in the years following the Second World War, when the operation of subsidiary plants in various parts of the country became common practice among the national brewers, the beer manufactured in California, the Midwest and New York, under one label, was sold as being identical in every respect. This was such an important consideration that Alvin Griesedieck, in his book about Falstaff, related candidly the difficulty encountered, at the beginning, in making the beer brewed at Omaha and New Orleans taste the same as that made in St. Louis.[11]

Schlitz, the third of the top three breweries right after the war, started its first subsidiary operation by buying the former George Ehret

----

* See Chapter Thirty.

brewery in Brooklyn in 1949.[12] Soon after this, there was an avalanche of purchases of breweries to be set up as subsidiaries.

Anheuser-Busch, in 1951, started yet another trend in the same direction by building a new plant in Newark from the bottom up. Then, in 1954, a second new home was built for Budweiser: a $20,000,000 brewery in Los Angeles.[13] The leaping growth of population on the West Coast, beginning during the war and continuing afterward, made it an important new market for expansion, and the economics of transportation forced the national brewers to establish locations there.

In 1953, the Theo. Hamm Brewing Co., having decided to enlarge its market, bought the plant of the Rainier Brewing Co. in San Francisco, thus adding the beer drinkers of four new states to its potential customers. Hamm's sales showed an appreciable rise at the same time: it went from eleventh place among the top sellers in 1953 to eighth in 1954, seventh in 1955 and then fifth in 1956.[14]

Schlitz also followed the move westward by building a new plant in Van Nuys, California, in 1954 (with a capacity of a million barrels); and Pabst, in the same year, completely overhauled the Los Angeles Brewing Co. (which had been an autonomous subsidiary since 1948) for the production of Blue Ribbon.[15] Falstaff, in 1953, made its bid for the West Coast market by buying the Pacific Brewing & Malting Co. in San Jose and retaining the president, William Knapp, as plant general manager.[16]

These westward expansions were justified by a population increase in California between 1950 and 1960 of 48.5%, according to the census figures; correspondingly, tax-paid withdrawals of beer went up about 56%. But a more startling change in the same category took place in Florida, where population took a 78.7% step up in the same period, and beer sales registered a climb even greater than that in California. It comes as no surprise, then, to discover that Anheuser-Busch, the National Brewing Co. of Baltimore, the Metropolis Brewing Co., International Breweries, Inc., and the Jos. Schlitz Brewing Co. have all either built new breweries or remodeled old ones in order to be right on hand as this market continues to develop.

One of the leaders in the multiple plant idea has been the Carling Brewing Co., a comparative newcomer among American breweries, having started operations in this country in 1933. On 12 September of that

year, the Peerless Motor Car Corporation announced to its stockholders
that arrangements had been made with the Brewing Corporation of
Canada, Ltd., to convert the Cleveland plant of the corporation (where
automobile manufacture had stopped in 1931) into a brewery.[17] Thus
the Carling business began, under the name of Brewing Corporation
of America. The Canadian Carling's, in London, Ontario, going back
as far as 1840, had become a subsidiary of Canadian Breweries, Ltd.,
one of several corporations headed by E. P. Taylor; and it was the Carling label which began to be marketed in Cleveland. The Brewing Corporation of America, operating entirely in that city, made a couple of
false starts in the beginning: one of these was an attempt to brew only
ale, and another was the decision to package the product exclusively in
nonreturnable bottles. From 1948 on, however, when Ian R. Dowie was
appointed vice president in charge of sales, the company started an
unusually swift advance toward a position among the industry's leaders.
The disappointing sales figure of just over 360,000 barrels in 1949 was
pushed up, in ten years, to nearly four and a half million — probably as
swift an ascent into the empyrean of the industry leaders as any brewing
combine has ever achieved.

There is no doubt that Carling has been helped to make its dramatic
bid for industry leadership by its wholehearted acceptance of the chain-
brewery conception. Starting in 1954, when the corporation name was
finally changed to the Carling Brewing Company, the management
has bought or built six additional Carling plants to saturate all regions
of the country with Red Cap Ale and Black Label Beer. The Griesedieck Western Brewing Co. at Belleville, Ill., was bought in 1954; the
next year a Frankenmuth, Mich., plant was bought from International
Breweries, Inc.; in 1956 a plant was built from the ground up in Natick,
Mass.; in 1958 a new plant was built in Atlanta, Ga., the same year the
Heidelberg Brewing Co. in Tacoma was taken over; and in 1961, a new
plant was opened in Baltimore.[18]

Though the idea has generally been to establish the two Carling
labels on a nation-wide basis, the company has seen fit to continue the
"Alt Heidelberg" label in Tacoma and the "Stag" label of Griesedieck
Western, because of their regional popularity; but eventually these may
well be dropped, too. Carling's, a spruce, aggressive and smoothly run-

ning organization, is one in which tradition counts for less than in those with a long historical background: one of its beliefs, as quoted by *Fortune* in 1959, is that the "200 or so firms now operating [in the United States] will be winnowed down to ten or twelve, with Carling's, of course, as top dog." [19] Presumably there are a number of "traditional" brewers in the country who have every intention of challenging this point of view.

In spite of the fact that size and capacity have become such vital considerations in modern brewing, statistics show that, as of 1959, the largest company in the brewing industry accounted for only 8% of the total business, and the fifteen leading companies combined were doing something like 55% of the business. According to an article written by Ian R. Dowie when he was still president of the Carling Brewing Co., "It is not uncommon in other brand name consumer goods industries to find one brand achieving something like that percentage [55%] of the total volume, and to find three or four together doing 80 per cent is commonplace." [20] In other words, the winnowing down to "ten or twelve" companies is certainly not going to happen right away — if ever.

Nevertheless, the phenomenon of brewery mortality (called euphemistically a "shakedown" by industrial analysts) has been constantly evident ever since Repeal. Each year has seen the closing or absorption of a number of breweries: even between so short a period as 1949 and 1958 more than 185 brewers were forced either to close down or sell out.[21] Out of the fifty-two top breweries listed in 1942, seventeen have been bought by others, four have simply failed or stopped functioning. As of 1961, there were approximately 230 in operation; and of those only some 140 were independently run. The trend toward larger and larger groupings of brewing companies is an undeniable fact, though it might best be seen as a tendency within industry in general. During the 'fifties, such combines have emerged in the railroad industry, in banking, in airlines, in the hotel business, in publishing — to mention only a few. While this is still going on, one cannot draw any firm conclusions about its significance for the future. Contemporary problems of financing, of public relations and promotion, in addition to an increasing uniformity of taste and activity which is brought about by better and closer communications, may be doing away with all that is local and independent. The sociologists will have to decide in the end whether this is a good or bad thing.

In the brewing industry, many of the plants that have gone entirely or been absorbed into one of the chains were poorly organized and lacking in a kind of dynamism which brewers had to a great degree before the first World War. The grandsons of founders were not always as interested in brewing as their ancestors — but it is amazing how many *have* been: August A. Busch, Jr., Rudolph J. Schaefer, Philip Liebmann, the Haffenreffers, the Olympia Schmidts, etc. These, the so-called "traditional" brewers, have not only held their own but kept up with contemporary developments and registered large increases in sales.

On the other hand, men from other professions and industries have in recent years become involved in brewing, a fact which has doubtless had its effect on the industry's attitudes. Richard G. Jones of the Jackson Brewing Co., for example, came into brewing from a banking background; Norman R. Klug of the Miller Brewing Co. was a lawyer. Datus E. Proper was an engineer in the petroleum industry before he joined the Pearl Brewing Co.; Harry Jersig, now with Lone Star Brewing Co., was a candy salesman; J. F. Lanser, chairman of the board of the Arizona Brewing Co., Inc., was an agronomist.*

The chain-brewery idea developed during the late 1950s at an accelerated pace. By 1961, the Lucky Lager Brewing Co. had four plants on the West Coast; the Pfeiffer Brewing Co. had three plants in Michigan and Minnesota producing mostly the one label; the National Brewing Co. of Baltimore, under Jerold C. Hoffberger, had plants in Orlando and Miami, Florida, and an affiliate in Detroit; International Breweries, Inc., operated six plants, Drewrys Limited, U.S.A., Inc., four, and Bohemian-Atlantic was a combine of four breweries.

The famous Blatz company has been absorbed by Pabst and the label

* A typical example of the sort of man who came into brewing from the outside is Richard T. Riney, now president of Sterling Brewers, Inc., in Evansville, who began in 1917 as assistant bookkeeper and order clerk, gradually worked his way into the sales department, then in 1925 started a series of posts in management which led, in 1934, to his election as president and general manager. Mr. Riney was also one of the founders of the Indiana Brewers Association and has served with the national organization in a variety of capacities for something like twenty years.

continued. The Krueger brand of Newark has been taken over by the Narragansett Brewing Co. of Cranston, R.I. The Miller Brewing Co. bought its neighbor in Milwaukee, the A. Gettelman Brewing Co. The C. Schmidt & Sons company in Philadelphia bought Adam Scheidt's Valley Forge Brewing Co. in Norristown, Pa. The Lone Star Brewing Co. of San Antonio owns and operates what was the Progress Brewery in Oklahoma City, and the Pearl Brewing Co. of San Antonio has taken over the famous St. Joseph, Missouri, plant of M. K. Goetz Brewing Co. The Metropolis Brewery Co., headed by Abraham Hertzberg, has three subsidiaries in addition to its main plant in Trenton, N.J.: the Spearman Brewing Co. in Pensacola, Fla., Hornell Brewing Co., Inc., of Hornell, N.Y., and the Century Brewing Corporation in Norfolk, Va. And in 1961, the F. & M. Schaefer Brewing Co., one of the most prominent of the "traditional" breweries, heretofore commanding a regional market that accounted in 1960 for sales of more than 3,000,000 barrels, made a move toward the national market by buying the Standard Brewing Co. in Cleveland, Ohio.[22]

While those who have put all their chips on the chain-brewery method naturally consider it the answer to the future, the possibility of existing successfully as a single-plant operation is admirably illustrated by P. Ballantine & Sons. Brewing only in the extensive plant at Newark and — what is more — bucking the traffic by producing a remarkably popular ale as well as beer, president Carl W. Badenhausen and his brother Otto have elevated the old-established business, which they bought and revived after Repeal, from annual sales of around half a million barrels to a figure well over four million. Since 1937, Ballantine has been consistently among the top ten brewers in the country, and since 1960 it has been the only single-plant brewery in that exalted group.

Buying new plants, opening new markets, absorbing other labels — these moves are not enough in themselves. They have to be supported by an enormous barrage of advertising on radio and television, in magazines, on billboards: the brewing industry's expenditure on advertising is estimated at about $95,000,000 a year. In 1938 it was only $6,000,000. Besides this straightforward attempt to keep the brand name in the public mind, the brewers find it worthwhile to spend time and money on campaigns of a public-relations nature — in particular, their support of sports events. The traditional link between beer and baseball may have been started by Colonel Jacob Ruppert, owner of the New York Yankees for so many years. Presumably Ruppert bought the club because of his love for baseball and especially the Yankees, rather than for any benefit he thought his brewery might derive from the association, but in any case his action created a highly favorable attitude toward beer and the industry — one which brewers since then have been wise to enhance.

Since the unquestionable emergence of packaged beer as the major portion of the market, packaging in itself has become an expensive and time-consuming problem for brewers. In the days of draught beer, the customer never saw or examined the barrel, and so there was no need to make it distinctive or dress it up. But the bottle and the can were quite different: they were handled by the customer and had to attract by their covers, so to speak, and so all the resources of labeling, coloring and design had to be called into play. In common with other industries that market their product, breweries have had to revamp and modernize the appearance of their packaged goods from time to time, and here too they have tried to combine the traditional with the new — to retain trademarks long associated with their names, but to incorporate these into patterns with an up-to-date look. In the case of brewers, it has gone even farther; the customer is tempted by large bottles and small bottles, king-sized cans and lilliputian seven-ouncers, six-packs, eight-packs, even three-packs. These devices, while they doubtless increase home-consumption sales and suit the public convenience, also lay an extra load on manufacturing expenses and cut pennies out of per-package profits.

Advertising has become a ruling consideration not only for each individual brewer but for the industry as a whole. In 1949, the Brewers Foundation set up an advertising committee to handle two major problems, defined at the 1950 convention by Carl W. Badenhausen as "1 — the ever-present threat of prohibition, and 2 — the need for getting a wider social acceptance of beer and ale." [23] These problems have apparently been met satisfactorily. Two campaigns in particular, based on the mottoes "Beer Belongs" and "America's Beverage of Moderation," helped in the late 'fifties to enlarge the acceptance of beer as an appropriate beverage in all situations. These campaigns illustrated the fact that the uses of beer were following the changes in social customs.

The struggle against the drys, though it has so far been successful for the brewing interests, is incessant. No victory is a sure and permanent one, because the drys keep up a tireless attack at all levels, in all areas. Their most persistent target has been advertising: bills with the purpose of outlawing the advertising of alcoholic beverages for interstate com-merce on radio and television, or in newspapers and periodicals, have been proposed in Congress time and time again.* The number of people living in dry areas was given as almost 8,000,000 in 1939 and about 14,500,000 in 1959 — an advance, to be sure, but one which took place mostly between 1939 and 1949. In the following ten years, the percentage of people in dry areas as compared with the rest of the country actually dropped from 10.4% to 9.6%, and the total has changed very little during that decade. It is well, besides, to recall that the cor-responding figure in 1910 was almost 44,000,000! [24]

In 1961, the association of brewers completed a kind of century-circle by voting to revert to its original name, United States Brewers Associa-tion. Since 1947, its pilot has been Edward V. Lahey, as president of the association and chairman of its board. In these offices, he has served longer than any other individual — a fact which has facilitated a con-sistency of approach to the industry's problems.

Ever since that first association in 1862, the brewers have been able to produce devoted men to serve their common interests: Fred Lauer, Henry Clausen, Jr., Henry H. Rueter and the many others who managed the affairs of the Association and sought to make the voice of the industry heard. The important figures were not only the presidents — but those men who served in less exalted offices, as secretary, treas-urer, committee member. Certainly Hugh F. Fox, carrying on through

---

* Examples of such bills are S.265, introduced by Senator Capper of Kansas in the 80th Congress, First Session, 1947; the Johnson-Reed bill, S.2365, 80th Con-gress, Second Session, 1948; S.1847, introduced by Senator Langer of North Dakota in the 81st Congress, First Session, 1949; S.2444, introduced by Senator Case of South Dakota and Senator Johnson of Colorado, 82nd Congress, Second Session, 1952; H.R.1227, introduced by Rep. Bryson of South Carolina in the 83rd Con-gress, First Session, 1953; S.3294, Senator Langer again, 83rd Congress, Second Session, 1954; S.923, Langer, and H.R.4627, Rep. Siler of Kentucky, 84th Con-gress, First Session, 1956.

Prohibition like the caretaker of an abandoned house, deserved special expressions of gratitude from the brewers.

In his summing up of the industry's progress and prospects, Mr. Lahey, at the 1960 convention, spoke of optimistic forecasts and remarked that "the brewing industry will share *fairly* in the prosperity predicted for the national economy." [25] The brewers appear willing to take this for the keynote of their current activities: they share in the good years and in the not-so-good years. The uncertain factors are the profit margin, the labor contract and the propaganda of the drys. The certain factor is the product; with modern laboratories in most breweries, with modern machinery and methods, the end result of the brewing process can always be depended on.

But for many years, brewing as an industry in the United States has been more than the making of beer. What has happened since Repeal and what will no doubt go on happening is that the selling techniques of other large successful industries are applied to brewing. If any changes occur in the product it will be because they contribute either to swelling the sales total or slimming down the cost of manufacture without compromising the product.

Curiously, one of the means by which beer sales have been pushed to record levels in recent times has been the successful campaign to bring beer back to its original social position: a universal beverage. It is no longer the workingman's drink, it is no longer a German drink, it is no longer exclusively a man's drink . . . most of these temporary labels have been removed by one method or another, and the acceptance of beer is closer than ever to where it was at the beginning. The kettle in the kitchen has given way to the tremendous factory covering several city blocks, but the drink in the glass fills the same purpose it always has.

Appendix One

JOHN WINTHROP, JR., ON THE
MALTING OF MAIZE, 1622*

The English have found out a way to make very good Beere of this Graine which they doe either out of Bread made of it, or by Maulting of it, that way of makeing Beere, of Bread, is onely by makeing the Bread in the manner as before described, and then breake it or Cutt it into greate Lumps, as bigg as a mans Fist or bigger (for it must not be broken small) then they Mash it and proceed every way about brewing of it, as is used in Brewing Beere of Mault, adding hopps to it as to make Beere.

In makeing Mault of it to make it good there is a singular way must be used. The Maulters that make Mault of Barly have used all their skill to make Mault also of this Corne, but cannot bring it the ordinary way to such a perfecion that the whole Graine is Maulted, and tender, and Flowry, as other Mault; Nor will the Beere made of it be well Coloured, but witish, the reason that it doth not come to the perfecion of good Mault in that way of Maulting as of other Graine, is this. It is found by experience, that this Corne before it be fully changed into the nature of Mault, must sprout out both wayes a great length the length of a Finger at least, but if more its better, so as it must put out the Roote as well as the upper sprout, and that it may so do, it is necessary that it be laide upon an heape a convenient time till it doth so sprout, but if it lieth of a sufficient thickness for this purpose, it will quickly heate and moulde, if it be stirred and opened to prevent the too much heating of it, those Sprouts that are begun to shoote out (if spread thin) cease growing, and consequently the Corne ceaseth to be promoted to that mellowness of Mault. If left thick till they grow any length they are so intangled one in the other and so very tender that

* *New England Quarterly*, vol. 10.

the least stirring and opening of the heape breaketh those axells of, and every Graine that hath the sprout, so broken ceaseth to grow to any further degree towards the nature of Mault, and soone groweth mouldy if not often stirred and spread thinn. To avoid all these difficulties, and to bring every sound Graine to the full perfection of good Mault, this way was tried, and found a sure and perfect way to it. In a Field or Garden or any where that there is loose Earth, take away the top of that Earth two or three Inches for so great a space as may be proportionable to the Quantity of Corne intended to be made into Mault, the Earth may be throwne up halfe one way, and halfe the other, for the more facility of that, and the following labour. Then upon the even Bed, or Floore of Earth where the upper part is so taken off, there lay the Corne intended to be maulted all over, that it may fully cover the Ground, then cover it over with the same Earth, that was taken thence, and then you have no more to doe, till you see all that plott of Ground like a greene Field covered over with the sprouts of the Corne, which within tenn dayes, or a Fortnight, more or less according to the time of yeare wilbe growne greene upwards, and Rooted downwards, and then there is no more to be done but to take it up and shake the Earth from it and drie it. It will by the Insnarlements of the Rootes one with another be like a Matt and hang so together that it may be raised in greate peices and the Earth shaken off from it (which is best to be done in a dry time) and then to make it very cleane, it may be washed and presently dried upon a Hill or in the Sun, or in that Countrey it selfe, spread thinn on a Chamber floore. This way every Graine that was sound, and good will grow and consequently become Mault, and no part of the Graine remains steely (as is alwayes in the other wayes of maulting it) but be mellow, and Flowry and very sweete, and the Beere that is made of this Mault wilbe of a very good browne Colour, and be a pleasant, and wholesome drinke. But because the other way of makeing Beere out of the Bread, as before sett downe, is found to be as well Coloured, and pleasant, and every way as good and very wholesome without any windy Quality, and keepeth better from Sowring then any other Beere of that Corne, therefore that way of Brewing is most in use in that Countrey, that way of Maulting being also yet little knowne.

Appendix Two

AN ACT TO ENCOURAGE THE MANUFACTURE AND CONSUMPTION OF STRONG BEER, ALE AND OTHER MALT LIQUORS *

Whereas the manufacture of strong beer, ale and other malt liquors, will promote the purposes of husbandry and commerce, by encouraging the growth of such materials as are peculiarly congenial to our soil and climate, and by procuring a valuable article of exportation: And whereas the wholesome qualities of malt liquors greatly recommend them to general use, as an important means of preserving the health of the citizens of this Commonwealth, and of preventing the pernicious effects of spirituous liquors:

1. *Be it therefore enacted by the Senate and House of Representatives in General Court assembled, and by the authority of the same,* That all brewhouses, wherein shall be made and produced for sale annually, a quantity of strong beer or ale, not less than one hundred barrels of thirty-one and an half gallons each, beer measure, with the utensils employed in such brewhouses and the immediate dependencies thereof; also all monies and stock of every kind employed and improved in such brewhouses, with the strong beer, ale and other malt liquors which shall be there made and produced for sale as aforesaid, with the faculty or annual profit of such manufacture, shall be, and they hereby are exempted from all taxes and duties of every kind, for the term of five years next after the passing of this act.

2. *And be it further enacted,* That all brewers or others, who shall be owners or occupiers of such brewhouses, shall, as soon as may be after the passing

* *The Perpetual Laws of the Common Wealth of Massachusetts — from the Establishment of its Constitution to the Second Session of the General Court, in 1798.* 2 vols., Worcester, 1799.

of this act, and afterwards, at least once in every year, produce to the several assessors of the towns and districts wherein such brewhouses shall be situate, satisfactory evidence of the quantities of beer or ale made in their said houses respectively, for one year then next preceding, in order that they may have the benefit of the exemption aforesaid.

[Passed *June* 22, 1789.]

References

These notes give, in the case of items included in the Bibliography, the short-est possible reference consistent with clarity — often the author's surname alone. Full bibliographical information on these items may be found by refer-ring to the section of the Bibliography indicated by the capital letter in paren-theses following such items.

ONE: THE UNIVERSAL BEVERAGE

1. Smith, *Travels*, I, 91-92. (C)
2. Bruce, *Econ. Hist. of Va.*, II, 263. (C)
3. Smith, *Travels*, I, 146. (C)
4. Bruce, *Econ. Hist. of Va.*, II, 211. (C)
5. Brown, *Genesis of the U.S.*, II, 660. (C)
6. Great Britain, *Calendar of State Papers*, pp. 26, 498. (C)
7. Hariot, p. 25. (C)
8. Smith, *Travels*, I, 39. (C)
9. "Letters from Va. in 1623," p. 238. (C)
10. Brown, *Genesis of the U.S.*, II, 883 (C); Hening, I, 84, 87. (C)
11. "Letters from Va. in 1623," p. 243. (C)
12. *Ibid.*, p. 375.
13. "Letter of Sir Francis Wyatt," p. 118. (C)
14. Bradford, p. 26*n*. (C)
15. *Ibid.*, p. 26.
16. *Ibid.*, p. 41.
17. *Ibid.*, p. 45.
18. *Ibid.*, p. 60 and *n*.
19. *Mourt's Relation*, p. 64. (C)
20. Bradford, p. 78. (C)
21. *Ibid.*, p. 65.
22. *Ibid.*, p. 143.
23. Wood, p. 16. (C)
24. Bradford, p. 78. (C)
25. Wood, p. 55. (C)
26. Andrews, *Colonial Period*, I, 270. (C)
27. *Winthrop Papers*, I, 371. (C)
28. *Ibid.*, II, 278.
29. Winthrop, *History*, I, 15. (C)
30. Mather, p. 30. (C)
31. Wood, p. 55. (C)
32. Winthrop, *History*, I, 25. (C)
33. *Winthrop Papers*, III, 136. (C)
34. Winthrop, *History*, I, 87. (C)

35. Boston, Record Commissioners, *Charlestown Land Records*, p. 10. (C)
36. Massachusetts, *Records of the Governor and Company*, I, 126. (C)
37. *Ibid.*, I, 140.
38. *Ibid.*, I, 213-214.
39. Boston, Record Commissioners, *Charlestown Land Records*, p. 2. (C)
40. Savage, p. 48 (C); *Dictionary of American Biography*; *New England Historical and Genealogical Register*, XLII, 184.
41. Massachusetts, *Records of the Governor and Company*, I, 238, 258. (C)
42. Smith, *Travels*, II, 176, 178. (C)
43. *A Perfect Description of Va.*, p. 62. (C)

TWO: THE ART AND MYSTERY OF BREWING

1. Emerson, II, 224-225. (B)
2. C. L. Shaw, "The Jolly Good Ale of Our Forefathers," in *Beer in Britain*, p. 85. (B)
3. *Ibid.*, p. 87.
4. "The High and Mighty Commendation of a Pot of Good Ale," *Studies in Philology*, XII, 10.
5. Hariot, p. 22. (C)
6. Worth, *The New and True Art of Brewing*. (B)
7. Deane, p. 20. (C)
8. Bruce, II, 213. (C)
9. Kimball, p. 349. (B)
10. Hariot, p. 21. (C)
11. Bruce, II, 212*n*. (C)
12. Bishop, I, 245. (C)
13. Mathias, pp. 63-78. (B)

THREE: BREWING IN NEW NETHERLAND

1. Innes, p. 34. (C)
2. Stokes, IV, 78. (C)
3. David Pieterssen De Vries, "Short Historical and Journal Notes, 1633-1643," in Jameson, p. 219. (C)
4. Kessler and Rachlis, p. 12. (C)
5. Stokes, IV, 78. (C)
6. Munsell, I, 36, 64. (C)
7. *Ibid.*, I, 24.
8. *Ibid.*, IV, 48.
9. *New York Genealogical and Biographical Record*, XVII, 82; Munsell, I, 69. (C)
10. Wheeler, pp. 87-88. (C)
11. Wilson, *Memorial History*, I, 229. (C)
12. Kessler and Rachlis, p. 17. (C)
13. Father Isaac Jogues, "Novum Belgium," in Jameson, p. 259. (C)
14. Kessler and Rachlis, p. 18. (C)
15. Wilson, *Memorial History*, I, 221 (C); Valentine, *History*, p. 30 (C); Innes, p. 176. (C)
16. Stokes, IV, 104. (C)
17. *Ibid.*, IV, 105.
18. Innes, pp. 145, 147. (C)
19. Valentine, *History*, pp. 89, 245. (C)
20. *Ibid.*, p. 114.
21. Fernow, *Records*, I, 90-93, 98, 126-130. (C)
22. White, *The Beekmans in Politics*, p. 33. (C)

23. Valentine, *History*, p. 133 (C); Innes, p. 325. (C)
24. Kouwenhoven, *Columbia Historical Portrait*, p. 41. (C)
25. Stokes, IV, 207. (C)
26. Fiske, *Dutch and Quaker Colonies*, II, 86. (C)
27. Innes, pp. 306-307. (C)
28. Fiske, *Dutch and Quaker Colonies*, I, 259 ff. (C)
29. Stokes, IV, 148, 153. (C)
30. Brodhead, I, 189. (C)
31. Fiske, *Dutch and Quaker Colonies*, I, 190. (C)
32. O'Callaghan, I, 598.
33. *New York Genealogical and Biographical Record*, III, 82-83.
34. *Ibid.*, XXVII, 82-83.
35. Fiske, *Dutch and Quaker Colonies*, II, 266 and *n*. (C)
36. O'Callaghan, IV, 29. (C)
37. Wilson, *Memorial History*, I, 330. (C)
38. Brodhead, II, 19-20. (C)
39. Myers, p. 28. (C)
40. Ward, *New Sweden*, p. 47. (C)
41. Myers, p. 98. (C)
42. Winsor, IV, 466. (C)
43. Myers, p. 165. (C)
44. Ward, *New Sweden*, p. 110. (C)
45. Brodhead, II, 193. (C)
46. *Ibid.*, II, 209.

FOUR: SEVENTEENTH-CENTURY BREWING

1. Hening, I, 374. (C)
2. Bruce, II, 213. (C)
3. John Hammond, "Leah and Rachel," in Hall, *Narratives*, p. 292. (C)
4. Bruce, II, 213. (C)
5. "Letters of William Byrd," p. 354. (C)
6. Frantz, p. 6*n*. (C)
7. Beverley, pp. 293, 316. (C)
8. Hening, I, 521-522. (C)
9. Bruce, II, 220, 228. (C)
10. Hening, II, 234. (C)
11. *York County Records, Deeds, Orders, Wills*, No. 13, p. 61.
12. *Ibid.*, No. 14, pp. 6-7.
13. *Ibid.*, No. 14, pp. 71-72.
14. Massachusetts, *Records of the Governor and Company*, III, 241. (C)
15. Winthrop, *History*, I, 124-125. (C)
16. Boston, Record Commissioners, *Boston Records, 1660-1701*. (C)
17. Massachusetts, *Records of the Governor and Company*, III, 173, 241. (C)
18. Massachusetts, *Acts and Resolves*, I, 30-33. (C)
19. *Ibid.*, I, 502, 513.
20. Boston, Record Commissioners, Second Report, Second part, p. 104. (C)
21. Colonial Soc. of Mass. *Publications*, XXIX, 1046-1049.
22. McElroy, pp. 248-249. (C)
23. Pope, p. 355. (C)
24. Hull, Account Books. (A)
25. Colonial Soc. of Mass. *Publications*, XXIX, 724.
26. Morison, *Founding of Harvard*, pp. 233, 448. (C)
27. Morison, *Harvard in the Seventeenth Century*, p. 90. (C)
28. Colonial Soc. of Mass. *Publications*, XV, 204.

29. Mass. Historical Soc. *Collections,* I, 259.
30. Morison, *Harvard in the Seventeenth Century,* p. 103. (C)
31. Boston, Record Commissioners, Second Report, p. 140. (C)
32. Walcott, pp. 218-252. (C)
33. Clark, I, 58-59. (C)
34. New Plymouth, *Records,* I, 38. (C)
35. *Ibid.,* I, 99, 137, 159.
36. Thomann, *Colonial Liquor Laws,* pp. 14n, 27n. (C)
37. New Plymouth, *Records,* II, 103 (C)
38. Dorr, p. 60. (C)
39. Staples, pp. 110 ff. (C)
40. Portsmouth, R.I., *Early Records,* p. 35. (C)
41. *Ibid.,* pp. 50.
42. Jameson, p. 203 (C)
43. *Ibid.,* p. 233.
44. Trumbull and Hoadly, I, 103, 154. (C)
45. *Ibid.,* I, 509 ff.
46. *Ibid.,* III, 437.
47. *Ibid.,* I, 444-507. (C)
48. *Winthrop Papers,* V, 323. (C)

FIVE: BREWING IN THE MIDDLE ATLANTIC COLONIES

1. Adams, *Album of American History,* I, 230. (C)
2. Donehoo, *Pennsylvania, a History,* I, 270. (C)
3. *Pennsylvania Magazine of History and Biography,* XXXVII, 121.
4. "The Restoration of Penn's Manor," p. 399. (C)
5. *Ibid.,* pp. 388-390. (C)
6. *Pennsylvania Magazine of History and Biography,* IX, 338.
7. "The Restoration of Penn's Manor," p. 391. (C)
8. "Letter of Thomas Paschall, 1683," in Myers, p. 252. (C)
9. Penn, "A Further Account," pp. 72-73. (C)
10. *Ibid.,* p. 74.
11. Myers, p. 268n. (C)
12. Watson, I, 50, 72. (C)
13. Gabriel Thomas, "An Historical and Geographical Account of Pennsylvania and West-New-Jersey" (1698), in Myers, pp. 327, 331. (C)
14. *Pennsylvania Magazine of History and Biography,* III, 455-456; IX, 377; LXIII, 97.
15. Leach, 19 January 1908. (C)
16. Francis Perot's Sons Co., pp. 9-10. (B)
17. Anthony Morris, Jr., MS Receipt [4 September 1731] (Collection of U.S. Brewers Association).
18. Scharf and Westcott, I, 153; III, 2278-2279 (C); Letter from T. Morris Perot to Wm. P. Smith, 22 March 1933 (A); Francis Perot's Sons Malting Co. (B)
19. Pennsylvania, *Minutes of Provincial Council,* III, 143. (C)
20. Stokes, IV, 426. (C)
21. O'Callaghan, I, 92, 163. (C)
22. Shourds, pp. 479-480. (C)
23. "The Present State of the Colony of West Jersey, 1681," in Myers, p. 191. (C)
24. Nelson, XIX, 208. (C)
25. *Ibid.,* XX, 97, 368.
26. "A Declaration of the Lord Baltimore's Plantation in Maryland, 1633," in Adams, *Album of American History,* I, 177. (C)
27. "A Relation of Maryland, 1635," in Hall, *Narratives,* pp. 82, 98. (C)

28. George Alsop, "A Character of the Province of Maryland," in Hall, *Narratives*, p. 352 and *n*. (C)
29. Browne, I, 438; II, 148-149. (C)
30. *Ibid.*, II, 407.
31. *Ibid.*, XV, 345.
32. Craven. (C)
33. Thomas Ashe, "Carolina, or a Description of the Present State of the Country, 1682," in Salley, pp. 146-147. (C)
34. "Letters of Thomas Newe, 1682," in Salley, p. 181. (C)

SIX: EIGHTEENTH-CENTURY DRINKING HABITS

1. Wilson, *Memorial History*, II, 89. (C)
2. O'Callaghan, I, 714. (C)
3. Jones, *Present State of Va.*, p. 86. (C)
4. Sherrill, p. 79. (C)
5. Angle, p. 56. (C)
6. "Journey of Francis Louis Michel," p. 118. (C)
7. Fisher, "Narrative," p. 108. (C)
8. Mathias, pp. 12 ff. (B)
9. *Ibid.*, p. 13.
10. Washington, Ledgers. (A)
11. Washington, *Writings*, II, 331. (C)
12. Jerdone, Letterbook. (A)
13. Earle, p. 92. (C)
14. Carroll, Account Book. (A)
15. Earle, p. 95. (C)
16. *Ibid.*, p. 98.
17. Adams, *Album of American History*, I, 56, 67, 89. (C)
18. Hatch, p. 119. (C)
19. *Encyclopaedia Britannica* (14th Edition).
20. *Great Industries of the U.S.*, p. 895. (C)
21. New York *Mercury*, 2 October 1752.
22. *Great Industries of the U.S.*, p. 895. (C)
23. Clark, I, 166.
24. *Ibid.*, p. 167.
25. Indenture of 17 January 1734, Penn Papers, Large Folio, p. 33. (A)
26. Roach, pp. 154-155. (C)
27. Agreement, 23 September 1751 (MS), (Historical Society of Pennsylvania).
28. Agreement, 13 August 1754 (MS), (Historical Society of Pennsylvania).
29. Philadelphia *Packet and Daily Advertiser*, 9 July 1788.
30. *Pennsylvania Magazine of History and Biography*, XLII, 336.
31. *Ibid.*, XXX, 33.

SEVEN: BREWING IN EIGHTEENTH-CENTURY NEW YORK AND PHILADELPHIA

1. Faneuil, Letter Book. (A)
2. "Burghers of New Amsterdam." (C)
3. "Muster Rolls of New York Provincial Troops." (C)
4. Wilson, *Memorial History*, II, 160. (C)
5. *New York Genealogical and Biographical Record*, XVII, 83, 88.
6. Stokes, V, 1097. (C)
7. New York *Packet*, 24 November 1783.
8. New York *Herald*, 12 December 1804.
9. *Rivington's Gazetteer*, 1 December 1774.

10. Atlee, Petition. (A)
11. Valentine, *History*, p. 293. (C)
12. Wilson, *Memorial History*, II, 477. (C)
13. Valentine, *History*, p. 304. (C)
14. New York *Gazette*, 17 June 1734.
15. Moss, II, 251. (C)
16. O'Callaghan, I, 726-727. (C)
17. *Ibid.*, I, 761.
18. "Letter of Thomas Paschall, 1683," in Myers, p. 252. (C)
19. Paschall, Papers, 1705-1711, and Accounts, 1713-1728. (A)
20. MS (American Philosophical Society Library, Philadelphia).
21. *Pennsylvania Magazine of History and Biography*, LVI, 164; LVII, 91.
22. *Ibid.*, XIV, 273.
23. Gillingham, pp. 108-110. (C)
24. Scharf, III, 2278-2279 (C); Watson, III, 176-177. (C)
25. *Pennsylvania Journal*, 14 July 1763.
26. *Ibid.*, 25 April 1765.
27. "Journey of Francis Louis Michel," p. 136.
28. "Account of Servants Bound and Assigned," XXXII, 240, 237, 368; XXXI, 446. (C)
29. Gilpin, p. 146. (C)
30. Fort Augusta, Pennsylvania, Quartermaster's Ledger. (A)
31. "Fort Pitt Account Book, 1765-67." (C)

EIGHT: BREWING IN EIGHTEENTH-CENTURY NEW ENGLAND

1. Samuel Adams Papers. (A)
2. Wells, I, 4-13. (C)
3. *Ibid.*, I, 24-36.
4. Faneuil, Daybook. (A)
5. Boston, Record Commissioners, 29th Report, p. 103. (C)
6. Lloyd, Letter Book. (A)
7. Hancock Family Manuscripts, Waste Book. (A)
8. Hancock Family Manuscripts, II, 2; II, 3; VIII, 8. (A)
9. Boston, Record Commissioners, 29th Report, pp. 197, 216 (C)
10. *Ibid.*, p. 191.
11. Boston, Record Commissioners, 11th Report, p. 122. (C)
12. *Ibid.*, p. 220.
13. Rhode Island Land Evidences. (A)
14. Records of Newport Historical Society.
15. Brown Family Papers. (A)
16. Rhode Island, Petitions to the General Assembly, XIII, 145. (A)
17. *Ibid.*, V, 110.
18. *Ibid.*, XXIX, 57.
19. Records of Newport Historical Society.
20. Rhode Island, Confiscated Estates. (A)

NINE: SUPPLYING BEER TO THE SOUTHERN COLONIES

1. Georgia, *An Account Showing the Progress*, p. 384. (C)
2. Jones, *History of Georgia*, I, 128. (C)
3. *Ibid.*, I, 229.
4. Stephens, *Journal of the Proceedings in Ga.*, p. 211. (C)
5. Stephens, *Journal of Wm. Stephens*, I, 86. (C)
6. Georgia, *An Impartial Enquiry*. (C)

7. "Bolzius Answers a Questionnaire," pp. 246-247. (C)
8. Beverley, p. 266. (C)
9. Swem, p. 235. (C)
10. William and Mary College, "Proceedings of the Faculty," p. 233. (C)
11. "Proposal in Regard to the Governor's House," p. 37. (C)
12. "Virginia County Records," p. 188. (C)
13. *Virginia Gazette*, 11 August 1774.
14. *Ibid.*, 10 July 1778.
15. *Ibid.*, 13 November 1779.
16. *Ibid.*, 29 October 1736.
17. *Ibid.*, 19 December 1777.
18. *Ibid.*, 10 February 1775.
19. *Ibid.*, 16 August 1776.
20. *Ibid.*, 8 May 1778.
21. *Ibid.*, 4 November 1773.
22. *Ibid.*, 25 September 1779.
23. *Ibid.*, 6 June 1745.
24. *Ibid.*, 25 August 1774; 16 October 1779.
25. "Diary of Col. Landon Carter," p. 178. (C)
26. Torrence, pp. 9, 11, 13. (C)
27. "Observations in Several Voyages and Travels in America," pp. 144, 145, 215. (C)
28. Wirt, pp. 36-37. (C)
29. Tyler, pp. 344-345. (C)

TEN: "BUY AMERICAN"

1. Riddell, p. 138. (C)
2. Receipt, dated 18 June 1767, Brown Family Papers, A30a. (A)
3. Hancock Family Manuscripts, VIII, 1 (1756). (A)
4. White, I, 141, 357. (C)
5. *Virginia Gazette* (Rind), 30 May 1766.
6. Boston *Evening Post*, 10 September 1750.
7. Andrews, "Boston Merchants," p. 181. (C)
8. Leach, 19 January 1908.
9. Fisher, "The Twenty-Eight Charges," p. 258. (C)
10. MS (Collection of U.S. Brewers Association).
11. *Virginia Gazette*, 25 May 1769.
12. *Ibid.*, 28 June 1770.
13. *Ibid.*, 14 December 1769.
14. *Ibid.*, 1 April 1775.
15. *Ibid.*, 10 August 1769.
16. Donehoo, *Pennsylvania, A History*, II, 1038. (C)
17. *Virginia Gazette*, 14 December 1769.
18. Brunhouse, p. 367. (C)
19. Donehoo, *loc. cit.*

ELEVEN: RECIPES FOR HOME BREWERS

1. Kimball, p. 117. (C)
2. Byrn, pp. 181-183. (B)
3. Benjamin Franklin Papers. (A)
4. *Benjamin Franklin on the Art of Eating* (Translation by editor), p. 57. (C)
5. Amherst, *Journal*, p. 152. (C)
6. MS (American Philosophical Society, Philadelphia).
7. Clarke, Letters. (A)

TWELVE: SUPPLYING THE BEER RATION

1. *Journals of the Continental Congress*, III, 322. (C)
2. Hart, II, 449. (C)
3. *From Cambridge to Champlain*, p. 21. (C)
4. Wildes, pp. 169, 172-173. (C)
5. *Virginia Gazette*, 19 August 1775.
6. "Donations to Boston," pp. 161, 165. (C)
7. Davidson, I, 141. (C)
8. *Virginia Gazette*, 5 January 1776.
9. *Ibid.*, 9 November 1775.
10. *Ibid.*, 24 August 1776.
11. *Ibid.*, 3 October 1777.
12. MS (Collection of U.S. Brewers Association).
13. "Letters of Robert Proud," p. 67. (C)
14. Hancock Family Manuscripts. (A)
15. "A Scrap of 'Troop' History," p. 227. (C)
16. "Memorial of John Lowry," p. 268. (C)
17. Washington, *Writings*, XXII, 441. (C)
18. Wilson, *Memorial History*, II, 468. (C)
19. Leach, 28 June 1908. (C)

THIRTEEN: THE PRESIDENT'S BEER

1. Clark, I, 481. (C)
2. Asbury, p. 23. (C)
3. Wilson, *Memorial History*, III, 55. (C)
4. Washington, *Writings*, XXX, 187. (C)
5. *Pennsylvania Magazine of History and Biography*, XXIV, 383.
6. Leach, 28 June 1908. (C)
7. Philadelphia *Packet and Daily Advertiser*, 10 May 1788.
8. *Ibid.*, 21 July, 22 July 1788.
9. *Ibid.*, 9 July 1788.
10. Wilson, *Memorial History*, III, 42. (C)
11. Philadelphia *Packet and Daily Advertiser*, 5 August, 6 August 1788.
12. Washington, *Writings*, XXX, 20. (C)
13. *Ibid.*, XXX, 35.
14. *Ibid.*, XXXI, 57.
15. *Ibid.*, XXXI, 149.
16. *Ibid.*, XXXV, 71.
17. "Washington's Household Account Book," XXX, 44, 462. (C)
18. Philadelphia *Packet and Daily Advertiser*, 27 June 1788.
19. Francis Perot's Sons Co., p. 10. (B)

FOURTEEN: ENCOURAGEMENT OF BREWING

1. Philadelphia *Packet and Daily Advertiser*, 24 July 1788.
2. Bordley, pp. 390 ff.
3. Spurrier, pp. 246-247. (C)
4. Deane, p. 21. (C)
5. O'Callaghan, II, 1184. (C)
6. Judd, Day Book. (A)
7. Tayloe Family Papers. (A)
8. New York *Daily Gazette*, 13 May 1789.

9. Angle, p. 151. (C)
10. Tolles, p. 263. (C)
11. Rush, p. 17. (C)
12. Massachusetts, *Perpetual Laws*, II, 33. (C)
13. *Western Brewer*, VII, 379.
14. Coxe, *A View of the U.S.*, pp. 386-389. (C)
15. Spurrier, pp. 246-248. (C)
16. Deane, *loc. cit.*
17. Bordley, p. 390. (C)
18. Hale, Account Book, 11 April 1801. (A)
19. Peterson, p. 304. (C)
20. Coxe, *An Address*, p. 14. (C)
21. Bordley, pp. 395-396. (C)
22. Hamilton, pp. 41, 68. (C)
23. *Ibid.*, p. 69.
24. Hening, II, 234. (C)
25. Coxe, *A View of the U.S.*, pp. 124-125, 209. (C)
26. Coxe, *Observations*, p. 31. (C)
27. Gallatin, p. 4. (C)
28. United States Treasury Department, *Tabular Statements*, p. 22. (C)
29. Mathias, p. 552. (B)
30. Carey, pp. 2-3, 7. (C)
31. United States Census Office, *Digest*, 1820. (C)

FIFTEEN: BREWERS AT THE TURN OF THE CENTURY

1. Bond, "Letters of Phineas Bond," I, 653. (C)
2. Brissot de Warville, I, 81. (C)
3. Sherrill, p. 79. (C)
4. *Moreau de St. Mery's American Journey*, p. 318. (C)
5. Sharswood, Account Book. (A)
6. Barrett, I, 300. (C)
7. See Dunlap, II, 296. (C)
8. Asbury, p. 13. (C)
9. Valentine, *Manual*. (C)
10. *The Old Brewery and the New Mission House*, p. 45. (C)
11. Stiles, II, 119-122. (C)
12. *Ibid.*, I, 217-218.
13. New York *Mercury*, 25 February 1770.
14. Stiles, II, 122. (C)
15. O'Callaghan, II, 239. (C)
16. United States Brew-Masters Association, *Souvenir of 20th Annual Convention*, Albany, 21-23 September 1908, p. 86.
17. *History of the Brewery and Liquor Industry of Rochester*, p. 7. (B)
18. *Kentucky Gazette*, 12 September 1789; *Pennsylvania Magazine of History and Biography*, LVI, 43n.
19. "Materials Relating to the History of the Mississippi Valley," p. 13. (C)
20. Quoted in Pittsburgh *Press*, 20 April 1901.
21. Shiras, p. 3. (C)
22. Pittsburgh *Gazette*, 17 October 1795.
23. Shiras, p. 4 (C); Pittsburgh *Gazette*, 23 January 1797.
24. Shiras, p. 6. (C)
25. Dahlinger, p. 78. (C)
26. Shiras, p. 6. (C)
27. *Ibid.*, p. 8. (C)

28. Strong to O'Hara, 31 July 1797, O'Hara Papers. (A)
29. Schramm, p. 77. (C)
30. *Ibid.*, pp. 78-80.
31. Pittsburgh City Directory, 1815, p. 140.
32. Pittsburgh City Directory, 1837.
33. Shiras, p. 15. (C)
34. Wilson, *Standard History of Pittsburg*, p. 198. (C)
35. Schramm, p. 69. (C)
36. Pears, p. 197. (C)

SIXTEEN: THOMAS JEFFERSON: GENTLEMAN-BREWER

1. Jefferson to Crawford, 10 November 1818 (Library of Congress). (A)
2. Jefferson, Account Books. (A)
3. Betts, p. 47 ff. (C)
4. Gray, II, 817. (C)
5. Jefferson to Meriwether, 17 September 1813 (Mass. Historical Soc.). (A)
6. Jefferson to Moore, 2 October 1813 (Library of Congress). (A)
7. *The London and Country Brewer*, Title-page, pp. 19-20. (B)
8. Jefferson to Dufief, 18 September 1813 (Library of Congress). (A)
9. Dufief to Jefferson, 23 September 1813 (Library of Congress). (A)
10. Jefferson to Dufief, 7 November 1813 (Library of Congress). (A)
11. Jefferson to Dufief, 20 March 1814 (Library of Congress). (A)
12. Dufief to Jefferson, 6 and 14 April 1814 (Library of Congress). (A)
13. Coppinger to Jefferson, 17 October 1802 (Library of Congress). (A)
14. Jefferson to Coppinger, 23 October 1802 (Library of Congress). (A)
15. Coppinger to Jefferson, 3 January and 18 February 1803 (Library of Congress). (A)
16. Coppinger to Madison, 16 December 1810 (Library of Congress). (A)
17. Coppinger to Madison, 20 December 1810 (Library of Congress). (A)
18. Coppinger to Jefferson, 6 April 1815, with attachment "Brewery Company" (Library of Congress). (A)
19. Jefferson to Coppinger, 25 April 1815 (Library of Congress). (A)
20. Coppinger to Jefferson, 15 September 1815, with attachment (Library of Congress). (A)
21. Jefferson to Barbour, 11 May 1821 (Library of Congress). (A)
22. Jefferson to Randolph, 25 January 1814 (Mass. Historical Soc.). (A)
23. Randolph to Jefferson, 18 February 1814 (Mass. Historical Soc.). (A)
24. Jefferson to Randolph, 27 September 1814 (Mass. Historical Soc.). (A)
25. Jefferson to Miller, 14 October 1816 (Library of Congress). (A)
26. Miller to Jefferson, 6 December 1816 (Library of Congress). (A)
27. Jefferson to Miller, 11 March 1817 (Library of Congress). (A)
28. Jefferson to Peyton, 11 March 1817 (Mass. Historical Soc.). (A)
29. Peyton to Jefferson, 17 March 1817 (Mass. Historical Soc.). (A)
30. Miller to Jefferson, 24 March 1817 (Library of Congress). (A)
31. Jefferson to Miller, 30 January 1819 (Library of Congress). (A)
32. Jefferson to Moore, 21 July 1814 (Library of Congress). (A)
33. Jefferson to Miller, 21 July 1814 (Library of Congress). (A)
34. Miller to Jefferson, 1 September 1815 (Library of Congress). (A)
35. Jefferson to Yancey, 15 October 1815 (Library of Congress). (A)
36. Jefferson to Cabell, 23 December 1815 (Library of Congress). (A)
37. Jefferson to Yancey, 6 January 1816 (Library of Congress). (A)
38. Jefferson to Miller, 17 February 1816 (Library of Congress). (A)
39. Miller to Jefferson, 29 February 1816 (Library of Congress). (A)

40. Miller to Jefferson, 22 August 1816 (Library of Congress). (A)
41. Jefferson to Miller, 14 October 1816 (Library of Congress). (A)
42. Miller to Jefferson, 6 December 1816 (Library of Congress). (A)
43. Jefferson to Miller, 11 March 1817 (Library of Congress). (A)
44. Jefferson to Madison, 11 April 1820 (Library of Congress). (A)
45. Barbour to Jefferson, 30 April 1821 (Library of Congress). (A)
46. Jefferson to Barbour, 11 May 1821 (Library of Congress). (A)

SEVENTEEN: MATTHEW VASSAR: BREWER-PHILANTHROPIST

1. Vassar, *Autobiography*, p. 22. (C)
2. Lossing, p. 18. (C)
3. Vassar, *Autobiography*, p. 24. (C)
4. James Vassar, Day Book, 1802-1805, Vassar Papers. (A)
5. Vassar, *Autobiography*, p. 27. (C)
6. *Ibid.*, p. 29.
7. James and Matthew Vassar, Daybook, 17 March 1808, 21 January 1811, Vassar
   Papers. (A)
8. *Political Barometer* (Poughkeepsie), 2 January 1811.
9. Platt, p. 86. (C)
10. Lossing, p. 25. (C)
11. *Ibid.*, p. 27.
12. Platt, *loc. cit.*
13. Poughkeepsie *Journal*, 10 June 1812.
14. *Ibid.*, 14 July 1813.
15. Platt, *loc. cit.*
16. Lossing, p. 33. (C)
17. *Ibid.*, p. 34.
18. Platt, p. 233. (C)
19. Hasbrouck, p. 237. (C)
20. Matthew Vassar, Jr., Journal and Brewing Book, 1833-1847, Vassar Papers. (A)
21. Lossing, p. 34. (C)
22. Poughkeepsie *Eagle*, Souvenir edition (1889).
23. Platt, p. 233. (C)
24. *Western Brewer*, XXIV, 431.

EIGHTEEN: THE AGE OF STEAM POWER

1. Mathias, pp. 85, 92-93. (B)
2. *Ibid.*, pp. 95-96.
3. Roll, p. 240. (C)
4. Coxe, *An Address*, p. 9. (C)
5. *Pennsylvania Magazine of History and Biography*, LXIII, 360.
6. Jordan, pp. 241-242. (C)
7. Graff. (C)
8. Betts, p. 369. (C)
9. Bathe, pp. 79-80. (C)
10. *Ibid.*, pp. 88-89, 91.
11. *Ibid.*, pp. 94, 117.
12. *Ibid.*, p. 207.
13. Mathias, p. 81. (B)
14. Francis Perot's Sons Co., pp. 17-18. (B)
15. Bordley, pp. 397-398. (C)
16. John Vaughan to Benjamin Vaughan, 4 July 1806, Vaughan Papers. (A)

NINETEEN: TOWARD THE MISSISSIPPI

1. Greve, I, 50. (C)
2. *Ibid.*, I, 418.
3. *Ibid.*, II, 441.
4. *Ibid.*, I, 431.
5. Cincinnati Directory, 1819.
6. Drake, p. 147. (C)
7. Greve, II, 436. (C)
8. *Ibid.*, I, 547.
9. *Ibid.*, I, 676.
10. Andreas, I, 100-132. (C)
11. Guyer, p. 40 (C); Andreas, I, 564 (C); Chicago *Sun-Times*, 16 August 1953.
12. Ogden to E. D. Perry, — January 1839 (Chicago Historical Soc.). (A)
13. Ogden to Edward Townsend, 15 July 1839 (Chicago Historical Soc.). (A)
14. Meeker, pp. 62-63 (B); Myrick, pp. 5-6. (B)
15. Ogden to E. Criswell, Albany, 13 August 1839 (Chicago Historical Soc.). (A)
16. Ogden to E. Townsend, 26 August 1839 (Chicago Historical Soc.). (A)
17. Ogden to E. Townsend, 17 September 1839 (Chicago Historical Soc.). (A)
18. Ogden to E. Townsend, 29 September 1840 (Chicago Historical Soc.). (A)
19. Ogden to Edward Townsend, 13 November 1840 (Chicago Historical Soc.). (A)
20. Ogden to William Haas, 22 August 1840 (Chicago Historical Soc.). (A)
21. Chicago *Daily News*, 16 March 1952.
22. Chicago *Tribune*, 1 September 1929.
23. Andreas, I, 564. (C)
24. Cleveland *Herald*, 14 May 1829.
25. Detroit *Daily Advertiser*, 21 November 1861.
26. Detroit *Free Press*, 15 August 1836.
27. Auburn and Russell, I, 165. (C)
28. Avery, vol. I. (C)
29. *Annals of the Early Settlers Association of Cuyahoga County*, I, No. 1, 83. (C)
30. Cleveland *Herald*, 29 May 1832.
31. *Ibid.*, 5 April 1834.
32. Cleveland *Herald and Gazette*, 1 June 1837; Cleveland City Directory, 1837.
33. Cleveland *Herald*, 10 December 1840.
34. *Ibid.*, 25 September 1843.
35. *Ibid.*, 1 July 1845.
36. Cleveland City Directory, 1850-1851; 1863.
37. Rose, p. 126. (C)
38. Cleveland City Directory, 1878.
39. Ste. Genevieve Archives, Wills No. 38. (A)
40. Scharf, II, 1330. (C)
41. *Louisiana Gazette*, 28 March 1812.
42. Will of Jacques Delassus de St. Vrain. (A)
43. From Wilt, Letter Book. (A)
44. Hab, Request for Naturalization. (A)
45. Scharf, I, 195. (C)
46. *Louisiana Gazette*, 6 June, 1 August 1812.
47. Scharf, I, 195. (A)
48. *Missouri Gazette*, 3 March 1819.
49. Hyde and Conard, II, 755. (C)
50. St. Louis *Enquirer*, 6 January and 10 February 1821.
51. Scharf, I, 195. (C)
52. *Ibid.*, I, 335n.

53. Darby, p. 73. (C)
54. Hab, Property in Sheriff's sale, 10 December 1828. (A)
55. Scharf, II, 1330. (C)
56. *Missouri Republican*, 23 February 1826, 11 December 1838.
57. Hyde and Conard, II, 755 (C); St. Louis City Directory, 1840-1841.
58. *Missouri Republican*, 22 November 1833, 3 July 1838.
59. *Ibid.*, 14 November 1835.

TWENTY: "LAGER BIER"

1. Bacon, p. 215. (B)
2. Roman, p. 90. (B)
3. *One Hundred Years*, p. 207. (B)
4. *Ibid.*, p. 248
5. *Ibid.*, p. 207.
6. Mathias, p. 4. (B)
7. Stiles, III, 588 *n.* (C)
8. Greve, I, 688. (C)
9. Galbreath, II, 177. (C)
10. Wittke, III, 52. (C)
11. Carl, *Texas*, pp. 95-96. (C)
12. *Ibid.*, pp. 115, 116.
13. *Ibid.*, p. 120.
14. House, p. 119. (C)
15. Curtis, p. 108. (C)
16. House, p. 120. (C)
17. French, p. 563. (C)
18. Martin, p. 50. (C)
19. *Loc. cit.*
20. Davidson, II, 374-375. (C)
21. *Ibid.*, II, 53. (Quoting from *Appleton's Journal*, 3 April 1869.)
22. Herancourt, Diary. (A)

TWENTY-ONE: THE FIRST LAGER BREWERS

1. Bacon, p. 214. (B)
2. *One Hundred Years*, pp. 209, 213. (B)
3. Stevens, *St. Louis*, p. 629 (C); Scharf, II, 1330 (C); St. Louis City Directory, 1840-1841.
4. *History of Milwaukee from Prehistoric Times*, p. 1457; Buck, IV, 344. (C)
5. Milwaukee *Sentinel*, 17 January 1872.
6. *Ibid.*, 18 May 1870.
7. *Ibid.*, 29 March 1870; Cochran, pp. 21-22. (B)
8. Greve, I, 688. (C)
9. *St. Paul, the Queen City*, p. 129. (C)
10. Pittsburgh *Dispatch*, 9 April 1911.
11. *Western Brewer*, III, 594.
12. Chicago *Sun-Times*, 16 August 1953.
13. Arnold, *History of the Brewing Industry*, p. 196. (B)
14. Buck, p. 344. (C)
15. Guyer, p. 43. (C)
16. *Ibid.*, p. 41.
17. Milwaukee *Daily Sentinel*, 30 March 1867.
18. Andreas, I, 564. (C)

19. Milwaukee *Daily Sentinel*, 10 December 1859.
20. Milwaukee City Directory, 1847, 1854-1855.
21. Milwaukee *Daily Sentinel*, 30 December 1859, 17 June 1861.
22. *History of Milwaukee from Prehistoric Times*, p. 1457. (C)
23. Milwaukee City Directory, 1847, p. 67.
24. *History of Milwaukee from Prehistoric Times, loc. cit.*
25. Milwaukee *Daily Sentinel*, 12 July 1867.
26. Bishop, II, 296; III, 244 (C); *One Hundred Years*, p. 193. (B)
27. United States Brew-Masters Association, p. 82. (B)
28. *One Hundred Years*, pp. 189-190. (B)
29. Utica City Directory, 1843-1844.
30. Pittsburgh *Leader*, 26 October 1895.
31. Hyde and Conard, IV, 2391. (C)
32. *One Hundred Years*, p. 216 (B); Stiles, II, 293. (C)
33. *One Hundred Years*, p. 238 (B); Bishop, II, 287. (C)
34. *One Hundred Years*, p. 256. (B)
35. French, p. 488*n*. (C)
36. Clark, I, 481. (C)
37. Guyer, pp. 39-40. (C)
38. Milwaukee *Daily Sentinel*, 30 March 1867.
39. Clark, I, 481. (C)

TWENTY-TWO: THE ORIGINS OF PROHIBITION

1. Fehlandt, p. 52. (C)
2. *Ibid.*, pp. 22-23.
3. Krout, p. 90. (C)
4. *Ibid.*, p. 78.
5. Daniels, p. viii. (C)
6. Fehlandt, pp. 56-57. (C)
7. Daniels, pp. 57-59. (C)
8. Krout, pp. 136-137. (C)
9. *Ibid.*, p. 151.
10. *Standard Encyclopedia of the Alcohol Problem*, I, 159. (C)
11. Fehlandt, pp. 80-81 (C); Cherrington, *Evolution of Prohibition*, p. 83. (C)
12. Krout, pp. 159 ff. (C)
13. Taylor, *A Report*, p. 6. (C)
14. Krout, p. 164*n*. (C)
15. Taylor, *A Report*, p. 44. (C)
16. Krout, pp. 182 ff. (C)
17. Daniels, p. 96. (C)
18. Gough, p. 135. (C)
19. *Standard Encyclopedia of the Alcohol Problem*, VI, 2475. (C)
20. Krout, pp. 194-196. (C)
21. Cherrington, *Evolution of Prohibition*, p. 127. (C)
22. Krout, pp. 201-206. (C)
23. Fehlandt, pp. 92-95. (C)
24. Krout, p. 215. (C)
25. Fehlandt, p. 119. (C)
26. Colvin, pp. 29-30. (C)
27. Krout, p. 284. (C)
28. Cherrington, *Evolution of Prohibition*, p. 30. (C)
29. *Ibid.*, p. 31.
30. Ostrander, p. 1. (C)
31. Fehlandt, pp. 125 ff. (C)

32. Cherrington, *Evolution of Prohibition*, p. 39. (C)
33. *Ibid.*, p. 40; Fehlandt, p. 132. (C)

TWENTY-THREE: THE PACIFIC COAST

1. Files of the Oregon Historical Society.
2. The *Oregonian*, Souvenir Issue, 1 October 1892.
3. Hines, *Illustrated History of Oregon*, p. 844. (C)
4. Weinhard, Vancouver Brewery Day Book. (A)
5. Weinhard, Vancouver Brewery Account Book. (A)
6. Portland City Directories, 1863, 1865.
7. *One Hundred Years*, p. 364. (B)
8. Bagley, p. 625. (C)
9. Hunt, I, 79-80. (C)
10. Reed, invoice, 20 September 1843. (A)
11. Bancroft, XXIV, 85. (C)
12. Cleland, p. 33. (C)
13. Ostrander, p. 4. (C)
14. San Francisco City Directory, 1856.
15. San Francisco *Merchant*, 22 May 1881.
16. San Francisco Mechanics Institute, *Report of the First Industrial Exhibition*, pp. 79-80. (C)
17. *History of Sacramento County*, pp. 42, 144. (C)
18. "Oregon and California Letters of Alden," p. 213. (C)
19. *History of Sutter County*, p. 47. (C)
20. *History of Yuba County, California*, p. 69 (C); Lithograph of Marysville, 1856 (Collection of Calif. Historical Soc.).
21. Marysville City Directory, 1855.
22. Gilbert, p. 71. (C)
23. Tinkham, p. 326. (C)
24. California Historical Society Collection.
25. Tinkham, *loc. cit.*
26. Gilbert, *loc. cit.*; *One Hundred Years*, p. 361. (B)
27. Buchner, p. 278. (B)
28. *History of Los Angeles County*, p. 69. (C)
29. *History of Plumas, Lassen and Sierra Counties*, pp. 464, 493. (C)
30. *Historical Souvenir of Eldorado County*, pp. 114, 187, 219. (C)
31. Placer County Directory, 1861.
32. Eagle to Margaret Eagle, 13 June 1852 (Huntington Library). (A)
33. Eagle to Margaret Eagle, 29 October 1852 (Huntington Library). (A)
34. Hittell, p. 282. (C)

TWENTY-FOUR: THE BREWERS JOIN FORCES

1. *One Hundred Years*, p. 252. (B)
2. Shih, p. 13. (B)
3. *History of Milwaukee from Prehistoric Times*, p. 1463. (C)
4. *Ibid.*, p. 1461; Milwaukee City Directories, 1848-1849, 1851-1852.
5. *History of Milwaukee from Prehistoric Times*, p. 1463. (C)
6. St. Louis *Post-Dispatch*, supplement, 25 December 1949; Scharf, II, 1333. (C)
7. *The City of Cincinnati and Its Resources*, p. 90. (C)
8. Stiles, III, p. 588n. (C)
9. Land, p. 110. (C)
10. *Ibid.*, p. 75; St. Paul City Directory, 1858, 1859.
11. Fehlandt, p. 72. (C)

12. *Ibid.*, p. 142.
13. Kouwenhoven, *Adventures of America*, Reproduction No. 58. (C)
14. Smith, *U.S. Federal Internal Tax History*, p. 1. (C)
15. *Documentary History*, p. 154. (B)
16. Lemp Family Papers. (A)
17. United States Brewers' Association, *Documentary History*, pp. 100, 116. (B)
18. *Ibid.*, p. 110.
19. *Report of the First Brewers' Congress*, in German (Collection of U.S. Brewers' Association, Inc.), p. 10.
20. United States Brewers' Association, *Documentary History*, pp. 115, 121.
21. *Ibid.*, p. 125.
22. *Ibid.*, p. 230.
23. *Ibid.*, pp. 148, 178 ff.
24. *Ibid.*, p. 98.
25. Fehlandt, pp. 172-173. (C)
26. *Ibid.*, p. 175.

TWENTY-FIVE: COMING OF AGE

1. Daniels, p. 205. (C)
2. Fehlandt, pp. 224-225. (C)
3. United States Brewers' Association, *Documentary History*, p. 183. (B)
4. *Record of the Sixth Annual Brewers' Congress* (Collection of U.S. Brewers' Association, Inc.), p. 5.
5. *Record of the Seventh Brewers' Congress* (Collection of U.S. Brewers' Association, Inc.), p. 10.
6. *Ibid.*, p. 3.
7. United States Brewers' Association, *Documentary History*, p. 203. (B)
8. Shih, Table 1.1.1. (C)
9. United States Brewers' Association, *Documentary History*, p. 174 (B)
10. Colvin, p. 49. (C)
11. *Ibid.*, p. 62.
12. *Ibid.*, pp. 62-63, 65.
13. United States Brewers' Association, *Documentary History*, p. 284. (C)
14. *Ibid.*, pp. 231-232.
15. *Ibid.*, pp. 243-244, 250.
16. *Ibid.*, p. 295.
17. *Ibid.*, pp. 262-263, 295.
18. *Ibid.*, pp. 301-302.
19. Daniels, p. 252. (C)
20. Fehlandt, p. 234. (C)
21. United States Brewers' Association, *Documentary History*, p. 341. (B)
22. Colvin, p. 118. (C)
23. United States Brewers' Association, *Documentary History*, pp. 365-366. (B)
24. Fehlandt, pp. 195-196. (C)
25. *Ibid.*, pp. 205 ff.
26. United States Brewers' Association, *Documentary History*, p. 401. (B)
27. Shih, *loc. cit.*
28. United States Brewers' Association, *Documentary History*, p. 403. (B)
29. *Ibid.*, p. 405.
30. McCabe, pp. 703-704. (C)
31. Brewers' Industrial Exhibition, 1876, *loc. cit.*
32. United States Centennial Commission, International Exhibition, 1876, *Reports and Awards: Group IV.* (C)
33. United States Brewers' Association, *Documentary History*, p. 409. (B)

TWENTY-SIX: THE BREWMASTER AS MECHANIC AND ENGINEER

1. Wyatt, pp. 4-5. (B)
2. *Western Brewer*, XXIII, 281.
3. New Orleans *Times*, 29 December 1865.
4. *Puck Weekly*, 7 December 1892. (In *Foam*, house organ of the F. and M. Schaefer Brewing Co., December 1956-January 1957, February 1958.)
5. Cincinnati *Enquirer*, 13 December 1960.
6. Pittsburgh *Dispatch*, 9 April 1911.
7. *Derrick's Hand-book of Petroleum*, p. 343. (C)
8. Land, p. 110. (C)
9. House, *loc. cit.*
10. Milwaukee *Daily Sentinel*, 19 May 1864.
11. Information from the Miller Brewing Co., Milwaukee.
12. *The City of Cincinnati and Its Resources*, p. 90. (C)
13. (Prescott) *Arizona Miner*, 5 March 1875.
14. Cummings, pp. 1-2, 17, 20, 51. (C)
15. Detroit *Free Press*, 15 February 1867.
16. Anderson, p. 38. (C)
17. *The Great Industries of the United States*, p. 157. (C)
18. *Western Brewer*, I, 61.
19. *Ibid.*, XXIII, 279.
20. Milwaukee *Daily Sentinel*, 17 January 1872.
21. *History of Milwaukee from Prehistoric Times*, p. 1459. (C)
22. *Ibid.*, pp. 1461-1463.
23. Guyer, pp. 42-43. (C)
24. Leadville *Herald Democrat*, 1 January 1899.
25. *Western Brewer*, I, 60-61.
26. Giedion, p. 599. (C)
27. ARW *Journal* (Air-Conditioning & Refrigeration Wholesalers), April 1958.
28. Arnold, *History of the Brewing Industry*, p. 93 (B); Giedion, p. 601. (C)
29. Phoenix *Herald*, 31 July 1890.
30. Anderson, p. 91. (C)
31. Cochran, p. 108. (B)
32. *One Hundred Years*, p. 556. (B)
33. Arnold, *History of the Brewing Industry*, p. 94. (B)
34. Young, p. 135. (C)
35. *Western Brewer*, I, 89-90.

TWENTY-SEVEN: THE BREWMASTER AS CHEMIST AND BIOLOGIST

1. Laufer and Schwarz, p. 79. (B)
2. Pasteur, p. vii. (B)
3. *Ibid.*, p. 142.
4. Roman, p. 13. (B)
5. Laufer and Schwarz, *loc. cit.*
6. Jörgensen, p. 431. (B)
7. Roman, p. 81. (B)
8. Laufer and Schwarz, pp. 76, 81-83. (B)
9. *Ibid.*, p. 83.
10. *Crown*, March 1942.
11. Cochran, p. 112. (B)
12. *Max Henius, a Biography*, p. 44. (B)
13. "St. Louis Business and Industry," p. 158. (C)

14. *Western Brewer*, II, 518.
15. *Ibid.*, IV, 972.
16. *Ibid.*, V, 167.
17. Ruff and Becker, pp. 126-127. (B)
18. *Western Brewer*, XX, 107.
19. Mobile City Directory, 1838.
20. Bottlers' and Soda Manufacturers' Association, Secretary's Records and Minutes. (A)
21. *Western Brewer*, II, 490.
22. *Ibid.*, II, 518.
23. *Ibid.*, III, 135; IV, 329.
24. Nurnberg, p. 1. (C)
25. *Ibid.*, p. 7.
26. *Ibid.*, pp. 11-12.
27. *American Brewer*, XVIII, 1122-1123.
28. Milwaukee *Sentinel*, 5 April 1877.
29. Cincinnati Business Directory, 1882.
30. *History of Milwaukee from Prehistoric Times*, p. 1464. (C)
31. Cochran, p. 123. (B)
32. Milwaukee *Sentinel*, 5 May 1877.
33. American Exposition of Brewing, Official Catalog, Chicago, 1911, p. 162.
34. *Western Brewer*, IV, 1092.
35. Pamphlet published by Anheuser-Busch Brewing Association, circa 1887, to establish its trademark.
36. Dreesbach, pp. 277-278. (B)
37. *Ibid.*, p. 276.
38. Cochran, pp. 126-127. (B)
39. Dreesbach, pp. 278-283. (B)

TWENTY-EIGHT: BEER IN THE WESTERN MINING TERRITORIES

1. Wilhelm. (C)
2. *Rocky Mountain News*, 6 July 1876.
3. *Ibid.*, 22 May 1861.
4. *Ibid.*, 19 April 1959.
5. *Tovey's Official Brewers' and Maltsters' Directory*, 1884, p. 21; *The Brewers Hand-Book*, 1890, p. 37.
6. Denver *Daily Gazette*, April 1866.
7. Denver City Directories.
8. *Rocky Mountain News*, 29 December 1957.
9. Watrous, p. 166. (C)
10. Hall, *History of Colorado*, III, 300. (C)
11. Kortright, p. 73. (C)
12. Ayers, p. 246. (C)
13. *History of Clear Creek and Boulder Valleys*, pp. 558-559. (C)
14. *Colorado Transcript* (Golden), 22 July 1874.
15. Hafen, II, 578 (C); Cornish, p. 180. (C)
16. *Pacific Coast Business Directory*, 1871.
17. *The Brewers Hand-Book*, 1890, p. 131.
18. United States Commissioner of Internal Revenue, *Report for the Fiscal Year ended June 30, 1892*, pp. 370-371.
19. Pamphlet issued by the Kessler Brewing Co. in 1952.
20. Interview with Frederick Schmidt, February 1961.
21. *Pacific Coast Business Directory*, 1871.
22. Barney, MSS. (A)

23. Tucson *Citizen*, 20 April 1872.
24. *Salt River Herald*, 28 December 1878.
25. Phoenix *Herald*, 24 May 1879.
26. *Ibid.*, 5 April 1879.
27. *Ibid.*, 3 May 1879.
28. *Ibid.*, 24 September 1879.
29. *Arizona Republican*, 2 August 1911.
30. *Arizona Democrat*, 1 August 1911.
31. *Arizona Gazette* (Phoenix), 26 January 1898.
32. Phoenix *Herald*, 26 January 1898.
33. *Brewery Gulch Gazette* (Special Edition), 1 June 1961, p. 25.
34. *Ibid.*, p. 10.

TWENTY-NINE: THE NATIONAL BREWERIES

1. United States Brewers Foundation, *The Brewing Industry in the U.S.: Brewers Almanac*, 1960, p. 10. (B)
2. Cochran, p. 73. (B)
3. Ehret, p. 51. (B)
4. Cochran, p. 180. (B)
5. *Crown*, March 1942, p. 25.
6. Krebs and Orthwein, p. 22. (B)
7. *Western Brewer*, XLVI, 171.
8. *Ibid.*, XL, 73.
9. *Ballantine's Breweries* (Brochure published by the company).
10. Pamphlet published by Wm. J. Lemp Brewing Co. in connection with the World's Columbian Exposition, Chicago, 1893.
11. New Orleans *Daily Picayune*, 6 December 1864.
12. Gray and Savage, pp. 88-91. (B)
13. *Daily Rocky Mountain News*, 19 July 1876.
14. Cochran, p. 173. (B)
15. *Texas Gazetteer*, 1884-1885.
16. New Orleans *Daily Picayune*, 1 April 1900; *Western Brewer*, XIX, 1164.
17. *Western Brewer*, II, 48.
18. Cochran, pp. 162-163. (B)
19. *American Brewer*, XVIII, 1039.
20. Krebs and Orthwein, p. 42. (B)
21. Philipp Papers. (A)
22. Adams & Hudson, Account Books. (A)
23. Homer & Palmer, Account Books. (A)
24. *Western Brewer*, I, 18.
25. *Budcaster* (Anheuser-Busch Brewing Co. house organ), March 1954.
26. *Western Brewer*, XVIII, 322.
27. American Exposition of Brewing, *Official Catalog*, Chicago, 1911, p. 168.
28. Cochran, p. 177. (B)
29. *Western Brewer*, XXIX, 543.
30. *Ibid.*, XXIX, 30.
31. Information from Sicks' Rainier Brewing Co., Seattle.
32. Information from the Pearl Brewing Co., San Antonio.
33. *Western Brewer*, III, 219, 423, 660.
34. *American Brewer*, XXVI, 583.
35. *Western Brewer*, XVIII, 111.
36. Harvey, p. 99. (C)
37. Catalogue of the Lewis and Clark Centennial Exposition, 1905.
38. *Brewers Journal*, XXX, 186.

39. Busch to Francis, 1902. Francis Papers. (A)
40. *American Brewer*, XXIX, 489.
41. *Ibid.*, XXIX, 77-78, 483, 501.

THIRTY: CONSOLIDATIONS AND SYNDICATES

1. Cochran, pp. 59-61. (B)
2. *Western Brewer*, II, 520.
3. *Ibid.*, III, 36.
4. Interview with John Gardiner, Jr., C. Schmidt & Sons Brewing Co., Philadelphia.
5. Interview with Datus Proper, Pearl Brewing Co., San Antonio, Texas.
6. *American Brewer*, XXVIII, 233.
7. *The Brewers and Texas Politics*, II, 1209. (B)
8. *The Brewers' Hand Book* (Supplement to *Western Brewer*), 1913, p. 63.
9. *Western Brewer*, XXVII, 116.
10. *Ibid.*, XXVII, 122.
11. *Southern Brewer and Bottler*, 10 April 1897; *One Hundred Years*, p. 526. (B)
12. *One Hundred Years*, p. 528. (B)
13. *The Brewers' Hand Book*, 1913, p. 23.
14. *Southern Brewer and Bottler*, 10 April 1897.
15. Seattle *Times*, 26 October 1950; Bagley, pp. 627, 1123. (C)
16. Seattle *Times*, 26 October 1950.
17. Bagley, p. 627. (C)
18. Information from Frederick W. Schmidt.
19. *Western Brewer*, XXIV, 34.
20. *Ibid.*, XVIII, 827.
21. *Ibid.*, IV, 1089.
22. *Der Amerikanische Bierbrauer*, XXI, 344.
23. *Western Brewer*, XVII, 2497.
24. Dulles, *The U.S. since 1865*, p. 45. (C)
25. United States Senate, 66th Congress, 1st Session, *Prohibiting Intoxicating Beverages*, Part 3, pp. 224-225. (C)
26. *Western Brewer*, XIV, 2248.
27. *Der Amerikanische Bierbrauer*, XXI, 279.
28. *American Brewer*, XXVIII, 631.
29. Cochran, pp. 153-159 (B); Pierce, III, 150. (C)
30. Cochran, p. 152 (B); Krebs and Orthwein, p. 24. (B)
31. *Western Brewer*, XVI, 1637.
32. United States Commissioner of Internal Revenue, *Annual Report*, 1901, pp. 442-443.
33. *American Brewer*, XXVIII, 631.
34. *Western Brewer*, XVII, pp. 1073, 1529; Cochran, p. 146. (B)
35. *Western Brewer*, XVII, pp. 2033, 2271.
36. *Ibid.*, XVIII, 109.
37. New Orleans *Times-Democrat*, 26 February, 27 April, 2 June 1890.
38. Pittsburgh Brewing Co., real estate and equipment ledger. (MS in archives of Pittsburgh Brewing Co.).
39. Pittsburgh *Bulletin Index*, 30 October 1941.
40. *Western Brewer*, February 1917, p. 53.
41. "The Brotherly Brewers," *Fortune*, April 1950, p. 101.
42. Cochran, pp. 143, 145. (B)
43. Scrap book of Erwin C. Uihlein.
44. Cochran, p. 198. (B)
45. Keitel. (B)
46. *Western Brewer*, XVII, 2033.

THIRTY-ONE: ORGANIZATION OF LABOR

1. United States Brewers' Association, *Year Book*, 1910, p. 19. (B)
2. Commons, *History of Labour*, I, 108-109, 169. (C)
3. *Ibid.*, I, 575.
4. Schlüter, p. 96. (B)
5. *Ibid.*, p. 97.
6. Commons, *History of Labour*, II, 86. (C)
7. Dulles, *The U.S. since 1865*, pp. 76-77. (C)
8. Schlüter, p. 112. (B)
9. Dulles, *The U.S. since 1865*, pp. 77-82. (C)
10. Schlüter, p. 89. (B)
11. Sandman & Lackman Co., Account Book. (A)
12. Cochran, p. 271. (B)
13. Weinhard, Account Books, 1858. (A)
14. Letter from Frederick Miller to relatives in Germany, July 1879 (Archives of Miller Brewing Co., Milwaukee).
15. United States Bureau of the Census, *Historical Statistics of the U.S., 1789-1945*, p. 70. (C)
16. Schlüter, p. 93. (B)
17. United States Bureau of the Census, *Historical Statistics of the U.S., 1789-1945*, p. 68. (C)
18. Cochran, p. 272. (B)
19. Schlüter, pp. 92-93, 101. (B)
20. *Ibid.*, p. 99.
21. Dulles, *The U.S. since 1865*, p. 83. (C)
22. Schlüter, pp. 100-101. (B)
23. *Ibid.*, pp. 100-106.
24. *Ibid.*, p. 116.
25. *Ibid.*, p. 117.
26. United States Brewers' Association, *Twenty-Sixth Brewers' Convention*, p. 12. (B)
27. Schlüter, pp. 119-127. (B)
28. United States Brewers' Association, *Year Book*, 1909, p. 19. (B)
29. Dulles, *The U.S. since 1865*, pp. 84-85. (C)
30. Schlüter, pp. 129-132, 135, 212. (B)
31. *Ibid.*, pp. 146-148.
32. United States Brewers' Association, *Twenty-Eighth Brewers' Convention*, p. 19. (B)
33. St. Louis *Republic*, 12 July 1889.
34. Schlüter, p. 150. (B)
35. *Western Brewer*, XIV, 95.
36. Schlüter, pp. 157-158. (B)
37. Document in archives of the Blitz-Weinhard Brewing Co., Portland, Oregon.
38. United States Bureau of the Census, *Historical Statistics of the U.S., 1789-1945*, pp. 67-68. (C)
39. United States Senate, 65th Congress, *Brewing and Liquor Interests and German Propaganda*, I, 84. (B)
40. *Ibid.*, p. 85.
41. Schlüter, pp. 220-221, 226-227. (B)

THIRTY-TWO: THE BREWING DYNASTIES AND THEIR ENEMIES

1. Anti-Saloon League *Year Book*, 1909, p. 5.
2. Odegard, p. 6. (C)

3. Merz, p. 3. (C)
4. United States Brewers' Association, *Twenty-Ninth Brewers' Convention*, p. 10. (B)
5. United States Brewers' Association, *Brewers' Almanac, 1960*, p. 10. (B)
6. *Western Brewer*, XXIX, 16.
7. Cochran, p. 425. (B)
8. *Western Brewer*, XXIX, 116.
9. Cochran, p. 262. (B)
10. *Brewer and Maltster*, April 1937, p. 20.
11. Fiftieth Anniversary publication of Jackson Brewing Co., "Jax Golden Jubilee," 1940.
12. Information from Miller Brewing Co., Milwaukee.
13. Information from Liebmann Breweries, Brooklyn.
14. "The Brotherly Brewers," p. 188; also information from Liebmann Breweries.
15. *Brewers Digest*, September 1954, pp. 42-47.
16. *Oregonian*, Souvenir issue, 1 October 1892; *History of the Columbia River Valley*, III, 782. (C)
17. *Brewers Journal*, 15 August 1941, pp. 41-43.
18. Milwaukee *Journal*, 1 March 1931.
19. Information from Jos. Schlitz Brewing Co., Milwaukee.
20. Tilton, pp. 13, 57. (C)
21. Letter and clipping in Taft Papers. (A)
22. National Anti-Saloon Convention, 1896, *Proceedings*.
23. Anti-Saloon League of America, Twelfth Convention, 1907, *Proceedings*, p. 10.
24. United States Brewers' Association, *Year Book*, 1909, pp. 147-159. (B)
25. Odegard, pp. 39-48. (C)
26. *Ibid.*, pp. 130-132.
27. Milwaukee *Sentinel*, 17 June 1861.
28. United States Brewers' Association, *Twenty-Eighth Brewers' Convention*, 1888, p. 42.
29. United States Brewers' Association, *Thirtieth Brewers' Convention*, 1890, p. 40.
30. "Adulteration of Malt Liquors," Hearing before the Committee on Ways and Means on H.R. 8522, defining Lager Beer, etc., p. 146.
31. United States Brewers' Association, *Thirty-Eighth Brewers' Convention*, 1898, p. 18.
32. United States Senate, 56th Congress, 1st Session, Report No. 516, *Adulteration of Food Products*, p. vi.
33. United States Brewers' Association, *Forty-Third Brewers' Convention*, 1903, p. 54.
34. United States Brewers' Association, *Thirty-Eighth Brewers' Convention*, 1898, pp. 13-14.
35. *Ibid.*, p. 16.
36. *Western Brewer*, XXIII, 1247.
37. *Ibid.*, XXIV, 115.
38. United States Brewers' Foundation, *Brewers Almanac*, 1960, p. 10. (B)
39. *Western Brewer*, XXIV, 341.
40. United States Brewers' Foundation, *Brewers Almanac*, 1960, p. 10. (B)
41. *Western Brewer*, XXVI, 299.
42. Roosevelt, IV, 1300-1301. (C)

THIRTY-THREE: VICTORY OF THE DRYS

1. Leech, p. 13. (C)
2. Quoted in *Western Brewer*, XII, 1499.

3. Roosevelt, VI, 1131. (C)
4. *Ibid.*, I, 464.
5. *American Brewer*, XXVIII, 393-394.
6. *Ibid.*, XXVIII, 588.
7. Roosevelt, III, 120. (C)
8. *Ibid.*, IV, 897.
9. *Ibid.*, VII, 773.
10. *Ibid.*, VIII, 927.
11. Odegard, p. 89. (C)
12. Steuart, pp. 67-68. (C)
13. H. C. Stunts to Taft, 5 September 1911, Taft Papers. (A)
14. Ferd. C. Iglehart to C. Hillis, 5 September 1911, Taft Papers. (A)
15. C. D. Hillis to Rev. P. A. Baker, 8 September 1911, Taft Papers. (A)
16. J. Wilson to Taft, 21 October 1911, Taft Papers. (A)
17. Odegard, pp. 145-146, 151, 155. (C)
18. Steuart, p. 144. (C)
19. Odegard, pp. 159-161. (C)
20. *Ibid.*, p. 163.
21. United States Brewers' Association, Fifty-second Convention, *Year Book and Proceedings*, pp. 3-4. (B)
22. United States Brewers' Association, *Year Book, 1915*, p. 2. (B)
23. *The Brewers and Texas Politics.* (B)
24. Odegard, pp. 182-186. (C)
25. *Western Brewer*, XLIV, 97-98.
26. Odegard, pp. 249-256. (C)
27. *Ibid.*, pp. 166-167.
28. Steuart, pp. 103-105. (C)
29. *Repeal Review*, June 1945.
30. Odegard, pp. 169-170. (C)
31. *Ibid.*, pp. 172-174.
32. Singer, p. 188. (C)
33. *Brewers Journal*, XLI, 35, 296.
34. *Ibid.*, XLI, 378, 380.
35. Steuart, pp. 121-122. (C)
36. United States Senate, 65th Congress, 2nd Session, *Brewing and Liquor Interests and German Propaganda*, I, 28-29. (B)
37. *Western Brewer*, LI, 101.
38. *Ibid.*, LI, 151.
39. Merz, p. 49. (C)

THIRTY-FOUR: THE UNPOPULAR LAW

1. Merz, p. 40. (C)
2. Krout, p. 302. (C)
3. *Western Brewer*, XLIX, 148.
4. *Brewers Journal*, XLI, 309.
5. United States Brewers' Association, *Year Book, 1919*, p. 50. (B)
6. United States Senate, 66th Congress, 1st Session, *Prohibiting Intoxicating Beverages*, Part 3, pp. 232, 334-341. (C)
7. United States Brewers' Association, *Year Book, 1919*, p. 23. (B)
8. *Repeal Review*, X, No. 2, 23, 24.
9. Nowak, *New Fields for Brewers*, pp. 7-8. (B)
10. *Brewers Journal*, XLI, 295.
11. Nowak, *New Fields for Brewers*, pp. 38 ff. (B)
12. Griesedieck, *The Falstaff Story*, p. 26. (B)

13. *Western Brewer*, LIII, 30, 77.
14. United States Treasury Department, Bureau of Industrial Alcohol, *Statistics Concerning Intoxicating Liquors, December 1932*, p. 126. (C)
15. *American Brewer*, XL, 1.
16. Scrapbook of Erwin C. Uihlein.
17. *Western Brewer*, LII, 25.
18. *Ibid.*, LIII, 31, 32, 76.
19. *American Brewer*, XL (1922), 114.
20. *Ibid.*, pp. 142, 162, 170-171, 186, 211, 282.
21. *Ibid.*, p. 275.
22. United States Treasury Department, Bureau of Industrial Alcohol, *Statistics Concerning Intoxicating Liquors, December, 1932*, p. 134. (C)
23. Merz, p. 127. (C)
24. *Ibid.*, pp. 90-91.
25. *Repeal Review*, June 1945, p. 25.
26. *Ibid.*, pp. 27-28.
27. *Ibid.*, pp. 26, 30.
28. Merz, p. 250. (C)
29. *Repeal Review*, June 1945, pp. 23-24, 27.
30. United States Senate, 69th Congress, 1st Session, *The National Prohibition Law*, II, 1588. (C)
31. Merz, p. 224. (C)
32. Dobyns, pp. 4-5. (C)
33. *Annals of the American Academy of Political and Social Science*, CLXIII (1932), 177.
34. Merz, p. 213. (C)
35. *Repeal Review*, June 1945, p. 31.
36. *Annals of the American Academy of Political and Social Science*, CLXIII (1932), 172.
37. *American Mercury*, XVI (1929), p. 151.
38. *Repeal Review*, June 1945, p. 30.
39. Gordon, *Wrecking of the Eighteenth Amendment*, p. 194. (C)
40. Fosdick and Scott, p. vii. (C)
41. *American Mercury*, XXV, 385.
42. United States House of Representatives, Committee on Ways and Means, 72nd Congress, 2nd Session, *Modification of Volstead Act*, p. 1. (C)
43. *Ibid.*, p. 229.
44. *Ibid.*, p. 526.
45. *Repeal Review*, June 1945, p. 32.
46. *American Brewer*, April 1933, p. 10.
47. *Ibid.*, p. 7.

THIRTY-FIVE: AFTER REPEAL

1. Griesedieck, *The Falstaff Story*, p. 106. (B)
2. United States Brewers Foundation, *Brewers Almanac*, 1960, p. 90. (B)
3. United States Brewers' Association, Fifty-Eighth Convention, *Proceedings*, p. 10. (B)
4. United States Brewers Foundation, *Brewers Almanac*, 1960, p. 17. (B)
5. *Brewer and Maltster*, 15 August 1917, p. 30.
6. United States Department of Commerce, Bureau of the Census, *Abstract of the Census of Manufactures*, 1919, p. 158; *Biennial Census of Manufactures*, 1931, p. 46. (C)
7. United States Department of Commerce, Bureau of the Census, *1958 Census of Manufactures* (Beverages, Industry Report MC58(2)-20G), p. 11. (C)

8. United States Brewers' Association, *Colonel Ruppert Looks at 1935*, p. 2. (B)
9. Quoted in *Western Brewer*, January 1933, p. 12.
10. *Ibid.*, April 1933, p. 35; June 1933, pp. 54-55.
11. United States Brewers' Association, Fifty-Eighth Convention, *Proceedings*, p. 9.
12. *Brewery Age*, January 1935, p. 27.
13. *Brewers Journal*, July 1935, p. 21.
14. U.S. Works Progress Administration, *State Liquor Legislation*, p. 13.
15. United States Brewers Foundation, *Brewers Almanac*, 1960, p. 17.
16. *Brewery Age*, March 1935, p. 85.
17. *Brewers Journal*, July 1935, p. 67; August 1935, p. 88.
18. *Brewery Age*, September 1935, p. 16.
19. United States Brewers' Association, Fifty-Eighth Convention, *Proceedings*, p. 5. (B)
20. *American Brewer*, January 1948, p. 48.
21. United States Brewers' Association, Fifty-Eighth Convention, *Proceedings*, p. 22. (B)
22. Cochran, p. 370. (B)
23. United States Brewers Association, Sixty-First Convention, *Proceedings*, pp. 49, 51. (B)
24. Cochran, p. 371. (B)
25. *Brewers Journal*, November 1935, pp. 40-41.
26. Griesedieck, *The Falstaff Story*, p. 189. (B)
27. *Brewery Age*, March 1936, pp. 11-14.
28. Cochran, p. 371. (B)
29. Griesedieck, *The Falstaff Story*, p. 191. (B)
30. *The Genesis and Execution of the Basic Public Relations Plan of Brewing Industry, Inc.*, p. 1. (Pamphlet in library of U.S. Brewers' Association.)
31. Badenhausen, p. 695. (B)
32. *Business Week*, 1 July 1939.
33. *Brewers Journal*, 15 July 1943, p. 22; 15 August 1940, p. 20.
34. *Ibid.*, 15 July 1940, p. 17; 15 August 1940.
35. *American Brewer*, January 1941, p. 17.
36. *Ibid.*, March 1941, p. 11.
37. United States Brewers Association, Sixty-Sixth Annual Meeting, *Proceedings*, pp. 40-41. (B)
38. *American Brewer*, March 1942, p. 13.
39. *Ibid.*, February 1942, pp. 25-26.
40. Texarkana *Gazette*, 1 June 1941.
41. *American Brewer*, January 1943, Supplement 1.
42. *Ibid.*, Supplement 3.
43. *Ibid.*, p. 42.
44. New York *Herald Tribune*, 15 January 1945.
45. *Brewers Almanac*, 1960, 1949.
46. *American Brewer*, May 1942, p. 9.
47. Griesedieck, "Beer and Brewing in a Nation at War," p. 300. (B)
48. United States Brewers Association, Sixty-Seventh Annual Meeting, *Proceedings*, p. 81. (B)
49. *American Brewer*, August 1943, p. 15.
50. United States Brewers Association, *Brewers Almanac*, 1960, p. 10.
51. United States Brewers Foundation, Seventieth Annual Meeting, 1946, *Proceedings*, p. 11.

THIRTY-SIX: NEW DIRECTIONS

1. United States Treasury Department, Internal Revenue Service, *Statistics Relating to the Alcohol and Tobacco Industries, Fiscal Year Ended June 30, 1960,* p. 40. (C)
2. United States Brewers Foundation, Seventieth Annual Meeting, 1946, *Proceedings,* p. 21.
3. Information from Theo. Hamm Brewing Co.
4. *American Brewer,* April 1937, p. 51; *Brewery Age,* January 1936, p. 73; October 1936, p. 85.
5. United States Department of Commerce, *Census of Manufactures: 1939,* II, 220; 1947, II, 132. (C)
6. *Ibid.,* 1947, pp. 159-166.
7. *Brewers Journal,* 15 July 1943, p. 22.
8. Griesedieck, *The Falstaff Story,* p. 138. (B)
9. *Ibid.,* p. 159.
10. Cochran, pp. 364, 376-377. (B)
11. Griesedieck, *The Falstaff Story,* pp. 163-166. (B)
12. *American Brewer,* March 1949, p. 10.
13. *Ibid.,* June 1954, p. 34.
14. *Advertising Age,* 16 January 1961, pp. 3, 67.
15. *Brewers Digest,* January 1954, pp. 55, 58.
16. *Ibid.,* p. 49.
17. Report to the Stockholders of Peerless Motor Car Corporation, 12 September 1933 (Archives of the Carling Brewing Co., Cleveland).
18. *Modern Brewery Age,* June 1961, pp. 44-45.
19. *Fortune,* August 1959, p. 168.
20. *Industrial Development,* October 1959.
21. United States Brewers Association, *Brewers Almanac,* 1960, p. 23. (B)
22. Information on firms from *American Brewer, Directory of Breweries,* 1960-1961; *Modern Brewery Age,* Blue Book Issue, March 1961.
23. United States Brewers Foundation, 74th Annual Meeting, *Report to Members,* p. 71. (B)
24. United States Brewers Association, *Brewers Almanac,* 1960, pp. 107-108. (B)
25. United States Brewers Foundation, Ninety-Eighth Convention, 1960, *Proceedings,* p. 18. (B)

Bibliography

A. UNPUBLISHED MATERIALS

Adams & Hudson, advertising agents, Boston. Account Books. (Baker Library, Harvard Graduate School of Business Administration).

Adams, Samuel. Papers. (New York Public Library).

Allen Family Papers, 1850-1910. (Virginia Historical Society).

Atlee, Samuel. Petition to General Assembly, New York State, April Term, 1795. (United States Brewers Association, Inc.).

Barney, James J. Manuscripts. (Arizona State Department of Library and Archives).

[Boston] Ledger of Exchange Coffee House. (Baker Library, Harvard Graduate School of Business Administration).

Bottlers' and Soda Manufacturers' Association. Secretary's Records and Minutes. Boston, 1866-1873. (Baker Library, Harvard Graduate School of Business Administration).

Brown Family Papers. (John Carter Brown Library).

Burkholder, Jonathan S., brewer, Smithville (Wayne Co.), Ohio. Business letters, 1882-1900. (Ohio Historical Society Library, Columbus).

Carroll, Charles, of Carrollton. Account book, 1735-1759. (Library of Congress).

Carter Family Papers. (Virginia Historical Society).

Clarke, Joseph. Letters. (Rhode Island State Archives, Providence).

Eagle, John H. Letters. (Henry E. Huntington Library).

Faneuil, Peter. Daybook. (Baker Library, Harvard Graduate School of Business Administration).

————. Letter Book. (Baker Library, Harvard Graduate School of Business Administration).

Faulkner, William D. Account books, 1772-1790. 3 vols. (New-York Historical Society).

Fort Augusta, Pennsylvania. Quartermaster's Ledger. (American Philosophical Society, Philadelphia).

Francis, David R. Papers. (Missouri Historical Society).

Franklin, Benjamin. Papers. (American Philosophical Society, Philadelphia).

Hab, Victor. Naturalization request paper (n.d.). (Missouri Historical Society).

————. Property in sheriff's sale, 10 December 1828. (Missouri Historical Society).

Hale, William, Jr., Tyringham, Mass., merchant. Account Book. (New York Public Library).

Hancock Family Manuscripts. (Baker Library, Harvard Graduate School of Business Administration).

Herancourt, George. Diary. (Historical and Philosophical Society of Ohio, University of Cincinnati).

Herring, John. Autobiography. (New-York Historical Society).

Homer & Palmer, Advertising agents, Boston. Account books. (Baker Library, Harvard Graduate School of Business Administration).

Hortiz, Joseph. Account with J. Coppinger, St. Louis, October 1807. (P. Chouteau Moffitt Collection, Missouri Historical Society).

Hull, John. Account Books of General Store Boston, 1685-1689, shop of John Hull, managed by Samuel Sewall, son-in-law. (Baker Library, Harvard Graduate School of Business Administration).

Jefferson, Thomas. Account Books. (New York Public Library).

———. Papers. (Library of Congress, Massachusetts Historical Society).

Jerdone, Francis. Letterbook. (William and Mary College Archives).

Judd, Jonathan, Jr., storekeeper & merchant, Southampton, Mass. Day Book. (Baker Library, Harvard Graduate School of Business Administration).

Larer, Melchior and John. Receipt Book, 1815-20. (Historical Society of Pennsylvania).

Lemp Family Papers. (Missouri Historical Society).

Lloyd, Henry, victualler, Boston. Letter book. (Baker Library, Harvard Graduate School of Business Administration).

Manning, William, tavern keeper, Billerica, Mass. Record Book. (Baker Library, Harvard Graduate School of Business Administration).

McHose & English, St. Louis brewers. Receipt. (Missouri Historical Society).

Naso [pseudonym] Recipe for pumpkin ale. February 1771. (American Philosophical Society, Philadelphia).

New Jersey [Colony] An Act appointing Commissioners for Supplying the several Barracks erected in the Colony of New Jersey . . . December 6, 1769. (United States Brewers Association, Inc.).

Non-Importation Agreements. (American Philosophical Society, Philadelphia).

Ogden, W. B. Letter Book. (Chicago Historical Society).

O'Hara Papers. (Historical Society of Western Pennsylvania, Pittsburgh).

Orn, James, Captain: Disbursements for ship *Nancy*. (Boston). (Baker Library, Harvard Graduate School of Business Administration).

Paschall, Thomas. Accounts, 1713-1728. (Historical Society of Pennsylvania).

———. Papers 1705-1711. (Historical Society of Pennsylvania).

Penn Papers. (Historical Society of Pennsylvania).

Perot, T. Morris. Letter to Wm. P. Smith, Philadelphia, March 22, 1933. (Historical Society of Pennsylvania).

[Philadelphia] Brewery Ledgers, 1733-35. (Historical Society of Pennsylvania).

Philipp, Emanuel Lorenz (1861-1925)—33rd Governor of Wisconsin. Papers, 1887-1925. (Wisconsin Historical Society, Madison).

Reed, Benjamin T. Invoice of Merchandise shipped by Benjamin T. Reed. 20 September 1843. (California Historical Society).

Rhode Island. Confiscated Estates.
        Land Evidences.
        Law Cases.
        Petitions to the General Assembly.
   (Rhode Island State Archives, Providence).

de St. Vrain, Jacques Delassus. Will: November 1804. (Missouri Historical Society).

Ste. Genevieve Archives, Wills No. 38. Will of Michel Livernois, 28 December 1779. (Missouri Historical Society).

Sandman & Lackman Brewery, 1855-1858. Account Book. (Historical and Philosophical Society of Ohio, University of Cincinnati).

Sharswood, William. Account Book, Oct. 1811 to June 1812. (Historical Society of Pennsylvania).

Taft, William H. Papers. (Library of Congress).

Tayloe Family Papers (Mount Airy). Minute Book, 1805-55. (Virginia Historical Society).

Tibbetts, Henry. Ledger. (Baker Library, Harvard Graduate School of Business Administration).

Vassar Family Papers. (Adriance Memorial Library, Poughkeepsie).
Vaughan Papers. (American Philosophical Society, Philadelphia).
Washington, George. Ledgers A and B. (Library of Congress).
———. Note Book, 1757. (New York Public Library).
Weinhard, Henry. Day Book and Account Book. (Archives of Blitz-Weinhard Brewing Co.).
Wiley, Harvey W. Papers. (Library of Congress).
Wilt, Christian. Letter Book. (Missouri Historical Society).
Zoar Society, sometimes called Society of Separatists. Zoar (Tuscarawas Co.), Ohio. Account Books, 1830-1900. (Ohio Historical Society Library, Columbus).

B. BOOKS AND ARTICLES DEALING WITH BREWING

American Brewing Academy, Chicago. Tenth anniversary reunion, alumni and former students. Chicago, 1901.
American Burtonizing Co. *Brewing Water, Its Defects and Their Remedy*. New York, c. 1909.
———. *The Treatment of Brewing Waters in the Light of Modern Physical Chemistry*. New York, c. 1913.
Arnold, John P. *History of the Brewing Industry and Brewing Science in America*. Begun by John P. Arnold; completed by Frank Penman. Chicago, 1933. (Prepared as Part of a Memorial to the Pioneers of American Brewing Science —Dr. John E. Siebel and Anton Schwarz.)
———. *Origin and History of Beer and Brewing*. Chicago, 1911.
The Art of Brewing on Scientific Principles . . . London, n.d.
Augenstein, Moritz. *Augenstein's Manual for Brewers and Distillers*. Washington, D.C., 1872.
Bacon, J. Burnitz. "Lager Beer in America." *Frank Leslie's Popular Monthly*, August 1882, vol. 14, no. 2.
Badenhausen, Carl W. "Self-Regulation in the Brewing Industry." *Law and Contemporary Problems*, vol. 7.
Bailey, R. Douglas. *The Brewer's Analyst*. London, 1907.
Baverstock, James H. *Treatises on Brewing* . . . *and on Malting*. London, 1824.
Beer in Britain. [Compiled from a special supplement of *The Times*, April 1958.] London, 1960.
Bickerdyke, John (pseud. of Charles Henry Cook). *The Curiosities of Ale and Beer*. London, 1886.
Black, William. *A Practical Treatise on Brewing*. London, 1875.
Brande, W. *The Town and Country Brewery Book*. London, 1840.
Brasenose Ale: A Collection of Verses annually presented on Shrove Tuesday, by the Butler of Brasenose College, Oxford. Boston, England, 1878. (Printed for Private Circulation by Robert Roberts.)
The Brewer, Distiller, and Wine Manufacturer. London, 1883.
The Brewers and Texas Politics. 2 vols. San Antonio, 1916.
The Brewing and Malting Industry of Chicago. Chicago, 1882.
Brown, Adrian John. *Laboratory Studies for Brewing Students*. London, 1904.
Brown, B. Meredith. *The Brewer's Art*. London, 1948.
Buchner, John. "California Steam Beer." *Western Brewer*, vol. 23.
Byrn, Marcus Lafayette. *The Complete Practical Brewer*. Philadelphia, 1852.
Campbell, Andrew. *The Book of Beer*. London, 1956.
Chapman, Alfred Chaston. *Brewing*. Cambridge, Eng., 1912.
Cochran, Thomas C. *The Pabst Brewing Company, The History of an American Business*. New York, 1948.
Combrune, Michael. *The Theory and Practice of Brewing*. London, 1762.
Coppinger, Joseph. *The American Practical Brewer and Tanner*. New York, 1815.

Dreesbach, Philip. *Beer Bottlers' Handy Book*. Chicago, 1906.

Edwardson, John R. "Hops — Their Botany, History, Production and Utilization." *Economic Botany*, April-June 1952.

Ehret, George. *Twenty-Five Years of Brewing*. New York, 1891.

Emerson, Edward Randolph. *Beverages, Past and Present*. 2 vols. New York, 1908.

"The Family Brewer." *Universal Magazine*, January-April 1748.

Feuchtwanger, Lewis. *Fermented Liquors: A Treatise on Brewing, Distilling and Rectifying* . . . New York, 1867.

Forty Years A-Brewing. New York, 1950. (Privately printed by Wallerstein Company, Inc.).

Foy, C. F. *The Principles and Practice of Ale, Beer and Stout Bottling*. London, 1955.

Gallobelgicus (pseud.). "*Wine, Beere, Ale, and Tobacco*: A Seventeenth Century Interlude." [Printed 1630.] Ed. by James Holly Hanford. In *Studies in Pholology*, vol. 12.

Gocar, Marcel. *Formulaire Technique & Technologique du Brasseur-Malteur*. Brussels, 1949.

Gray, Barry, and John Savage. *Ale in Prose and Verse*. New York, 1866.

Griesedieck, Alvin. "Beer and Brewing in a Nation at War." *Quarterly Journal of Studies on Alcohol*, vol. 3.

——. *The Falstaff Story*. Privately printed, 1951.

Hackwood, Frederick W. *Inns, Ales, and Drinking Customs of Old England*. London, 1909.

Ham, John. *The Theory and Practice of Brewing from Malted and Unmalted Corn, and from Potatos*. London, 1829.

Haring, Frank. *Knowing Alcoholic Beverages*. New York, 1954.

Hayman, E. N. *A Practical Treatise to Render the Art of Brewing More Easy*. London, 1819.

A History of the Brewery and Liquor Industry of Rochester, N. Y. Rochester, 1907.

Hopkins, Reginald Haydn, and B. Krause. *Biochemistry Applied to Malting and Brewing*. New York, 1937.

How to Carve, Serve a Dinner, and Brew. [Norman Munro's Ten Cent Handy Books, No. 15. New York, n.d.]

Hughes, E. *A Treatise on the Brewing of Beer*. London, 1796.

Importance of the Brewery. Edinburgh, 1770.

In Praise of Ale. Collected and arranged by W. T. Marchant. London, 1888.

Jörgensen, Alfred. "Hansen's System of Pure Yeast Culture in English Top-Fermentation," *American Brewer*, vol. 27.

Keitel, Adolph. *Government by the Brewers?* Chicago, 1918.

Kimball, Marie. "Some Genial Old Drinking Customs." *William and Mary College Quarterly*, Third Series, vol. 2.

Krebs, Roland, and Percy J. Orthwein. *Making Friends is Our Business: 100 Years of Anheuser-Busch*. Privately printed, c. 1953.

Laufer, Stephen, and Robert Schwarz. *Yeast Fermentation and Pure Culture Systems*. New York, 1936.

Lichtenberg, Bernard. *The Genesis and Execution of the Basic Public Relations Plan of Brewing Industry, Inc*. August 1938.

The London and Country Brewer. London, 1759.

Lovibond, Thomas Watson. *Brewing with Raw Grain*. London, 1883.

Mathias, Peter. *The Brewing Industry in England, 1700-1830*. Cambridge, Eng., 1959.

Matthews, Charles George, and Francis Edward Lott. *The Microscope in the Brewery and Malt-House*. London, 1889.

Max Henius: A Biography. Chicago, 1937.

McCulloch, John. *Distillation, Brewing and Malting.* San Francisco, 1867.

Meeker, E. *Hop Culture in the United States.* Puyallup, Washington Territory, 1883.

Morewood, Samuel. *A Philosophical and Statistical History of the Inventions and Customs of Ancient and Modern Nations in the Manufacture and Use of Inebriating Liquors.* Dublin, 1838.

Moritz, Edward Ralph, and George Harris Morris. *Text-Book of the Science of Brewing.* London, 1891.

Myrick, Herbert. *The Hop.* Springfield, Mass., 1914.

Nowak, Carl A. *Modern Brewing.* St. Louis, 1934.

———. *New Fields for Brewers.* St. Louis, 1917.

One Hundred Years of Brewing. Chicago and New York, 1903.

Parkes, B. *The Domestic Brewer and Family Wine-Maker.* London, 1821.

Pasteur, Louis. *Etudes sur la Bière.* Paris, 1876.

Peeke, Hewson J. *Americana Ebrietatis.* Privately printed. New York, 1917.

Francis Perot's Sons Malting Co. *The Oldest Business House in America.* Privately printed. Philadelphia, n.d.

Riley, Walter A., Jr. *Brewery By-Products.* London, 1913.

Roman, W., ed. *Yeasts.* The Hague, 1957.

Ross-Mackenzie, John. *A Standard Manual of Brewing and Malting and Laboratory Companion.* London, 1927.

Ruff, Donald G., and Kurt Becker. *Bottling and Canning of Beer.* Chicago, 1955.

"The St. Louis Brewing Industry After a Fifty Year Development Period." St. Louis *Post-Dispatch*, supplement, 25 December 1949.

Salem, Frederick William. *Beer, its History and its Economic Value as a National Beverage.* Hartford, Conn., 1880.

Scamell, George. *Breweries and Maltings: Their Arrangement, Construction, and Machinery.* London and Edinburgh, 1871.

Schlüter, Hermann. *The Brewing Industry and the Brewery Workers' Movement in America.* Cincinnati, 1910.

Shannon, Robert. *A Practical Treatise on Brewing, Distilling, and Rectification.* London, 1805.

Shih, Ko Ching, and C. Ying Shih. *American Brewing Industry and the Beer Market.* Brookfield, Wisc., 1958.

Shore, A. *A Practical Treatise on Brewing.* London, 1804.

Siebel, J. E. "Historical Outlines of Brewing in the United States." *Western Brewer*, vol. 23.

Stopes, Henry. *Malt and Malting.* London, 1885.

Sykes, Walter J. *The Principles and Practice of Brewing.* London, 1897.

Thausing, Julius E., *et. al. The Theory and Practice of the Preparation of Malt and the Fabrication of Beer.* Philadelphia, 1882.

[Thomann, Gallus]. *American Beer.* New York, 1909.

Thomson, Thomas. *Brewing and Distillation.* Edinburgh, 1849.

Tizard, W. L. *The Theory and Practice of Brewing.* London, 1843.

The Town and Country Brewery Book. London, 1840.

Travers, George W. *A Century of Brewing, Hudson Ales, and the Evans' Brewery.* New York, 1886.

Tuck, John. *The Private Brewer's Guide to the Art of Brewing Ale and Porter.* London, 1822.

United States Brewers Association (United States Brewers Foundation). *The Brewing Industry in The United States: Brewers Almanac.* New York, 1940, 1944, 1946, 1949, ———.

———. *Colonel Ruppert Looks at 1935.* Brewers' Educational Service Bulletin No. 3. New York, 1934.

———. *Convention Proceedings*. New York, 1862 ———.

———. *Documentary History of the United States Brewers' Association*. Parts I and II. New York, 1896-1898.

———. *Year Book of the United States Brewers' Association*. New York, 1909-1921.

United States Brew-Masters Association. *Souvenir of the 20th Annual Convention*. Albany, 21-23 September 1908.

United States Senate. 56th Congress, 1st Session. *Adulteration of Food Products*. Report No. 516. Washington, 1900.

———. 65th Congress. 2nd Session. Hearings Before the Sub-committee on the Judiciary. *Brewing and Liquor Interests and German Propaganda*. 3 vols. Washington, 1919.

Vaizey, John. *The Brewing Industry 1886-1951*. London, 1960.

Wahl, Robert, and Max Henius. *American Handy Book of the Brewing Malting and Auxiliary Trades*. 3rd ed. 2 vols. Chicago, 1908.

Wallace, A. P. (pseud. of Vrest Orton). *Proceedings of the Company of Amateur Brewers*. Privately printed for members of the Company, 1932.

Weeks, Morris, Jr. *Beer and Brewing In America*. New York, 1949.

Word for Word, an Encyclopaedia of Beer. Introduction by Ivor Brown. London, 1953.

Worth, W. Y. *Cerevisiarii Comes; or, the New and True Art of Brewing*. London, 1692.

Wright, Herbert Edwards. *A Handy Book for Brewers*. London, 1897.

Wyatt, Francis. "The Influence of Science in Modern Beer Brewing." *Journal of the Franklin Institute*. Philadelphia, 1900.

C. GENERAL BOOKS AND ARTICLES

"Account of Servants Bound and Assigned before the Mayor of Philadelphia." *Pennsylvania Magazine of History and Biography*, vols. 31, 32.

Adams, James Truslow, ed. *Album of American History*. 4 vols. New York, 1944.

Adams, James Truslow. *The Founding of New England*. Boston, c. 1921.

Adams, John Quincy. *Report upon Weights and Measures*. Washington, D.C., 1821.

Adams, Leon D. *The Commonsense Book of Drinking*. New York, 1960.

Amherst, Jeffrey. *The Journal of Jeffrey Amherst*. Ed. by J. Clarence Webster. Toronto, c. 1931.

Anderson, Oscar Edward. *Refrigeration in America, a History of a New Technology and its Impact*. Princeton, 1953.

Andreas, A. T. *History of Chicago*. 3 vols. Chicago, 1886.

Andrews, Charles M. "The Boston Merchants and the Non-Importation Movement." Colonial Society of Massachusetts *Publications*, vol. 19.

———. *The Colonial Period of American History*. 4 vols. New Haven, 1934, 1936, 1937.

Angle, Paul M. *The American Reader*. New York, 1958.

Annals of the Early Settlers Association of Cuyahoga County. Cleveland, 1880.

Anti-Saloon League of America. *Proceedings*. Washington, D.C., 1895-1916.

Arnold, Isaac N. *William B. Ogden*. Fergus Historical Series No. 17. Chicago, 1882.

Asbury, Herbert. *The Gangs of New York*. New York, 1928.

Auburn, Wilfred Henry, and Miriam Russell. *This Cleveland of Ours*. 4 vols. Cleveland, 1933.

Avery, Elroy McKendree. *A History of Cleveland and its Environs*. 3 vols. Chicago, 1918.

Ayers, Mary C. "Howardsville in the San Juan." *Colorado Magazine*. vol. 28, No. 4.

Bagley, Clarence B. *History of Seattle*. Chicago, 1916.

Bail, Hamilton Vaughan. *Views of Harvard, A Pictorial Record to 1860.* Cambridge, Mass., 1949.

Bailyn, Bernard. *The New England Merchants in the Seventeenth Century.* Cambridge, Mass., 1955.

Baldwin, Leland D. *Pittsburgh, the Story of a City.* Pittsburgh, 1938.

Bancroft, Hubert Howe. *Works.* 39 vols. San Francisco, 1882-1890.

Barrett, Walter (pseud. of Joseph A. Scoville). *The Old Merchants of New York.* New York, 1885.

Bathe, Greville and Dorothy. *Oliver Evans: A Chronicle of Early American Engineering.* Philadelphia, Historical Society of Pennsylvania, 1935.

Benjamin Franklin on the Art of Eating. Printed for the American Philosophical Society by Princeton University Press, 1958.

Bernhard, Duke of Saxe-Weimar. *Travels through North America 1825-26.* 2 vols. Philadelphia, 1828.

Berthoff, Rowland Tappan. *British Immigrants in Industrial America, 1790-1950.* Cambridge, Mass., 1953.

Betts, Edwin Morris, ed. *Thomas Jefferson's Farm Book.* Princeton, N.J., 1953.

Beverley, Robert. *The History and Present State of Virginia.* Ed. by Louis B. Wright. Chapel Hill, 1947.

Billings, John Davis. *Hardtack and Coffee.* Boston, 1888.

Bishop, John Leander. *A History of American Manufactures from 1608 to 1860.* 3 vols. Philadelphia, 1866.

Bolzius, Johann Martin. "Johann Martin Bolzius Answers a Questionnaire on Carolina and Georgia." *William and Mary College Quarterly,* Third Series, vol. 15.

Bond, Phineas. "Letters of Phineas Bond, British Consul at Philadelphia, to the Foreign Office of Great Britain, 1787-1794." (In American Historical Association *Annual Report,* 1896-1897.)

The Book of Milwaukee: "Feeds and Supplies the World." Milwaukee, 1901.

The Book of Minnesotans. Ed. by Albert Nelson Marquis. Chicago, 1907.

Bordley, John Beale. *Essays and Notes on Husbandry and Rural Affairs.* Philadelphia, 1799.

Boston Directory, 1796. Boston, 1796.

Boston. Record Commissioners. *Boston Records from 1660 to 1701.* Boston, 1881.

———. Second Report. *Boston Town Records, 1634-1660, and the Book of Possessions.* Boston, 1877.

———. *Charlestown Land Records, 1638-1802.* Boston, 1883.

———. *Miscellaneous Papers.* Boston, 1886.

———. 11th Report. *Records of Boston-Selectmen, 1701 to 1715.* Boston, 1884.

———. 29th Report. *A Volume of Records Relating to the Early History of Boston, Containing Miscellaneous Papers.* Boston, 1900.

Boston. *Records of the Suffolk County Court, 1671-1680.* In Colonial Society of Massachusetts *Publications,* vol. 29.

Bottomley, Edwin. *An English Settler in Pioneer Wisconsin: The Letters of Edwin Bottomley, 1842-1850.* Ed. by Milo M. Quaife. State Historical Society of Wisconsin, *Collections,* vol. 25. Madison, 1918.

Bradford, William. *Of Plymouth Plantation.* Ed. by Samuel Eliot Morison. New York, 1952.

Braintree, Mass. *Records of the Town of Braintree.* Ed. by Samuel Austin Bates. Randolph, Mass., 1886.

Brissot de Warville, Jacques Pierre. *New Travels in the United States of America.* 2 vols. London, 1794.

Brodhead, John Romeyn. *Documents Relative to the Colonial History of the State of New York.* Ed. by E. B. O'Callaghan. Albany, 1856.

Brown, Alexander. *The Genesis of the United States.* 2 vols. Boston, 1890.

Browne, William Hand. *Archives of Maryland*. 68 vols. Baltimore, 1883 ——.

Bruce, Philip Alexander. *Economic History of Virginia in the 17th Century*. 2 vols. New York, 1896.

Bruce, William George. *History of Milwaukee-City and County*. Chicago, 1922.

Brunhouse, R. L. "The Effect of the Townshend Acts in Philadelphia." *Pennsylvania Magazine of History and Biography*. vol. 54.

Buck, James S. *Milwaukee Under the Charter*. 4 vols. Milwaukee, 1876-1886.

"The Burghers of New Amsterdam and the Freedmen of New York, 1675-1866." New-York Historical Society *Collections*, vol. 18.

Burlingame, Roger. *The American Conscience*. New York, 1957.

Calverton, Victor Francis. *Where Angels Dared to Tread*. Indianapolis, 1941.

Carey, Mathew. *Address of the Philadelphia Society for the Promotion of National Industry, to the Citizens of the United States*. New Series, No. 2. Philadelphia, 1819.

Carl, Prince of Solms-Braunfels. *Texas, 1844-1845*. Translated from the German. Houston, 1936.

Cherrington, Ernest Hurst. *The Anti-Saloon League Year Book*. Chicago, 1908-1930.

——. *The Evolution of Prohibition in the United States of America*. Westerville, O., 1920.

The City of Cincinnati and its Resources. Cincinnati, 1891.

Clark, Victor S. *History of Manufactures in the United States*. 3 vols. New York, 1929.

Cleland, Robert Glass, ed. *Apron Full of Gold: The Letters of Mary Jane Megquier, 1849-1856*. San Marino, Calif., 1949.

Cobden, Richard. *England, Ireland, and America*. London, 1835.

Cochran, Thomas C., and William Miller. *The Age of Enterprise*. New York, 1942.

Colonial Society of Massachusetts. *Collections*, vols. 15-16. Boston, 1925.

Colorado and Southern Railway. Office Guide 1901-02.

Colton, Julia M. *Annals of Old Manhattan, 1609-1664*. New York, 1901.

Colvin, D. Leigh. *Prohibition in the United States*. New York, 1926.

Commager, Henry Steele, and R. B. Morris, eds. *The Spirit of "Seventy-Six."* 2 vols. Indianapolis, 1958.

Commons, John R., *et al.*, eds. *A Documentary History of American Industrial Society*. 10 vols. Cleveland, 1910-1911.

Commons, John R., *et al. History of Labour in the United States*. 4 vols. New York, 1918-1935.

Cornish, Dudley Taylor. "The First Five Years of Colorado's Statehood, 1876-1881." *Colorado Magazine*, vol. 25, No. 4.

Cox, James. *Old and New St. Louis*. St. Louis, 1894.

Coxe, Daniel. *A Description of the English Province of California, by the Spaniards Call'd Florida, and by the French La Louisiane*. London, 1727. In *Occasional Papers*, Reprint Series No. 11. Sutro Branch, California State Library. San Francisco, 1940.

Coxe, Tench. *An Address to an Assembly of the Friends of American Manufactures*. Philadelphia, 1787.

——. *Observations on the Agriculture, Manufactures and Commerce of the United States*. New York, 1789.

——. *A View of the United States of America*. Philadelphia, 1794.

Craven, Wesley Frank. *Southern Colonies in the Seventeenth Century, 1607-1689*. Vol. 1 of *A History of the South*. Baton Rouge, 1949.

de Crèvecoeur, Michel-Guillaume Jean. (John Hector St. John.) *Letters from an American Farmer*. Originally published 1782. New York, 1904.

Cummings, Richard O. *The American Ice Harvests*. Berkeley, Calif., 1949.

Curtis, Albert. *Fabulous San Antonio*. San Antonio, 1955.

Dabney, Thomas Ewing. *One Hundred Great Years, the Story of the Times-Picayune from its Founding to 1940.* Baton Rouge, 1944.

Dacus, Joseph B., and James W. Buel. *A Tour of St. Louis; or, The Inside Life of a Great City.* St. Louis, 1878.

Dahlinger, Charles William. *Pittsburgh, a Sketch of its Early Social Life.* New York, 1916.

Daniels, Rev. W. H., ed. *The Temperance Reform and Its Great Reformers.* New York, 1878.

Darby, John F. *Personal Recollections.* St. Louis, 1880.

Davidson, Marshall B. *Life in America.* 2 vols. Boston, 1951.

Davis, Andrew McFarland. *John Harvard's Life in America; or, Social and Political Life in New England in 1637-1638.* In Colonial Society of Massachusetts *Publications,* vol. 12. *Transactions 1908-9.* Boston, 1911.

Deane, Samuel. *The New-England Farmer.* Worcester, Mass., 1790.

Depew, Chauncey Mitchell, ed. *One Hundred Years of American Commerce.* 2 vols. New York, 1895.

De Ros, Lt. the Hon. Fred. Fitzgerald, R.N. *Personal Narrative of Travels in the United States and Canada in 1826.* London, 1827.

The Derrick's Hand-book of Petroleum . . . Developments from 1859 to [1899]. Oil City, Pa., 1898-1900.

"Diary of Colonel Landon Carter." *William and Mary College Quarterly,* First Series, vol. 20,

Dickinson, Henry W. *A Short History of the Steam Engine.* New York, 1939.

Dobyns, Fletcher. *The Amazing Story of Repeal: An Exposé of the Power of Propaganda.* Chicago and New York, 1940.

"Donations to Boston During the Siege." Massachusetts Historical Society *Collections,* Second Series, vol. 9.

Donehoo, George Patterson. *Harrisburg, the City Beautiful, Romantic and Historic.* Harrisburg, 1927.

Donehoo, George P., ed. *A History of the Cumberland Valley in Pennsylvania.* 2 vols. Harrisburg, 1930.

———. *Pennsylvania, a History.* Chicago, 1926.

Dorr, Henry Crawford. *The Planting and Growth of Providence.* (Rhode Island Historical Tracts, No. 15.) Providence, 1882.

Dowell, Stephen. *A History of Taxation and Taxes in England.* 4 vols. London, 1888.

Dow, George Francis. *Everyday Life in the Massachusetts Bay Colony.* Boston, 1935.

Drake, Daniel. *Natural and Statistical View, or Picture of Cincinnati.* Cincinnati, 1815.

Dugas, Vera Lea. "Texas Industry, 1860-1880." *Southwestern Historical Quarterly,* vol. 59, No. 2.

Dulles, Foster Rhea. *Labor in America.* New York, 1960.

———. *The United States Since 1865.* Ann Arbor, 1959.

Dunlap, William. *A History of the Rise and Progress of the Arts of Design in the United States.* 3 vols. Boston, 1918.

Earle, Alice Morse. *Home Life in Colonial Days.* New York, 1899.

Eaton, Clement. *A Study of the Southern Confederacy.* New York, 1954.

The Economic History of the United States. 5 vols. New York, 1945-1951.

Eighty Years' Progress of the United States. (Original edition 1861) New York, 1864.

Faulkner, Harold Underwood. *American Economic History.* Eighth edition. New York, [1960].

Faust, Albert Bernhardt. *The German Element in the United States.* 2 vols. New York, 1927.

Fehlandt, August F. *A Century of Drink Reform in the United States*. Cincinnati, 1904.

Fernow, Berthold, ed. *Documents Relative to the History and Settlement of the Towns along the Hudson and Mohawk Rivers*. Albany, 1881.

———. *The Records of New Amsterdam from 1653 to 1674 Anno Domini*. 7 vols. New York, 1897.

The First Century of the Republic. New York, 1876.

Fisher, George. "Narrative of George Fisher." *William and Mary College Quarterly*, First Series, vol. 17.

Fisher, Sydney George. "The Twenty-eight Charges Against the King in the Declaration of Independence." *The Pennsylvania Magazine of History and Biography*, vol. 31.

Fiske, John. *The Dutch and Quaker Colonies in America*. 2 vols. Boston, 1900.

———. *Old Virginia and Her Neighbors*. 2 vols. Boston and New York, 1897.

Flick, Alexander C., ed. *History of the State of New York*. 10 vols. New York, 1932-1937.

"Fort Pitt Account Book, 1765-67." *Western Pennsylvania Historical Magazine*, vol. 29, Nos. 3 and 4.

Fosdick, Raymond B., and Albert L. Scott. *Toward Liquor Control*. New York and London, 1933.

Frantz, Joe B. *Gail Borden, Dairyman to a Nation*. Norman, Oklahoma, 1951.

French, J. H. *Gazetteer of the State of New York*. Syracuse, 1860.

Fritsche, Louis Albert, ed. *History of Brown County, Minnesota*. 2 vols. Indianapolis, 1916.

From Cambridge to Champlain: A Manuscript Diary. Privately printed. Middleboro, Mass., 1957.

Galbreath, Charles Burleigh. *History of Ohio*. 5 vols. Chicago and New York, 1925.

Gallatin, Albert. *Report from the Secretary of the Treasury, on the Subject of American Manufactures*. Boston, 1810.

Gaston, Joseph. *Portland, Oregon, its History and Builders*. 2 vols. Chicago, 1911.

Gazlay, David M. *American Biography for 1861*. San Francisco, 1861.

Georgia. *An Account Showing the Progress of the Colony in Georgia in America from its first Establishment*. (London, 1741). In *The Colonial Records of the State of Georgia*, vol. 3. Atlanta, 1905.

———. *An Impartial Enquiry into the State and Utility of the Province of Georgia*. (London, 1741). In *Occasional Papers*, Reprint Series No. 13. Sutro Branch, California State Library. San Francisco, 1940.

Giedion, Siegfried. *Mechanization Takes Command*. New York, 1948.

Gilbert, Col. F. T. *History of San Joaquin County, California*. Oakland, 1879.

Gillingham, Harrold E. "Pottery, China and Glass Making in Philadelphia." *The Pennsylvania Magazine of History and Biography*, vol. 54.

Gilpin, Joshua. "Journey to Bethlehem, 1802." *Pennsylvania Magazine of History and Biography*, vol. 46.

Goodspeed, Thomas W. "William B. Ogden." *University Record*, New Series, April 1918.

Gordon, Ernest. *The Wrecking of the Eighteenth Amendment*. Francestown, N.H., 1943.

Gordon, Thomas F. *Gazetteer of the State of New York*. Philadelphia, 1836.

Gough, John B. *Autobiography and Personal Recollections of John B. Gough*. Springfield, Mass., 1869.

Graff, Frederick. *Notes upon the Water Works of Philadelphia, 1801-15*. Philadelphia, 1876.

Gray, Lewis Cecil. *History of Agriculture in Southern United States to 1860*. 2 vols. New York, 1941.

Great Britain, Public Record Office. *Calendar of State Papers, Colonial Series* (America and West Indies). London, 1860.

The Great Industries of the United States. Hartford, 1872.

Greeley, Horace. *Art and Industry as Represented in the Exhibition at the Crystal Palace, New York 1853-4.* New York, 1853.

Greve, Charles Theodore. *Centennial History of Cincinnati and Representative Citizens.* 2 vols. Chicago, 1904.

Guyer, I. D. *History of Chicago; its Commercial and Manufacturing Interests and Industry.* Chicago, 1862.

Hacker, Louis M. *The Triumph of American Capitalism.* New York, 1940.

Hafen, Leroy R., ed. *Colorado and Its People.* 4 vols. New York, 1948.

Hall, Clayton Colman, ed. *Narratives of Early Maryland, 1633-1684.* New York, 1910.

Hall, Frank. *History of the State of Colorado.* 4 vols. Chicago, 1891.

Hamilton, Alexander. *Report on the Subject of Manufactures, made the 5th of December 1791.* Philadelphia, 1827.

Hamlin, Paul M., and Charles E. Baker. *Supreme Court of Judicature of the Province of New York, 1691-1704.* 3 vols. New York, 1959.

Hariot, Thomas. *Narrative of the First English Plantation of Virginia.* (First printed in London, 1588) London, 1893.

Harlow, Alvin F. *Old Bowery Days.* New York, 1931.

Harrington, Virginia D. "The Colonial Merchant's Ledger." In Alexander C. Flick, *History of the State of New York.* New York, 1932-37. Vol. 2.

Hart, Albert Bushnell, ed. *Commonwealth History of Massachusetts.* 5 vols. New York, 1927-1930.

Harvey, Mrs. James R. "The Leadville Ice Palace of 1896." *Colorado Magazine,* vol. 17, no. 2.

Hasbrouck, Frank, ed. *The History of Dutchess County, New York.* Poughkeepsie, 1909.

Hatch, Charles E., Jr. "Glassmaking in Virginia, 1607-1625." *William and Mary College Quarterly,* Second Series, vol. 21.

Hawgood, John A. *The Tragedy of German-America.* New York, 1940.

Hazard, Samuel. *Annals of Pennsylvania, 1609-1682.* Philadelphia, 1850.

Hening, William Waller. *Statutes at Large.* 13 vols. New York, 1823.

Higginson, Francis. *New-Englands Plantation.* (Reprint of London, 1630, edition) Salem, Mass., 1908.

Hines, Rev. Harvey K. *An Illustrated History of the State of Oregon.* Chicago, 1893.

———. *An Illustrated History of the State of Washington.* Chicago, 1893.

Historical Souvenir of Eldorado County, California. Oakland, 1883.

History of Clear Creek and Boulder Valleys, Colorado. Chicago, 1880.

History of the Columbia River Valley. 3 vols. Chicago, 1928.

History of Los Angeles County, California. (Originally published 1880) Berkeley, Calif., 1959.

History of Milwaukee, Wisconsin, from Pre-historic Times to the Present Date. Chicago, 1881.

History of Plumas, Lassen and Sierra Counties, California. San Francisco, 1882.

History of Sacramento County, California. Oakland, 1880.

History of St. Paul. St. Paul, 1890.

History of Siskiyou County, California. Oakland, 1881.

History of Sutter County, California. Oakland, 1879.

History of Yuba County, California. Oakland, 1879.

Hittell, John S. *The Commerce & Industries of the Pacific Coast of North America.* San Francisco, 1882.

Hodge, Paul R. *The Steam Engine.* New York, 1840.

Hofstadter, Richard and others. *The United States: The History of a Republic.* Englewood Cliffs, N.J., 1957.

Hollister, Gideon H. *The History of Connecticut.* 2 vols. Hartford, 1857.

Hosmer, James K. *Samuel Adams.* Boston, 1885.

House, Boyce. *City of Flaming Adventure: The Chronicle of San Antonio.* San Antonio, 1949.

Hunt, Herbert. *Tacoma, Its History and Its Builders: A Half Century of Activity.* Chicago, 1916.

Hyde, William, and Howard L. Conard, eds. *Encyclopedia of the History of St. Louis.* 4 vols. St. Louis, 1899.

Industries and Wealth of the Principal Points in Rhode Island. New York, 1892.

Innes, John H. *New Amsterdam and its People.* New York, 1902.

"Isle of Wight County Records." *William and Mary College Quarterly,* First Series, vol. 7.

Jameson, John Franklin, ed. *Narratives of New Netherland, 1609-1664.* New York, 1909.

Jefferson, Thomas. *The Domestic Life of Thomas Jefferson, compiled from Family Letters and Reminiscences by his Great-Granddaughter.* Cambridge, Mass., 1939.

Jewell, Edwin L. *Jewell's Crescent City Illustrated.* New Orleans, 1874.

Jones, Charles C. *History of Georgia.* 2 vols. Boston and New York, 1886.

Jones, Hugh. *The Present State of Virginia.* Ed. by Richard L. Morton. Chapel Hill, 1956.

Jordan, John W. "Moravian Immigration to Pennsylvania 1734-1765." *Pennsylvania Magazine of History and Biography,* vol. 33.

Journals of the Continental Congress, 1774-1789. 34 vols. Washington, 1904-1937.

"The Journey of Francis Louis Michel." *Virginia Magazine of History and Biography,* vol. 24.

Kargau, Ernest D. *Mercantile, Industrial and Professional Saint Louis.* St. Louis, 1902.

Kessler, Henry H., and Eugene Rachlis. *Peter Stuyvesant and His New York.* New York, 1959.

Kimball, Gertrude Selwyn. *Providence in Colonial Times.* Boston, 1912.

Knight, Sarah (Kemble). *The Journal of Madam Knight, on a Journey from Boston to New York in 1704.* New York, 1935.

Knittle, Walter A. *The Early Eighteenth Century Palatine Emigration.* Philadelphia, 1936.

Kortright, S. E. "Historical Sketch of the Bonanza Mining District." *Colorado Magazine,* vol. 22, no. 2.

Kouwenhoven, John A. *Adventures of America, 1857-1900, A Pictorial Record from Harper's Weekly,* New York, 1938.

———. *The Columbia Historical Portrait of New York.* Garden City, N.Y., 1953.

———. *Made in America.* New York, 1948.

Kraus, Michael. *The United States to 1865.* Ann Arbor, 1959.

Krout, John Allen. *The Origins of Prohibition.* New York, 1925.

Land, Jonathan E. *Industries of St. Paul, 1882-3.* St. Paul, 1883.

Langdon, William Chauncy. *Everyday Things in American Life.* 2 vols. New York, 1937-1941.

Leach, Frank Willing. "The Philadelphia of our Ancestors." *North American* (Philadelphia), 19 January 1908, 28 June 1908, 13 December 1908.

Leech, Margaret. *In the Days of McKinley.* New York, 1959.

"Letter of Sir Francis Wyatt, Governor of Virginia, 1621-1626." *William and Mary College Quarterly,* Second Series, vol. 6, no. 2.

"Letter Written by Mr. Moray, a Minister, to Sir R. Moray, from Ware Diver in Mock-jack Bay, Virginia, Feb. 1, 1665." *William and Mary College Quarterly,* Second Series, vol. 2, no. 3.

"Letters from Virginia in 1623." *Virginia Magazine of History and Biography*, vol. 6.

"Letters of Charles Stevens." Ed. by E. Ruth Rockwood. *Oregon Historical Quarterly*, v. 88, no. 3.

"Letters of Robert Proud." *Pennsylvania Magazine of History and Biography*, vol. 34.

"Letters of William Byrd." *Virginia Magazine of History and Biography*, vol. 25.

Lossing, Benson J. *Vassar College and its Founder*. New York, 1867.

Mackay, Alexander. *The Western World; or, Travels in the United States in 1846-47*. London, 1849.

Macpherson, David. *Annals of Commerce*. 4 vols. London, 1805.

Marquis, Albert Nelson, ed. *The Industries of Cincinnati*. Cincinnati, 1883.

Marryat, Capt. Frederick. *Diary in America*. 3 vols. London, 1839.

Marsh, Edward A. *The Evolution of Automatic Machinery as Applied to the Manufacture of Watches*. Chicago, 1896.

Martin, Edward Winslow (pseud. of James Dabney McCabe). *The Secrets of the Great City*. New York, 1868.

Massachusetts. *The Acts and Resolves of the Province of the Massachusetts Bay*. 21 vols. Boston, 1869-1922.

——. *The Perpetual Laws of the Commonwealth of Massachusetts from the Establishment of its Constitution to the Second Session of the General Court, in 1798*. 2 vols. Worcester, 1799.

——. *Records of the Governor and Company of the Massachusetts Bay in New England*. Nathaniel B. Shurtleff, ed. 6 vols. Boston, 1853-54.

"Materials Relating to the History of the Mississippi Valley from the Minutes of the Spanish Supreme Councils of State, 1787-1797." *Louisiana Historical Quarterly*, vol. 21, no. 1.

Mather, Richard. *Journal of Richard Mather, 1635*. Boston, 1850.

May, Colonel John. *Journal and Letters of Colonel John May of Boston*. Ed. by Richard S. Edes and William M. Darlington. Cincinnati, 1873.

McCabe, James D. *The Illustrated History of the Centennial Exhibition*. Philadelphia, c. 1877.

——. *New York by Sunlight and Gaslight*. New York, 1882.

McElroy, John William. "Seafaring in Seventeenth Century New England." *New England Quarterly*, September, 1935.

Mease, James. *Picture of Philadelphia*. Philadelphia, 1831.

"Memorial of John Lowry, to the Governor and Council." *Calendar of Virginia State Papers*, vol. 3.

Merz, Charles. *The Dry Decade*. Garden City, N.Y., 1931.

Millan, John. *Coins, Weights and Measures*. London, 1749.

Miller, John C. *Sam Adams, Pioneer in Propaganda*. Boston, 1936.

[Milwaukee] *The City of Milwaukee Guide: A Souvenir of the Milwaukee Exposition and of the Great National Saengerfest*. Milwaukee, 1886.

Milwaukee's Industries, 1892.

Mittelberger, Gottlieb. *Journey to Pennsylvania in 1750*. Philadelphia, 1898.

Mood, Fulmer. "John Winthrop, Jr., on Indian Corn." *New England Quarterly*, vol. 10.

Moreau de St. Mery's American Journey, [1783-1798]. Ed. and tr. by Kenneth and Anna M. Roberts. Garden City, N.Y., 1947.

Morison, Samuel Eliot. *The Founding of Harvard College*. Cambridge, Mass., 1935.

——. *Harvard College in the Seventeenth Century*. Cambridge, Mass., 1936.

——. *Three Centuries of Harvard, 1636-1936*. Cambridge, Mass., 1936.

Morrison, Andrew. *The Industries of New Orleans*. New Orleans, 1885.

Moss, Frank. *The American Metropolis, From Knickerbocker Days to the Present Time*. New York, 1897.

[Mourt's Relation]. A *Relation or Iournall of the beginning and proceedings of the English Plantation settled at Plimoth in New England, by certaine English Aduenturers both Merchants and others.* London, 1622.

Munsell, Joel. *Annals of Albany.* 10 vols. Albany, 1871.

"Muster Rolls of New York Provincial Troops, 1755-1764." New-York Historical Society *Collections,* vol. 24.

Myers, Albert Cook, ed. *Narratives of Early Pennsylvania, West New Jersey and Delaware, 1630-1707.* New York, 1912.

Neill, Rev. Edward D. *History of Washington County and the St. Croix Valley, including the Explorers and Pioneers of Minneapolis.* Minneapolis, 1881.

Nelson, William, ed. *Documents relating to the Colonial History of the State of New Jersey.* Vols. 19 & 20 of *New Jersey Archives,* Series 1. Paterson, 1897-1898.

New Orleans and the New South. New Orleans, c. 1887.

[New Plymouth Colony]. *Records of the Colony of New Plymouth.* 12 vols. Boston, 1855-1861.

Newson, T. M. *Pen Pictures of St. Paul, Minnesota and Biographical Sketches of Old Settlers.* St. Paul, 1886.

Nurnberg, John J. *Crowns: The Complete Story.* 2nd. ed. Philadelphia, 1955.

"Observation in Several Voyages and Travels in America." *William and Mary College Quarterly.* First Series, vol. 15.

O'Callaghan, E. B. *The Documentary History of the State of New York.* 4 vols. Albany, 1849-1851.

Odegard, Peter H. *Pressure Politics: The Story of the Anti-Saloon League.* New York, 1928.

The Old Brewery, and the New Mission House at The Five Points. By Ladies of the Mission. New York, 1854.

"The Oregon & California Letters of Bradford Ripley Alden." *California Historical Society Quarterly,* vol. 28, no. 3.

Ostrander, Gilman M. *The Prohibition Movement in California, 1848-1933.* Berkeley and Los Angeles, 1957.

Owens, Richard N. *Business Organization and Combination.* New York, 1951.

Pears, Thomas Clinton, Jr. "Visit of Lafayette to the Old Glass Works of Bakewell, Pears & Co." *Western Pennsylvania Historical Magazine,* vol. 8, no. 4.

Pen and Sunlight Sketches of Saint Louis. Chicago, c. 1892.

Penn, William. "A Further Account of the Province of Pennsylvania and its Improvements." *Pennsylvania Magazine of History and Biography,* vol. 9.

[Pennsylvania]. *Minutes of the Provincial Council of Pennsylvania.* 10 vols. Philadelphia, 1852.

Pennsylvania Archives, Fourth Series. *Papers of the Governors, 1681-1747.* Harrisburg, 1874-1900.

Pennypacker, Morton. *General Washington's Spies on Long Island and in New York.* Brooklyn, 1939.

A Perfect Description of Virginia. London, 1649. In *Virginia Historical Register,* vol. 2.

Peterson, Arthur G. "Commerce of Virginia, 1789-91." *William and Mary College Quarterly,* Second Series, vol. 10.

Pierce, Bessie Louise. *A History of Chicago.* 3 vols. New York, 1937.

Platt, Edmund, *The Eagle's History of Poughkeepsie.* Poughkeepsie, 1905.

Pope, Charles Henry. *The Pioneers of Massachusetts.* Boston, 1900.

[Portsmouth, R.I.]. *The Early Records of the Town of Portsmouth, Rhode Island.* Providence, 1901.

Postlethwayt, Malachy. *The Universal Dictionary of Trade and Commerce,* by M. Jacques Savary des Bruslous. 2 vols. London, 1751.

"Proposal in Regard to the Governor's House." *Virginia Magazine of History and Biography,* vol. 17.

"Proposal of an Arctic Expedition in the Seventeenth Century." *Pennsylvania Magazine of History and Biography*, vol. 31.

Rawle, Francis. "Ways and Means for the Inhabitants of Delaware to Become Rich." *Pennsylvania Magazine of History and Biography*, vol. 53.

Reavis, L. U. *Saint Louis: The Future Great City of the World.* St. Louis, c. 1875.

"The Restoration of Penn's Manor." *General Magazine and Historical Chronicle*, vol. 41.

Riddell, William Renwich. "Suggested Governmental Assistance to Farmers Two Centuries Ago, in Pennsylvania." *Pennsylvania Magazine of History and Biography*, vol. 53.

Roach, Hannah Benner. "Benjamin Franklin Slept Here." *Pennsylvania Magazine of History and Genealogy*, vol. 84.

Robertson, Ross M. *History of the American Economy.* New York, 1955.

Robinson, W. W. *Los Angeles from the Days of the Pueblo.* San Francisco, 1959.

Rogers, John William. *The Lusty Texans of Dallas.* New York, 1960.

Roll, Erich. *An Early Experiment in Industrial Organization, Being a History of the Firm of Boulton & Watt, 1775-1805.* London, 1930.

Roosevelt, Theodore. *The Letters of Theodore Roosevelt.* Ed. by Elting E. Morison. 8 vols. Cambridge, Mass., 1951-1954.

Rose, William Ganson. *Cleveland: The Making of a City.* Cleveland, 1950.

Rush, Benjamin. *An Inquiry into the Effects of Ardent Spirits upon the Human Body and Mind.* Brookfield, Mass., 1814.

"St. Louis Business and Industry, 1877." *Missouri Historical Society Bulletin*, vol. 16.

Saint Paul, the Queen City of the Northwest. St. Paul, c. 1893.

Salley, Alexander S., Jr., ed. *Narratives of Early Carolina, 1650-1708.* New York, 1911.

[San Francisco. Mechanics Institute] *Descriptive Numerical Catalogue of the 5th Industrial Exhibition of the Mechanics' Institute of the City of San Francisco.* San Francisco, 1865.

———. *Report of the First Industrial Exhibition of the Mechanics' Institute of the City of San Francisco.* San Francisco, 1858.

———. *Report of the Eighth Industrial Exhibition of the Mechanics' Institute of San Francisco.* San Francisco, 1872.

Santerre, George H. *White Cliffs of Dallas: The Story of La Reunion, the Old French Colony.* Dallas, 1955.

Savage, James. *A Genealogical Dictionary of the First Settlers of New England.* 4 vols. Boston, 1860-1862.

Scharf, J. Thomas, and Thomas Wescott. *History of Philadelphia, 1609-1884.* 3 vols. Philadelphia, 1884.

Scharf, J. Thomas. *History of Saint Louis City and County.* 2 vols. Philadelphia, 1883.

Schlesinger, Arthur Meier. *The Colonial Merchants and the American Revolution, 1763-1776.* New York, 1918.

Schramm, Eulalia Catherine. "General James O'Hara, Pittsburgh's First Captain of Industry." Thesis, University of Pittsburgh, 1931.

"A Scrap of 'Troop' History; Memoranda of Thomas Peters, made in his copy of 'By-Laws of the First Troop Philadelphia City Cavalry.'" *Pennsylvania Magazine of History and Biography*, vol. 15.

Seybert, Adam. *Statistical Annals . . .* Philadelphia, 1818.

Sheppard, William. *Of the Office of the Clerk of the Market, of Weights and Measures, and of the Laws of Provision.* London, 1665.

Sherrill, Charles H. *French Memories of 18th Century America.* New York, 1915.

[Shiras, George, Jr.]. *Justice George Shiras Jr. of Pittsburgh.* Pittsburgh, 1953.

Shourds, Thomas. *History and Genealogy of Fenwick's Colony.* Bridgeton, N.J., 1876.

Shurtleff, Nathaniel B. A *Topographical and Historical Description of Boston.* Boston, 1891.

Simley, Jerome C., ed. *History of Denver.* Denver, 1901.

Singer, Michael. "Deutschamerika in den Kriegsjahren." *Jahrbuch der Deutsch-amerikaner für das Jahr 1918.* Chicago, 1917.

Sketches and Business Directory of Boston and its Vicinity for 1860 and 1861. Boston, c. 1860.

Smiles, Samuel. *Lives of Boulton and Watt.* Philadelphia, 1865.

Smith, Harry Edwin. *The United States Federal Internal Tax History from 1861 to 1871.* Boston, 1914.

Smith, John. *The Travels of Captaine John Smith.* 2 vols. Glasgow, 1907.

Spurrier, John. *The Practical Farmer.* Wilmington, 1793.

Standard Encyclopedia of the Alcohol Problem. 6 vols. Westerville, Ohio, 1925-1930.

Staples, William Reed. *Annals of the Town of Providence.* Rhode Island Historical Society *Collections,* vol. 5.

Stephens, Ann S. (pseud. Jonathan Slicker). *High Life in New York,* New York 1843.

Stephens, William. A *Journal of the Proceedings in Georgia.* In *The Colonial Records of the State of Georgia,* vol. 4.

————. *The Journal of William Stephens.* 2 vols. Athens, Ga., 1958.

Steuart, Justin. *Wayne Wheeler, Dry Boss.* New York, 1928.

Stevens, Sylvester K. *Pennsylvania, Titan of Industry.* New York, 1948.

Stevens, Walter B. *St. Louis, The Fourth City, 1764-1911.* St. Louis, 1911.

Stewart, George R. *American Ways of Life.* Garden City, N.Y., 1954.

Stiles, Henry R. A *History of the City of Brooklyn.* 3 vols. Brooklyn, 1867-1870.

Still, Bayard, *Milwaukee: The History of a City.* Madison, Wis., 1948.

Stokes, Isaac Newton Phelps. *The Iconography of Manhattan Island, 1498-1909.* 6 vols. New York, 1915-1928.

Swem, E. G. "Some Notes on the Four Forms of the Oldest Buildings of William and Mary College." *William and Mary College Quarterly,* Second Series, vol. 8.

Taylor, John, plaintiff. A *Report of the Trial of the Cause of John Taylor vs. Edward C. Delavan, prosecuted for an alleged Libel, tried at the Albany Circuit, April, 1840.* Albany, 1840.

Tenner, Armin. *Cincinnati Sonst und Jetzt.* Cincinnati, 1878.

Thomann, Gallus. *Colonial Liquor Laws.* New York, 1887.

————. *Liquor Laws of the United States: Their Spirit and Effect.* New York, 1885.

Tilton, Alice Busch. *Remembering.* Privately printed, 1947.

Tinkham, George H. *History of San Joaquin County, California.* Los Angeles, 1923.

Tolles, Frederick B. "George Logan, Agrarian Democrat." *Pennsylvania Magazine of History and Biography,* vol. 75.

Torrence, Robert M. *The Barnitz Family.* Printed for private distribution to members of the family. Baltimore, 1961.

Trollope, Frances. *Domestic Manners of the Americans.* New York, 1949.

Trumbull, Benjamin. A *Complete History of Connecticut.* 2 vols. New London, 1898.

Trumbull, J. Hammond, and C. J. Hoadly. *The Public Records of the Colony of Connecticut.* 15 vols. Hartford, 1850-1890.

Trumbull, L. R. A *History of Industrial Paterson.* Paterson, 1882.

Tyler, Moses Coit. *Patrick Henry.* Boston, 1887.

United States Department of Agriculture. *Growing and Curing Hops.* Farmers' Bulletin No. 304. Washington, 1910.

United States Census Office. *Digest of Accounts of Manufacturing Establishments in the United States.* Fourth Census, 1820. Washington, 1823.

United States Department of Commerce, Bureau of the Census. *Abstract of the Census of Manufactures, 1919.* Washington, 1923.

————. *Biennial Census of Manufactures, 1931.* Washington, 1935.

————. *Census of Manufacturers:* 1939. 2 vols. Washington, 1942.

————. *Historical Statistics of the United States, 1789-1945.* Washington, 1949.

————. *1958 Census of Manufactures, Beverages, Industry report* MC58(2)-20G. Washington, 1961.

United States Centennial Commission. *International Exhibition, 1876.* Ed. by Francis A. Walker. Washington, 1880.

————. *Reports and Awards.* Philadelphia, 1877.

United States House of Representatives. 72nd Congress, 2nd Session. Hearings before the Committee on Ways and Means. *Modification of Volstead Act.* Washington, 1932.

United States Senate. 69th Congress, 1st Session. Hearings before the Sub-committee of the Committee on the Judiciary. *The National Prohibition Law.* 2 vols. Washington, 1926.

————. 66th Congress, 1st Session. Hearings before the Sub-committee of the Committee on the Judiciary. *Prohibiting Intoxicating Beverages.* 3 vols. Washington, 1919.

United States Treasury Department. *Annual Report of the Commissioner of Internal Revenue.* Washington, 1863 ————.

————. *Documents Relative to the Manufactures of the United States.* Executive Document No. 308. Ed. by Louis McLane. 2 vols. Washington, 1833.

————. Bureau of Prohibition. *Statistics Concerning Intoxicating Liquors.* Washington, 1928-1932.

————. Internal Revenue Service. *Statistics Relating to the Alcohol and Tobacco Industries for the Fiscal Year Ended June 30, 1960.* Washington, 1960.

————. *Tabular Statements of the Several Branches of American Manufactures, 1810.* Philadelphia, 1813.

Usher, Abbott Payson. *A History of Mechanical Inventions.* New York, 1929.

Valentine, David T. *History of the City of New York.* New York, 1853.

————. *Manual of the Corporation of the City of New York.* New York, 1865.

[Vassar, Matthew] *The Autobiography and Letters of Matthew Vassar.* Ed. by Elizabeth Hazelton Haight. New York, 1916.

[Virginia] *Calendar of Virginia State Papers.* 11 vols. Richmond, 1875-1893.

"Virginia County Records, March 25, 1770." *Virginia Magazine of History and Biography,* vol. 12.

Wainwright, Nicholas B. *Philadelphia in the Romantic Age of Lithography.* Philadelphia, 1958.

Walcott, Robert R. "Husbandry in Colonial New England." *New England Quarterly,* June 1936.

Ward, Christopher. *New Sweden on the Delaware.* Philadelphia, 1938.

Ward, Townsend. "North Second Street and its Associations." *Pennsylvania Magazine of History and Biography,* vol. 4.

Washington, George. *The Writings of George Washington.* Ed. by John C. Fitzpatrick. 39 vols. Washington, 1931-1944.

"Washington's Household Account Book, 1793-97." *Pennsylvania Magazine of History and Biography,* vols. 29, 30.

Watrous, Ansel. *History of Larimer County, Colorado.* Fort Collins, 1911.

Watson, John F. *Annals of Philadelphia and Pennsylvania.* Revised by Willis P. Hazard. Philadelphia, 1905.

Weeden, William. *Economic and Social History of New England, 1620-1789.* 2 vols. Boston, 1891.

Wells, William V. *The Life and Public Services of Samuel Adams.* 3 vols. Boston, 1865.

Western Reserve Historical Society. *Publication No. 100.* Cleveland, 1919.

Wheeler, Robert G. "The House of Jeremias van Rensselaer, 1658-1666." *New-York Historical Society Quarterly,* vol. 45.

White, Philip L. *Beekman Mercantile Papers*. 3 vols. New York, 1956.

———. *The Beekmans of New York in Politics and Commerce*. New York, 1956.

Wildes, Harry Emerson. *Valley Forge*. New York, 1938.

Wiley, Harvey W. *Beverages and Their Adulteration*. Philadelphia, c. 1919.

Wilhelm, David O. *History of the City of Denver*. Denver, 1866.

[William and Mary College] "Proceedings of the Faculty, July 11, 1798." *William and Mary College Quarterly*, Second Series, vol. 27.

Williams, J. Fletcher. *A History of the City of St. Paul*. In *Minnesota Historical Society Collections*. vol. 4.

———. *History of Washington County and the St. Croix Valley*. St. Paul, 1881.

Wilson, Erasmus, ed. *Standard History of Pittsburg, Pennsylvania*. Chicago, 1898.

Wilson, James Grant, ed. *Memorial History of the City of New York*. 4 vols. New York, 1892.

Winsor, Justin, ed. *Narrative and Critical History of America*. 8 vols. Boston, 1884-1889.

Winthrop, John. *History of New England*. Ed. by James Savage. 2 vols. Boston, 1825-1826.

Winthrop Papers. 5 vols. Massachusetts Historical Society. Boston, 1929-1947.

Wirt, William. *The Life of Patrick Henry*. New York, 1831.

Wittke, Carl. ed. *The History of the State of Ohio*. 6 vols. Columbus, 1941-1944.

Wood, William. *New-England's Prospect*. (First published 1635.) Boston, 1865.

Young, S. O. *A Thumb-nail History of the City of Houston, Texas from its founding in 1836 to the year 1912*. Houston, 1912.

Index

Index

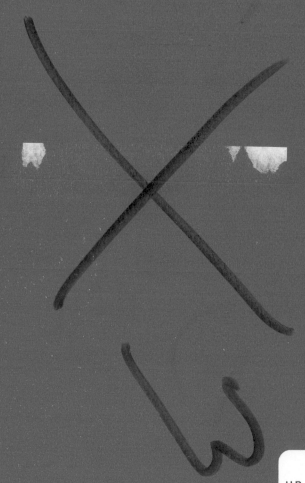